MEDICINE, CHARITY A

IN MEMORY OF BERYL DAVID (1918–2004)

Medicine, Charity and Mutual Aid
The Consumption of Health and Welfare in Britain, c.1550–1950

Edited by

ANNE BORSAY
University of Wales Swansea, UK
and
PETER SHAPELY
University of Wales Bangor, UK

Routledge
Taylor & Francis Group

LONDON AND NEW YORK

First published 2007 by Ashgate Publishing

2 Park Square, Milton Park, Abingdon, Oxon OX14 4RN
711 Third Avenue, New York, NY 10017, USA

Routledge is an imprint of the Taylor & Francis Group, an informa business

First issued in paperback 2016

British Library Cataloguing in Publication Data

Medicine, charity and mutual aid : the consumption of
   health and welfare in Britain, c.1550–1950. – (Historical urban studies)
   1. Charities – Great Britain – History 2. Charities,
   Medical – Great Britain – History 3. Great Britain – Social
   conditions
   I. Borsay, Anne II. Shapely, Peter
   361.7'0941

Library of Congress Cataloging–in–Publication Data

Medicine, charity and mutual aid : the consumption of health and welfare in Britain,
c.1550–1950 / edited by Anne Borsay and Peter Shapely.
     p. cm. – (Historical urban studies series)
   Includes bibliographical references.
   ISBN–978–0–7546–5148–2 (alk. paper)
   1. Charities – Great Britain – History. 2. Voluntarism – Great Britain – History. 3. Public welfare – Great Britain – History. 4. Social service – Great Britain – History. 5. Medical care – Great Britain – History. I. Borsay, Anne. II. Shapely, Peter.

HV245.M386 2007
362.94109'03–dc22

2006030263

ISBN 13: 978-0-7546-5148-2 (hbk)
ISBN 13: 978-1-138-27565-2 (pbk)

Contents

List of Figures and Tables

Figures

Tables

Notes on Contributors

Ian Atherton is a Senior Lecturer in History at Keele University.

Anne Borsay is Professor of Healthcare and Medical Humanities in the School of Health Science at Swansea University.

Flurin Condrau is a Lecturer in the History of Medicine in the Centre for the History of Science, Technology and Medicine at the University of Manchester.

Sheila Cooper is Associate Dean Emeritus of the Indiana University Graduate School and taught history on the Indianapolis and Bloomington campuses of Indiana University.

Barry Doyle is Assistant Dean of Research in the School of Social Sciences and Law at the University of Teeside.

Stuart Hogarth is a Research Associate in the Department of Public Health and Primary Care at the University of Cambridge.

Eileen McGrath is a Postgraduate Student in History at Keele University.

Sylvia Pinches is Team Leader for England's Past for Everyone, Herefordshire, a project of the Victoria County History Trust, and Honorary Visiting Research Fellow in the Centre for English Local History at the University of Leicester.

Jonathan Reinarz is a Wellcome Trust Research Fellow and Lecturer at the Centre for the History of Medicine at Birmingham Medical School.

Peter Shapely is a Lecturer in the Department of History and Welsh History at the University of Wales, Bangor.

Anne C. Shepherd, who is completing her PhD at Oxford Brookes University, is a Research Assistant at the Centre for Suicide Research, Department of Psychiatry, University of Oxford.

Pat Starkey teaches in the School of History at the University of Liverpool.

Andrea Tanner is a Research Fellow at Kingston University and Honorary Archivist at Fortnum and Mason.

Alannah Tomkins is a Lecturer in History within the School of Humanities at Keele University.

Acknowledgements

This book has its origins in the Fifth International Conference of the European Association of Urban Historians, which was held in Berlin in the summer of 2000 on the theme of 'European Cities: Networks and Crossroads'. At this conference, Anne Borsay and Peter Shapely arranged a main session called 'History from Below: The Urban Poor and the Reception of Medicine and Charity in Western European Cities'. We are indebted to the conference organizers for the opportunity to explore a subject that had been identified as a neglected area in the history of medicine and charity at the previous conference of European Association in Venice two years before. Thanks are also due to the Berlin participants who agreed to develop their papers into chapters for the book and to those who accepted our invitation to join the team in order to expand the range of issues covered. We are grateful to Series Editors of 'Historical Urban Studies', Richard Rodger and Jean-Luc Pinol, for their support of the project, and to Tom Gray and the editorial staff at Ashgate for their efficient processing of the manuscript. Above all, the editors and the contributors thank Penny David for the patience, skill and enthusiasm that she brought to copy-editing the typescript.

Historical Urban Studies
General Editors' Preface

Density and proximity are two of the defining characteristics of the urban dimension. It is these that identify a place as uniquely urban, though the threshold for such pressure points varies from place to place. What is considered an important cluster in one context - may not be considered as urban elsewhere. A third defining characteristic is functionality - the commercial or strategic position of a town or city which conveys an advantage over other places. Over time, these functional advantages may diminish, or the balance of advantage may change within a hierarchy of towns. To understand how the relative importance of towns shifts over time and space is to grasp a set of relationships which is fundamental to the study of urban history.

Towns and cities are products of history, yet have themselves helped to shape history. As the proportion of urban dwellers has increased, so the urban dimension has proved a legitimate unit of analysis through which to understand the spectrum of human experience and to explore the cumulative memory of past generations. Though obscured by layers of economic, social and political change, the study of the urban milieu provides insights into the functioning of human relationships and, if urban historians themselves are not directly concerned with current policy studies, few contemporary concerns can be understood without reference to the historical development of towns and cities.

This longer historical perspective is essential to an understanding of social processes. Crime, housing conditions and property values, health and education, discrimination and deviance, and the formulation of regulations and social policies to deal with them were, and remain, amongst the perennial preoccupations of towns and cities - no historical period has a monopoly of these concerns. They recur in successive generations, albeit in varying mixtures and strengths; the details may differ.

The central forces of class, power and authority in the city remain. If this was the case for different periods, so it was for different geographical entities and cultures. Both scientific knowledge and technical information were available across Europe and showed little respect for frontiers. Yet despite common concerns and access to broadly similar knowledge, different solutions to urban problems were proposed and adopted by towns and cities in different parts of Europe. This comparative dimension informs urban historians as to which were systematic factors and which were of a purely local nature: general and particular forces can be distinguished.

These analytical and comparative frameworks inform this book. Indeed, thematic, comparative and analytical approaches to the historical study of towns and cities is the hallmark of the Historical Urban Studies series which now extends to over 30 titles, either already published or currently in production. European urban historiography has been extended and enriched as a result and this book makes another important addition to an intellectual mission to which we, as General Editors, remain firmly committed.

Richard Rodger   *University of Leicester*
Jean-Luc Pinol   *Université de Lyon II*

CHAPTER ONE

Introduction

Anne Borsay and Peter Shapely

In 1500, only 3.1 per cent of the population of England and Wales lived in settlements of over 10,000 people. By 1800 the figure was 20.3 per cent. In the decades to 1890, however, the proportion trebled to 61.9 per cent and by 1951 more than three-quarters of the population were resident in towns of at least this size. Compounding the general effects of urbanization was the growth of large-scale cities and conurbations. In 1800, 10.7 per cent of the English and Welsh population occupied settlements of over 100,000. By 1851 it was 24.9 per cent, by 1891 39.5 per cent, and by 1951 52.7 per cent.[1] Mary Lindemann has cautioned against exaggerating the differences between these new urban areas and traditional rural communities. But, as she concedes, towns and cities did tend to have more medical practitioners and play host to hospitals, asylums and other institutions.[2] Thus urbanization was associated with the dramatic growth of voluntary charities, responding to social dislocation and the emergence of what was perceived as a myriad of good causes.[3]

This book explores the consumption – as opposed to the production – of charitable assistance, medical care, parish poor relief and mutual aid, focusing on the perspectives of those who received support in urban environments. As such, it addresses the strategies and methods of the bodies that dealt with poor and working-class members of society who were allocated benefits or who were members of mutual-aid organizations. Too many studies in the past have taken an institutional stance, concentrating on the benefactors and officials who were responsible for implementing policies. But this was a two-way relationship in which recipients were not passive in the face of whatever was put before them.[4] In capturing this relationship, the book moves beyond the paternalistic approach to give due weight to the attitudes and feelings of those who were meant to benefit. However, it is not enough simply to counterbalance the 'top person's' version of history because 'the history of the "common people" ... cannot be divorced from the wider considerations of social structure and social power'. Therefore, our reconfiguration of the recipient or consumer of medicine, charity and mutual aid, seeks 'a richer synthesis of

---

1   J. de Vries, *European Urbanization, 1500–1800* (London, 1984) pp. 39, 45–7; L. H. Lees, 'Urban Networks', in M. Daunton (ed.), *Cambridge Urban History of Britain: Volume 3, 1840–1950* (Cambridge, 2000) p. 70; P. Corfield, *The Impact of English Towns* (Oxford, 1982) p. 9.

2   M. Lindemann, *Medicine and Society in Early Modern Europe* (Cambridge, 1999) p. 232.

3   P. Shapely, *Charity and Power in Nineteenth-century Manchester* (Manchester, 2000).

4   A.J. Kidd, 'Philanthropy and the Social History Paradigm,' *Social History*, 21/2 (1996): 180–92; P. Shapely, 'Urban Charity, Class Relations and Social Cohesion: Charitable Responses to the Cotton Famine,' *Urban History*, 28/1 (2001): 46–63.

historical understanding' that engages personal agency with economic, social and political relations.[5]

The historiographical context

The reappraisal of the post-war welfare state from the late twentieth century has promoted a mixed economy of provision in which scaled-down public services are offset by an expansion of the voluntary and commercial sectors, and consumer choice features prominently in the evaluation of performance.[6] The extent to which the fragmentation of supply has liberated the contemporary user is open to debate. However, it does add fresh impetus to the 'history from below' that Edward Thompson advocated so forcefully from the 1960s. 'I am seeking', he wrote in *The Making of the English Working Class*, 'to rescue the poor stockinger, the luddite cropper, the "obsolete" hand-loom weaver, the "utopian" artisan, and even the deluded followers of Joanna Southcott, from the enormous condescension of posterity.'[7] Continental Europe fashioned a micro-historical response to this agenda. In France, for instance, Le Roy Ladurie's *Montaillou* (1975) used inquisitorial records from the bishopric of Poitiers to reconstruct the life of a Pyrenean peasant community between 1318 and 1325, while Carlo Ginzburg's *The Cheese and the Worms* (1976) employed similar sources to explore the spiritual and intellectual world of a miller from north-eastern Italy who was born in 1532.[8] In Britain, on the other hand, 'history from below' took a different turn, drawing on the tradition of labour history and its Marxist inheritance. The consequence was a preoccupation with the popular radicalism of the modern period, which led to the neglect of not only pre-modern voices but also of non-élite groups outside the arena of mainstream politics.[9] As Roy Porter observed of medical history, 'it was what the doctor did to, and for, the sick that counted; the patient was just the raw material, the unwitting bearer of a disease or lesion'.[10]

The history of charity has not avoided this myopia. There have been many valuable studies in recent years covering a wide range of issues, including medical care, welfare provision, gender, religion, power, authority and both class formation and inter-class relations.[11] Among the key themes to emerge has been the role of

---

5   J. Sharp, 'History from Below', in P. Burke (ed.), *New Perspectives on Historical Writing* (Cambridge, 1991) pp. 32–3.

6   See, for example, G. Finlayson, *Citizen, State and Social Welfare in Britain, 1830–1990* (Oxford, 1994).

7   E. Thompson, *The Making of the English Working Class* (London, 1965) pp. 12–13.

8   Le R. Ladurie, *Montaillou: Cathars and Catholics in a French Village 1294–1324*, English edn (London, 1978); C. Ginzburg, *The Cheese and the Worms: The Cosmos of a Sixteenth-century Miller*, English edn (London, 1980).

9   Sharpe, 'History from Below', pp. 27–31.

10   R. Porter, 'Introduction', in R. Porter (ed.), *Patients and Practitioners: Lay Perceptions of Medicine in Pre-Industrial Society* (Cambridge, 1985) p. 2.

11   See, for example, P. Joyce, *Work, Society and Politics* (London, 1980); F. Prochaska, *Women and Philanthropy* (Oxford, 1980); J. Garrard, *Leadership in Victorian Industrial Towns*, (Manchester 1983); G. Stedman-Jones, *Outcast London* (Cambridge, 1983); A. Borsay, *Medicine and Charity in Georgian Bath: A Social History of the General Infirmary*

charitable institutions as extensions of the power relations and policy developments in urban society. Yet, while these studies have given an insight into the impact and function of charities in Britain, the nature of the source materials means that research continues to be largely from the perspective of institutions, donors, administrators and professionals. Annual reports, newspapers, contemporary journals and personal accounts provide the staple source base, but they give a very one-sided account, which emphasizes either the positive characteristics of benefactors and officials, or how charitable involvement underpinned their power in the urban arena. Charity was thus reduced to a 'history of kindness' or a way of achieving greater influence and status; it helped women to get out of the home, or it reinforced their feminine role; it was an altruistic act or a vehicle for social control. However, missing from such critiques was the reciprocal, two-way relationship between donor and recipient highlighted by Alan Kidd's seminal study of the social history of philanthropy.[12]

The 'gift' of charity not only involved donating time and money to a specific cause but also demanded some return either in the form of status and self-satisfaction or in terms of deference. This deference from the recipient, a display of gratitude and indebtedness, was also part of the reciprocal nature of the charitable relationship. But if grasping the impact and role of urban charity requires an appreciation of recipients, there is a basic problem with putting them into the picture.[13] The poor left few records and their perspectives were generally unrepresented through other media. Methodologically, therefore, studying recipients is fraught with difficulties; they remain an elusive group. Nevertheless, Peter Mandler's edited volume – looking at recipients of charity from struggling labourers in Antwerp to pregnant women impoverished in Paris and destitute children abandoned in New York – has demonstrated the possibilities for excavating their attitudes and positions.[14] Research may have to rely on middle-class interpretations, brief first-hand snippets or behavioural patterns, but this does not diminish its importance.

The book in outline

In examining the consumption of health and welfare, each chapter in this volume assesses the impact of charity from the perspective of the poor, exploring a range of suppliers that include social agencies, medical institutions and mutual-aid networks. Central to the charitable relationship that underpins this process are its consequences for social relations. Charities are often envisaged as a mechanism for controlling recipients, but this is a product of a predominantly 'top-down' history. The reality is more complex, as Chapter 2 shows with reference to cathedral almsmen in England between 1538 and 1914. Despite the belief that Henry VIII's assault on the Catholic

---

c.1739–1830 (Aldershot, 1999); M. Gorsky, *Patterns of Philanthropy: Charity and Society in Nineteenth-century Bristol* (Woodbridge, 1999); Shapely, *Charity and Power in Nineteenth-century Manchester*.

12   Kidd, 'Philanthropy'.

13   Shapely, 'Cotton Famine': 47–9.

14   P. Mandler (ed.), *The Uses of Charity: The Poor on Relief in the Nineteenth-century Metropolis* (Philadelphia, 1990).

church fractured the link between poor relief and cathedrals, the tradition continued. Post-Reformation cathedrals were thus charged with a range of philanthropic duties, including the maintenance of a fixed number of almsmen. Henry's intention was that the main beneficiaries would be aged and impotent poor men, old or wounded soldiers appointed by the crown, who received a regular stipend (and sometimes accommodation) in return for very light duties at the cathedral church. In practice and over time, however, successful applicants departed from the Tudor stereotype; and though sick, injured or disabled, they were neither typically ex-servicemen nor necessarily poor. The lengthy and bureaucratic application process favoured applicants who were assertive, persistent and capable of manufacturing a persuasive case – qualities that may have taxed the less healthy and robust. Furthermore, it generated a constituency of sometimes unruly men, who were unwilling to conform to the idealized image of the grateful and powerless poor set out in the founding rhetoric of the cathedrals. Therefore, the uncritical acceptance of concepts like discipline, subservience and social control is challenged.

The poor did not invariably behave consistently towards middle- and upper-class munificence; some regarded charity more as a right than as a gift. This attitude was evident in the response to allotments during the eighteenth and nineteenth centuries. At the time of enclosure, the landless poor were given small plots as awards in lieu of rights of pasturage and fuel gathering. Chapter 3 examines popular reaction to how the trustees managed these allotments. Struggles over compensation for common rights, and over their reduction to 'charity', were not confined to rural parishes. On the contrary, the enclosure of the common fields surrounding market towns and cities was also contentious. What had once been a benefit for all landless cottagers too often became restricted to the deserving poor not in receipt of poor relief. Fuel charities were also frequently established in parishes soon after enclosure and from the 1830s there was a proliferation of coal clubs, set up by local élites to encourage thrift in the needy. The poor, however, retained a sense that the Town Lands (as these allotments were often called) and the profits were theirs by right. Opposition to this denial of rights was expressed not only by hedge-breaking at the time of enclosure but, later in the nineteenth century, by public protest, including formal complaint to the Charity Commissioners. Local élites had reneged on the exchange of rights implicitly agreed at enclosure. Therefore, trust had been eroded and the charitable relationship had broken down.

Trust was also pivotal to the reciprocal aid that passed between relatives and friends. As Chapter 4 contends, these private exchanges were pervasive during the early modern period, despite being largely undocumented and hence invisible to the historical eye. A broad, anthropological definition of kinship is adopted with three categories: cognatic (blood relatives); agnatic (affines including spouses, step-relatives and in-laws); and fictive (agnates' agnates, servants). These bonds, it is argued, eclipsed the modest role of public welfare, discrediting claims that kinship systems were weak. Engaging in such relationships was economically rational at a time when life was precarious, not just for the lower orders but also for the middling sort and the gentry who were also vulnerable to a sudden deterioration in their circumstances. Furthermore, these commitments were rooted in social norms that transcended genealogical distance and crossed the generations. This did not mean that kinship support was without tensions. Nevertheless, at points of strain in the life cycle – which often coincided with childbearing, the early death of parents, or old age – the nuclear family plugged into a raft of assistance from relatives and friends. Children were educated; households welcomed servants and apprentices who were kin; jobs were found; and help in cash and in kind was given. Donors as well as recipients benefited, earning public approval and future security from their investment in a system of reciprocal aid.

Complementing informal kinship relations in the mixed economy of welfare was the formal charitable organization, which emerged during the early modern period to sit beside traditional forms of benevolence like the cathedral almshouse. As Chapter 5 suggests, however, the implications for recipients were at best ambivalent. By 1828 a dozen towns and cities in Britain had educational institutions for deaf children. Since their survival depended upon a mixed economy of commercial fees and charitable donations, effective marketing was essential. Therefore, pupils were regularly put on public display. Not only were the institutions open to inspection by interested parties, but their patrons also elected children for admission on the basis of published biographical notes, and those who subsequently acquired communication skills were paraded before annual meetings of benefactors and subscribers to demonstrate their proficiency. The image presented on such occasions, and in the printed materials that the institutions produced, was of a disciplined but caring community. However, these 'voices' bore little resemblance to the experiences of deaf children, who were subjected to teaching methods that were harshly imposed and living conditions that were of a low standard. Although some pupils did occasionally participate in acts of defiance, age, class and disability left them largely powerless to confront the structures through which their schooling was delivered.

Medical institutions were also perceived as controlling environments, but as Chapters 6, 7 and 8 illustrate, adults negotiating treatment for themselves and their families were not inevitably reduced to grateful beneficiaries of a knowledgeable benefactor. Chapter 6 penetrates the in-patient experience from the autobiographical viewpoint of Joseph Townend, a textile worker who spent several months in the Manchester Royal Infirmary during 1827. According to historical orthodoxy, the rise of modern medicine from the later eighteenth century disempowered patients who in the early modern period had bargained with doctors in a commercial marketplace. Townend's encounter with the Manchester Infirmary revises this interpretation. Admitted via the recommendation of his employer, he not only negotiated his status as an in-patient but also secured surgery for a long-term disability as well as for his more recently injured wrist. Only when he disobeyed medical orders was traditional authority imposed. The disciplinary regime was also mediated through relationships between patients, the fitter of whom engaged in the day-to-day running of the hospital and in carnivalesque inversions of institutional roles that contributed to a sense of compassionate solidarity and set limits on the extent of medical domination. But for Townend – a dedicated Methodist – sickness went hand-in-hand with salvation. Critical of the pastoral care delivered by the Established Church, he saw his hospital stay as a spiritual journey in which surgery was the cure for a previous life of levity.

Whereas Chapter 6 catches an autobiographical glimpse of the hospital, the next two chapters unpick its procedures. Chapter 7 compares the gatekeeping function at five Birmingham institutions, two general and three specialist. Though the rules stressed helping the deserving poor, governors struggled to control entry. The discovery of abuse was difficult at the General Hospital (founded in 1779) because often patients were known only by the sponsor who had supplied their ticket, and they became adept at depicting themselves as worthy applicants. The Women's Hospital (founded in 1871) deliberately recruited beyond the deserving poor, providing comfortable wards and a relaxed discipline in its bid to break new ground in pelvic surgery. Similarly, misuse was less of concern to the Eye Hospital (founded in 1823) where out-patients predominated and maximizing the numbers treated took precedence. A large out-patient population did not stop the Children's Hospital (founded in 1861) from becoming the first medical institution in Birmingham to begin systematic enquiries into the financial status of patients' families. Significantly, children were not always rejected because their families were able to pay for treatment; occasionally they were of the wrong age, but the primary cause of rejection was the threat of biological infection. However, it was the Queen's Hospital (founded in 1841) that pushed investigative procedures furthest when the introduction of free access in 1876 was underpinned by a subsequent assessment in which hospital almoners identified those who could afford to pay or who were covered by the corporate subscriptions of employers or mutual-aid societies.

The success of such procedures in managing admission is open to question, as Chapter 8 reveals for the Great Ormond Street Hospital for Sick Children in London during the second half of the nineteenth century. While the rules represented patients and their parents as passive recipients of the hospital's attention, the intake pattern indicated that they were customers rather than powerless petitioners. Unlike the majority of the metropolitan voluntary hospitals, governors' recommendations were relatively unimportant in admitting children, this responsibility resting principally with the medical profession. Incurable cases, babies and the chronic sick were supposed to be refused because the founders did not wish the hospital to become a refuge for chronically sick children. In practice, however, doctors responded favourably to the parents' desire to treat children who were poorly, rather than acutely sick. Furthermore, though parents were allowed to visit for just two hours each week, they retained the right to remove their children at any time. This right was exercised frequently, the most common reasons for taking children home being that they were not thriving under the hospital regime, and that the family missed them too much to permit any further separation. Therefore, in contrast to the depiction of the recipient as passive, suffering and dependent in Victorian fund-raising campaigns, patients – through their families – did have a voice, exercising choice in accepting treatment and influencing the admission decisions made by the hospital.

Contrary to popular opinion, not all charities were rooted in a relationship between different socio-economic classes; some were formed by the middle classes for the middle classes, throwing up important variations in attitudes, forms of relief, and social relations. Chapter 9 looks at one such charity, the Holloway Sanatorium, which was founded by the wealthy patent-medicine manufacturer and philanthropist, Thomas Holloway, and opened in Surrey in 1885 to offer quality care exclusively to the insane middle classes. Though Holloway believed that these patients were excluded from asylum provision that was easily purchased by the wealthy and freely available to the poor, he feared that they were not immune to the demeaning effects of charity. Therefore, his Sanatorium was reserved for the 'deserving' middle classes, who had remained faithful to the work ethic until overtaken by unavoidable predicaments. Charges were variable. From 1889, when the Sanatorium was registered as a charity, a minimum of 25 per cent of all admissions were on charitable rates, those who paid fees subsidizing patients who were of good social status but of limited means. The more affluent enjoyed additional privileges. However, all experienced the Sanatorium's impressive architecture with its elaborate public rooms and luxurious conditions. Extensive programmes of entertainment were also drawn up to take the place of manual labour in the asylums that catered for the lower orders. Patients were thus invited to participate in a range of sporting and cultural activities, and in outside excursions. According to the rules, length of stay was limited to one year. But, in practice, longer terms of residence and repeated re-admissions were negotiated as part of the collaborative relationship that grew up between recipients, their families and the Sanatorium's management.

Whereas Chapter 9 examines a sanatorium for insane patients, so-called to lessen the stigma that the term 'asylum' conveyed for the middle classes, Chapter 10 considers sanatoriums for working-class patients with the physical condition of tuberculosis. Britain's campaign from around 1900 to build TB institutions specifically for the treatment of the urban poor led, ultimately, to the inclusion of a specific 'sanatorium benefit' in the National Insurance Act of 1911. Recent historiography has focused on the explication of policy making in tuberculosis control. Under this scenario, the sanatorium has been read as a futile therapeutic instrument, whose real function was subjecting the working class to disciplinary regimes; and sanatorium doctors have been accused of aiming for psychological influence over the patient, which in practice implied a broadly understood hygienic education. However, the long-term effects of tuberculosis treatment have not received much attention. While this evaluation is initially a quantitative question about the survival rates of patients, it raises questions simultaneously about changing definitions of health, treatment, and the ensuing quality of life. Therefore, statistical evidence of the short- and long-term effects of sanatorium care is set against the historical construction of 'medical success'; and biographical material from patients who underwent clinical interventions like chest surgery, and failed to escape the stigma that likewise afflicted the mentally ill, is absorbed into a qualitative assessment of TB treatment.

From the end of the nineteenth century – in parallel with the development of a more collectivist state – a different kind of charitable relationship began to evolve as recipients started to assert a greater level of influence with donors and staff, and mutual aid started to undermine existing networks and relationships. Chapter 11 teases out this transition for urban medical provision between 1900 and 1948, drawing on two institutions in Middlesbrough: the North Ormseby Hospital (NOH) and the North Riding Infirmary (NRI). Both founded in the 1860s as the town was expanding rapidly, they were a response to the health needs generated by heavy industry with its record of workplace accidents and environmental pollution. Lacking the urban élite that traditionally supported voluntary hospitals, Middlesbrough shaped an alternative politics of health care in which employers joined with workers belonging to flourishing mutual-aid organizations. By the 1930s, 70 per cent of contributions were coming from workers' clubs. This changing nature of the financial base left neither the mission nor the management of the hospitals unaffected, as conflicts arose over the meaning of voluntarism, charity and mutual aid. In 1929, for example, public controversy broke out at the NRI after the honorary medical staff disputed the right of the house committee to investigate complaints that they were neglecting patients. As the hospitals grew in popularity – with three times as many patients in 1946 as 1900 – trade unions played an increasing role in their reform. The result was a shift in the balance of power between medical staff, patients and managers, and the creation of a more democratic medical infrastructure.

With recipients effectively turning into customers who bought into charity, relationships changed for all those involved. Mutual aid conferred the ability to pool resources and become actively involved in the management of networks that formed a 'third wing' of support for the poor. The democratic structure also meant that different norms and systems operated from either charity or the state. Issues of power, social cohesion and class management were no longer applicable because the 'recipient' was also a 'member'. Therefore, the organizations provided greater scope for an expansion of civil society, greater empowerment, and greater social inclusion; and members were purchasers, paying for a service with the expectation of a specific return. Chapter 12 applies this analysis to attempts by the Co-operative Men's Guild to educate and politicize their members during the mid twentieth century. The objective of the Guild was to mobilize working-class men, to make them active members of society, and to promote their interests through the political system. However, while other groups were relatively effective in advancing their agendas, the Guild enjoyed only limited success because its methods of communication and its policies failed to appeal to the Co-operative Movement's substantial working-class membership. After the Second World War, many branches were criticized for degenerating into glorified social clubs, while workers in the 1950s were themselves attacked for preferring the delights of television. The inability to develop a mass popular appeal, which led to the eventual demise of the Guild, demonstrated that mutual-aid organizations and charities could be a positive force for reform only if there were clear and obvious benefits; they functioned on a two-way basis as a system of mutual exchange and gains, and if there were no tangible and obvious advantages recipients disengaged. Consequently, the Guild's promotion of 'citizenship' was in vain because the concept was neither marketed in an attractive manner nor recognized as relevant to the needs of members in the post-war world.

Professionals, like donors, often overlooked the importance of reciprocity in the success of their care and support, ignoring the fact that the execution of power over patients and clients could seriously restrict the attainment of their goals. Chapter 13 underlines the commanding position of the professional in social-work charities during the later twentieth century. Narratives of the lives of those who became clients were constructed for them within the files of the social-work agency; there they were out of reach to their central characters who were unable to correct misunderstandings, protest at misrepresentations or comment on the quality of the care that they received. Although the post-war period gave rise to research into social work and social workers, the views of clients were still not taken into account. Major reports on the training of social workers in 1959, and on the reorganization of social-work services in 1968, also signally failed to ask clients about their experiences. Research attempts to redress this one-sided record, and ostensibly to privilege the views of the powerless, were made in the 1970s and early 1980s, and greeted with acclaim by the social-work profession. However, revisiting this research refutes the claim that it retrieved the voices of clients from obscurity, because the priorities of the interviewers, and the ambitions of the agencies, all too often overshadowed the concerns of the recipients. Furthermore, there was the potential for gender distortion to arise from an all-male cast of interviewers interrogating predominantly female respondents. The process of transcription also embodied the unequal control over the outcome endemic to all such interviews. Therefore, the research methodology was unable to offset the professional power that drove the relationship between social workers and the poor in need of support.

Conclusion

This book is a counterweight to histories of medicine, charity and mutual aid that are told from the narrow perspective of those with power and authority. Britain after 1500 gradually developed a plethora of charitable organizations, akin to those that had previously emerged in the larger towns and cities of Europe.[15] With the onset of industrialization from the late eighteenth century, the vertical divisions of a mature class society slowly superseded the 'horizontal cleavage[s]' of the early modern period.[16] Even before the Industrial Revolution, however, charity was welcomed as a force for social cohesion, which defended the established hierarchy against instability and disruption. The 'deserving' poor, who had demonstrated their commitment to economic independence and self-help, were supported; the 'undeserving' poor, who were feckless and work shy, were left to rely on stigmatized poor relief. Thus the value system that underpinned social relations was reinforced.

In these circumstances, it was difficult – if not impossible – for recipients of charity to overturn its principles and policies through protest or resistance. Nevertheless, this does not imply that simplified notions of social control give an adequate account of the charitable relationship. Firstly, patients and clients contested the disinterested altruism claimed by their alleged benefactors and became increasingly inclined to see the 'generosity' of more wealthy members of the community as a right to which they were entitled rather than a gift for which gratitude was expected. Secondly, passivity in the face of donor and professional power was not uniform. Consumers manipulated services to achieve an acceptable package and rejected aid that was unpalatable. Finally, the rise of mutual-aid organizations presented opportunities for democratic participation. It follows that the starting point for research into the charitable relationship has to be its diversity. Individual narratives have depicted a variety of experiences, some more positive than others. These multiple experiences – whether expressed in language or observed in behaviour – were negotiated within

---

15 See, for example, J. Barry and C. Jones (eds), *Medicine and Charity Before the Welfare State* (London, 1991); O. P. Grell and A. Cunningham (eds), *Health Care and Poor Relief in Protestant Europe 1500–1700* (London, 1997).

16 H. Perkin, *The Origins of Modern English Society 1780–1880* (London, 1969) p. 24.

a dynamic exchange, which was shifting, unpredictable, and constructed from 'bottom-up' as well as from the 'top-down'. Consequently, traditional pictures of the recipient, which peddle generalized assumptions of docile submission, do scant justice to the historical complexities of medicine, charity and mutual aid.

CHAPTER TWO

'Pressed down by want and afflicted with poverty, wounded and maimed in war or worn down with age?' Cathedral almsmen in England 1538–1914

Ian Atherton, Eileen McGrath and Alannah Tomkins

It is the assumption of many historians that in Protestant England the link between the church and the poor was broken at the Reformation, and that, therefore, the traditions of almsgiving and poor relief of medieval English cathedrals became negligible after the 1530s.[1] In this way the English Reformation contributed to 'the wreckage of traditional charity', and the experience of poverty became more challenging, especially for those in urban poverty, given the location of most cathedrals.[2] In fact, charitable traditions continued in cathedrals, but in forms altered (and admittedly attenuated) by Henry VIII. Between 1538 and 1542 Henry refounded eight English cathedrals which had previously been monastic foundations: Canterbury, Carlisle, Durham, Ely, Norwich, Rochester, Winchester and Worcester. At the same time the king founded six entirely new cathedrals out of the ruins of the dissolved monasteries: Bristol, Chester, Gloucester, Oxford, Peterborough and Westminster.[3] The charters and statutes of these cathedrals set out a vision of a commonwealth infused with charitable endeavour. The letters patent refounding Winchester Cathedral, for example, stated that Henry was taking especial care that henceforth 'old age, specially of those who have served Us well and faithfully, [will

---

1   O. Hufton, *Bayeux in the Late Eighteenth Century* (Oxford, 1967), p. 89. See O.P. Grell, A. Cunningham and R. Jutte (eds), *Health Care and Poor Relief in 18th and 19th Century Northern Europe* (Aldershot, 2002), p. 3, for the generalization that welfare in northern Protestant countries became characterized by government rather than church control, whereas in southern and Catholic Europe the church retained or eventually reasserted control over charity. In this chapter, all dates before 1752 are old style except that the new year is taken to have begun on 1 January.

2   P. Slack, 'Hospitals, Workhouses and the Relief of the Poor in Early Modern London', in Grell, Cunningham and Jutte (eds), *Health Care and Poor Relief*, p. 235.

3   S.E. Lehmberg, *The Reformation of Cathedrals: Cathedrals in English Society, 1485–1603* (Princeton, 1988), pp. 81–91. Westminster lost its status as a cathedral in 1556 but was re-erected as a collegiate church in 1560 and it continued to support almsmen: see C.S. Knighton (ed.), *Acts of the Dean and Chapter of Westminster, 1543–1609* (Westminster Abbey Record Series, 1–2, 1997–9), i, p. xviii; ii, *passim*. Cambridge, not to be outdone by Oxford, was also granted 24 almsplaces to be attached to Trinity College even though it lacked a cathedral: see J.P.C. Roach (ed.), *Victoria County History of Cambridge and Ely*, Vol. 3 (Oxford, 1959), p. 463.

be] cherished, and lastly that Christ's poor should be succoured ... and all other such works of piety overflow far and wide into neighbouring places, to the glory of God and the benefit and welfare of our subjects'.[4]

As part of this vision, Henry's cathedrals were charged with providing for a fixed number of almsmen (known also as bedesmen), appointed by the crown. Each almsman received from the dean and chapter a stipend (between £4 10s. and £6 13s. 4d. annually, depending on the cathedral),[5] a gown and, generally, accommodation, either in a specific almshouse connected to the cathedral or in whatever rooms the cathedral had to hand. Henry ordained that the almsmen were to be 'poor men pressed down by want and afflicted with poverty, wounded and maimed in war, or worn down with age, or otherwise weakened and reduced to poverty and wretchedness'.[6] Edward VI re-emphasized the point in his charter to Norwich, decreeing that one of the purposes of the cathedral was 'that the old, whose strength is exhausted – they especially, who in the defence of Our Person, or otherwise employed in the affairs of Our Kingdom, have served Us publicly, well and faithfully – should be properly sustained with the necessaries of life'.[7] The numbers of almsmen ordained by the crown at each cathedral varied between four and 24, in relation to the institution's wealth: poorly endowed Gloucester, for example, had only four, while wealthy Canterbury had 12 and Christ Church Oxford (an anomaly in being both a cathedral and a college of the university) 24.[8] In a small cathedral city such as Ely (with a population of perhaps 2,000 in the mid seventeenth century and no almshouse before the mid eighteenth century) the six almsrooms provided by the cathedral were highly significant and the dean and chapter were the main benefactors in the town,[9] but in a larger city like Gloucester (with a population of around 5,000 in the later seventeenth century), the four cathedral almsrooms were but small beer compared to the more than 90 other places in almshouses in the city.

None the less, between 1609 and 1756 the dean and chapter of Gloucester typically spent around £80 a year (about 8 per cent of its rental income) on all charity, ranging from the stipends of the almsmen to small sums given to those begging at

---

4   G.W. Kitchen and F.T. Madge (eds), *Documents relating to the Foundation of the Chapter of Winchester A.D. 1541–1547* (London, 1889), p. 44.

5   The stipend was £4 10s. at Carlisle and Worcester, £6 at Oxford, and £6 13s. 4d. at Chester, Ely, Peterborough and Westminster. J.E. Prescott (ed.), *The Statutes of the Cathedral Church of Carlisle* (London, 1903), pp. 72–4; J. Curthoys, '"To Perfect the College ..." – the Christ Church Almsmen 1546–1888', *Oxoniensia*, 60 (1995), p. 383; Cheshire Record Office [hereafter CRO], EDD 3913/1/1, p. 25; Cambridge University Library [hereafter CUL], EDC 2/1/4 (b), f. 11v; National Archives (Public Record Office) [hereafter PRO], PC1/3/87; Westminster Abbey Library, Muniment Book 15, f. 99r.

6   W.T. Mellows (ed.), *The Foundation of Peterborough Cathedral* (Northamptonshire Record Society, 13, 1941), p. 114.

7   Norfolk Record Office [hereafter NRO], DCN 28/1, p. ix.

8   This chapter considers only cathedral and collegiate almsrooms in the gift of the crown. Other royal almshouses, such as Ewelme or the poor knights of Windsor, and almshouses at cathedrals not in the gift of the crown, such as the matrons' colleges at Salisbury and Winchester or St Ethelbert's Hospital, Hereford, are beyond the scope of this chapter.

9   *Victoria County History of Cambridgeshire*, iv, pp. 42, 45, 89.

the cathedral or on briefs and money spent on repairing roads (often in the cathedral precincts and usually much less than the £20 a year laid on them by Henry VIII for road repairs).[10] In this way, cathedral charity formed an integral part of a wider pattern of urban charity. Philanthropic effort was noticeably concentrated in large urban centres, particularly London, Norwich and Bristol, with an observable shift after 1660 towards Warwickshire and the West Riding (suggesting 'a direct connection between the stage of economic development and the sources of charity').[11] Yet, in addition to considerations of its impact, cathedral charity is worth studying because it does not suffer from one of the key problems bedevilling much previous work on the history of charity that aims to reach beyond the individual foundation – namely, the patchy and disparate survival of documentation, with wide variations in both geographical spread and typology of manuscript survivals. Cathedrals combined relative financial security with longevity (except for the period from 1649 to 1660, when they were abolished by the Interregnum regime) and they preserved their records systematically and continuously, with few gaps after 1660.[12] A comparative study of English cathedral almsmen thus permits investigation of the role and position of the recipient of urban charity that has hitherto been little explored, and allows consideration of matters of social control and social cohesion, and the themes of the relationships between donors and recipients which are central to this collection.

Therefore this chapter will examine the points of connection and disjunction between the founding intentions of charity, the charity administrators (in this case represented by the joint forces of the crown and cathedral deans and chapters), and their beneficiaries. In doing so it will analyse in some detail the process of application for a place in a cathedral almshouse, particularly the forms of words adopted by applicants and the additional information which they added (in writing or in person) to maximize their chances of appointment. It will then go on to contrast these supplicatory forms with the prosperity, behaviour and demeanour of almsmen once they were in post. It becomes clear that cathedral authorities were not above manipulating the rules governing appointments to suit their own ends, but that almsmen were similarly adept at utilizing the charity benefits flexibly. Furthermore, blatant 'misbehaviour' may often have inspired chagrin among deans and chapters, but rarely prompted almsmen's expulsion from the charity.

Admission as an almsman

Since all the almsrooms were in the gift of the crown, admission was through a complex procedure involving petitioning the monarch; many successful petitions

---

10   Gloucestershire R[ecord] O[ffice], D936 A1/1–7; *Victoria County History of Gloucestershire*, iv, pp. 102, 351–6.

11   C. Wilson, 'Poverty and Philanthropy in Early Modern England', in T. Riis (ed.), *Aspects of Poverty in Early Modern Europe* (Florence, 1981), pp. 256, 268.

12   A. Tomkins, 'Cathedral Almsmen: A New Prosopographical Project', *History and Computing*, 12/1 (2000): 99–107. The almshouses at Christ Church Oxford and Gloucester continued through the 1650s: see Curthoys, 'Christ Church Almsmen', p. 382; S. Eward, *No Fine but a Glass of Wine: Cathedral Life at Gloucester in Stuart Times* (Salisbury, 1985), pp. 106–7.

survive in cathedral archives and the files of the Signet Office, Home Office and State Paper Office in the National Archives, though the absence of failed applications limits the conclusions that can be drawn. Like Sokoll's Essex pauper letters, these petitions were highly strategic documents.[13] Recent writings on the strategies used by the poor to obtain poor relief or medical assistance discuss a number of approaches: stressing worthiness and/or honesty; playing for sympathy, even making threats. The petitions for cathedral almsrooms tapped into a range of these modes of expression but tended towards humble supplication. No petitions employ threats; a quiescent stance was probably advisable, given the discretionary nature of the almsplace awards (in contrast with poor relief that, after the Restoration, the poor came to regard as a right).[14] The format of petitions varied little, and most adopted the same strategy, stressing the military service of the petitioner and the wounds they had received which had rendered them incapable. If Taylor's categorization of the voices of pauper authors is used (formal, informative, insistent and desperate) then these petitions show a mixture of the first two, emphasizing that the petitioners were the respectable, deserving poor: honest, worthy and loyal to the crown and the established church.[15]

These petitions display a characteristic rhetoric of deferential gratitude but also adopt the unctuous wording of petitions to the crown, and most conclude with the promise of daily prayers for the sovereign and the royal family.[16] In the wake of the British civil wars and, to a lesser extent, the Glorious Revolution and the Jacobite revolts, petitioners were eager to stress their loyal service to church and crown against rebels. The petition of Edward Lloyd to Charles II for an almsroom at Chester was particularly fulsome. He was wounded while serving as a Royalist trooper in the 1640s, and ever thereafter he 'continued Loyall to your Majesties interest, and zealous for the Government of the church of England by Bishops in opposition to all the enemies thereof; and for so doeing is reduced to very great poverty' and by 1681 he was unable to support himself, his aged wife, or his three children. Signing himself 'your loyall, suffering, and almost perishing Subiect, and Servant', he promised to 'ever pray to give you the Hearts of your Subiects, and the necks of your Enemies'.[17] In some cases, details of other family members who had also served were

---

13   T. Sokoll, 'Old Age in Poverty: The Record of Essex Pauper Letters, 1780–1834', in T. Hitchcock, P. King and P. Sharpe (eds.), *Chronicling Poverty: The Voices and Strategies of the English Poor, 1640–1840* (Basingstoke, 1997), pp. 127–54.

14   P. Slack, *The English Poor Law* (Cambridge, 1999), p. 29. For an eighteenth-century view, see *The Gentleman's Magazine*, 9 (1739), p. 233. See also S. Hindle, 'The Political Culture of the Middling Sort in English Rural Communities, *c*.1550–1700', in T. Harris (ed.), *The Politics of the Excluded c.1500–1850* (Basingstoke, 2001), p. 78.

15   J.S. Taylor, 'Voices in the Crowd: The Kirkby Lonsdale Township Letters, 1809–36', in Hitchcock, King and Sharpe (eds), *Chronicling Poverty*, pp. 111–12. Additional voices are now being identified: A. Tomkins, 'Poverty, Kinship and the Case of Ellen Parker, 1818–1827', in S. King and R.M. Smith (eds), *Poverty and Relief in England, 1500–1880* (Woodbridge, forthcoming).

16   For example, PRO, SP36/50, f. 394.

17   PRO, SO8/15. In 1664 Charles II had ordered cathedrals to refuse to admit as almsmen any that did not have a record of loyal service to him or his father: Durham University Library Archives and Special Collections, GB-0033-COL, Cosin Letter Book 1B, 114.

thrown in for good measure: William Friend lost two sons in the Williamite wars in Ireland, Richard Cox 'bred up two sons who are now in your majesty's service', while Edward Robinson was supporting his daughter-in-law and grandson when his soldier son was killed in Flanders.[18] Most of the almsmen had allegedly served in the navy or the army: in a sample of 183 petitions and warrants between 1660 and 1769, 127, or 69 per cent, mention military service, and 56 (31 per cent) do not.[19] In all periods there were those who had served the crown in other ways, such as two Elizabethan almsmen at Oxford who had worked in the royal kitchens, while at Westminster there was a tradition of rewarding watermen as well as old soldiers and sailors.[20] From the 1730s, however, decay of trade became increasingly common grounds for petitioning for an almsroom, and in such cases it was necessary to counter any contemporary belief that the poor were profligate and idle, or wilfully unemployed. Many petitioners stressed their previous hard work – 'has been industrious and laborious in his calling and careful in educating his children' – and their endeavours to maintain their family without recourse to outside help.[21]

The petitions were, however, by no means the start of the process of application, which must have begun for applicants with a realization that such places existed and a calculation whether to apply for formalized charity at all, and if so, whether for a cathedral almsroom or a different form of relief.[22] In addition to local charities, there were from 1593 until the later seventeenth century county pensions for soldiers and from 1692 the pensions of the Royal Hospital, Chelsea, while for sailors there were the almshouses and pensions of Trinity House, the pensions provided by the Chest at Chatham between the 1590s and 1803, and from the 1690s, the Royal Hospital for Seamen at Greenwich. Though a pension from the Chatham Chest could be held with other bounty, most of these were mutually exclusive.[23] If cathedral charity was chosen (even though others might be quicker, more generous or more freely available),[24] which cathedral? Most requested a place in a named cathedral, usually that closest to them, though a few mentioned more than one possibility or merely pleaded for any almsroom in the crown's gift.[25] A few applicants clearly lacked

---

18   PRO, SO8/23, SO8/26, SO8/29.

19   Petitions and warrants in PRO, SO8/5, 12, 15, 29–31, 42, 45; SO5/31; SP34; SP36.

20   Curthoys, 'Christ Church Almsmen', p. 382; PRO, SO5/31, ff. 46r, 48r; SO8/31, Thomas Burnham (1709).

21   PRO, SO8/26, Richard Nelmes (1695); SO8/38, John Lines (1726); SP36/30, f. 323 (Charles Allen, 1733).

22   In 1915 the Worcester dean and chapter began advertising vacancies in the local press: Worcester Cathedral Archives [hereafter WCA], C[hapter] A[cts], A299, p. 380.

23   S.B. Black, 'The Chest at Chatham, 1590–1803', *Archaeologia Cantiana*, 111 (1993), pp. 263–80; S. Brumwell, 'Home from the Wars', *History Today*, 52/3 (March 2002): 41–7; R.E. Scouller, *The Armies of Queen Anne* (Oxford, 1966), pp. 323, 328–36; PRO, PROB11/1346, f. 269; SP36/22, f. 39.

24   PRO, SO8/31, John Foster (1709). In the mid eighteenth century the nearly 15,000 Chelsea out-pensioners received 5d. a day (£7 7s. 5d. a year): Brumwell, 'Home from the Wars', p. 44.

25   PRO, SP12/262/149; SP34/28, f. 108r; SO8/5, Thomas Head (1670), Thomas Paine (1670).

local knowledge and were merely casting round in the dark for anything they might obtain. The grant to Benjamin Hessellwood in 1697 of an almsroom in Lincoln Cathedral in consideration of the loss of a leg at sea while fighting the French five years earlier shows both the lack of detailed information of some petitioners and the lax supervision of the system sometimes operated by the royal clerks, for as it was later admitted after the grant had passed the Signet Office, there was 'No such Place in the Kings Guift'.[26] Nevertheless, most successful petitioners had already obtained the support of the dean and chapter of the cathedral at which they sought an almsroom, suggesting that the first control point over applications was exercised by the cathedral itself before any approach was made to the crown: at Worcester all bar one of the successful petitions between 1664 and 1769 were supported by at least one of the cathedral canons.[27] At Norwich in the 1880s (and probably elsewhere, then and earlier) candidates for almsrooms were interviewed by the dean before the crown was petitioned, though even then it was advantageous to have secured the support of a canon (or his wife).[28]

In the following decade the dean and chapter of Worcester decreed that any applicant for a bedesman's place was to serve on probation for three months before being recommended to the crown for an official appointment.[29] Though most cathedrals were eager to retain control over applications for their own almsrooms – in 1747 the dean and chapter of Chester insisted that no vacancies were to be disposed of by the crown without their recommendation[30] – other individuals and bodies might also exercise some patronage over the process. Many petitions were supported by the mayor and aldermen of the cathedral city or other town, while almsrooms at Durham in the early nineteenth century were effectively in the gift of the MPs for the city, who prepared a list of six or eight names who were then advanced in turn as vacancies arose; if an MP lost his seat before all his nominees had received almsrooms, there might then be a struggle to see whether his nominees, or those of his successor as MP, were favoured.[31]

A petition for a place had then to be prepared. Many are beautifully written documents,[32] and all follow the conventions of petitions to the crown. Few, if any, can have been written by the applicants themselves, and the cost of a professional scribe is further evidence that most petitioners must have had the backing of the dean and chapter or other wealthy support. Some petitions were penned by one of

---

26   PRO, SO5/31, f. 58r. As a secular cathedral, Lincoln had no royal almsmen. For a similar case see *Calendar of State Papers, Domestic, 1703–4*, p. 480.

27   PRO, SO8/2–52.

28   S.J.N. Henderson (ed.), *The Goulburn Norwich Diaries* (Norwich, 1996), p. 408.

29   WCA, CA A299, p. 6. For further details about the charitable provision of Worcester Cathedral and its bedesmen, see Eileen McGrath's forthcoming Keele PhD thesis.

30   PRO, SO5/31, rear flyleaf.

31   PRO, SO5/31, f. 22r; SO8/29, Peter Milner (1704); SO8/30, Peter Taylor (1707), Richard Hornsby (1708) and Joshua Hurst (1708); SO8/31, John Colthrand (1709); West Yorkshire Archive Service, Bradford, SpSt 11/4/4/4. At least one petition for a Norwich almsroom was addressed to the city's MPs: SO8/42, Thomas Potter (1738).

32   For example, PRO, SO8/30, Robert Allfeild (1707), Robert Tuffe (1707), Joseph Nixon (1708).

the notaries at the cathedral such as the chapter clerk: in the mid eighteenth century the dean and chapter of Winchester had a habit of compiling joint petitions on behalf of between six and ten men at a time, and doing so in their own name rather than that of the applicants.[33] Petitions may also have been penned centrally, presumably by clerks in Whitehall, for in 1708 petitions for places at Peterborough, Rochester, Oxford and Exeter are all in the same hand.[34] Certificates and testimonials needed to be appended, from former commanding officers to testify to their service or wounds (such petitions were similar in form and content to those to quarter sessions for maimed soldiers' pensions between the 1640s and 1680s),[35] or local notables (the minister, churchwardens, mayor or other borough officials, leading parishioners) to witness their need and loyalty to church and crown. Then the petition could be presented to the crown, often through the master of requests. In the 1630s the dean of the Chapel Royal and the Archbishop of Canterbury vetted each petition;[36] thereafter it is not clear how the merits of each case were judged.

If a petition were successful, then an order for the patent of an almsroom would have to be subscribed, signified and procured, often by three different officials (usually including one of the secretaries of state, who might intervene directly to appoint his own nominee),[37] and the clerk of the signet would be ordered to prepare a king's bill for the grant before the grant itself, known as an almsman's patent, would be issued.[38] This bureaucratic process was not necessarily lengthy – in 1707 Peter Taylor had his petition for a place at Chester Cathedral supported by the mayor and aldermen there on 28 March, by the dean and chapter on 31 March, and on 8 April the order to prepare a bill for the place was issued[39] – but it presumably needed someone to oil the Whitehall bureaucracy and pay the clerks' fees: in the mid eighteenth century a patent cost £1 6s. 6d., while at the beginning of the next century the total cost of the petition, patent and all the fees appears to have been £2 8s. 6d.[40] Despite the pressures of patronage, the initiative might still sometimes lie with the petitioner, as the case of Exeter Cathedral suggests. It was a secular cathedral and so had no almsrooms in the crown's gift, though at the Restoration the dean and chapter converted the cloisters into a six-place hospital for those 'fallen into distresse chiefly for their loyaltie to his Majestie'. The patronage was vested in the dean and chapter, but at least three industrious claimants secured royal nomination to the almshouse

33   PRO, EXT6/14; HO118/4; SO8/45, John Ealy and others (1747); SO8/52, Roger Upton and others (1768).

34   PRO, SO8/30, Henry Hinde, William Hixon, James Till, Joseph Rook and John Satchwell.

35   M. Stoyle, "'Memories of the Maimed": The Testimony of Charles I's Former Soldiers, 1660–1730', *History*, 88 (2003): 204–26; D.J. Appleby, 'Unnecessary Persons? Maimed Soldiers and War Widows in Essex, 1642–1660', *Essex Archaeology and History*, 32 (2001): 209–21.

36   PRO, SP16/520/5, f. 5.

37   PRO, SP36/22, f. 39.

38   PRO, SO5/31; HO118/4.

39   PRO, SP8/30, Peter Taylor (1707).

40   WCA, A45 and A127; CRO, EDD 2/38, Edward Peake (1809).

through the route reserved for king's bedesmen, no doubt trusting that the king's warrant would add weight to their suit to the cathedral.[41]

Being granted a patent of a place was by no means the end of the process for the would-be almsman. Reversionary grants had to be navigated; despite the king's order in 1635 revoking all grants in reversion and insistence that no petition would be heard unless a place was void, from the Restoration to 1815 it became the norm to grant patents in reversion. Other applicants had to be stymied: the petition of the 88-year-old Robert Curley for an almsman's place at Durham in 1788 is endorsed with the claim that he was more infirm than another petitioner.[42] Then the next vacancy had to be waited for, which might be several years. John Reynolds had to wait 21 years between the grant of his patent in 1743 and his admission to an almsroom at Worcester in 1764.[43] Thomas Wade was granted a patent for an almsman's place at Rochester on 29 November 1684; a few days later he appeared at the cathedral to demand his place, only to be disappointed with the news that there was no vacancy and, moreover, there were several men with earlier patents who would be preferred first. Over seven years later, on hearing a rumour that an almsman had died, his wife Margaret came to the chapter in April 1692 to demand her husband's place, but Thomas was again disappointed for the rumour proved to be false. He was finally admitted in 1699.[44] Not all were as eager as Wade.

Thomas Andrews must have seen his patent issued in 1792 for a place at Chester as a form of insurance policy, for by the time was admitted in 1810 he had twice consented to allow another to take the place.[45] It might even be the responsibility of the aspirant to inform the chapter that a vacancy had occurred: in 1707 Thomas Sayer appeared before the dean of Norwich brandishing his patent (issued four years previously); he was accompanied by one of the residents of the Close to testify that his uncle, a bedesman, was dead; Sayer was thereupon admitted.[46] Although the typical delay between patent and vacancy at Oxford was three years, longer waits were not uncommon, so it is not surprising that a number of grantees died before a vacancy occurred,[47] especially given that many grantees were over 60 when

---

41   A. Erskine, V. Hope and J. Lloyd, *Exeter Cathedral: A Short History and Description* (Exeter, 1988), p. 66; R.W. Parker, *Archaeo-Historical Assessment of Exeter Cathedral Cloisters* (Exeter Archaeology Report no. 97.42, 1997), pp. 21–3; PRO, SO5/31, ff. 23, 26r; SO8/25, Joseph Rook (1708). We are grateful to Prof. Nicholas Orme for discussion and references about the Exeter almshouse. For another case suggesting the initiative of the petitioner, see *Calendar of State Papers, Domestic, 1702–3*, p. 423.

42   NRO, DCN 115/9 (1635); PRO, SP12/255/41; SP16/255/2; West Yorkshire Archive Service, Bradford, SpSt 11/4/4/4; CRO, EDD 3913/3/1, ff. 25r, 96r; PRO, DURH20/130/14; CUL, EDC 2/4/1, ff. 66r, 86v. From 1815 patents were issued by the crown only on a vacancy: PRO, HO118/4.

43   WCA, A90 and D821.

44   N. Yates and P.A. Welsby (eds), *Faith and Fabric: A History of Rochester Cathedral, 604–1994* (Woodbridge, 1996), p. 106.

45   CRO, EDD 2/38; EDD 3913/1/12, p. 94. He was still in place in 1827: EDD 2/44.

46   NRO, DCN 24/4, f. 138v; PRO, SO8/29, Thomas Sayer (1703).

47   A. Tomkins, *The Experience of Urban Poverty 1723–1782: Parish, Charity and Credit* (Manchester, 2006); PRO, SO5/31, f. 18r; there are additionally many patents granted

they petitioned for a place.[48] The final hurdle to navigate before admission was the oath to be sworn to the dean to perform his duty and yield obedience to the dean and prebendaries. For most this was a formality, but not for one at Chester who in 1671 refused the oath. He was judged contemptuous 'haveing neither performed due reverence to his Governour, nor devotion to his God in this quire, openly avowing that hee careth not for the place & is not onely a person of a bad example but of an evill life being much given to excessive drinking vile detracting & severall other vicious habits', and was expelled before he began.[49]

From ailment to application to admission as an almsman was, as we have seen, often a long period. George Wilde lost a leg in the ill-fated attack on Cadiz in 1625 but continued in the navy until at least 1648; he was granted a warrant for a place at Rochester in 1669. Thomas Tyler lost both his legs serving in the navy against the Dutch in 1666; he received his patent for a place at Worcester in June 1687 and was admitted in September.[50] It is not clear how some of the almsmen supported themselves between their discharge from the army or navy and their admission to an almsroom; many must have been reduced to begging, as was the case with William Granger in the 1580s before he was admitted to Christ Church Oxford; a few, like Richard Smyth in 1603, may have received a small pension from the cathedral while they waited for a vacancy.[51] A number of almsmen had already had stays in the London hospitals. Robert Ellis was injured in the knee on board the *Pembroke* in February 1696; in March 1704 Dr Thomas Gardner certified that he had been 'turn'd out of Hospitall as Uncurable'; in July 1707 a warrant for a place in Westminster Abbey was ordered.

Thomas Johnson, also granted an almsman's place at Westminster in 1668 (though he died before a vacancy occurred), had been wounded in the left leg on the *Leopard* two years earlier in an engagement with the Dutch, and then 'Lay Nyne Months in St Thomas' Hospitall'. James Keats spent time at St Bartholomew's and Guy's Hospitals, and in the London and Westminster Infirmaries, but without being successfully cured of the lameness in his left leg he suffered while on campaign in Flanders; he was granted a place at Oxford.[52] Others had sought their own cure: Arthur Crispin was lame in his right arm and petitioned for a place at Westminster in 1688 on the grounds that he 'hath wasted what he had in trying to gett it cured'.[53]

---

but no record at the cathedral of an almsroom being entered.

48 PRO, SO5/31, ff. 22r, 27r; SO8/29, Henry Smith (1703); SO8/30, Thomas Sands (1706), Christopher Denton (1707), William Hixon (1708). There were a few almsmen in their 20s and 30s, though Charles I had ordered that no place was to be granted to anyone under '50. Or 60' except in cases of great impotency: Historical Manuscripts Commission, *Report on Manuscripts in Various Collections* (8 vols, London, 1901–13), vii, p. 63; PRO, PRO, SP16/520/1, f. 5; SO8/30, Richard Apley (1707).

49 WCA, A89; CRO, EDD 3913/3/2, pp. 86, 88.

50 PRO, SO5/31, ff. 22r, 47r; WCA, A89.

51 Curthoys, 'Christ Church Almsmen', p. 382; W.T. Mellows and D.H. Gifford (eds), *Elizabethan Peterborough* (Northamptonshire Record Society, 18, 1956), p. 43.

52 PRO, SO 8/52, James Keats (1768).

53 Curthoys, 'Christ Church Almsmen', p. 381; PRO, SO8/15, William Harper (1680), Nathaniel Sayer (1680) and John Marshall (1680); SO8/30, Robert Ellis (1707); SO5/31, ff. 18r, 48r.

There were those almsmen who, maimed in royal service, were quickly admitted to an almsroom, especially in the wake of the Second Anglo-Dutch War of 1665–7 when, the Interregnum having largely wiped the slate clean of almsmen, there were few holding reversionary grants. Jeffrey Boldock, for example, lost an arm on the *Charles* in 1666, received a patent for Norwich in March 1669, and was admitted there in June 1670.[54] Most petitioners, however, were victims of life-cycle poverty exacerbated by (often severe) disabilities caused by military service, and having maintained themselves by their own labour for many years, petitioned for a place only in old age. Many veterans of the civil wars of the 1640s were granted patents of almsrooms in the 1670s and 1680s. Francis Calverley's was a typical case: he lost his limbs at Brentford in 1642, but it was on account of his failing eyesight, which meant he could no longer earn his living by his penmanship, that he petitioned for a place at Peterborough in 1675.[55]

Aspiring almsmen had, therefore, to negotiate a long and tortuous process, attracting the support of their commanding officer, local MP, cathedral dean or mayor, navigating the standardized procedures of the royal bureaucracy while remaining sensitive to the particular custom and practice of their chosen cathedral. Failure to secure a grant in the correct form could mean that the dean and chapter refused to admit the aspiring almsman, even though he bore royal letters for his admission.[56] The tenacity and sometimes longevity required were somewhat in contrast with the self-fashioning required to present themselves as grateful, deserving and helpless poor, 'incapable of doing any act of his own towards his support' in the words of one petition.[57] They were also rather at odds with the benefits yielded by an almsman's place.

Rewards for almsmen

The rewards garnered by almsmen were not necessarily commensurate with the efforts required to secure them. The main benefit came in the form of a stipend. The stipend granted in the 1540s remained fixed and was rarely augmented: at Norwich, for example, it rose from £6 to £8 a year in 1808 and to £10 in 1818, where it remained in 1854. By that year small increases had also been made at Bristol, Durham, Gloucester, Rochester, Westminster, Winchester and Worcester; at Canterbury, Chester, Ely, Oxford and Peterborough there had been no augmentation at all; and at Carlisle the stipend had actually decreased.[58] What started as a fair pension was significantly degraded over this period. Almsmen also received other benefits, such

---

54 PRO, SO5/31, f. 19r; NRO, DCN 24/3, f. 91r.

55 PRO, SO8/10, Francis Calverley (1675) and Anthony Gold (1675); SO8/12, Thomas Spink (1677), SO8/15, Edward Lloyd (1681) and William Castle (1681).

56 CUL, EDC 2/4/1, f. 86v.

57 PRO, DURH20/130/14.

58 NRO, DCN 26/10/7, 6 December 1808; Curthoys, 'Christ Church Almsmen', pp. 390–91; *First Report of Her Majesty's Commissioners ... to Inquire into the State and Condition of the Cathedral and Collegiate Churches*, Parliamentary Papers, 1854 [1821] xxv, 1, pp. xxxv, 1–36; *Third and Final Report*, Parliamentary Papers, 1854–5 [1936] xv, 39, p. 10. By the mid nineteenth century some cathedrals were having difficulties filling almsrooms.

as a gown (blue at Norwich, purple at Westminster, black at Chester) with a red silk rose on the left shoulder.[59] Henry VIII's intention had been that almsmen should be housed in the cathedral close and this seems to have been common practice for the first century.[60] Though sixteenth-century regulations for the almshouse of Oxford Cathedral imply that the wives of almsmen lived in the town rather than the almshouse, almsmen and their families did live in, for example at Worcester (where Gabriel Mence and his family occupied rooms over the north porch of the cathedral) and, in the eighteenth and nineteenth centuries, at Oxford.[61] From the Restoration, however, a number of cathedrals, like Worcester, no longer housed all (or indeed any) of their almsmen, who thereby became a species of out-pensioner.[62] Some cathedrals, however, continued to provide accommodation. Christ Church Oxford had a two-storey almshouse for its bedesmen, standing opposite the college in St Aldate's parish, on the ground now occupied by the east end of Pembroke College. Nevertheless, the almshouse housed a maximum of 16 of the 24 almsmen: Anthony Wood described the buildings of Christ Church hospital as incomplete in 1662; drawings dating from the early nineteenth century depict the almshouse partly in ruins and at that time no more than four almsmen resided there with other parts of the building let as a timber yard.[63] By 1865 no cathedral housed its almsmen except Oxford, which accommodated 12 of its 24 bedesmen.[64]

Though the value of a bedesman's place declined significantly, such almsrooms still had worth. First, almsmen might receive a variety of informal charity in addition to their entitlements under the cathedral's statutes. There might be small payments for additional duties such as blowing the organ, caring for the churchyard and dealing with tourists;[65] there might be a share of the offerings received at communions or

59 NRO, DCN 24/5, f. 108v (1767); Westminster Abbey Library, WAM 46755 (1749); CRO, EDD 2/44 (1827).

60 Westminster Abbey Library, Muniment Book 15, f. 99r; G.A. Metters (ed.), *The Parliamentary Survey of Dean and Chapter Properties in and around Norwich in 1649* (Norfolk Record Society, 51, 1985), p. 36; I. Atherton, 'The Dean and Chapter, Reformation to Restoration: 1541–1660', in P. Meadows and N. Ramsay (eds), *A History of Ely Cathedral* (Woodbridge, 2003), p. 176; R.V.H. Burne, *Chester Cathedral* (London, 1958), p. 63; Eward, *Cathedral Life at Gloucester*, pp. 98, 107.

61 WCA, CA A76, p.67; William Green's wife apparently gave birth to four children in the almshouse in the 1760s and 1770s, see Oxford RO, Mss dd par Oxford St Aldate's baptismal register, baptisms of 9 September 1763, 6 October 1765, 4 May 1772 and 21 March 1775; Curthoys, 'Christ Church Almsmen', pp. 384–5 (though this author thinks that the families of Oxford almsmen continued to live out).

62 J. Noake, *The Monastery and Cathedral of Worcester* (London, 1866), pp. 575–7.

63 D. Macleane, *A History of Pembroke College* (Oxford Historical Society, 33, 1897), pp. 435–7; *Wood's City of Oxford* (Oxford Historical Society, 15, 1890), pp. 193–4; J. Skelton, *Oxonia Antiqua Restaurata* (Oxford, 1823), vol. 2; Curthoys, 'Christ Church Almsmen', pp. 380–81, 388.

64 *Return from the Deans and Chapter of the Several Cathedral and Collegiate Churches*, Parliamentary Papers, 1865 (206) xli, 439.

65 Gloucestershire RO, D936 A12/2; P. Barrett, *Barchester: English Cathedral Life in the Nineteenth Century* (London, 1993), pp. 110–11; Curthoys, 'Christ Church Almsmen', pp. 390–91.

other extra payments;[66] there might be doles of money or in kind on special occasions such as a bishop's enthronement or dean's installation, or on church feasts such as Christmas.[67] Like many of the poor, the bedesmen subsisted on an economy of makeshifts.[68] Second, being an almsman brought a variety of intangible but none the less important benefits. There was the status of being known as a 'king's almsman' which, in a status-conscious society, might have been considered important by some.[69] The portraits of two Chester almsmen painted in 1827, or the photograph of all ten of Worcester's almsmen taken in 1891, suggest something of the status, authority and pride that an almsman might derive from his post.[70] In addition, the almsmen of Westminster Abbey had a place in processions at royal funerals.[71] Being a cathedral almsman may have helped to unlock access to a range of other preferment in the gift of the dean and chapter for the bedesmen's family, such as appointment as a cathedral officer,[72] or admission to the cathedral school,[73] or even for the bedesman himself.[74]

In 1898 John Hammerton, formerly a colour sergeant in the Worcestershire regiment, was admitted as a bedesmen at Worcester. His talents were quickly spotted: he was rapidly appointed verger; then the custos (who had both charge of

---

66 Gloucestershire RO, D936 A1/3, p. 281; NRO, DCN 24/3, ff. 92r, 220–1r; S.E. Lehmberg, *Cathedrals under Siege: Cathedral in English Society, 1600–1700* (Exeter, 1996), p. 244; Historical Manuscripts Commission, *Various Collections*, vii, p. 68; NRO, DCN 24/3, ff. 220-1r, DCN 24/5, ff. 139v, 284r; WCA, A102–3.

67 Henderson (ed.), *Goulburn Norwich Diaries*, pp. 80, 93, 289, 327–8; Norwich Dean and Chapter Library, Dean Goulburn's diaries, 31 December 1881 (a reference we owe to the Revd Noel Henderson); WCA, CA A76 (1675).

68 S. King and A. Tomkins (eds), *The Poor in England 1700–1850: An Economy of Makeshifts* (Manchester, 2003).

69 West Yorkshire Archive Service, Bradford, SpSt 11/4/4/4; CRO, EDD 3913/1/1, p. 12. Similarly membership of the Welsh charity school in London carried status implications along with the benefit of free schooling; see S. Lloyd, '"Agents in their own Concerns"? Charity and the Economy of Makeshifts in Eighteenth-Century Britain', in King and Tomkins (eds), *The Poor in England*, pp. 100–36.

70 CRO, EDD 2/44; WCA, G1, reproduced in Barrett, *Barchester*, pl. 13.

71 Historical Manuscripts Commission, *Various Collections*, iv, p. 164; W.S. Lewis (ed.), *The Yale Edition of Horace Walpole's Correspondence* (London, 1937–83), xi, p. 322.

72 John Coates, senior, was almsman at Norwich in the 1660s; another man of the same name, probably his son, was subsacrist there from 1665 to 1695: NRO, DCN 11; ANW admon. John Coates 1672, 100.

73 Although the evidence is often only circumstantial, there are examples of the admission of a scholar shortly after the admission of a bedesman of the same name: *Calendar of State Papers, Domestic, 1598–1601*, p. 198; *1661–2*, p. 9; PRO, SO8/31, Thomas Robins (1709); D.M. Owen and D. Thurley (eds), *The King's School Ely* (Cambridge Antiquarian Records Society, 5, 1982), pp. 22, 52–3, 94; CRO, EDD 3913/3/2, pp. 16, 57; C.D. Watkinson, 'Thomas Ebdon', *Oxford Dictionary of National Biography* (Oxford, 2004).

74 Hugh Dod, a bedesman of Chester from 1661, was also appointed porter (1662) and verger (1665). Henry Hughes, another Chester bedesmen admitted in 1676, was the following year made verger and trooper for the cathedral in the county militia: CRO, EDD 3913/3/2, p. 16, f. 29r; EDD 3913/1/5, pp. 17, 221, 227, 341.

the bedesmen, vergers and cleaners, and a salary of £100, many times that of a bedesman) was forced to resign in his favour, and then he was asked to undertake the duties of subsacrist and clerk of works.[75] There might be other benefits for bedesmen. At Worcester in the later nineteenth century cathedral almsmen were regularly promoted to the cathedral's hospital of St Oswald, an almshouse which provided accommodation.[76] Third was the profit that an enterprising almsman (or his family) might make from his place. At the end of Elizabeth's reign at least one Oxford almsman was able to procure a room in the almshouse for another in return for a payment of £10, while an Ely almsman was able to resign his place to a nominated successor. Where accommodation was provided, it might be sublet: in the 1720s the Oxford bedesmen sublet a part of their almshouse as a brewhouse.[77] It was sometimes even possible for the family of an almsman to continue in the almshouse after his death: Elizabeth Crosier continued as a lodger in Christ Church almshouse for 16 years after the death of her almsman father in 1745.[78] Almsmen and their relations clearly made creative use of the makeshifts at their disposal.

None the less, the depth of almsmen's poverty (particularly after their election to a cathedral place) was probably limited. Research in this area to date suggests that, notwithstanding the falling relative value of the almsmen's stipend, few became so impoverished that they made a successful call on parish poor relief. With careful husbanding, an almsman's stipend would have represented a small but sufficient income for a single person in the mid eighteenth century for example, and the majority portion of a poor family's income, though not enough on its own for a family's survival. Even so, a comparison between the 70 almsmen who received stipends from Oxford at some time during the period 1740–70 and the identities of those receiving some form of parish relief in Oxford city in the mid eighteenth century showed very little overlap between the two groups. Only three almsmen can definitely be identified among city paupers; the great majority of Christ Church almsmen avoided the need for parish relief altogether.[79] This resilience was not obviously impaired by Christ Church men having young families. The presence of nuclear families might arguably have provided insurance against parish relief: wives and children may even have supplied the additional income that rendered parish support unnecessary. If this virtual separation of cathedral poor from parish poor was a feature of the welfare picture nationwide, it may well have arisen from apprehensions about the appropriate groups targeted by different support agencies. Cathedral almshouses catered for a subsection of the poor slightly out of kilter with the parish definition of the deserving poor in that, broadly, adult men were not

75 Cathedral Commission, *Report ... upon the Cathedral Church of Worcester*, Parliamentary Papers, 1884 [C3939], xxii, 159, p. 18, app. p. 4; WCA, CA A299, pp. 51–2, 79, 84, 88–90.

76 WCA, CA A168 and St Oswald's lists of residents.

77 Curthoys, 'Christ Church Almsmen', pp. 386–8; CUL, EDC 2/4/1, ff. 66r, 112v; Metters (ed.), *Parliamentary Survey*, p. 36.

78 Oxford RO, Mss dd par Oxford St Aldate's marriage of 13 December 1761 (when Elizabeth Crosier was married to James Gardiner, and both were described as lodgers in Christ Church almshouse).

79 Tomkins, *The Experience of Urban Poverty*.

typical recipients of parish relief; instead payments were concentrated on the elderly (particularly women) and children.

When the amounts of parish money paid to the three apparently pauperized Oxford almsmen are investigated, their claim to impoverishment becomes even more tenuous. Two of the three known pauper almsmen took very little parish money.[80] The third pauper, Henry Huntingdon, arguably became a victim of the contemporary practice of selling pensions; if people in receipt of some regular benefit like an almshouse pension needed to approach a parish for additional relief, the parish might insist on receiving the pension or payment to offset its costs.[81] On 20 April 1756, St Mary Magdalen parish in Oxford paid 2s. 6d. to have Huntingdon's pension made over to them. The parish may have been afraid that he would run away and leave his wife and family to be relieved, as he had done on one occasion already in 1755, when he had been followed to Abingdon, apprehended and committed to one of Oxford's gaols. It should be noted, however, that there were no entries on the credit side of the St Mary Magdalen overseers' accounts during Huntingdon's life to suggest that the pension was actually received by the parish. He might have been forced to sign his charity pension over as a sort of insurance or indemnity; the parish could either hold it in abeyance indefinitely or enforce its right to his money if need arose.

In his satirical poem of 1740, John Woodman was heavily critical of the system that purportedly allowed Chelsea Hospital pensioners to sell their pensions. At Chelsea, pensions could be paid a year or more in advance, but the money was allegedly squandered in a fraction of the time it was supposed to last, leaving pensioners destitute as 'there is not the one Half of them who are inclined to be careful or frugal'. Creditors would supply money until the next pension payment was due and then demand all of this income in repayment, forcing pensioners into a cycle of borrowing. Woodman deplored the fact that from the pensions that poor men should have received from the hospital, 'their overseers and others may get above £6,000 a year'.[82] But it remains to be proved that significant numbers of Chelsea pensioners or cathedral almsmen fell into this sort of poverty trap. The implication that Chelsea pension sales to parish officers were so notorious as to merit satire is itself the only evidence of wholesale dependency on poor relief.

Indeed, cathedral statutes that ordained that almsmen should be poor and infirm or aged could be bent or contradicted and some claims to poverty were patently nominal. The laconic and formulaic phraseology of the petition could hide a different story. At the beginning of 1708 Aaron Alcock petitioned for an almsroom at Norwich on the grounds of his poverty and good reputation and his suit was supported by the dean and chapter who certified that Alcock was 'a poor man and a fit object for her Majestys Charity'; that August he was admitted as an almsman. The dean's diary, however, reveals the true reason for Alcock's preferment. Minding his own business

---

80   Oxford RO, Mss dd par Oxford St Martin St Martin b.17–b.21 overseers' accounts 1725–72, entries concerning Ralph Pettit; St Mary Magdalen, Mss dd par Oxford St Mary Magdalen, b.71 overseers' accounts 1750–66 entries concerning Edward Maiden.

81   For example, see P. Anderson, 'The Leeds Workhouse under the Old Poor Law: 1726–1834', *Publications of the Thoresby Society*, 56/2 (1980), p. 90.

82   J. Woodman, *The Rat-Catcher at Chelsea College* (London, 1740), pp. vii, 24.

one day in Norwich, the dean's coach had raced towards Alcock after the horses had bolted and the coachman had been thrown to the ground. As it sped past Alcock had grabbed the reins and stopped the coach. The dean, convinced that Alcock had saved his life, repaid him with a grant of the next almsroom to fall vacant.[83] Alcock's was but a particularly dramatic case of a dean and chapter rewarding someone already connected with the cathedral or its higher clergy. Daniel Goodwyn's appointment as a Norwich almsman in 1711 was secured by the bishop of Norwich because he was a creditable tradesman in the city who had fallen into decay, and because his son was the archdeacon of Oxford.[84] In the early eighteenth century the dean and chapter of Winchester secured grants of almsrooms to one who had been maimed while fighting a fire at the cathedral and to another injured while repairing one of the canon's houses.[85] Almsrooms were also regularly used as a reward for old cathedral retainers. One of the first bedesmen at Ely was a former servant to the bishop there, while an Elizabethan bedesman at Canterbury had been keeper of the bishop's palace;[86] in the eighteenth century Ely almsrooms were regularly granted to those described as 'a poor retainer' to Ely Cathedral.[87]

Almsrooms might be a way of pensioning off cathedral officers too old to carry out the duties of their office, such as William Geast, a verger at Norwich from 1680 until his appointment as almsman in 1688.[88] They might even be used in an underhand way: in 1677, in a bid to reduce the number of conducts (lay clerks) they had to maintain, the dean and chapter of Chester had the grant of an almsroom to Francis Watson fraudulently revoked and procured the appointment of John Penn, one of their 'unserviceable' conducts, in his place – without Penn's knowledge and against his wishes (the stipend of an almsmen being less than half that of a conduct). However, on Watson's appeal to the crown the appointment of Penn was declared void (it being discovered that the petition on behalf of Penn made a number of untrue claims about his having fought for Charles I when he was, in fact, too young to have participated in the civil wars); Watson was restored as an almsman, and Penn as a conduct.[89] There was also a tendency to use almsmen's places merely as a means of supplementing the stipend of favoured cathedral officers even though they met none of the qualifying conditions. James Hawkins, organist at Ely 1682–1729, was granted an almsman's patent in 1708; William Kirk, senior verger of Norwich 1715–27, was also an almsman there from 1719.[90] Isaac Miller was one of the dean of Norwich's

83   PRO, SP34/38, ff. 73–4; NRO, DCN 115/2, p. 221; DCN 24/4, f. 145v.

84   NRO, DCN 11; DCN 115/2, pp. 326–7.

85   PRO, SO8/30, Richard Rose (1707), Richard Jones (1708).

86   *Letters and Papers, Foreign and Domestic, of the Reign of Henry VIII*, xvi, no. 985, p. 477; *Diocesis Cantuarensis Registrum Matthei Parker* (Canterbury and York Society, 1907–33), vii, p. 665.

87   PRO, SO8/29, John Knowles (1705); SO8/31, Thomas Robins (1709); SO8/42, Thomas Kempton, Francis Fern, Richard Lucas (1738).

88   NRO, DCN 11; Dean and Chapter Peculiar, Register of Wills, iv, ff. 156–7r.

89   CRO, EDD 3913/3/2, p. 94; EDD 3913/3/3, pp. 14, 17–18; PRO, SO8/12, Francis Watson (1677).

90   Meadows and Ramsay (eds), *Ely Cathedral*, p. 225; PRO, SO8/30, James Hawkins (1708); NRO, DCN 11; DCN 115/3, p. 62; Dean and Chapter Peculiar, Register of Wills,

most trusted servants: described by him as 'a person very fitt to serve ye church on any occasion that may happen', he garnered a sheaf of positions to be held in plurality: keeper of the cathedral prison from 1702, bailiff of the chapter's woods from 1707, and almsman from 1716.[91] Half of those holding almsrooms at Chester in 1665 were already members of the choir: two as minor canons and one as conduct.[92]

A few even made wills: Thomas Sayer, a Norwich almsman and worsted weaver, for example, made bequests in his will in 1708 totalling £30 in cash, besides his household goods.[93] One of Chester's bedesmen in 1827 was Nathaniel Harrison, one of the substantial cheesemongers of the city.[94] Henry VIII's mid sixteenth-century vision of a scheme of charitable relief for those afflicted with poverty was, in the long eighteenth century, in danger of becoming a provision for the old age of some of the middling sort.

Almsmen, control and power relationships

If deans and chapters disrupted Henrician expectations about the likely beneficiaries of cathedral charities, almsmen in their turn could contradict expectations about their behaviour once in post. Having acquired places by fashioning themselves as powerless, weak and deserving, the documentary evidence of the bedesmen's subsequent behaviour does not necessarily conform to the idealized notion of the grateful, powerless poor. As Andy Wood has noted, everyday power relations demanded of plebeians that they disguise their feelings. Deference to a lord or employer could secure work, land, credit, gifts, charity or patronage. And the converse was equally true: misplaced truculence, a willingness to speak out of turn, or a refusal to follow the public behaviour expected of subordinates, could all lead to trouble.[95]

Bedesmen were accused of four main types of misbehaviour: neglect of duty (the most chronic), intoxication, begging, and disrespectful conduct. Deans and chapters sought to advance those with whom they already had connections to almsrooms in part because, in return for the benefits they received, bedesmen were expected to perform certain duties. They were expected to attend services daily and to pray

---

v, f. 67. For a similar practice at Gloucester at the Restoration, see Historical Manuscripts Commission, *Various Collections*, vii, p. 63.

91   NRO, DCN 11/6–7, extraordinaries, 1724 and *passim*; DCN 115/1, pp. 181–2; DCN 115/2, pp. 189–90; DCN 24/4, ff. 101r, 170r. At Gloucester James Sayer, a former soldier, tailor and tenant of one of the cathedral's houses in the precincts, was appointed subsacrist in 1686, bedesman in 1689, porter in 1690; he was also library keeper and paid to keep order in the churchyard; all these offices he kept until his death in 1713. His son was chapter auditor from 1702. Eward, *Cathedral Life at Gloucester*, pp. 214, 221–2, 271, 277.

92   CRO, EDD 3913/1/5, pp. 15, 17.

93   NRO, Dean and Chapter Peculiar, Register of Wills, iv, ff. 231v–2r. See also Curthoys, 'Christ Church Almsmen', pp. 385–6.

94   CRO, EDD 2/44; James Pigot & Co.'s *National Commercial Directory* (1828–9; 1834), Chester.

95   A. Wood, '"Poore Men Woll Speke One Daye": Plebeian Languages of Deference and Defiance in England, *c.*1520–1640', in T. Harris (ed.), *The Politics of the Excluded c. 1500–1850* (Basingstoke, 2001), pp. 78–9.

for the monarch, to assist at those services, toll the bells and clean the cathedral church.[96] Repeatedly, however, cathedrals reported that the bedesmen neglected their duties and were absent from the cathedral.[97] Individuals were admonished for neglect of duty,[98] but so chronic was the neglect that often it was tackled as a group problem. Prior to the civil war at Worcester, Robert Davis, Richard Dirram and Walter Evans were all suspended for non-attendance and for 'manifest contumacy' in not appearing in chapter to answer their case, resulting in a suspension of salary until the dean 'pleases to restore them again'.[99] Again at Worcester, in 1735 Henry Phillips, Richard Jelley, Henry Glover and John Lines were admonished by the dean for not attending services and John Child was given a special warning for his lack of diligence regarding both cleaning and attendance.[100]

Prochaska has argued that outbreaks of institutional resistance expressed themselves most notably in the form of drunken and disorderly conduct,[101] and though this can be seen in the case of the almsmen, his judgement underestimates the degree to which moral codes and their implementation changed over time. Drunkenness among the almsmen was a persistent problem from the Reformation, but in the Victorian period cathedral authorities appear to have taken a sterner view of the abuse. John Allgate resigned his almsroom at Worcester in 1880 when given an ultimatum to cease occupying or managing the public house where he was then living,[102] while William Edmund Linton, after three admonitions for drunkenness, was expelled from Worcester in 1896. In Linton's case his misbehaviour was the more egregious for being public: he was intoxicated in the street and was uncivil to visitors.[103] The closer supervision of almsmen seen at Worcester and elsewhere from the mid nineteenth century was a reflection of the development of a sterner moral code and the rise of cathedral tourism (which made the role of bedesmen – and any misdemeanours – more public). At Worcester, for example, begging by bedesmen became a punishable offence. James Barnes, having been reported to the canon in

---

96   Gloucestershire RO, D936 X16, art. 22. In the mid and late nineteenth century many cathedrals sought to increase the duties of the bedesmen, sometimes also increasing their stipend: *Return from the Deans and Chapter of the Several Cathedral and Collegiate Churches*, Parliamentary Papers, 1865 (206) xli, 439, pp. 30–1, 46; Cathedral Commission, *Report ... upon the Cathedral Church of Carlisle*, Parliamentary Papers, 1884 [C3937], xxii, 99, pp. 18–19; *Report ... upon the Cathedral Church of Gloucester*, Parliamentary Papers, 1884–5 [C4307], xxi, 213, p. 13, app. p. 4.

97   Gloucestershire RO, D936 A1/1, p. 139; Historical Manuscripts Commission, *Various Collections*, vii, p. 67; Westminster Abbey Library, Muniment Book 14, f. 11r.

98   For example, WCA, CA A77, p. 149; A299, p. 3b; Gloucester Cathedral Library, MS 2, ff. 139r, 141r.

99   WCA, CA A75, p. 121.

100 WCA, CA A77, p. 148.

101 F. Prochaska, 'Philanthropy', in F.M.L. Thompson (ed.), *The Cambridge Social History of Britain, 1750–1950, Volume III: Social Agencies and Institutions* (Cambridge, 1990), p. 375.

102 *Registrum Matthei Parker*, vii, pp. 665–6; Curthoys, 'Christ Church Almsmen', pp. 385, 390; WCA, CA A298, pp. 80b, 83.

103 WCA, CA, A298, pp. 132, 214, 216; A299, p. 3b.

residence for asking for and receiving money from a visitor in the cathedral, was suspended for one month in 1882 and John Beckwith was suspended for over two weeks in 1874 as a result of having been seen merely to accept money from a visitor to the cathedral.[104] The increased numbers of admonitions of almsmen was also in response to the attempt of the first Cathedral Commission in 1855 to reinvigorate the role of bedesmen and increase the powers of deans and chapters over them.[105]

Lack of deference was perceived as a problem by chapters. In 1687 Hugh Prescott, a Worcester almsman, was charged with having written and sent a 'scandalous letter' to the dean, wherein he had 'falsely charged his superiors with defaming his wages' (presumably as a result of some misdemeanour not specified in the chapter acts) 'with other false and disobedient imputations' and that he had further offended by 'causing the names of some persons of honour to be forged and subscribed to the said letter'. On this occasion Prescott 'confessed himself very sorry for it, submitted and desired pardon'. His punishment was merely a recorded admonishment   the equivalent of a written warning.[106] As Prescott's case suggests, disrespectful behaviour by the bedesmen was only rarely dealt with harshly, even in the late nineteenth century.

The rule of deans and chapters over their almsmen was generally tolerant, even lax. Though regulations for the Christ Church almshouse in Oxford were occasionally promulgated, there is little evidence that they were consistently enforced.[107] Deans and chapters did have a range of sanctions from deduction of stipends for absence to admonishment, suspension and expulsion, but they were often hesitant to employ these. Expulsion was rarely used, as the case of William Mence of Worcester illustrates. He enjoyed a running battle with the chapter over a period of seven years between 1734 and 1741. What began as an issue of the neglect of duty escalated to a matter of 'insolent behaviour in chapter and … his manifest contumacy and contempt' of former admonitions. What is interesting about his case is the number of repeated chances that the chapter give him to mend his ways – which he failed to do. The chapter was very reluctant to impose the extreme penalty even though he was 'incorrigible' and was expelled, not once, but twice – in 1735 and 1741 – the second time being six years after his third (and by the cathedral statutes final) admonition.[108] At Norwich between 1615 and 1718, there were 54 admonitions of cathedral officers, only one being of an almsman, and eight expulsions, none of them an almsman; it was the minor canons and the lay clerks who were most frequently punished – mainly for drunkenness, negligence, absence, sexual immorality or disrespect to the dean.[109]

Such tolerance was born of a number of factors. In the first place, before the mid nineteenth century the interest of many deans and chapters in their almsmen was sporadic, or confined to particular individuals, for a number of reasons. Their

---

104 WCA Chapter Acts, A298, pp. 12, 100.

105 Cathedral Commission, *Third and Final Report*, pp. xx–xxi.

106 WCA, CA A76, p. 143.

107 Curthoys, 'Christ Church Almsmen', pp. 385–7, 394–5.

108 WCA, CA A 77, pp. 141, 143, 174.

109 NRO, DCN 24/2–4; DCN 115/1–3. There were 6 minor canons, 8 lay clerks and 6 bedesmen.

appointment was not wholly in chapter hands. Their stipends were a fixed charge on the chapter's income, laid down by the cathedral statutes and ordained by the crown; as cathedral revenues grew dramatically from the late seventeenth century until the late nineteenth, chapters could easily sustain such a small outgoing.[110] Many of their statutory duties could be quietly dropped (such as the saying of particular prayers)[111] or more easily discharged by deputies: between the Restoration and the early eighteenth century at Norwich, Chester, Peterborough and Rochester, for example, deductions were made from the stipend of each almsman to pay a deputy to undertake their duties of sweeping the church and tolling the bells.[112] Deans and canons did not always know who their almsmen were. Dean Goulburn of Norwich, for example, rarely mentioned the bedesmen in his late Victorian diaries and when he did, it was rarely by name – lay clerks and minor canons, those who celebrated divine service in the cathedral with him, by contrast, feature much more regularly.[113] Similarly, almsmen themselves might not know who the dean and canons were. In 1631 Edmund Taylor, a Norwich almsman for four years, thought that his stipend came from 'the paymaster to his Majesties Maymed souldiars' rather than the canon-treasurer, while 40 years later four Norwich almsmen procured a third party to write on their behalf to the dean to inquire of the name of the current treasurer from whom they might receive their wages.[114] In such low regard did they hold their bedesmen that Carlisle and Rochester from the 1770s and Ely a little later stopped appointing almsmen altogether (though all recommenced appointments in 1851, anticipating the recommendations of the Cathedral Commission).[115] Even after the Cathedral Commission, some cathedral clergy wished an end to bedesmen: in 1884 Dean Perowne of Peterborough castigated their appointment as 'an almost unmitigated evil',[116] while Christ Church Oxford ceased providing accommodation for its almsmen in 1876, converting the almshouse into a canonry.[117]

---

110 The annual receipts of Norwich Cathedral, for example, grew five-and-a-half-fold between the 1670s and the 1860s: see I. Atherton and B.A. Holderness, 'The Dean and Chapter Estates since the Reformation', in I. Atherton *et al.* (eds), *Norwich Cathedral: Church, City and Diocese, 1096–1996* (London, 1996), p. 687.

111 Curthoys, 'Christ Church Almsmen', p. 389. The statutory prayers of the bedesmen are set out in Mellows (ed.), *Peterborough Cathedral*, p. 121 and CUL, EDC 2/1/4, (b) f. 14v, (c) f. 13v.

112 Bodleian Library, MS Tanner 133, f. 144r; CRO, EDD 3913/3/3, pp. 69, 100; Burne, *Chester Cathedral*, p. 180; PRO, PC1/3/87/5; Yates and Welsby (eds), *Faith and Fabric*, p. 107. After the Restoration almsmen at Bristol and Ely also used deputies: PRO, SO8/29, Richard Perryman (1703); CUL, EDR F/5/41, f. 176r.

113 Henderson (ed.), *Goulburn Norwich Diaries*.

114 NRO, DCN 12/27, Edmund Taylor's receipt, 8 December 1631; J.F. Williams and B. Cozens-Hardy (eds), *Extracts from the Two Earliest Minute Books of the Dean and Chapter of Norwich Cathedral, 1566–1649* (Norfolk Record Society, 24, 1953), p. 65; Bodleian Library, MS Tanner 134, f. 136.

115 Yates and Welsby (eds), *Faith and Fabric*, p. 107; Prescott (ed.), *Statutes of Carlisle*, p. 65 n. 1; PRO, HO45/8541-2.

116 Cathedral Commission, *Report... upon the Cathedral Church of Peterborough*, Parliamentary Papers, 1884–5 [C4308] xxi, 249, app., p. 13.

117 Curthoys, 'Christ Church Almsmen', pp. 390–92.

Second, the relatively low financial value of an almsroom caused problems to almsmen and chapters alike. Some bedesmen were allowed to carry on a trade in order to supplement their stipend, though Gabriel Mence was expelled from Worcester for carrying on his – shoemaking – in his rooms above the north porch of the cathedral in 1670.[118] An alternative solution was employed at Ely as early as the 1560s: the dean and chapter allowed its almsmen to 'go abroad for their better living'.[119] In the seventeenth century it became common practice for many almsmen at Ely, Norwich, Peterborough and Rochester, and possibly elsewhere, rarely or never to attend, preferring life in London and expecting their stipends to be paid there or to a third party who would then forward the money to the capital.[120] In the 1670s four of Norwich's complement of six bedesmen and four of Ely's six were absent.[121] Absenteeism became such a problem that the canons might lose track of their almsmen. In 1673 one of the minor canons of Gloucester reported that 'As for the poore men We have sometimes none of them at prayers, sometimes one, sometimes two, but seldome three, as for the 4th I know not where he is, or whether there be a 4th'.[122] Norwich almsman John Rochester died in London in 1695, but it was five and a half years before the chapter discovered what had happened to him, while one canon candidly informed the dean about another in 1718: 'As to William Parker our Beadsman, I cannot yet learn where his abode was ... Tis 3 yeares at Michaelmas last since he has been with me.'[123] If losing one bedesman may be regarded as misfortune, losing two looks like carelessness.

Cathedrals, in fact, were not wholly to blame, for the third reason for the lax discipline often enforced was that bedesmen were not wholly under the control of the dean and chapter. The four absentee almsmen at Ely in 1679 all had the king's dispensation to continue in their almsrooms without attending the cathedral.[124] Though bedesmen were supposed to be obedient to the dean and chapter, their patents were granted for life (until 1812, when they were amended to during the king's pleasure), giving them security of tenure: many contemporaries suspected that the relative certainty of keeping an almsroom once admitted (compared with, say, a one-off charity) encouraged complacency and disorderly conduct.[125] Moreover, the process of their appointment, requiring them to collect the support of former commanding officers or town and parish notables, and their position as almsmen of

---

118 WCA, CA A76, p. 67. In Mence's case the issue appears to have been that his trade was carried on in the church, not that he was at work. In 1821 Thomas Jolley was allowed by the Worcester chapter to continue his trade while continuing as an almsman: WCA, CA A81, p. 28.

119 Atherton, 'Dean and Chapter 1541–1660', p. 184.

120 CUL, EDC 3/5/2, Richard Dudley's acquittance; Bodleian Library, MSS Tanner 133, ff. 25v, 144r, Tanner 134, f. 106; Mellows (ed.), *Peterborough Cathedral*, pp. lviii–lix; PRO, PC1/3/87; Yates and Welsby (eds), *Faith and Fabric*, p. 107.

121 Bodleian Library, MS Tanner 134, f. 136; CUL, EDR F/5/41, f. 176r.

122 Eward, *Cathedral Life at Gloucester*, p. 147.

123 NRO, DCN 115/1, p. 113; DCN 32/32, Martin to Prideaux, 29 November 1718.

124 CUL, EDR F/5/41, f. 176r.

125 PRO, HO118/4; A. Tomkins, 'Almshouse versus Workhouse: Residential Welfare in 18th-Century Oxford', *Family and Community History*, 7/1 (May 2004): 50.

the crown, meant that many were able to seek outside support in any dispute with the cathedral authorities.

They were, thus, in a different position from the recipients of private or local charity. When the dean and chapter of Christ Church Oxford sought to close their almshouse, the almsmen petitioned the queen in 1867 (sending their petition via the Duke of Cambridge, commander-in-chief of the army) and the lord chancellor in 1873.[126] Though neither petition was successful, cathedral almsmen had channels to higher authorities. Moreover, individually and as a group, they tended to be belligerent (and examples of this span the centuries under consideration here). When, in 1822, John Dawson, almsman of Chester, felt himself wronged over deductions of his stipend for absence from the cathedral (explaining 'my health is in such a precarious state that I am under the necessity of leaving Chester this week for some time, to be under the Care of the Whitworth doctors'), he threatened the chapter clerk that unless he received payment immediately he would petition Parliament 'for a full investigation and redress'.[127] In 1590 Thomas Arundel tired of waiting for a vacancy at Durham and 'greatlie abused' the Durham chapter 'with verie vnsemelie termes, threatninge also to fetche [them] all vpp one after another by Pursevant and to crie out vpon [them] to her majestie'.[128] At Worcester the bedesmen worked as a group to obtain or improve their rights, jointly petitioning the dean and chapter at least twice, in c.1660 and 1695.[129] That neither petition resulted in material gain for the bedesmen takes nothing away from their readiness to challenge the authorities, strongly suggesting that both petitioners' claims of humility and historiographical notions of subservience and social control would be misplaced here. As has been seen, most almsmen were old soldiers and sailors, and it has been suggested that experience of life in the armed forces may have effectively constituted assertiveness training, helping them to express a claim or negotiate for relief from charity.[130]

What is perhaps more surprising is that on a number of occasions the case of almsmen both individually and as a group was taken up by the Privy Council and resolved in the almsmen's favour. In 1600 the Privy Council ordered that Christ Church pay a pension to William Booth until an almsroom in the cathedral became vacant, and in 1677 the Privy Council restored Francis Watson to the Chester almsroom from which he had unjustly been ejected.[131] In 1720 the dean of Peterborough sought to deduct the wages of three almsmen who had been absent

---

126 Curthoys, 'Christ Church Almsmen', p. 391.

127 CRO, EDD 2/38, Dawson to Eaton, 29 May 1822. The Whitworth doctors comprised several generations of the Taylor family, working at Whitworth near Rochdale in Lancashire. They treated rich and poor alike, including Princess Elizabeth, daughter of George III. J.L. West, *The Taylors of Lancashire: Bonesetters and Doctors, 1750–1890* (Manchester, 1977).

128 Westminster Abbey Library, Muniment Book 14, f. 62r.

129 Noake, *Worcester*, pp. 575–7; Worcestershire RO, 712.17147 3945.

130 G. Hudson, 'Negotiating for Relief: Strategies used by Victims of War in Seventeenth-Century England', paper delivered at the Oxford University Social History of Early Modern Britain seminar, October 1991; T. Harris, 'Introduction', in Harris, *Politics of the Excluded*, p. 8; Stoyle, '"Memories of the Maimed"'.

131 Curthoys, 'Christ Church Almsmen', p. 386; PRO, SO8/12, Francis Watson (1677). See Westminster Abbey Library, Muniment Book 14, f. 62 and Mellows and Gifford (eds),

from the cathedral for about a dozen years unless they returned to Peterborough and served the church by 'the duty of picking of Stones'. The three almsmen, all former sailors, petitioned the king in council through one of the secretaries of state early the following year claiming that the dean had no precedent for his action, showing that absentee almsmen had long been paid through a third party, and asserting that they, like other almsmen, had 'served the Crown, either by Sea or Land and were disabled, And Consequently thereby Rendred incapable, to do the least duty whatever, And on that Account have ever been Permitted to Live with their Wives or Friends at any distance, to help Support them, it being impossible that £6 13s. 4d. can buy them common necessarys for Life'. The almsmen backed up their petition with two certificates, one which they had sworn before a master in chancery, and one from the current bishop of Peterborough (and former dean) supporting their version of the facts. The Privy Council heard the case and decided in the almsmen's favour, ordering that, in respect of their poverty and service to the crown, no residence requirement should be enforced upon them and that they should all be paid in full.[132] The message was clear: almsmen belonged to the crown and cathedrals should only concern themselves with seeing them paid.

Almsmen were, on many counts, in an odd position. First, they were appointed by one body (the crown) to be a part of another (a cathedral). Second, their creation in the midst of the English Reformation froze in time a particular moment and theological view for three and a half centuries. Henry VIII had envisaged them as a part of a Catholic model for his new cathedrals, living a quasi-monastic corporate life, practising intercessory prayer for the royal family in a daily round of services. Within two decades of their institution in the early 1540s, the progress of the English Reformation had swept away their theological rationale. Third, the duties they were expected to perform were often at odds with their claims of incapacitation and injury sustained in royal service – a contradiction fully exploited by many, including the three Peterborough almsmen in 1720–21. Fourth, almsmen occupied an ambiguous position within the cathedral and its precincts. In theory they represented the idealized poor, loyal to the crown and obedient to their betters, passing their years in the service of the church and in supplications to the Almighty for the prosperity of their prince. Meanwhile the real poor were often castigated as the undeserving and vilified by the dean and chapter, who felt themselves crowded out by floods of poor persons flocking to live in the cathedral close. In 1698 the bishop of Worcester ordered that the cathedral almsmen keep the cathedral porch clear from the 'disturbance of clamorous cripples, vagabonds and beggars', clearly illustrating the distinction between the deserving and undeserving poor; at Norwich the dean and chapter worked strenuously but vainly to keep the poor out of the Close and in 1703 the dean lamented that there were in the Close an 'abundance of poor which we cannot get rid of'.[133] Cathedral almsmen might find a variety of ways of avoiding

---

Elizabethan Peterborough, pp. 35–6 for further examples of royal intervention on behalf of bedesmen.

132 PRO, PC1/3/87; PC2/87, pp. 139, 236.

133 WCA, CA A76, p. 205: Worcestershire RO, 7147:2073; NRO, DCN 115/1, p. 231; I. Atherton, 'The Close', in Atherton *et al.* (eds), *Norwich Cathedral*, pp. 641–2.

such decanal strictures, for example by being poor only in name, by not living in the close, or by never coming to the cathedral, but none were within the spirit of the original foundation.

Conclusion

Charity is often contrasted with poor relief: the former being private and particular (both in its aims and in its recipients), the latter the sphere of government, local or national. Cathedral almsrooms disturb this neat binary opposition, for they blur the boundaries between the state and other institutions. Their history also unsettles other categories by which historians have frequently sought to explain charity and the treatment of the poor. Much of the study of charity has been focused on the donor–recipient paradigm, but the history of cathedral almsrooms is more complex, resting on a three-way relationship between the crown, the cathedral, and the almsman. Some cathedral bedesmen were able to reformulate the demands placed upon them with considerable success, but they did so not as Edward Thompson and others have suggested through their 'imperfect empowerment' as an expression of the 'pre-history of class formation', nor by a process of negotiation between rich and poor as an expression of an exchange relationship,[134] but with the support of the crown itself. Cathedral authorities, however, did not lack agency and ingenuity themselves. Their definitions of 'the poor' could vary considerably from the original royal injunction to reward those 'pressed down by want'. They might use the gift of almsrooms to recognize old cathedral employees or to reward men for services to the cathedral almost without regard to their poverty. In Oxford the almshouse did continue to cater for maimed servicemen, but the majority were not destitute; instead they inhabited the shadowy space between the solidly prosperous and the undeniably poor who were forced to resort to their parish for regular welfare. Cathedral almsmen were not necessarily destitute, but they occupy a liminal and little-studied place in the urban economy of welfare.

Moreover, the attitudes by deans and chapters towards the behaviour of their bedesmen suggest that the emphases on notions of discipline, subservience and social control, so prominent in much of the literature, need nuancing and adapting. It seemed axiomatic to commentators of the seventeenth and eighteenth centuries that charity was preferable to parish relief because of the impact it had on recipients; it was thought that charity engendered gratitude and social cohesion, whereas relief was looked on as a right and gave rise to undesirable demands by the poor. In fact the very reliability of cathedral charity to bedesmen encouraged a casual attitude among bedesmen, but also more surprisingly cathedral authorities, and the crown. At least before the 1850s, men absented themselves from their cathedral duties and even from the cathedral city. From the viewpoint of the almsmen, cathedral charity

---

134 See E.P. Thompson, 'Eighteenth-Century English Society: Class Struggle without Class?', *Social History*, 3 (1978): 133–65; E.P. Thompson, *Customs in Common* (Harmondsworth, 1993); D. Eastwood, 'History, Politics and Reputation: E.P. Thompson Reconsidered', *History*, 85: 280 (2000): 650.

represented a flexible form of welfare, since neither their personal actions nor their geographical movement were limited.

And yet, elements of Henry VIII's original vision for his bedesmen and his cathedrals regularly, if occasionally, resurfaced. Some bedesmen, worshipping twice a day in the choir alongside the other members of the cathedral, were tied in to an idealized vision of a holy commonwealth, arrayed before God within the cathedral, seated according to rank, from the highest, the dean, down to the lowliest, the almsmen. Such a vision might be re-enacted in other ways outside services. Almsmen, for example, occasionally witnessed the wills of other members of the cathedral, even members of the chapter.[135]

Thomas Sayer, the old soldier who had brandished his patent so successfully to become a Norwich almsman in 1707, lived in the cathedral close there, worked for the dean and chapter, and was tied by bonds of friendship with other cathedral officers and almsmen such as Isaac Miller, almsman and keeper of the precincts gaol, and Richard Wharfe, porter.[136] When John Wykyns, a resident of Christ Church's almshouse, died in the mid sixteenth century, he made bequests to the dean, one of the clerks, some of the cathedral servants, and the other almsmen.[137] Almsmen might genuinely draw support, collegiality and respect from their position. The traditional amalgam of royal mercy and Christian charity was so deeply rooted it could even find expression into the twentieth century: on 19 July 1912 the dean and chapter of Worcester ordered that the name of one of their recently deceased almsmen, James Newman (who had been admitted August 1885 and appointed a verger in December 1897) be inscribed on one of the stones in the cloisters as a permanent memorial, a bede in stone.[138]

---

135 Henry Andrews, a Norwich almsman, witnessed the will of Prebendary Jeffrey Spendlove in 1665: NRO, DCN 11; Dean and Chapter Peculiar, Register of Wills, iii, ff. 72–4r.

136 PRO, SO8/29, Thomas Sayer (1703); NRO, DCN11/5 (1705–6); Dean and Chapter Peculiar, Register of Wills, iv, ff. 231v–2r; DCN 115/1, p. 137; DCN 24/4, ff. 133r, 138v, 149v.

137 Curthoys, 'Christ Church Almsmen', p. 385.

138 WCA, CA A299, p. 310.

CHAPTER THREE

From common rights to cold charity: enclosure and poor allotments in the eighteenth and nineteenth centuries

Sylvia Pinches

The enclosure movement in England, long the object of praise for its perceived modernizing effects as part of the 'Agricultural Revolution', has also been the subject of much criticism.[1] Enclosure affected not only areas of open-field farming but also ancient royal forests and towns, for, as Henry French has concluded, 'the importance of urban agriculture and agrarian resources has been underestimated'.[2] The opposition of those directly affected manifested itself in many ways, from grumbling and foot-dragging through petitions and physical obstruction to downright riot.[3] Even at the peak of enclosure activity in the late eighteenth century it was not without its critics, especially for its effects on the poor. This criticism was taken up by the Hammonds in the early twentieth century, and was revived later by E.P. Thompson and J.M. Neeson among others. Some attention was paid to the deleterious effects of enclosure on the yeoman farmer and the smallholder, but only over the last twenty years or so have historians seriously begun to reassess the consequences for the cottagers and

---

1   J.D. Chambers and G.E. Mingay, *The Agricultural Revolution, 1750–1880* (London, 1966), pp. 88–104; M.E. Turner, *English Parliamentary Enclosure: its historical, geographical and economic history* (Folkestone, 1980); J.A. Yelling, *Common Field and Enclosure in England, 1450–1850* (London, 1977).

2   H. French, 'Urban agriculture, commons and commoners in the seventeenth and eighteenth centuries. The case of Sudbury', *Agricultural History Review*, 2nd Series 48 (2000): 171–99.

3   J.M. Neeson, 'An eighteenth-century peasantry', in J. Rule and R. Malcolmson, (eds), *Protest and Survive. The Historical Experience. Essays for E.P. Thompson* (London, 1993), pp. 24–59; J.M. Neeson, *Commoners, Common Right, Enclosure and Social Change in England, 1700–1820* (Cambridge, 1993), pp. 262–80; J.W. Anscomb, 'An eighteenth century inclosure and foot ballplay at West Haddon', *Northamptonshire Past and Present*, 4 (1968/69): 17–18. For seventeenth-century opposition to enclosure, see B. Sharp, 'Common rights, charities and the disorderly poor', in G. Eley and W. Hunt (eds), *Reviving the English Revolution: Reflections and elaborations on the work of Christopher Hill* (London, 1988), pp. 107–37.

the landless poor.[4] The effect of enclosure on the commoners and the landless in forest areas and towns is only just beginning to be examined in detail.[5]

Compensation for cottagers' rights extinguished by enclosure often took the form of small plots of land held on trust for the benefit of the poor, in the manner of charities, and the way in which these 'poor's allotments' were subsequently managed by the parish élite could cause resentment. As Dunbabin says, 'great store was set by "rights" derived from the past. It really mattered to the inhabitants of Shipston-under-Wychwood that an eight-acre fuel allotment should be recognized not as a charity but as compensation for the 1851 enclosure act'.[6] Villagers and townsfolk often retained a sense that the Town Lands (as these allotments were often called) and the profits therefrom were theirs by right. Long-remembered grievances over enclosure resurfaced during the early nineteenth century in the form of complaints to the Charity Commission and were taken up later by trades unionists and parish councillors. The enclosure of the common fields and wastes surrounding market towns and cities was also the cause of dispute. This paper seeks to explore the way in which common rights, once an integral part of the subsistence economy of the poor and of the parish and manorial infrastructure, became transformed into institutional charity, with some reflections on the resistance to that transformation in both town and country.[7] Examples will be taken from rural fuel allotments and the enclosure of urban commons.

Common rights and their value

Common rights were part of the manorial structure and fell into two main categories: appendant and appurtenant. Rights appendant went with land, so that ownership of land in the common fields also gave certain rights of pasture for sheep, pigs and geese. So-called ancient cottages had rights appurtenant allowing pasturage over the

---

4   J.L. Hammond, *The Village Labourer 1760–1830: a study in the government of England before the Reform Bill* (London, 1927); W.G. Hoskins, *Midland Peasant* (London, 1957); J.M. Martin, 'The small landowner and parliamentary enclosure in Warwickshire', *Economic History Review* 2nd series, 32 (1979): 328–43; Neeson, *Commoners*; K.D.M. Snell, *Annals of the Labouring Poor: Social Change and Agrarian England, 1660–1900* (Cambridge, 1985); E.P. Thompson, *Customs in Common* (Harmondsworth, 1991).

5   J. Broad, 'The smallholder and cottager after dissafforestation: a legacy of poverty', in J. Broad and R. Hoyle (eds), *Bernwood. The Life and Afterlife of a Forest* (Preston, 1997), pp. 90–107; French, 'Urban agriculture'; H. French, 'Urban common rights, enclosure and the market: Clitheroe Town Moors, 1764–1802', *Agricultural History Review*, 2nd Series, 51 (2003).

6   J.P.D. Dunbabin (ed.), *Rural Discontent in Nineteenth-Century Britain* (London, 1974), p. 248.

7   S. Birtles, 'Common land, poor relief and enclosure: the use of manorial resources in fulfilling parish obligations 1601–1834', *Past and Present*, 165 (1999): 75–106. Even as late as 1890 a report on the town charities of Warwick stated that 'the common lands of the two parishes should be taken into account, in the consideration of the question of the charitable institutions of the town'. Anon., *A Report of the Charities of the Borough of Warwick Presented to the Town Council and ordered to be printed* (Warwick, 1890), p. 6.

common fields and wastes for stinted numbers of cows and horses and often other rights, varying from place to place, depending on the custom of the manor. These included piscary (fishing), estover and firebote (wood gathering for house repair and fuel) and turbary (cutting of turves). Some rights, such as the inter-commoning of cattle, arose not from property ownership but from vicinage, that is, from occupation of neighbouring property. A further type of common right was common in gross, vested in a person not a property, either through a grant or by prescription (that is, 20 years of unchallenged use).[8] Access to the common wastes allowed the poor to gather other products of the land, which could be of benefit to those eking out an existence.[9] However, such use right could legally be vested only in an individual, not in the body of the 'inhabitants' or the 'poor' generally and 'the inability of the poor to claim common right *in gross* by prescription lay at the heart of much of the acrimony surrounding enclosure'.[10]

The process of enclosure entailed the assessment of the extent and value of the land to be enclosed and all the rights held in and over it. Then the land was apportioned in consolidated allotments according to the value of land held before and the value of rights that would be extinguished by the enclosure.[11] Just how valuable a part these rights played in the economy of the poor was, and is, unclear.[12] The keeping of a cow or two on the common was a significant matter, although partisans for enclosure might deny it. Arthur Young estimated the value of a cow to a family at as much as 5–6s. a week, not far short of a week's wages for a labourer at the time. The pages of the *General Report on Agriculture* and the *General Views of Agriculture* in various counties are full of comments highlighting the effects of the loss of cow commons. One such states that 'the poor seem the greatest sufferers; they can no longer keep a cow, which before many of them did, and they are now maintained by the parish'.[13] While the emphasis in the literature is mainly on rural cottagers, many townsfolk also once kept a cow.

When considering the value of gathering fuel a wide range of factors needs to be examined – the types of fuel available and their relative calorific values and the time and effort expended in gathering them. (It was not just wood that was collected for fuel – gorse, also known as furze, and fern and bracken were all gathered, as

---

8   E.C.K. Gonner, *Common Land and Inclosure* (London, 1912; 1966); G.D. Gaddsden, *The Law of Commons* (London, 1988).

9   Neeson, *Commoners*, pp. 45, 158–75.

10   Birtles, 'Common land', p. 83.

11   Turner, *English Parliamentary Enclosure*; J.W. Anscomb, 'Parliamentary Enclosure in Northamptonshire: processes and procedures', *Northamptonshire Past and Present*, 8.6 (1988–89): 409–23; J. Chapman, 'Enclosure Commissioners as landscape planners', *Landscape History*, 15 (1993): 57–69.

12   See, for example, J. Howlett, *Enclosures, a cause of improved agriculture, of plenty and cheapness of provisions* (London 1787; 1973), published as a refutation of the anonymous tract *A Political Enquiry into the consequences of enclosing common lands*, which praised the benefit of common rights.

13   Quoted in Snell, *Annals*, pp. 174–9.

was peat and even dried dung.[14]) To this should be added the availability and cost of purchased fuel, and the availability of employment sufficiently well paid for such purchases to be made. Contemporary estimates for the cost of having to buy fuel rather than gather it for a poor family varied widely. In the 1790s the Revd David Davies of Barkham in Berkshire suggested that a family could cut enough fuel for a year in one week, but that it would cost anything from £1 15s. to £4 3s. a year to purchase, which was about one-tenth of the annual income of a labourer.[15] Fifty years later, in 1844, a Mr Keen, giving evidence to the Committee on Commons' Inclosure, reported that the average annual expenditure on fuel of a cottager with a four-roomed dwelling in Godalming, Surrey (enclosed 35 years previously) was £3 12s. 4d. This was based on an estimate of two tons of coal at £1 12s. a ton and a hundred faggots at £1 0s. 10d. a hundred, recouping 12s. 6d. by selling the ash to a farmer. In other parts of the country coal was more generally available at £1 a ton and faggots at 12s. a hundred, so that the average cost of a year's fuel would be £2 10s.[16] This latter evidence points out that coal varied enormously in cost around the country, and according to the time of year, depending on the proximity of the coalfields. Before the advent of canals, coal was carried by packhorse or mule, severely limiting its distribution and keeping the cost high. By the 1860s it was 70 per cent cheaper to move coal by rail than canal.[17] Although the availability of coal was increasing and its cost diminishing, it was not always the most suitable form of fuel. It would not burn well on the simple hearths under a wide chimney which were still common in cottages in the late eighteenth and early nineteenth centuries – iron grates and tall narrow chimneys were necessary, but expensive to acquire. There were other factors to consider in the relative merits of coal and wood fires – despite being so much cheaper, wood has a lesser calorific value (3.5) than coal (6.9) and requires much more constant attention and stoking. However, it is a cleaner fuel to handle and burn, and the ash could be used (or sold) for agricultural and industrial purposes.[18] Furze or gorse, one of the fuels most commonly used by the poor, has similar properties to wood, but must have been particularly unpleasant to gather and bring home on one's back. One cannot help wondering whether the women and children, who had the main responsibility of supplying the hearth, were not

---

14   Dung has a higher calorific value than wood (4.0 compared to 3.5), but using it for fuel obviates its use as fertilizer. Land stewards in the early eighteenth century were advised 'to narrowly watch and observe that the Tenants do not gather Cowdung ... in order first to dry it, and then to burn it ... to the no small prejudice of the Farm'. C. Davidson, *A Woman's Work is Never Done: A History of Housework in the British Isles, 1650–1950* (London, 1983), p. 77; E. Lawrence, *The Duty of a Steward to his Lord* (1727; Farnborough, 1971), p. 29; P. Warde, 'Woodland fuel, demand and supply', in J. Langton and G. Jones (eds), *Forests and Chases of England and Wales c.1500–c.1850. Towards a survey and analysis* (Oxford, 2005), pp. 80–86.

15   Neeson, *Commoners*, p. 165.

16   J. Humphries, 'Enclosure, common rights and women: the proletarianization of families in the late eighteenth and early nineteenth centuries', *Journal of Economic History*, 50 (1990): 32–3.

17   Davidson, *A Woman's Work*, pp. 87, 90.

18   For example, fertilizer and lye. Davidson, *A Woman's Work*, pp. 90–100.

sometimes relieved at no longer having to go and cut furze, but to have an annual delivery from the coal charity.

Despite denials by some contemporary theorists of the value to the poor of gathering fuel, there does seem to have been a general recognition that enclosure resulted in increased hardship. There was also fear that this hardship increased dishonesty, and wood-stealing was a constant complaint of landowners.[19] The number of enclosure agreements making provision for fuel will be discussed below, but it is also remarkable that a considerable number of fuel charities were established between the mid eighteenth and the mid nineteenth centuries, and that pre-existing charities diverted their income to the provision of fuel. There is also evidence of increased amounts of money being paid for fuel by the overseers of the poor in parishes recently enclosed.[20] In some areas, at least, allowances were paid to the poor when engaged in gathering their fuel rather than being in paid employment.[21] By the 1820s there were 64 endowed charities in Warwickshire distributing fuel, either free or at a subsidized price. However, the reasons given for establishing these charities could sometimes be disingenuous. At Boughton, Northamptonshire, the Earl of Strafford gave a rent charge of £5 a year to the poor. It was still being distributed entirely in fuel in the mid nineteenth century, although it had been noted in 1786 that:

> as the deed was never inrolled, as directed by the Statute of Mortmain, it is said, the heirs of Lord Strafford are not bound by the Deed, which charges his estate with an annuity for divers good considerations, and not in lieu of the poor's right to cut furze, &c as should have been expressed.[22]

In addition to endowed charities, a number of 'coal clubs' were set up. They seem to have proliferated from the 1830s, the same period as the great flourishing of friendly societies.[23] Many of them were a combination of savings club and voluntary charity, the sums saved by the poor being 'topped up' or matched by wealthy parishioners

---

19 B. Reay, *The Last Rising of the Agricultural Labourers. Rural Life and Protest in Nineteenth-century England* (Oxford, 1990), pp. 8, 44, 54, 58, 71–3, 138, 172. A reporter to the Poor Law Commissioners in Northamptonshire complained that men set to work on the roads only worked when supervised and that 'if there is a wood near ... they run into the woods to steal firing, which they hide and carry off at a convenient time'. *Report of the Royal Commission on the Poor Laws* (1834; Harmondsworth, 1974), Part I, p. 111.

20 J. Lane, 'Administration of the Poor Law in Butlers Marston, Warwickshire, 1713–1822' (unpublished master's dissertation, University of Wales Cardiff, 1970), p. 19.

21 In North Elmham, Norfolk, it was recorded on 7 June 1824 that 'Cha⁵ Mash, wants an allowance during the time he has been cutting his firing, he states 6 days on Turf common, 3 days being sufficient for cutting his own, for which he is [to] have an allowance 5s'. Birtles, 'Common land', p. 92.

22 *Returns of Charitable Donations*, Parliamentary Papers (PP) 1816 (511) XVIa; see Northamptonshire County Record Office (NCRO) CAM 1059; *Supplementary Inquiry of the Charity Commissioners*, 1867–75, PP 1877 LXVI; NCRO CAM 1058. See note 26.

23 P.H. Gosden, *The Friendly Societies in England, 1815–1875* (Manchester, 1961).

as an encouragement to self-reliance and providence.[24] When the Burton Dassett, Warwickshire, clothing and coal club was revived in January 1884, more than 70 people wanted to join and the vicar hoped 'to obtain the help of landowners and others in the parish, in order to encourage the poor in these acts of providence'.[25] Sometimes additional money was given to these funds from endowed charities in the parish, thus blurring even further the distinction between charities and self-help organizations. However, when the trustees drew up a scheme for regulating the parish charities in Stretton-on-Dunsmore, Warwickshire, in 1859, they were criticized by counsel for their intention to continue generous support for the village clubs. The scheme approved by the Court of Chancery in 1859 restricted the amount they could give each year to no more than £25 for the Sick Club, £25 to the Coal Club and only £16 to the Clothing Club.[26]

Self-reliance of the type encouraged by support of such funds had its critics, as some commentators debated the moral value of the independence given by rights of common. Did some measure of independence from wage-labour make a man hard-working and self-reliant, as some contended, or did it make him work-shy and constantly seeking a share in the goods of others (be it the common land, poor relief or charity)? Similar considerations also informed the debate on the reform of the Poor Law in the late eighteenth and early nineteenth centuries and the investigations into the state of endowed charities that were conducted at the same time as enquiries into the administration of the Poor Law. In the 1780s Thomas Gilbert not only promoted the act which permitted parishes to combine to establish workhouses, but also introduced the act which sent out enquiries into charities for the relief of the poor.[27] In the 1810s Lord Brougham began a campaign to investigate the state of the poor, which culminated in a series of royal commissions, running from 1819 to 1837, to enquire into endowed charities in England and Wales, usually referred to collectively as the Brougham Commission.[28] John Howlett, a clergyman who wrote widely on political economy in the closing years of the eighteenth century, was in no doubt about the pernicious effects of both common rights and public charities. He refuted the 'trite and common objections to enclosures, that they are inevitably ... a great diminution of the privileges and happiness of the poor' by insisting that all

24   S.M. Pinches, 'Charities in Warwickshire in the eighteenth and nineteenth centuries' (unpublished doctoral thesis, University of Leicester, 2001), pp. 170–72.

25   Warwickshire County Record Office (WCRO), DR 220/35, *Burton Dassett Parish Magazine*, 1885.

26   WCRO CR700/8, Charity Commission Scheme, 1859.

27   26 Geo. III, *c*.56 and 26 Geo. III, *c*.58. The results of the enquiry were published in 1816, at the instigation of Lord Brougham, as *Abstract of the Returns of Charitable Donations 1786*, PP 1816 XVIa. The Warwickshire returns, reprinted from the foregoing, are at WCRO QS 69/4; Northamptonshire at NCRO CAM 1059.

28   *Analytical Digest of the Reports of the Commissions of Inquiry into Charities, 1819–37*, PP 1843 XVI, XVII. The original parish by parish reports of the Brougham Commission appear scattered throughout the Parliamentary Papers series. County volumes were published by HMSO in 1890, combining the original reports with the answers to the Supplementary Inquiry of the Charity Commissioners, 1867–75, PP 1877 LXVI (*Brougham*). R. Tompson, *The Charity Commission and the Age of Reform* (London, 1979).

common rights did was to encourage 'servants, &c. in the neighbourhood, allured by these temptations, [to] try every stratagem in order to gain a settlement in so flattering a situation'. The end result was only an increase in the poor rate. He went on to say that parish charities were often 'highly injurious' to the poor themselves, by removing a spur to industry, and consequently injurious to the ratepayers of the parish.[29] The 1834 Poor Law Commissioners' Report reiterated the belief that charity made men lazy and improvident: 'wherever, indeed, public charities are profusely administered, we hear, from those who are engaged in their administration, complaints of the discontents and disorders introduced'.[30]

Rural enclosures

Firstly, a distinction needs to be made between charity estates consolidated by enclosure and those created by it. Examination of the 1787 Return of Charitable Donations and the reports of the Brougham Commission of Enquiry into Charities 1819–37 shows that there were many charities known variously as 'Town Lands', 'Poor's Land', 'Poor's Plot', 'Fuel Land' and so on. Over the years confusion sometimes arose over the origins of these town lands and the Gilbert Returns occasionally cited enclosure as the foundation, whereas the enclosure merely awarded an allotment in exchange for existing charity property. The later Charity Commissioners made much more thorough investigations, and their reports for Warwickshire listed nine such misidentified charity estates, referring to trust deeds stretching back to the Tudor period and beyond without necessarily being able to identify a specific donor or foundation date. The use of the income varied from church repairs, maintenance of bridges and highways, to support of the poor rates and doles to the poor.[31] For example, a part of the parish of Clifton-on-Dunsmore was enclosed by agreement in 1648 and by the time of the Gilbert enquiry it was believed that this had created the Town Lands. However, the later Charity Commissioners' ascertained that 20 acres had been exchanged for scattered parcels 'generally called Town Grounds' and that they:

> should be set by the churchwardens and the constables for the time being, at a reasonable rate, to such of the poor inhabitants of Clifton as had no other land … if they should be willing to be tenants … the yearly rent … should be received half by the churchwardens and half by the constable … and employed by them in defraying such charges as were incident to their offices … as formerly accustomed.[32]

Many charity estates were affected by enclosure. Just like any other person or legal body owning land in the common fields, they had their scattered strips of arable

---

29 Howlett, *Enclosures, A Cause of Improved Agriculture.*

30 *Royal Commission on the Poor Laws*, Part I, p. 121.

31 *Brougham*, Barford, pp. 148–9; Barston, p. 241; Clifton-on-Dunsmore, p. 703; Haseley, pp. 133–4; Hatton, pp. 288–9; Ladbrooke, p. 193; Nuthurst, p. 277; Southam, pp. 205–9; Stretton-on-the-Fosse, pp. 177–8. The Poor's Land at Ladbrooke was returned as common land to the Royal Commission on Common Land (1955–8). W.G. Hoskins and L. D. Stamp, *The Common Lands of England and Wales* (London, 1963), p. 330.

32 *Brougham*, p. 703.

and doles of meadow exchanged for a consolidated holding. Extra allotments were made in exchange for any rights of common attaching to their property. Also like individuals, charities were liable to shoulder their share of the cost of enclosure, which could bear heavily on them, just as it did on small farmers.[33] Sometimes even large charities objected to the cost of enclosure, as did the Lord Leycester's Hospital, Warwick, at the proposal to enclose the common fields of Harbury, where it held an estate.[34] The trustees of the Hospital did agree to shoulder their share of the cost of hedges and fences when Napton was enclosed in 1778, but took out mortgages to pay for them.[35]

Fuel charities created by enclosure

However, there *were* some entirely new charities created by the allotment of land to be held on trust for the poor, usually in lieu of their extinguished rights to gather fuel on the common lands. The parliamentary acts specified that the beneficiaries were not to include anyone who occupied any of the land about to be enclosed.[36] Martin, in his extensive studies of Warwickshire enclosures, detected 'a distinct decline in generosity over time in the compensation meted out to the village poor by enclosure commissioners'.[37] However, there were variations around the county, and he suggested that the enclosures of the eastern parishes, with their bias towards animal husbandry, not only preserved extensive common grazing rights but also provided 'relatively generous allotments to the poor'.[38]

The Gilbert Return for Warwickshire correctly listed only eleven charity estates created by enclosure, although others had certainly been created before 1786. Many such allotments may have been 'lost', as their purposes became less relevant in later years,[39] An examination of the Brougham Reports and the enclosure records held by the Warwickshire County Record Office has brought to light a further 18 examples. There may be still more to be identified, especially in those parishes that were enclosed by agreement at an early date. Similar research in Northamptonshire

---

33   J.M. Martin, 'The cost of parliamentary enclosure in Warwickshire', in E.L. Jones (ed.), *Agriculture and Economic Growth, 1660–1815* (London, 1967), pp. 121–51.

34   WCRO CR 410, Objections of Leycester's Hospital to enclosure of Harbury, 1766. (Harbury was not finally enclosed until 1779.)

35   WCRO CR 1600/83–87, 90, Agreements re hedges and expenses 1778–79, mortgages 1779–1806.

36   For example, Tysoe Fuel Land 'for such poor people residing in the said parish as should not occupy any part of the lands intended to be enclosed, in lieu of a right to cut furze or gorse upon the waste land of the said parish'. *Brougham*, p. 320; WCRO CR 224/ 92, Tysoe Enclosure Act 1798.

37   J.M. Martin, 'Village traders and the emergence of a proletariat in South Warwickshire, 1750–1850', *Agricultural History Review*, 32 (1984): 179–88, 185.

38   J.M. Martin, 'The small landowner and parliamentary enclosure in Warwickshire', *Economic History Review.* 2nd series, 32 (1979): 328–43, 331.

39   By the 1950s many allotments 'for specific purposes now of no importance' had been forgotten and the rights attached to them obliterated. Hoskins and Stamp, *Common Lands*, p. 99.

has so far revealed 25 charities established by enclosure. In both counties the peak period of activity was 1751–1800, with 18 and 15 examples respectively.

Some enclosures took into consideration the rights of the poor by confirming their rights to gather fuel in certain restricted areas rather than creating a new allotment. The 1757 enclosure award for the market town of Kenilworth, Warwickshire, preserved as common 35 acres 36 perches of hilly waste on Tainter Hill Common on the outskirts of the town itself and another 4 acres 3 roods and 4 perches near the hamlet of Burton Green. The award stated that the land:

> shall remain common and unenclosed to the intent and purpose that the poor belonging to the said parish of Kenilworth shall from time to time for ever hereafter use exercise and enjoy a free and constant right to get furze goss [sic] or fern ... and that the Lord of the Manor of Kenilworth ... shall ... make such plantations for ornament on the said allotments or either of them as he or they shall think proper.[40]

In Stretton-on-Dunsmore, which was enclosed by agreement in 1704, the Poor's Plot was an exchange for existing charity land, but was consistently let in parcels of 20 perches to poor cottagers and the income used since at least the late eighteenth century to supply coal, which does imply an awareness of the consequences of the loss of fuel-gathering rights. The enclosure agreement certainly referred to the provision of fuel. Although confirming the rights of the lord of the manor to the herbage of the banks and roadsides, it excepted 'the Bushes that at any time hereafter shall grow therein which shall be applied to such uses as the Bushes which grow on the Poor's Plot'.[41] On the other hand, the parishioners of Long Lawford, Warwickshire, believed that they had the right to cut 'furze on a strip of land, eight yards wide, running parallel with the public road, leading over the Long Lawford heath, which right they asserted was awarded to them under the act for enclosing it'. The Brougham Commissioners examined the award for the enclosure of Lawford Heath dated 23 March 1774 and determined that 'there is, however, no such right awarded to them, and if they have exercised such a power, it can only have been by sufferance of the owners'.[42]

However, the Commissioners did support the villagers over the mismanagement of the Poor Plot. The liberties of Long Lawford had been enclosed some time before 1719 and 20 acres set aside for the benefit of the poor. For over a hundred years the income had been used to subsidize the poor rates, until a public meeting in

---

40 WCRO Y1/50, Transcript of Kenilworth Enclosure Award, 27 January 1757. The parish charity board erected in the St Nicholas church porch in 1867 records that the local railway company had paid £50 to set up a Gorse and Fern Fund in 'lieu of the rights of the Poor over the portion of ground taken by the Common near Mill End'. By 1956 Kenilworth Common had dwindled to 29.6 acres but the common right of estover (wood gathering) and taking gravel remained. Hoskins and Stamp, *Common Lands*, pp. 124, 328.

41 WCRO CR 498, Agreement of Enclosure of Stretton-on-Dunsmore, 2 June 1704; CR 700/1-65 Stretton-on-Dunsmore charity records, 1787–1905.

42 *Brougham*, pp. 719–20. For a discussion of roadside wastes, see G. S. Lefevre, *English Commons and Forests* (London, 1894), pp. 288–98; Hoskins and Stamp, *Common Lands*, pp. 115, 123, 124, 143, 221.

1833, following the bitter complaints of the poor, decided to spend £4 a year on the rent of the school and to distribute the rest of the income in coal and bread. The poor still complained that they were not allowed to rent quarter-acre plots and the Commissioners, while maintaining that 'they can have no *right* to the occupation of this land', were nevertheless sympathetic:

> considering that the poor of this parish have been for many years, wrongfully deprived of the rents of the land in question … we have recommended to the parish to take this question into consideration, and to allot to the poor as may have a fair claim thereto, a small portion of this land … The poor of this parish seem entitled to a liberal exercise of the discretion in such cases vested in the parish officers as a compensation for what they have been deprived of for so long.[43]

However, many feared that such allotments would lead to men becoming too independent, and in the nearby parish of Thurlaston, also in Warwickshire, the Commissioners recommended that in future:

> a portion of the poor's land should be divided into small allotments, at low rents, for the use of such deserving poor as were not already provided for, keeping them within such bounds as should not hold out the temptation to become small farmers, or to deprive their employer of the due benefit of their time and strength, *and at the same time especially discouraging the idea (very prevalent in this district), that the term 'Poor's Land' of itself implies a right in the poor parishioner to demand occupation, instead of the participation in the benefits of the produce of the land* [my italics].[44]

The administration of the charities

The trustees of these poor's lands were usually either some of the major landowners and their heirs, or some combination of the minister, churchwardens and overseers of the poor. In the Warwickshire sample, 13 had a combination of churchwardens, constables and overseers of the poor as their trustees. Four others included the minister with the parish officers. Even when there were private trustees, usually the lord of the manor or major landholders, they were often advised by the minister and parish officers about who should benefit from the land. The land allocated was usually on the heath or 'furze ground' on which the cottagers had once gathered fuel, often on the extreme edge of the parish, alongside a main road. In nine of these places, at least, this seems to have been so.[45] Some parishes stipulated that the land was to be maintained as furze ground, the cottagers retaining the right of cutting it themselves, as at Harborough Magna, Thurlaston and Stretton-under-Fosse, or, as

---

43 *Brougham*, pp. 719–20. The Commissioners referred to the powers of creating small allotments in the Acts 2 Will. IV, c. 42 and 59 Geo. III, c. 12, which they felt were both applicable to this case.

44 *Brougham*, pp. 712–13.

45 Avon Dassett, Bilton, Bourton and Draycott, Dunchurch, Harborough Magna, Long Compton, Napton, Thurlaston and Tysoe. Similar distributions of Poor's Plots have been identified in other counties, for example Ashby Parva, Leicestershire (private communication from Dr John Goodacre).

at Ilmington, the churchwardens cutting it and distributing it at the rate of two kids (bundles) per head.[46] Even when there was no requirement to maintain furze thickets, this land tended to be of poor quality and so the rental value was not very great, though it could be improved. By the time of the Brougham Charity Commission the Poor's Land at Stretton-under-Fosse had been cleared and improved, and the annual rent of £12 was distributed in coal, 'each poor cottager in the village of Stretton having a portion delivered at his door'.[47] However, if allotments were left entirely to the management of the poor they could be neglected, suffering from the common case that what is everybody's is nobody's when it comes to taking care of it.[48]

An increasingly discriminatory approach to the distribution of the fuel charities developed as the provisions of the New Poor Law hardened the distinction between the deserving and the undeserving poor.[49] No longer was it enough merely to be a poor inhabitant to benefit. In many parishes the charity was reserved for widows and families, the amount given depending on the number of children. Lists could be drawn up excluding men seen to be 'trouble-makers' or otherwise undeserving. Only occasionally is it possible to catch a glimpse of the reaction to this, varying as it did from outright threats to more subtle protest. In Milton, Cambridgeshire, in 1843 it was decided to deprive able-bodied single men of the benefit of the coal charity. Two threatening letters were picked up in the parish and published in the *Cambridge Chronicle* on 16 December. One read, 'You shall see a good blase before Christmas day old David I will give five or six a tase [taste] the coles for that. You may prepare yourselfs for a fire old David yard shall be on fire before nex Mondy old Nix Lawson Webstter Adam Jennings they shall have tast before winter gone for taken me of coles'.[50] A more temperate and articulate, though none the less determined, reaction was displayed by Joseph Arch, the leader of the Agricultural Workers Union. In the parish of Barford, Warwickshire, a public right of way had been closed by the Earl of Warwick and

The Earl offered to give two hundredweight of coal every year to each working man in the village. This was to buy us out. The villagers agreed to it so it was a fair bargain. My birthright was sold before I was born; still, the coals were there to claim if I chose, and I did choose. For two or three years I did not have any, but one day when they were distributing these coals I happened to be at home, and thought I might just as well go for my two hundredweight. So I got my barrow, and went to the man that was giving them out. 'I have come for my coals', I said. 'Oh', said he, looking at me. 'Have you?' 'Yes',

---

46 *Brougham*, p. 161.

47 *Brougham*, pp. 698–9.

48 Birtles, 'Common land', p. 97.

49 Some parishes had long made clear distinctions of who could and could not receive the benefit. The enclosure decree of 1669 for Leamington Hastings, Warwickshire, set aside 108 acres for the benefit of the church, schoolmaster and other good works. In 1683 it was decided to distribute the rent 'every Sunday from All Saints Day to Easter about twenty shillings by sixpences and shillings. No one to receive it who were not at church'. G.I. MacFarquhar, *Leamington Hastings Almshouses and Poors Plot, 1607–1987* (no place, no date, *c*.1984), p. 8.

50 Cited in A.J. Peacock, 'Village Radicalism in East Anglia, 1800–1850', in Dunbabin, *Rural Discontent*, pp. 27–61, 58.

I said 'and I mean to have them too'. He looked at his list. 'Your name is not down on my list', said he. 'Oh, it's not, is it? Who makes out that list, I should like to know?' 'The parson', said he. 'I thought so', said I. 'Well, I have come here to do business, let there be no mistake about that. It is now about a quarter past one – if I do not receive an order to fetch my coals by three o'clock, I'm going across the park, and if they summon me, I will tell the reason why. All the world hereabouts shall know why I went.' I said no more but went off. I had said quite enough, however, before three o'clock had struck, up comes a lad with a message, 'please will you come down and fetch your coals.' Down for my coals I went and had no more bother about it.[51]

Urban enclosures

Many small towns were part of a large rural parish, and even larger towns could have significant outlying areas of open field and common land. Between 1720 and 1870 some 160 towns sought to obtain parliamentary acts of enclosure.[52] There was a balance to be struck between the needs of the surrounding farmers and those of the inhabitants of the towns, although these were not mutually exclusive. While overall the towns won and expanded into the surrounding areas, there were regional and temporal variations. In the seventeenth century the urban wastes around Bromsgrove, Worcestershire,

> were sufficiently abundant to serve both the farming community and meet the various demands of the cottagers, weavers and glovers of the industrial townships. However, as the second phase of agricultural expansion gained momentum, the extensive common wastes of Bromsgrove, like those elsewhere in the area, were controlled more carefully for the benefit of the farming population. By the 1670s a number of farmers considered their common rights on the Lickey to be worth up to one-third of the yearly value of their holdings.[53]

Despite the growth of Bromsgrove and the southernward sprawl of Birmingham, the Lickey Hills are still open land and 524 acres form the Lickey Hills Country Park. On the other hand, in Northamptonshire, the small town of Kettering enclosed 2,262 acres (82 per cent of the land in the parish) in 1804. The 1801 census recorded 641 houses, and the fact that there were only 102 claimants under the enclosure act, 'suggests that only about 16 per cent of the families in the town were directly concerned with the enclosure of the fields. It is a small percentage and reflects the great growth and importance of trade and commerce in the town in relation to agriculture'. The disputes that this led to rumbled on for years.[54]

---

51   J. Arch, *From Ploughtail to Parliament: an Autobiography* (London, 1898; 1986), pp. 53–4.

52   French, 'Urban agriculture', p. 173.

53   P. Large, 'Urban growth and agricultural change in the West Midlands', in. P. Clark (ed.), *The Transformation of English Provincial Towns 1600–1800* (London, 1984), pp. 169–89, 182.

54   R.A. Martin, 'Kettering Inclosure, 1804–5', *Northamptonshire Past and Present* 5. 5 (1977): 413–24; NCRO KPL 14-59, Kettering dispute over Town Lands 1818–23.

The motives for enclosure varied from place to place, as did the compensation of the commoners and provisions for the poor. Some urban enclosure occurred to facilitate the expansion of the town, to allow the building of a road, railway or canal, or to pay for some local improvement scheme.[55] Warwick comprised two parishes, St Mary's and St Nicholas. St Mary's was mostly contained within the borough, with commonable land in the Lammas Field and Saltisford Common, both of which remained common until the twentieth century.[56] St Nicholas, however, was an extensive parish largely outside the town. It had two large commonable meadows, of which St Nicholas remained common until 1928. However, in 1772 an Act was obtained for the enclosure of the St John's Meadow. A claim was made on behalf of the poor before the ground was staked out, of their right to cut furze on Warwick Heath. A 15-acre plot was awarded to the Earl of Warwick and other trustees for the benefit of the poor of Bridge End Ward in St Nicholas, laid out beside the Warwick to Whitnash road. By the time of the Charity Commission enquiry in the 1820s this had been cleared and was let to a farmer at £27 6s a year, which was distributed in coal; coal was still being distributed in 1875, and the rent had increased to £36.[57]

Not all towns made such allotments. When 66 acres belonging to the town of Atherstone in the parish of Mancetter, Warwickshire, were enclosed in 1765 no provision was made for the poor specifically, although 100 acres was allotted to the cottagers in lieu of their rights of common pasturage. First proposed in 1730, enclosure was delayed by the concerted opposition of the cottagers and some of the 60 or so freeholders for 35 years.[58] Interestingly, the enclosure of Bedworth, Warwickshire, in 1769 was not only to enclose the common fields, but also 'for the regulating of the charity estates within the said parish'. The seven trustees 'should be incorporated by the name of "The Governors of the Hospital of Mr. Nicholas Chamberlaine, and the Possessions and Revenues thereof"'. Although no allotment was made specifically for the poor, two heaths, amounting in all to about 24 acres, were exempted from the award as they 'belong and are promiscuously enjoyed by all the Inhabitants and landowners'.[59]

The question of precisely who owned the rights to these commons was particularly complex in urban settings, especially in chartered boroughs. Were all the inhabitants

---

55   For example, the enclosure act for Bolton, Lancashire, in 1792, was unusually specific in stipulating that the profits of enclosing 270 acres of Bolton Moor should be applied in 'widening, paving, lighting, watching, cleansing, and otherwise improving the streets of Great Bolton and on supplying water for the free use of the inhabitants. Any surplus was to go to the Poor Rates.' J.L. and B. Hammond, *The Bleak Age* (1934; Harmondsworth, 1947), p. 79.

56   *Victoria County History of Warwickshire*, 8 vols (1904–1969), pp. 8, 436–7.

57   *Brougham*, p. 842; WCRO CR 928/1, Bill of Enclosure of St Nicholas, Warwick, 1772; CR 1707/92, Act of Enclosure; QS 75/123, Enrolment of award, 1773.

58   WCRO Y1/21/1, Typescript of Atherstone Enclosure Award, 11 September 1765; HR 35, papers re enclosure of Atherstone, 1730–65. 'Opponents of enclosure had valued the fuel and sand which women collected at £3 3s a year, and a child able to work brought in the same again – together they earned almost a third of a labouring family's income', quoted in Neeson, *Commoners*, p. 165. See also the discussion of Atherstone enclosure in E.P. Thompson, *Customs in Common* (London, 1991; 1993), pp. 152–8.

59   *Brougham*, pp. 684–5. WCRO QS 75/10, Enclosure award for Bedworth, 1769.

to benefit, freemen only, or the corporation itself, standing for 'the inhabitants'? For example, at Sudbury, Suffolk, two local craftsmen, a goldsmith and a turner, brought a case in Chancery against the corporation. They claimed that 'the original grant from Richard de Clare had vested control in *all* the free burgesses and their successors, not merely the mayor and corporation'. They also claimed that the income from the commons had been distributed as the corporation thought fit, rather than for the benefit of 'the poorer sort' (though still begging the question of whether this meant the poorer sort of burgess or the poorer sort of inhabitant). The mayor and corporation riposted that the lands were not a public charity or intended for the relief of the poor, but were held in common by all the free burgesses for depasturing their animals.[60] In the radical days of the 1790s even female voices could be raised claiming an interest in the commons. In 1792 the Derby Corporation proposed the sale of Nun's Green to finance town improvements. This led to a fierce war of pamphlets in the town, some purporting to be written by women. One of them stated 'Nun's green, say I, I hate the name of it! – What have we to do with Nuns in these days. – Besides, brother, it belongs to us, as well as to you; women have rights as well as men; and the act of Parliament says, the Nun's green belongs to every inhabitant of Derby'.[61] Certainly the women of Sudbury benefited from the commons, though in the early eighteenth century female heads of households were more likely to receive distribution money than to depasture animals upon them.[62]

Similar arguments over who had access to the commons and who should benefit from the profits obtained in Coventry. From the earliest times the common fields of Coventry had been known as the Michaelmas Lands, being enclosed for cultivation from Candlemas (2 February) till Michaelmas Day (29 September), and the common meadows were known as Lammas Lands, being closed from Candlemas till Lammas Day (1 August).[63] Both were common pasturage for the citizens (increasingly interpreted as the freemen only) for the rest of the year. The adjacent wasteland was also held in common, with a stint of two cows and a horse or two horses and a cow. Citizens of Coventry could, and many did for centuries, avail themselves of these rights, though the regulation of the lands and wastes caused some bitter disputes between individual citizens, the body of freemen and the corporation from time to time. As late as 1836 J. Carter, the Town Clerk, was in dispute with the freemen, represented by T. Hands and the Freemen's Protection Committee, who alleged damage through Carter's having opened a quarry where the Lammas right of pasture was enjoyed.[64] These ancient rights were fiercely defended, even though they had the deleterious effect of restricting the outward growth of the city, leading to much overcrowding and poor housing in the centre.

---

60 French, 'Urban agriculture', pp. 180–83.

61 R. Sweet, 'Women and civic life', in R. Sweet and P. Lane (eds), *Women and Urban Life in Eighteenth-Century England 'On the Town'* (Aldershot, 2003), p. 37.

62 French, 'Urban agriculture', p. 191.

63 A. Brian, 'Lammas Meadows', *Landscape History* 15 (1993): 57–69.

64 Coventry Archives, PA 14/10/92 10 Sept. 1836. See also the case before the King's Bench in 1811 between Thomas Hodierne and James Higgins over the enclosure of the Poddy Croft, where Hodierne claimed right of pasture. WCRO CR 1311.

The first moves towards enclosure occurred in 1828 and 1834, with the cutting of Telford's turnpike road and then the London and Birmingham railway through part of the land. Compensation was paid for the loss of both strips of land which, with interest, had amounted to £2,476 4s. by 1843. A public meeting of the freemen in that year decided that it should form a fund called 'The Freemen's Seniority Fund', out of the interest of which a payment of 6s. a week should be paid to the most aged freemen according to their seniority.[65]

During the 1840s the fifty or so landowners attempted to enclose the Lammas and Michaelmas Lands, but failed to get the agreement of the freemen who clung to their rights of pasturage, even though the majority of them no longer had cattle of their own, but 'fathered' other people's for a consideration. Agreement was finally reached in 1860, and 976 acres were enclosed, the largest allotment going to the freemen as a body, the corporation and some charity estates receiving other shares.[66] Within six years 'an influential body of non-freemen citizens formed the view that, so far as concerned the area of the Lammas and Michaelmas lands allotted to the freemen in 1860, the allotment ought really to have been made to the corporation, on behalf of the city as a whole'.[67] Eventually a second Act of 1875, enclosing the remaining common land, allotted half to the corporation for the benefit of the whole city and half to the freemen for the benefit of the Seniority Fund.[68] The manorial wastes remained common and the last were finally designated public open spaces in 1927.[69] A report from the Select Committee on Commons in 1913 had described Gosford Green, Coventry, as 'nineteen acres of common land with rights of over 3,000 freemen, who were willing to relinquish what had become valueless rights in favour of the City of Coventry whose intention it was to lay out the land as a recreation ground'.[70] The rights may have been described as 'valueless' by the commissioners in 1913, but even in the late 1970s there were, albeit erroneous, memories of the pasture rights. An apprentice just about to become a freeman told the author of this article that he would have the right to keep a cow and a horse on Hearsall Common.

---

65   In later years, at least, advertisements were placed in the local paper seeking applications from aged freemen. For example, on 7 October 1891 an appeal appeared in the *Midland Daily Telegraph* asking for applications from freemen enrolled in 1840 and 1841.

66   F. Smith, *Coventry, Six Hundred Years of Municipal Life* (Coventry, 1945), pp. 2, 11, 137–44. WCRO QS 75/37, Enrolment of Coventry enclosure award, 1860.

67   Smith, *Coventry*, p. 143. Similar disputes obtained in Gateshead, about whether the common rights belonged to the borough and freemen or for 'the common good'. Six hundred acres were first enclosed in 1809, and a further 200 acres in 1814, of which ten were vested in the borough and freemen. Eventually in 1861 they agreed to hand over the ten acres to the Corporation as 'an agreeable place of resort to the public'. Hammond and Hammond, *Bleak Age*, p. 80.

68   Smith, *Coventry*, p. 144; WCRO QS 75/38, Enrolment of awards, 1875.

69   Smith, *Coventry*, p. 171.

70   *Report from the Select Committee on Commons (Elmstone Hardwicke Common Fields and Gosford Green Regulations)*, (HM Stationery Office, 1913; 22 September 2004), http://www.bopcris.ac.uk/bop1900/ref204.html.

Legal and political battles over charities

The reports of the nineteenth-century charity commissioners contain occasional but very telling examples of poor inhabitants themselves making their complaints known to 'officials'. There are sometimes glimpses of what must have been very lively town meetings when the local élite was called to task over the running of parish charities, including those established by enclosure. Some of these disputes simmered from the time of enclosure until the end of the nineteenth century, only occasionally erupting into the view of the historian, but no doubt the frequent talk of fireside and taproom. As the rural workers became more self-confident, with increased educational opportunities and political awareness, the rise of the trades unions in the 1870s gave them a voice. It is sometimes difficult to tell which came first. J.P.D. Dunbabin has suggested that it was 'disputes over charities and riots over enclosure' in Norfolk and Lincolnshire that led to the formation of the local unions.[71] On the other hand, Pamela Horn has suggested that waning success over wages and working hours led the National Agricultural Labourers Union in Oxford to turn its attention to village charities. They used the published accounts of the Charity Commission from the earlier part of the century to glean details of the history of the charities and then made enquiries into their current state. For example, the minute book of the Horspath branch records that in 1881 the secretary 'who was also a churchwarden, approached the charity commissioners over an alleged maladministration. The matter was investigated and a proper distribution of the funds secured'.[72]

There were other ways by which inhabitants could challenge the administration of local charities. Legislation was passed in 1597 and 1601, which gave the Lord Chancellor the power to establish a commission of enquiry when a case of maladministration was brought to his attention. The findings of the commission would then be sealed in Chancery and have the authority of parliament. The alternative was for individuals to lay information before the Attorney-General, leading to often lengthy and expensive proceedings in Chancery.[73] The costs involved generally meant that the undertaking was usually that of wealthier inhabitants, acting on behalf of their poorer neighbours. In Berkswell, Warwickshire, a long-brewing dispute between the lord of the manor and the local inhabitants over the village school resulted in a case in Chancery in 1586. In the time of Charles II it was the turn of the churchwardens to be investigated by a Royal Commission. In 1754 a number of inhabitants brought a case in Chancery against the vicar and churchwardens for misapplying the funds. In 1794 the overseer of the poor was complaining about the management of the charity estate.[74] Sladiburn, a large moorland parish in Lancashire, was enclosed in 1619 and

71   Dunbabin, *Rural Discontent*, pp. 72, 74.

72   P. Horn, 'Agricultural Trade Unionism in Oxfordshire', in Dunbabin, *Rural Discontent*, pp. 85–129, 116–17.

73   39 Eliz. I, *c*.6, An act for erecting hospitals, or abiding and workhouses for the poor; 43 Eliz. I, *c*.4, An act to redress the mis-employment of lands, goods and stocks of money heretofore given to certain charitable uses. Pinches, 'Charities in Warwickshire', pp. 47–50, 62–3; G. Jones, *History of the Law of Charity, 1532–1827* (London, 1969), pp. 33, 52, 161.

74   *Brougham*, pp. 637–40; WCRO CR 2037/1–2, Inquisition into charities, 14 Jan. 20 Car. II; DR 720/20, letter from Joseph Liggins, overseer of the poor, 1794.

60 acres allocated for the relief of the poor, probably in lieu of grazing rights. By the mid eighteenth century cowgates, or grazing rights, were rented to poor inhabitants and the income used by the overseers to pay the parish pensioners, which had the effect of keeping down the poor rates for the more prosperous inhabitants. In 1745 six inhabitants brought a case to the Court of the Duchy of Lancaster, protesting that the income should benefit all the poor inhabitants (that is, not ratepayers). The dispute ran on unresolved until at least the 1830s.[75] The cost and difficulty of challenging maladministration or peculation on the part of trustees was reduced with the establishment of the permanent Charity Commission in 1853. The Commission had the power to investigate the administration of endowed charities, to arbitrate between trustees and, if necessary, to certify cases into Chancery. It could also draw up new schemes and appoint trustees.[76]

In a number of corporate towns, including Coventry and Warwick, there were long-drawn out disputes and in both towns it was not until the Municipal Reform Act of 1835 that the running of the charities vested in the corporation were put on a sound footing. Even then, the opposition of sections of the community, especially with regard to the enclosure of the commons, led to further dispute, as discussed below. In Warwick much of the property formerly belonging to the religious guilds of the town had been given to the Corporation in 1545, forming what was known as the King Henry VIII Estate. It is not clear whether there was originally any intention for payments for the support of the poor to be made from this estate, or whether it really was, as the Corporation felt, income for the general purposes of the town. However, by a Chancery decree in 1618 the Corporation was obliged to distribute at least £16 a year to the poor and raise a stock of £100 to put them to work.

The estate continued to cause dispute and friction in the town until in 1736 the estate was sequestered by the Court of Chancery. It was another 12 years before a Chancery Order restored the administration of the estate to the Corporation, with the stipulation that at least £1 a week should be distributed in bread, and such other help given to the poor as might from time to time be deemed necessary. Thereafter the estate was administered reasonably well and the Charity Commissioners were not too scathing in their report of 1826.[77] The Municipal Reform Act 1835 removed control of this and the other charities from the Corporation. The Municipal Charities were formed under an independent group of trustees, but an inspection in 1854 found a number of serious faults in their administration.[78] The administration of the estate still caused furious rows nearly 30 years later when it was proposed to transfer 13 charities to the estate of the King's School Foundation. Two pamphlets were published. One held that 'of late years the existing charities in the Town would

75 Unpublished paper by R.W. Hoyle and C.J. Spencer, 'The Sladiburn Poor Pasture: changing configurations of popular politics in the eighteenth- and early nineteenth-century village'. I am grateful to Prof. Hoyle for allowing me to read this paper.

76 16 & 17 Vict., *c*.137, Charitable Trusts Act, 1853. Tompson, *Charity Commission.*

77 *Brougham*, pp. 747–66.

78 *Reports of Public Inquiries Respecting Warwick Charities, held under the authority of the Charity Commissioners by Walter Skirrow, Esq. ... in July 1854 and July 1868* (Warwick, 1868).

seem to have been fairly administered'.[79] The other stated that 'There has been a lot
of crooked and cunning scheming during the last 130 years to deprive the poor of
the rich charities left them by better men than those who have grabbed them from the
poor and destitute ... Thirteen of the best charities were carried from the people to
the High Schools – £3,600, leaving the poor penniless'.[80] This pamphlet war was not
unique to Warwick. Gorsky has made a study of 'the politics of charity' in Bristol, in
which he examined the way in which the distribution of charity funds could be used
to influence elections. Even after the electoral and municipal reforms of the 1830s
the mismanagement of charity funds was a weapon in the political armoury.[81]

Conclusion

Despite the differences between the experiences of urban and rural enclosures
there are certain common themes. For the inhabitants of town and village, access
to the pasture of the common fields and to the produce of the wastes was both
an economic benefit and a symbolic representation of their full belonging to the
community. The level of economic independence conferred by rights of common
may be debatable and no doubt varied from place to place and time to time, but the
independence of spirit and sense of both ownership and of belonging gained from
them was important. When these rights were extinguished by enclosure the levels
of compensation also varied tremendously, both in their economic value and their
social significance. In rural parishes the reduction of 'the common' to a small fuel
allotment administered manipulatively as a charity was of limited benefit. In urban
areas the land allocated either to the corporation or to the wider body of freemen in
lieu of rights of pasture over the common fields could and in many cases did become
valuable building land, forming a considerable investment, endowing pension funds
for freemen or financing civic improvements. The enclosure of the common wastes,
on the other hand, and their transformation into parks and recreation grounds was
of less economic value, but no less beneficial in other ways. In the crowded and
smoky towns of the nineteenth and early twentieth centuries such urban lungs were
important and gave the town dweller an access to land in some ways denied to their
rural cousin.

The resentment of the rural poor about their loss of access to the land and the
fruits of it expressed itself in many ways. At the time of the enclosure itself it could
take the form of petitioning, hedge-breaking or riot. Thereafter the resentment could
be expressed more covertly, by actions ranging from grumbling, sullen ingratitude on
receipt of 'charity' which they saw as theirs by right, or by criminal acts. F. Liardet,
writing about the 'peasantry' of Kent in 1839, described how 'charities are regarded
but as the return of a miserable fraction of the wealth they have extorted from their
own labours, and are received by them with ingratitude and sullenness'. He also noted

---

79 *Report of the Charities of the Borough of Warwick* (Warwick, 1890).

80 *A Full and Complete History of the Warwick Charities showing the Result of
Misapplications and Charity Grabbing* (Coventry, 1890).

81 M. Gorsky, *Patterns of Philanthropy: Charity and Society in Nineteenth-century
Bristol* (Woodbridge, 1999), pp. 63–85.

the 'very erroneous notions prevailing respecting the rights of property'.[82] The wood-stealing, and also poaching, which were so severely punished during the eighteenth and nineteenth centuries can be seen as no more than the traditional sharing of the produce of the land, criminalized by the enclosing landlords in defence of their newly acquired individual property rights. It is a matter of debate as to why this opposition, occasionally violent, did not erupt into more widespread insurrection, especially in the 1790s or the 1830s. However, it is wrong to say with Roger Wells that 'by 1800 few English agricultural labourers, unlike their Irish counterparts and Irish peasants, had any concept of ever having owned land, whatever sentiments romantic radicals would have liked to instil in the nineteenth century'.[83] The examples quoted here show that, in some villages at least, Neeson is right to suggest that 'the result [of enclosure] was a memory of expropriation that informed, legitimized, and sharpened the class politics of nineteenth-century villages' and, one can add, of towns.[84]

---

82 F. Liardet, 'State of the Peasantry in the county of Kent' in *Central Society of Education, Third Publication* (London, 1839; London, 1968), pp. 98, 133–4, quoted in Reay, *The Last Rising of the Agricultural Labourers*, pp. 185–6.

83 R.A.E. Wells, 'The development of the English rural proletariat and social protest, 1700–1850', in M. Reed and R.A.E. Wells (eds), *Class, Conflict and Protest in the English Countryside, 1700–1880* (London, 1990), p. 34.

84 Neeson, *Commoners*, p. 330.

CHAPTER FOUR

Kinship and welfare in early modern England: sometimes charity begins at home

Sheila Cooper

The needy in early modern England had three principal sources of support: public welfare, self-help and their kin and 'friends'.[1] Of the three the first has received by far the most attention, the second virtually explains itself, while the third, kin and friends, has been a matter of some historical debate. None the less, several recent scholars have come to regard early modern public welfare as decidedly inadequate to have met the needs of the poor and distressed in England. The parish relief system, Steve Hindle notes, 'could never be anything like central to the survival strategies of the overwhelming majority of the indigent'.[2]

Public welfare commonly came either from the government or from privately funded charities, many of the latter providing education and medical care. Their records, which inform much of our work on the poor, necessarily focus on a particular subset that interacted with the authorities – petitioners, patients or the like.[3] Kin exchanges, on the other hand, were relatively private by their very nature unless there was a public need to record them, as in wills or deeds. Yet even wills share the problem of the more disparate, scattered evidence – the difficulty of seeing welfare or relief provided within the kin group in anything approaching its entirety.

Although scholars agree that the poor, the needy and the not so needy routinely received help from kin and friends, the nature of that help is not well defined and its extent largely unexplored. This chapter argues that English people responded very extensively to the needs of kin, broadly defined, as well as to their future security; that social norms would have been violated had they not done so; and that the exchange was generally in the interest of both the giver and the recipient.

---

1   Besides employment, which was often sporadic, self-help would have included gleaning, pawning, begging, prostitution and criminal activity. In early modern England the term 'friend' or 'friends' meant anyone close to the speaker or writer and was routinely used as a synonym for kin.

2   S. Hindle, *On the Parish? The Micro-Politics of Poor Relief in Early Modern England c.1550–1750* (Oxford, 2004), p. 8.

3   None the less, recent creative use of these sources aided by new technology and interdisciplinary approaches has resulted in a much more highly nuanced view of the early modern poor.

Kin and collectivity

Several historians, while acknowledging that kin provided assistance to the poor, have asserted the primacy of community help. They have posited a growing role for the collectivity over the course of centuries, especially in England after late Elizabethan parliaments passed the Poor Laws of 1598 and 1601.[4] Katherine Lynch, for example, has written that, over several hundred years before 1800, the creation of community groups in England and elsewhere in Europe filled a void left by the waning strength of kinship ties. She suggests that the 'extrafamilial forms of solidarity' visible in rural areas were even more pronounced in the growing urban ones, where, she thinks, kinship bonds were likely to have been weaker.[5]

Lynch finds support in Peter Laslett's belief that the nuclear family, common in early modern England, had shallow kinship ties. His nuclear-hardship hypothesis predicts that when young people married at late ages on average and then set up independent, nuclear-family households, they were especially vulnerable to life's stresses. Laslett, like B. Seebohm Rowntree before him, recognized that circumstances varied in synchrony with the individual's life-cycle and with that of the family, especially the family head.[6] Individuals were at greatest economic risk when very young, then again for a period after their mid thirties when their children were young and their surviving parents old, and finally in their own declining years. Laslett claimed that the simple-family household lacked the depth of kin to address the resulting problems. He argued that unlike more complex families or households, nuclear families would have needed substantial help from beyond the kin group.[7] When duress occurred, such families would necessarily have had to seek the support of the wider community or collectivity. 'The family and the collectivity complement each other', was Laslett's belief.[8]

Shallow kin density depends in part upon whom one includes as kin. Linking individuals primarily by male surname would lead one to find few relatives in the house or, for the most part, elsewhere. In a high-mortality environment with frequent remarriage, many kin would not have borne the male head's surname. Many of those not part of the nuclear family resident in households were servants. If we were able to find out more about them than their surnames, we often would find kin. Ralph Josselin, whom Alan Macfarlane found meaningfully connected to relatively few kin, had in addition to his servant sister one nephew Thomas Humphy as a servant for five years and probably his other nephew for about a year. The nephews were

---

4   Late Elizabethan legislation (39–40 Eliz. I, *c*.3 and 43 Eliz. I, *c*.2) framed poor relief until 1834.

5   K. Lynch, *Individuals, Families and Communities in Europe, 1200–1800* (Cambridge, 2003), pp. 2–14, and after.

6   B.S. Rowntree, *Poverty: A Study of Town Life* (London, 1922). See also J. Henderson and R. Wall, 'Introduction', in Henderson and Wall (eds), *Poor Women and Children in the European Past* (London, 1994), p. 9.

7   P. Laslett, 'Family, Kinship and Collectivity as Systems of Support in Pre-Industrial Europe: A Consideration of the Nuclear-Hardship Hypothesis', *Continuity and Change*, 3 (1988): 153–75.

8   Ibid., p. 166.

the only surviving sons of his sisters and did not carry the Josselin name.[9] Some of the problem with measuring kin depth depends on one's definition of kin, and the easiest marker of a consanguineous group is male surname, but it is inadequate even for cognates in a bi-lineal society.

Others have also posited weak kinship ties in England. Alan Macfarlane, for example, has claimed that lack of strong kin bonds in medieval England led to the long march of English individualism.[10] The failure of parish officers centuries later to enforce the law regarding kin obligation has pushed David Thomson to infer that early Victorian England expected little from kin.[11] However, scholars disagree about the weakness of kinship in England. Pat Thane, Lynn Botelho, and others have challenged Thomson, asserting that relatives provided significant aid to the elderly.[12] Sam Barrett's detailed study of six West Riding townships shows that kin in late eighteenth- and early nineteenth-century Yorkshire supplied material aid and that their presence procured access to other sources of relief.[13] It would seem that for every Keith Wrightson who finds low kin density and thus little kin support in early modern Terling, Essex, there is a David Cressy who argues that early modern kin were an important resource for the poor.[14]

Individuals and families were indeed at risk at certain periods in their life-cycles, as Laslett claimed. Moreover, real wages were low from the late sixteenth until the early eighteenth century. Even then the real-wage level was not as good as it had been two hundred years earlier. Mortality was high throughout most of the seventeenth century and again in the earlier eighteenth, often claiming family breadwinners.[15] In a computer simulation of parental mortality by age of child, James Oeppen has found that from 1600 to 1750, roughly a quarter of youths under 15 and one-third of those under 20 would have lost at least one parent, sometimes both. In the last half

9   R. Josselin, *The Diary of Ralph Josselin* 1616–1683,(ed.) Alan Macfarlane (London, 1976), pp. 217–349.

10   A. Macfarlane, *The Origins of English Individualism: The Family, Property, and Social Transition* (New York, 1978), esp. pp. 3–5, 140–47.

11   D. Thomson, 'The Decline of Social Welfare: Falling State Support for the Elderly since Early Victorian Times', *Ageing and Society*, 4 (1984): 451–82.

12   P. Thane, *Old Age in English History* (Oxford, 2000), pp. 134–9; P. Thane, 'Old People and Their Families in the English Past', in M. Daunton (ed.), *Charity, Self-Interest, and Welfare in the English Past* (London, 1996), p. 134; L.A. Botelho, *Old Age and the English Poor Law, 1500–1700* (Woodbridge, 2004), pp. 132–7. The Poor Law of 1601 required members of three vertical generations – grandparents, parents and children – to contribute to each other's need unless such help threatened their own children's welfare.

13   S. Barrett, 'Kinship, Poor Relief and the Welfare Process in Early Modern England', in S. King and A. Tomkins (eds), *The Poor in England 1700–1800: An Economy of Makeshifts* (Manchester, 2003), pp. 199–207, esp. 221.

14   K. Wrightson, 'Kinship in an English Village: Terling, Essex 1550–1700', in R. M. Smith (ed.), *Land, Kinship, and Life-Cycle* (Cambridge, 1984), pp. 313–32; D. Cressy, 'Kin and Kin Interaction in Early Modern England', *Past and Present*, 113 (1986): 38–49.

15   E.A. Wrigley and R.S. Schofield, *The Population History of England 1541–1871* (London, 1981), pp. 642–3, Table A9.2: 'A real-wage index for England 1500–1912'. According to Steve Hindle, public funds were insufficient for the poor at least before 1660: see Hindle, *On the Parish?*, p. 4.

of the eighteenth century, the mortality rate declined to where one in five children under age 15 and more than one in four under age 20 had suffered parental loss.[16] The age of first marriage was dropping, so on average children had younger parents. However, although lessening, a parental deficiency, for which others needed to compensate, remained.

Public relief was one form of compensation, both for parental deficiency and for general need. Public relief, however, was not free. As Marco van Leeuwen has written, accepting charity meant accepting forms of social control.[17] In England the forms varied – wearing a pauper badge, giving up a child, attending church, among others. While the demands placed on petitioners by parish officers would have been unwelcome, those who accepted them would have weighed the alternative of doing without and found it less attractive. For those who lacked adequate options, aid from the collectivity was worth the cost. The many others in need who had sufficiently rewarding alternatives would have pursued them.

To be sure, help from kin and friends often had its own issues of control. The poor, especially the elderly poor, might well have preferred relief from the parish to being subject to the inverse relationship that could have occurred when they had to rely on children or the lack of independence incurred in living under someone else's thatch. On the other hand, the norm of reciprocity functioned in kin groups in a way that it did not in the collectivity, and shame at asking for relief must have produced much reluctance.

Kinship and aid

Scholars who define kin too narrowly can easily miss or underestimate the importance of friends and family in addressing loss in such a perilous society. Anthropologists frequently divide kin into three categories: cognatic (blood relatives); agnatic (affines including spouses, step-relatives and in-laws); and fictive kin (agnates' agnates, life-cycle and other servants, among others).[18] In seventeenth- and eighteenth-century England, it was common for an individual to have relationships in each category. Genealogical distance has often been considered the key variable in determining the intensity of kinship relationships. However, genealogical distance may not always have been the primary factor in that intensity.

Today, members of families broken by divorce or enlarged by adoption frequently have limited relationships with cognates and intense relationships with agnates or fictive kin. The same may be said for early modern families broken by death or enlarged by apprenticeship and service. The success of non-consanguineous families lends merit to C.C. Harris's suggestion that common household membership might be the

---

16   The author is indebted to James Oeppen of the Max Planck Institute for Demography, Rostock, Germany and of the University of Cambridge Group for running the Camsin simulation for her.

17   M.H.D. van Leeuwen, 'Logic of Charity: Poor Relief in Pre-Industrial Europe', *Continuity and Change* 24: 4 (1994): 606.

18   Will Coster discusses these kinship terms and the concentric circles of kin more fully in *Family and Kinship in England, 1450–1800* (Harlow, 2001), pp. 40–41.

most vital determinant of kin closeness.[19] As the nuclear-hardship hypothesis would lead us to expect, the average late age of first marriage in the early modern period, coupled with high mortality rates, meant that early modern sibling sets (and thus aunt and uncle groups) were usually small, and surviving grandparents problematic. However, rather than distancing agnates and fictive kin, that demographic reality could have brought survivors closer together. In such cases, agnates and fictive kin would have helped to compensate for the paucity of cognates.

One of the key ways that agnates and fictive kin, including godparents, became involved in helping their relatives was in being surrogate parents to their children. In a society that suffered substantial parental loss, agnatic and fictive kin such as godparents and masters were an important source of immediate relief and a bulwark against future insecurity for countless young people.

Life-cycle service was a very important mechanism mitigating the problem of nuclear hardship. Such service occupied young people from all social strata; and households across the social spectrum, even many very poor ones, had servants at some time, often parish apprentices.[20] Sometimes, especially in first placements, the sending family and the receiving family were well acquainted, often kin of some sort, even if quite removed. For example, Elias Ashmole, who was concerned about his deceased first wife's newly orphaned young sister, brought her to London from the West Country to serve him and his third wife.[21] When he died some years later, he left her one hundred pounds. At other times service and apprenticeships were arranged through a third party who knew the two parties. While many of these arrangements did not work out well, others developed into strong relationships.

Young people left home in droves.[22] At any given time about two-thirds of English households would have included a servant, usually a life-cycle one. Approximately 60 per cent of pre-industrial English youth between the ages of 15 and 25 were in life-cycle service, including apprenticeship, for varying lengths of time. Many who did not enter service left to go to school or to stay with relatives. Some did both at the same time, like Richard Kay's cousin, William Taylor, who boarded with the Kays for about six years, during which the cousins 'were both Schoolfellows and Bedfellows'.[23]

Having adolescents and young adults leave home to live with other families well before their expected late marriages was a brilliant solution to a demographic, economic and social dilemma. Late age of marriage itself worked as a population depressant; and keeping young people occupied during the long wait for adult status dampened what today would be called the jobless rate as well as possible

---

19   C.C. Harris, *Kinship* (Minneapolis, 1990), p. 74.

20   Many of these would have been parish or pauper apprentices, young people who were a charge on the parish and placed in residents' homes, sometimes against objection and generally with some abatement of tax or some other consideration.

21   *Elias Ashmole, His Autobiographical and Historical Notes, His Correspondence, and Other Contemporary Sources*, ed. by C.H. Josten (5 vols.) Oxford: Clarendon Press, 1966. For the legacy to a former sister in law, see vol. 1, p. 294 and vol. 2, p. 632.

22   For the nature of the adolescent exodus, see S.M. Cooper, 'Intergenerational Social Mobility in Late-Seventeenth- and Early-Eighteenth-Century England', *Continuity and Change* 7:3 (1992): 283–301.

23   R. Kay, *The Diary of Richard Kay, 1715–51* (Manchester, 1968), p. 21.

restiveness. Life-cycle service differed from lifetime service.[24] The latter was an adult occupation, the former a passing stage on the road to a young person's future employment. Life-cycle service provided training, moved labour from where it was often superfluous to where it was generally needed, and acted as an exogenous marriage market while giving young people a surrogate family. Once resident with masters and mistresses, apprentices, servants and journeymen had joined a family, whether born into it or not, and 'family' is what the resulting group was called by its members and others.[25]

Reciprocity and trust

Kinship involves reciprocity and trust to a high degree, which helps to make it different from public welfare. Aid given to and by kin differs qualitatively from relief that the commonalty provides. Reciprocity is a fundamental social norm – *the* fundamental norm, some social scientists believe. Reciprocity goes much further than exchange of gifts or favours. It oils the machinery of social life so that individuals aid each other, understanding that a good deed today incurs credit redeemable in the future – if the debtor is able, available and agreeable. This might include material help, physical assistance or emotional support. Repayment need not be made in kind and may be made to another individual – a person's spouse or kin, for example – and may also extend across generations. Bulstrode Whitelocke's beloved servant and confidant William Cooke died beside his cart returning from a Whitelocke errand. Whitelocke was crushed and, when Cooke's widow asked that he give their surly grandson Cooke's old tenancy, Whitelocke acquiesced, albeit reluctantly.[26]

Trust also plays a central role in relationships, especially in those where interaction is frequent and where physical space is shared. The most fundamental group in which trust resides is usually the family, whether consanguineous or not. Trust is essential to stable social relationships, and in Niklas Luhmann's words, it is 'a basic fact of social life'.[27] Trust forms an important part of the web that sustains social interaction and leads one to expect that the world will generally function in a predictable fashion. If not misplaced or violated, trust simplifies life, for it is the unexpected and unpredictable that present the greatest problems.

---

24   On life-cycle *vis à vis* lifetime service, see S. Cooper, 'From Family Member to Employee: Aspects of Continuity and Discontinuity in English Domestic Service, 1600–2000', in A. Fauve-Chamoux (ed.), *Domestic Service and the Formation of European Identity* (Bern, 2004), esp. pp. 278–9.

25   The well-known diaries of Samuel Pepys, Thomas Turner and Ralph Josselin as well as many others use the term family in this way. For further discussion, see N. Tadmor, 'The Concept of the Household-Family in Eighteenth-century England', *Past and Present,* 151 (1996): 111–40.

26   B. Whitelocke, *The Diary of Bulstrode Whitelocke* (ed.) R. Spalding (Oxford, 1990), pp. 295, 638, 645.

27   P. Blau, *Exchange and Power in Social Life* (New York, 1964), p. 99. N. Luhmann, *Trust and Power* (New York, 1979), p. 4.

Some theorists distinguish between two forms of trust: the expectation of technically competent performance and the expectation of what has been called fiduciary obligation and responsibility.[28] Technical competence is the easier to understand, for it is often scheduled and is generally evident – mail delivery or cooking dinner, for example. There are usually minimally acceptable performance levels, and often performance does not have to be very high. The expectation of technical competence is the kind of trust a master would have in a servant to perform a job, or the servant in the master in regard to job training.

Fiduciary trust, which is moral in nature, is far more important than that of expectation of performance. Fiduciary trust helps to equalize relationships because it is built on reciprocity. One person trusts another to be willing to help him and expects to return help at a later time, often in a different form. Trust is analogous to a savings account upon which a person may draw, except that the account is not limited to money and immediate repayment is seldom necessary. Yet expectation of reciprocation at some point remains.

If trust is well placed, the truster will be better off than he otherwise would have been, but the decision to trust, James Coleman has pointed out, 'is nearly always problematic'.[29] Trust is less problematic with kin groups, however, because they are based on it. The kin group's strength depends in part on its members' awareness that relationships between kin are known to many of the group beyond the two principals. Thus kinship networks have the 'propensity to ensure that commitments entered into by kinsfolk are discharged'.[30] The group's opportunity for observation and shared intelligence serve as an enforcement mechanism, encouraging reciprocation of trust.

Trust extends to fictive kinship, where ritual often plays an important role. In England baptisms and confirmations were common rituals. Their relatively public nature again made others besides the principals aware of their obligation. However, ritual was not essential to fictive kinship, as it often developed quite naturally, for example between life-cycle servants and their masters or mistresses, who served *in loco parentis*. Like cognatic and agnatic relationships, fictive relationships could last a lifetime and into the next generation.[31] They, too, helped to mitigate nuclear hardship.

---

28   B. Barber, *Logic and Limits of Trust* (New Brunswick, 1983), p. 9.

29   J.S. Coleman, *Foundations of Social Theory* (Cambridge, Mass., 1980).

30   Harris, *Kinship*, p. 74. James Coleman notes that employing relatives results in a lower average quality of performance because the pool from which they are picked is small. Coleman, *Foundations*, pp. 111–12. However, performance trust is not as important as fiduciary trust and there we expect relatives and friends to be more trustworthy.

31   Apprenticeship and pauper apprenticeship was in effect a form of life-cycle service and apprentices were often referred to as servants. See Cooper, 'English Domestic Service, 1600–2000', pp. 277–96.

The poor, the needy and the at-risk

In 1689, the demographer Gregory King estimated that those persons in contemporary families decreasing England's wealth outnumbered those increasing it. Besides paupers and vagrants the 'decreasers', so to speak, included many families of those either fitfully employed or under-employed, like labourers, seamen and soldiers.[32] It is tempting to take King's analysis as accurate, for his 1695 estimate of England's population has been found to be remarkably on target.[33] However, while King's 'decreasing' occupational groups were economically challenged, many of them, like seamen or agricultural labourers, were essential to the nation's increasing prosperity. Moreover, the occupations of the 'increasers' did not necessarily give them economic stability or financial comfort. Shopkeepers, tradespeople, artisans, craftsmen – indeed, merchants, gentry and other putative increasers – were at risk of poverty, often from forces beyond their ken, as Wrigley and Schofield's analysis of relationship between real wages and population growth confirms.[34]

'Poor' and 'needy' are relative terms, for which we have no single definition in this period except in narrow contexts. Hindle suspects that roughly 20 per cent of the population, the 'conjectural poor', were 'in need'; and he calls about another 5 per cent, those on relief, the 'structural poor'.[35] Defining the poor in such a way for a period when parish records are probably our most cohesive source facilitates analysis. However, Keith Wrightson's term, the 'poorer sort', reflects more felicitously the indeterminacy of those in, those sometimes in, and those who might not be too far from need.[36] The poor were a very fluid group; a large body of needy was scraping together a living outside of the poor records' purview. If the 'poor' were not a stable group, neither were the 'middling sort'. Moreover, another sizable body of those living in comfort or even affluence was at risk. In early modern England poverty could envelop an individual or family relatively quickly.

The gentry at risk

Even those at the top of the economic ladder could slip. Landed aristocracy and gentry who were not given to gambling, drink or political ambition could find themselves in penury from sequestration, bad harvests, poor investments or a surfeit of unmarried sisters and younger brothers. The siblings, for their part, quite often descended socially and economically over their lifetimes.

---

32   G. King, '"Scheme of the income & expence of the several families of England" calculated for the year 1688', in P. Laslett, *The World We Have Lost: England before the Industrial Age* (New York, 1984), Table 1, pp. 32–3, 34.

33   See Wrigley and Schofield, *Population History*, pp. 159, 175, 181.

34   Ibid., pp. 407–12.

35   Hindle, *On the Parish?*, p. 4.

36   K. Wrightson, 'The Social Order of Early Modern England: Three Approaches', in L. Bonfield, R.M. Smith and K. Wrightson (eds), *The World We Have Gained: Histories of Population and Social Structure* (Oxford, 1986), pp. 177–202.

The slide of many aristocratic and gentle families is well known and well documented. Personal failings aside, they generally could not control the effects on their landed income of economic, political and other disruption. The cliché of 'three generations up and three generations down' often proved an optimistic overstatement. Individuals as well as families rose and fell. In the early modern period heads rolled relatively easily and very publicly. However, many of the less spectacular difficulties of those with high status were more private.

Fatherless members of the gentry had a common problem. If the father died young or improvident, his younger children often had to put together their own economy of makeshifts.[37] Usually that included appeals to the heir as well as to other kin and friends. Quite often older as well as younger survivors lived off social, not actual, capital while they penned begging letters. The heir's inability or unwillingness to salvage enough from an encumbered estate to pay portions or to provide schooling could relegate his siblings to financial uncertainty and single working lives.

Some of Sir Ralph Verney's relatives, including his brother Henry, were among those so relegated.[38] Two of their nieces, Cary Stewkeley and Peg Adams, and a cousin, Doll Leeke, became lifetime servants to others within the family. Cary, companion to Sir Ralph's incapacitated daughter-in-law, had hoped that her service would result in a sizable legacy. In this regard she had misplaced trust in her uncle.[39] Her sister Pen Stewkeley was luckier. She was the namesake of their childless aunt, Penelope Verney Osborne, who left Pen over seven thousand pounds. This caused her surprised uncle to abandon his plan to get his sexually wayward niece off to some remote location.[40] Pen was not the first Verney to profit from her Christian name. Sir Ralph's maternal aunt, the childless Lady Margaret Eure, settled nine hundred pounds on Ralph's sister Margaret, who lived with her.[41]

For his part Sir Ralph had barely lived with his sisters, for his generation was not theirs. The oldest, Susan, was his junior by eight years, and he was 16 years senior to Cary and Pen's mother, and 20 years older than the mother of Peg

---

37   This term, first used by Olwen Hufton to apply to economic strategies in early modern France, has been lifted by historians of England to describe the various ways in poor people pieced together a living.

38   Material on the Verneys comes from two modern studies, S.E. Whyman, *Sociability and Power in Late-Stuart England: The Cultural World of the Verneys, 1660–1720* (Oxford, 1999), and M. Slater, *Family Life in the Seventeenth Century: The Verneys of Claydon House* (London, 1984); read together with F.P.N. Verney, *Memoirs of the Verney Family during the Civil War*, 4 vols (New York, 1970).

39   Whyman, *Sociability*, pp. 37, 53–4.

40   Whyman, *Sociability*, p. 126. Had any of Aunt Osborne's three children survived, Pen might have had to remove. Rather, Sir Ralph involved himself in securing Pen's inheritance. Earlier he had invested Aunt Eure's money for his sister Margaret, then he clandestinely borrowed much of it back. Slater, *Family Life*, p. 97.

41   Ibid., p. 97. Children were very commonly given their godparent's Christian name at baptism. It is likely that Margaret Eure was Margaret Verney's godmother as well as aunt. The same can be said below for Lady Joan Barrington and her niece, Joan or Jane Whalley.

Adams.[42] He had been gone from home for most of their childhoods and had married young. As a result there had been little occasion for reciprocal exchange and no great reservoir of affection. When he inherited, the contest between the king and Parliament was threatening the family's investments. In exile in France with a wife and children to support, Sir Ralph found his sisters and their needs to be little more than irritants. Their maternal uncle, Dr William Denton, an eminent physician, served as intermediary when he could and also dispensed medical treatments freely to them. Close to Ralph's age, he was much loved in the family. Vertical lineage was important to Ralph; his lateral vision was seriously limited.

This kind of limbo and distance between siblings was not uncommon for the landed. Sir Robert Walpole's sisters languished in the Norfolk countryside awaiting their portions. They begged their brother for money for clothes, which even their mother's letters to her son could not elicit.[43] In their prolonged dependency they may have been worse off than the granddaughter of Sir Walter Kirby, Walpole's predecessor as Member of Parliament for King's Lynn, Norfolk. His elder son had become indigent, so Lady Alice Kirby, Sir Walter's widow, left money in trust at interest to apprentice her step-grandsons as well as for their sisters at 21.[44] One of the latter, Elizabeth Kirby, petitioned the Lynn authorities early for forty shillings 'to releise her in a present extreme necessity' and collected the rest of her legacy two years later.[45] The Walpole girls were unable to petition.

The Verney family was one of several great gentry networks. Another included a complicated group of agnates, cognates and fictive kin much involved in Puritan politics. While she lived, Lady Joan Barrington, *née* Cromwell, was at its heart. She educated many young relatives including her niece, Jane Whalley.[46] When the litigiousness of Jane's father Richard Whalley impoverished him, he could no longer pay Jane's board. Neither could he see a way to maintain her at home, so he asked Lady Joan to retain Jane as a servant. Thus her aunt kept Jane on, aborted the chaplain Roger Williams's wooing of her, and in time married her off with a large portion to a minister not bound for America.[47] Jane's sister Mary, living with her father and desperately trying to find a lost legacy, fared less well.[48]

---

42   Ibid., pp. 80ff. Only two of Sir Ralph's five brothers, generally closer to him in age, lived long, and all died without heirs. For genealogies, see Whyman, *Sociability*, p. xiii; and Slater, *Family Life*, pp. 202–3.

43   The Walpole Correspondence is held in two parts, one in the manuscript collections of the University of Cambridge Library and the other in the rare books division of the University of Chicago Library.

44   Norfolk Record Office, ANW Will Register MF/312, Will of Alice Kirby, 1691. She forgave a debt of forty pounds owed by her improvident stepson, Sir Walter's elder son.

45   Norfolk Record Office, KL/C7/12/f.152.o.

46   Most of the young women, as godchildren, were named Jane or Joan, names that were interchangeable.

47   Lady Joan found Williams arrogant and self-serving and was not unhappy when he departed for America. There he became a controversial religious figure, famous for opposing the religious establishment and for the founding of the colony of Rhode Island.

48   A. Searle (ed.), *Barrington Family Letters*, Camden Society fourth series vol. 28 (London: Royal Historical Society, 1983), pp. 15ff.

The middling sort at risk

Luck, social capital and austere personal habits were sometimes all that kept many of the diverse middling sort from becoming certifiably poor. In his autobiography, William Stout of Lancaster listed 25 who were 'broke', many of them other tradesmen with whom he had been long involved and whose affairs he was asked to settle.[49] Stout was quick to note that conviviality and risk-taking played a role in many of these disasters. One might be tempted to dismiss Stout, a dour Quaker, if some of the temptations open to a shopkeeper did not also appear in apprentice Roger Lowe's rare diary.[50] Lacking supervision when he ran a village shop for his master, Lowe indulged his sociable traits in plentiful visits to ale-houses among other diversions, often closing the shop to do so. His friends and master cautioned him fruitlessly. Sociability built custom, Lowe rationalized, but he knew it could be dangerous. Shortly after taking over his master's shop, he gave it up to become a waged journeyman for another shopkeeper. For him it was the safer course.

Sociability fueled with alcohol felled many of Stout's acquaintances. At the same time many of the Lancaster men had also overreached, tempted by investment opportunities on a scale that would never have existed for Roger Lowe in Ashton. Some of Stout's fallen acquaintances had been worth thousands of pounds a year at their height, including two Lancaster mayors and the collector of customs – men who had had the 'direction of affairs of this burrow'. Robert Lawson, a Sunderland merchant who traded in Lancaster, might have been worth three or four thousand pounds, Stout thought, but 'overshot himself' in the 'superfluity of buying land at great prices and building …'.[51]

Henry Coward, Stout's former master and good friend, had at one time been 'very much respected and trusted'. He increasingly took risks where his knowledge was weak and increasingly stood surety for too many local gentry who subsequently defaulted. He fell into debt, went into seclusion, and avoided jail by dying.[52] Like others, his financial failure had repercussions for family and kin. Coward's grocer son-in-law, William Godsalve, also stood surety too often for a questionable set of cronies. He fled, leaving wife and son to the 'charity of friends'. Stout loaned Godsalve's deserted wife money to trade in smallwares. Her little shop supported her, her son, her infirm sister, and their mother, Coward's impoverished widow. Hearing of his wife's success, Godsalve returned and took over the shop, but his convivial habits had not changed; he failed and left once more.[53]

Failures pepper the pages of Stout's autobiography, some of his one-time apprentices among them, in spite of their former master's aid. He assisted when his first apprentice, John Troughton, took over his shop, but John's lack of discipline drove him away, as it did John's widowed mother and sister, who replaced Stout.

---

49   W. Stout, *The Autobiography of William Stout of Lancaster, 1665–1752* (Manchester, 1967).

50   R. Lowe, *The Diary of Roger Lowe* (ed.) W.L. Sachse (New Haven, 1938) p. 118.

51   Stout, *Autobiography*, p. 202.

52   Ibid., pp. 74–5, 81, 111, 120–21.

53   Ibid., p. 156.

After Troughton was jailed for debt, Stout helped to satisfy his creditors, bought his shop goods, and arranged his release. Unfortunately when Robert Troughton, bound with his brother John for a loan, had to sell his estate to pay it, the family, 'which had been as much in substance and reputation as any family in Overton or the neighbourhood', finally broke. John 'roved about' for a while, then became a ship's steward and was lost with the ship on an American voyage. His wife moved in with her parents.[54]

Stout's parish apprentice, John Robinson, came to him as a ten-year-old. Stout sent him to school for four years, then apprenticed him to a worsted weaver. When in trade on his own, Robinson 'was not so industrious or carfull as he ought, fell to drinking and broke...'. He married, but thereafter he too sailed to America, leaving his wife in London to support herself.[55]

For Stout the most troublesome failure of an apprentice, however, was that of his namesake nephew. He too took over his uncle's shop and failed. His uncle kept him out of jail and restocked the shop for him, only to see him fail again. Thereafter the enabling, albeit despairing, Stout settled an annuity on him, which young Stout and his wife overspent. When Stout refused to pay their debts, they successfully appealed to the wife's brother. Thereafter Stout contained their spending by paying the annuity in small amounts for specific purposes. Meanwhile Leonard, another Stout nephew, took his brother's small son to raise and educate. A third brother, John, having finished his apprenticeship to a Manchester woollen draper, took over his uncle's shop. Stout paid three hundred pounds for yet another restocking, this one successful. John Stout prospered and later became mayor of Lancaster.[56]

Stout's continued care of his nephew was not unique. More than a few of Stout's insolvents depended on the charity of kin and friends. Benjamin Borrow fled to his Westmorland relations and died, leaving his wife and child to his father-in-law. Quakers took on Joseph Green's daughter. Robert Carter overran his credit and subsequently died poor, but his MP brother-in-law gave Carter's daughter a thousand-pound portion. John Hull's father, a vicar, paid his debts and found him a job in the Customs. He soon drank himself to death, leaving his widow and six children 'mostly to the care and dependence of his father'.[57]

Mental illness for those genetically programmed for it often strikes young adults. Fraud triggered tanner Benjamin Casson's depression. He had to be 'confined and bound' for some time before he improved. Then, through distant relatives, he gained a position in the Customs.[58] Stout had arranged a London apprenticeship for his first cousin's son, Peter Wilson. Once in trade, he flourished; Stout alone gave him over a hundred pounds' worth of business each year. In about six years, however, he started randomly passing out his shop goods. His 'friends' summoned his father, who took Peter home to Kendal and settled an annuity on him.[59]

---

54   Ibid., pp. 99–100, 110–18.
55   Ibid., p. 154.
56   Ibid., p. 222.
57   Ibid., pp. 100, 144, 150.
58   Ibid., p. 152.
59   Ibid., p. 166.

Any strong drink made William Coward, a quiet and 'fully imployed' tailor, go on spending sprees while 'roaring about the town loudly as a mad man', the prey of opportunists. His protective father left such estate as he had to two executors, one of them Stout, for the use of his son. They gave public notice that they would not pay any more creditors even if Coward ended in jail. There they would maintain him permanently if need be. Publicly a credit risk, Coward had only his earnings and the odd gift to spend. Stout, the surviving executor, used the interest on Coward's small inheritance to maintain 'that unruly man', protecting the principal against the time 'when he came to old age'.[60]

Although kin and friends rescued some of the disturbed, others sank. They and their dependents had to fall back on public support. William Lawson, Stout's fellow apprentice, never recovered his 'right capacity' and was 'reduced to poverty'. As a trustee, Stout had bound a currier's orphaned son to his shoemaker uncle. The boy worked well when he was not 'frandish', but his fits prevented him from moving beyond journeyman's work. Thus he died poor and left his wife and children as charges to Lancaster.[61]

The poor at risk

In 1657, at 'about twelve or thirteen years' Edward Barlow started a six-day walk from rural Lancashire to London. Although he had never seen the sea, he fancied a sailor's life. His parents, 'being poor and in debt', had six children that they could ill afford to support. Edward had aborted his father's attempt to place him with a Manchester whitester but knew he needed to support himself.[62] He located his father behind the parish clerk's plough and asked if he would lend him six shillings on his half-interest in a fowling piece, shared with a neighbour boy. Offering his share in the gun as collateral let Edward pretend that he was not asking for a gift and gave his father opportunity to give his son something of a parting present.[63]

London was not the nearest port, but Edward's sister Anna and his younger brother were servants there, the latter a tapster for their uncle who kept the Dog and Bear, a Southwark inn. Edward arrived penniless, having spent his money on food, and quickly located Anna, who sent him to their uncle. The latter had had word that he was coming and had been out searching for him. Before long Edward reluctantly had replaced his homesick brother at the inn's tap.[64]

Edward's uncle quickly began to discourage Edward's yen for the sea. He interfered when a spirit posing as a ship's surgeon needing a helper would have

---

60   Ibid., p. 164.

61   Ibid., p. 72.

62   The whitening or bleaching trade in Manchester was largely seasonal, depending on supplies of brown Irish yarn, so an apprenticeship involved incidental labour, much of it agricultural, and the master could have hired Edward out.

63   E. Barlow, *Barlow's Journal of His Life at Sea on the King's Ships ... from 1659 to 1703*, vol. I (ed.) B. Lubbock (London, 1934), pp. 19–21.

64   Ibid., pp. 22–5.

kidnapped the naive Edward.[65] He arranged service with a vintner to see if that would appeal. He urged the life of a Thames waterman as equivalent to a sailor's and much safer. Edward remained fixed. 'At last, ... not being willing that I should go I could not tell whither', Edward would later write, his uncle capitulated and found him a mariner master.[66]

After eight years Edward gained his freedom and could keep his wages. When in port he left a 'token' with his uncle to send home to the Barlows – a pound apiece for his parents, 'ancient and poor and being in debt', one for his brother, and another for a sister and his brother's children to share. However, his uncle 'being in a straight' and losing his inn, had kept the token. Edward surely felt aggrieved but blamed his spendthrift cousins for his uncle's downfall along with his going surety too easily. He determined not to leave such a large sum with his uncle again and requested its return, which took about two years. His uncle had gone to some lengths with him for little reward. Although the 'borrowing' had violated trust, he may have felt free to use Edward's money as repayment for his investment in Edward as Edward was at sea and could not be asked. Edward may have sensed an obligation and directed his anger at the cousins.[67]

Cutting a fine figure in new clothes 'too high for my calling', Edward at last visited his parents, winning their poor neighbours' envy as well as admiration. On his departure, he gave his family another token. His next voyage, for the East India Company, was extremely difficult, ending with his ship's capture and his imprisonment. He lost his wages and virtually all of what he had on board. To 'try' his friends and relations, he wrote to his parents to see if they could raise ten pounds to sustain him until his next voyage. None was 'able or willing', which he considered a lesson learned. Yet Anna, lately dead and much mourned, had left pay she had collected for him, which, with some petty trade and minor funds, gave him enough money for himself and to send a small amount to his parents. The sending of his token betrayed hurt and seemed a reprimand, 'showing them how kind I was to supply their wants'.[68]

Conclusion

The Old Poor Law framed by Elizabethan Parliaments has been justly admired. Although perhaps not quite the unique arrangement that once was thought, it was a remarkable piece of legislation and a very early attempt to organize a relief system nationally and administer it locally. The relief it provided was targeted – both in type

---

65   'Spirits' haunted the docks, enticing naïve young people on to ships, where they remained captive until sold as indentured servants in American ports.

66   Barlow, *Journal*, I, pp. 28–30.

67   Ibid., pp. 139, 146–7. Others found that spendthrift children created trouble for parents. Henry Purefoy wrote to a London debtor on behalf of Hunt the baker's family to ask him to take a small sum to satisfy the debt. 'I could compel old Mr. Hunt to pay, but hee has been so great a loser by his extravagant son that hee has scarce left enough to buy himself and his wife bread.' G. Eland (ed.), *The Purefoy Letters*, vol. I (London, 1931), p. 34.

68   Barlow, *Journal* I, pp. 174–8.

of need and in type of applicant. While philanthropic associations met some of its gaps, they too were directed at a limited target and a particular kind of recipient.

Help from family or friends was a different, much more comprehensive kind of aid. It is more difficult to document because it was often silent and pervaded daily life. There was also often an unplanned element in it. Ralph Lowe recounted many little incidents of kindness from unplanned gifts – a few pennies, a cooked meal, his brother's support when a rumour swept the village that he was a bastard, and the like. And William Stout gave of himself, his knowledge and his goods not only to his namesake but to the other six of his brother's children. When, at 79, he was run down by a horse, there they were – a nephew making sure his goods were secure, a niece's doctor husband seeing to his injuries, a great-niece keeping his house – worth all his trouble over them.[69]

It is not surprising that the vignettes above make little mention of the collectivity in terms of aid. While many of those mentioned were in need, there appeared to be few, if any, starving or naked. Other than two or three of William Stout's broken tradesmen, they were not to our knowledge turning to the collectivity. Instead they were turning to family or friends, or in some cases family and friends were trying to help them in spite of themselves. A loan or a gift from kin or friends was much more desirable than a hand-out from the parish. Transactions with kin left open the possibility of repayment, and for the poorer members of a kin network the payment did not have to be made in the same currency, so to speak, as the original gift.

Sir Ralph Verney did not need, nor did he think that he needed, much that his sisters had to offer, so he could be somewhat oblivious even to their legitimate needs. On the other hand he could not totally ignore them, however, and not only because he was controlling money that was legally theirs: among others, he had Dr Denton, whom he respected, judging him.

Receiving aid had the potential to affect many recipients' views of their status negatively. Moreover, having to sign away the few goods that a poor person owned, or being forced to send others away from home as a condition for relief, was unpalatable. Aid from kin was not only much more varied, it was more extensive, even multi-generational. Furthermore, the recipient could believe that some day he or she would reciprocate.

---

69   Small gifts, including drink, are scattered through Lowe's *Diary* after p. 13. Stout, *Autobiography*, esp. pp. 237, 229.

CHAPTER FIVE

Deaf children and charitable education in Britain 1790–1944

Anne Borsay

The origins of deaf education in Britain are obscure, but there is evidence that children from prosperous families were receiving personal tuition during the Tudor period, while the publication of John Bulwer's *Deaf and Dumb Man's Friend* in 1642 stimulated a further rash of private activity, with Alexander Popham and Daniel Whalley allegedly becoming the first prelingually deaf people to be taught to speak. It was not until 1764, however, that a school was founded, when Thomas Braidwood dedicated his former mathematical academy in Edinburgh to the education of deaf children after being persuaded by a wealthy local merchant to admit his deaf son. Twenty years later, Braidwood moved his school to the London suburb of Hackney; in 1792, another was opened, this time in Bermondsey, south of the river;[1] and by 1828, institutions for deaf pupils had been set up as far afield as Aberdeen, Birmingham, Doncaster, Dundee, Edinburgh, Exeter, Glasgow, Liverpool, Manchester and Perth. Part of a wider movement that by the same date had delivered 128 institutions in Europe and North America as a whole,[2] these establishments applied teaching methods that had multiple roots. As the French guru Abbé de l'Epée conceded, 'I find no difficulty in believing that Amman invented the art in Holland, Bonnet in Spain, Wallis in England, and other ingenious men in other countries; without, perhaps, having seen each other's works'.[3] Yet whereas elsewhere, public institutions for the application of these techniques were 'sanctioned and supported by different States', in Britain 'the benevolence of individuals' had 'superseded the necessity of legislative interference'.[4]

This chapter explores the implications of this charitable benevolence for deaf children before the Education Act of 1944. Special education in the era of the welfare

---

1   P. Beaver, *A Tower of Strength: Two Hundred Years of the Royal School for Deaf Children, Margate* (Lewes, Sussex, 1992), pp. 23, 28–9; B. Grant, *The Deaf Advance: A History of the British Deaf Association, 1890–1990* (Edinburgh, 1990), pp. 1–4; P. Jackson, *A Pictorial History of Deaf Britain* (Winsford, Cheshire, 2001), pp. 15–16, 52, 55; P. Ladd, *Understanding Deaf Culture: In Search of Deafhood* (Cleveden, Bristol, 2003), pp. 102–5; J. Rée, *I See A Voice: Language, Deafness and the Senses – A Philosophical History* (London, 1999), pp. 137–9.

2   W.C. Fenton, *A Brief View of the Institutions for the Deaf and Dumb in Europe and America with some remarks relative to the Yorkshire Institution for the Deaf and Dumb* (Doncaster, 1833), p. 18.

3   *Gentleman's Magazine*, Supplement (1803): 1204.

4   Fenton, *Brief View*, p. 5. See also *Gentleman's Magazine*, 62 (February 1792): 134.

state has been the subject of a number of studies,[5] the most recent of which is Paddy Ladd's compelling interpretation of residential schools and the construction of deaf culture.[6] Earlier accounts are more difficult to retrieve. Given their non-statutory status, however, deaf institutions did engage in vigorous marketing campaigns to achieve financial solvency. In so doing, they utilized child recipients for advertising material designed to sell the virtues of their service from the standpoint of donors and educationalists. Nevertheless, the texts that emerged from this process do allow us to compare the imagery of deaf schooling with the experiences of deaf pupils, shedding light on the role of spectacle in vending charity and the use of rhetoric in articulating its aims and methods. Therefore, we can grasp the perspectives of children caught up in the pedagogic and institutional regimes through which deaf education was delivered.

Spectacle: constructed perceptions

In 1848 John William Lashford, a pupil at the Brighton and Sussex Institution for the Deaf and Dumb, died of consumption at the age of 17. Strapped for cash, the master of the institution published a memoir to put 'on record the wonderful dealings of the Lord toward one ... of whose future success and usefulness great hopes had been entertained'. Despite being called *A Voice from the Dumb*, John's story was told from the perspective of the deaf institution. In a style epitomizing Victorian sentimentality, he was depicted as a child who had achieved piety through adversity. '[T]his dear boy had been in the habit of assembling his little mute companions around him every morning, and spelling before him a prayer, previously to leaving their bedroom.' When death was imminent, he returned home to a 'humble but clean and comfortable sick room'.

> He was quite sensible to the last; and about an hour before his death, he signed for all in the room to kneel around his bed and pray; after which, he took his mother's hand and spelled *soul* on her fingers, and looking steadfastly upwards, he pointed to heaven and signed, 'Glory, glory.' Such was the joy with which *he* stood on the brink of death, and all was peace to the very end.[7]

By portraying a 'good death' of the sort promoted by the Evangelical Revival and captured by the Romantic Movement, the Brighton Institution converted John

---

5   See, for example, S. French with J. Swain, 'Institutional Abuse: Memories of a Special School for Visually Impaired Girls – A Personal Account', in J. Bornat, R. Perks, P. Thompson and J. Walmsley (eds), *Oral History, Health and Welfare* (London, 2000), pp. 159–79; T. Cook, J. Swain and S. French, 'Voices from Segregated Schooling: Towards an Inclusive Educational System', *Disability and Society*, 16 (2001): 293–310.

6   Ladd, *Understanding Deaf Culture*, pp. 297–331.

7   W. Sleigh, *A Voice from the Dumb: A Memoir of John William Lashford, Late a Pupil of the Brighton and Sussex Institution for the Deaf and Dumb* (London, 1849), pp. i, 45, 64, 79.

Lashford into a marketable product whose appeal to the spiritual anxieties of less challenged believers generated valuable funds.[8]

Living pupils were also used as merchandise. Some accounts of their activities were anonymous. Letters were 'now and then' arriving that bore witness to 'the pleasing change which the few years training ... produces', reported the Committee of the West of England Institution at Exeter in 1866. 'Boys who were before regarded as vagrants, suspected of thefts and mischief, unwilling to work, have returned to their homes in quite a different spirit.'[9] On other occasions, letters penned by named pupils were reproduced. On 23 March 1833, for instance, John Harrison wrote to his father from the Yorkshire Institution for the Deaf and Dumb at Doncaster. As well as enquiring into the health of his family, he thanked them for gifts received in December and explained that the tailor was making him a new coat. Most striking, however, was a religious piety akin to that of John Lashford's *Memoir*. 'If I pray to God morning and night, and love him, and seek Jesus to make intercession for me, when I die I shall go to heaven, and be eternally happy with Jesus Christ.' Murderers and the wicked, on the other hand, 'go to hell'.[10] As Arthur Dimmock has remarked, had such letters been genuine, they 'would have put modern teaching results to shame'.[11]

The display of pupils in the flesh was more intrusive than paper publicity. Despite condemning parents for allowing their children to beg,[12] deaf institutions were happy to brandish them for charitable purposes. First, admission was through a public selection process. Benefactors and subscribers voted for candidates – typically aged between six and 12 – on the basis of biographical notes, which were circulated in advance of electoral meetings.[13] In this way, interest in the charity was kept alive and distant governors were made aware of the 'many most distressing cases' that had to be turned away.[14] Second, deaf institutions opened their doors to regular inspection[15]

---

8   P. Jalland, 'Victorian Death and its Decline: 1850–1918', in P.C. Jupp and C. Gittings, *Death in England: An Illustrated History* (Manchester, 1999), pp. 232–42.

9   West of England Institution for the Instruction of Deaf and Dumb Children of the Counties of Devon, Cornwall, Somerset and Dorset, *Report for the Year 1865: Fortieth Report* (Exeter, 1866), p. 9.

10   Fenton, *Brief View*, p. 28.

11   A.F. Dimmock, *Cruel Legacy: An Introduction to the Record of Deaf People in History* (Edinburgh, 1993), p. 26.

12   S. Koven, 'Remembering and Dismemberment: Crippled Children, Wounded Soldiers, and the Great War in Great Britain', *American Historical Review*, 99 (1994): 1177–8.

13   Brighton Institution for the Instruction of Deaf and Dumb Children of the Counties of Sussex, Hampshire, and Kent, *Seventh Report for 1848* (Brighton, 1848), p. 13–15. See also Asylum for Deaf and Dumb Children of the Poor, *Address to the Governors, and to the British Public* (London, 1835); *Twenty-Fifth Report of the General Institution for the Instruction of Deaf and Dumb Children at Edgbaston, near Birmingham* (Birmingham, 1838), pp. 12–14; West of England Institution, *Report for the Year 1899: 74th Report* (Exeter, 1900), p. 11.

14   *A Report of the Purposes, Progress, and Present State of the Asylum for the Support and Education of Indigent Deaf and Dumb Children, situated in the Kent Road, Surrey* (London, 1859) p. 5.

15   *Twenty-Fifth Report of the General Institution for the Instruction of Deaf and Dumb Children at Edgbaston, near Birmingham*, back cover; Brighton Institution, *Seventh Report*,

long after the Bethlem Asylum, or Bedlam, had put a stop to such voyeurism.[16] 'Visitors', intoned the 1822 *Annual Report* of the London Asylum,

> may there see Children in all the progressive states of mental improvement, advancing from the dull blank of solitary ignorance, as received by the Institution, to the several degrees of opening intellect in the expanding mind of a communicative, useful, rational, moral, and religious being; acquiring, with the use of language, a participation in the comforts of social intercourse, and in the consolations of Christian hope.[17]

During the early years of the Exeter Institution, this opportunity was eagerly seized, the 'number of persons ... of first respectability, who daily visit ... [being] a further confirmation of the powerful excitement to which it has given rise'.[18]

But it was the public examination of pupils to sell the 'modern miracles ... of instruction'[19] that created the most dramatic spectacles. In December 1806, Weeden Butler attended such an exhibition at Thomas Braidwood's private academy. He 'was most highly gratified with the examination of a fine youth of thirteen years of age, who was born deaf ... [but] he wrote, ciphered, and conversed *viva voce* before a large company with the utmost fluency and readiness'.[20] The charitable institutions followed this example. Therefore, in his retrospective *Memoirs* of 1865, Alexander Atkinson recalled how in 1815, when he had first visited the Edinburgh Institution with his mother and her 'oldest friend', 'my future master presented his best pupils ... and caused them to exhibit the best part of their progress in education, and, by means of their fingers, carry on conversations with each other. In this', he concluded, 'they acquitted themselves with the aid of cheerful faces and intelligent looks, to the wonder and admiration of these ladies'. Subsequently, Alexander himself was recruited to promote the Institution's wares after the committee decided to despatch the master and a group of proficient pupils on a tour of the north of Scotland.[21]

The display of deaf children was most elaborate when attempts were being made to found an institution. During the campaign for the London Asylum, a deaf boy was summoned to recite the Lord's Prayer at churches and chapels where collection sermons were being preached.[22] In 1812, an audience at the Birmingham Philosophical Institution was presented with more theatre when a deaf girl – who 'could read and write; and by the use of signs ... communicate her own sentiments, and comprehend those of others' – was put through her paces. There was much interest in 'this little child'.

---

p. 2; Royal Cambrian Institution for the Deaf and Dumb, *Annual Report: Eighty-Third Year 1929–30* (Swansea, 1930) p. 30.

16 A. Scull, *The Most Solitary of Afflictions: Madness and Society in Britain, 1700–1900* (New Haven and London, 1993) pp. 51–2.

17 *Gentleman's Magazine*, 92 (April 1822): 305–7.

18 *Second Report of the West of England Institution for the Instruction of Deaf and Dumb Children of the Counties of Devon, Cornwall, Somerset, and Dorset* (Exeter, 1828) pp. 11–12.

19 *The Welshman* (5 February 1847).

20 *Gentleman's Magazine*, 77 (January 1807): 36–8.

21 A. Atkinson, *Memoirs of My Youth* (1st pub. 1865; Feltham, Middlesex, 2001), pp. 11, 29–31.

22 Beaver, *Tower*, p. 37.

Her appearance ... was remarkably engaging. Her countenance was full of intelligence, and all her actions and attitudes in the highest degree animated and expressive; while the eagerness with which she watched the countenances of her instructors, and the delight with which she sprang forward to execute, or rather anticipate their wishes, afforded a most affecting spectacle.

The performance had the desired effect and a few days later the decision to open a deaf institution in Birmingham was taken.[23]

With the growth of institutional provision, existing pupils were exhibited to inspire the funds for new establishments. Thus the initial success of the Doncaster Institution was attributed to a visit by Mr Vaughan with two pupils from Manchester who 'instantly convinced the inhabitants of the usefulness' of the project. At first, there were only 20 in the audience, 'but when the interesting nature of the examination of the children was made known throughout the town, the spectators became very numerous'. Before the meeting closed, £70 had been given in annual subscriptions and the Institution opened in 1829.[24] Past as well as present pupils were displayed. In February 1847 Francis Hancock, a former pupil of the London Asylum who was working as an engineer in west Wales, joined William Wrathmell, a 16-year-old pupil from Doncaster, at a meeting in Aberystwyth. According to *The Welshman* newspaper, '[t]he examination of the two, gave the most satisfactory proof of the astonishing effect of culture upon the minds of those whom nature has deprived of so important an inlet to knowledge as the sense of hearing'.[25]

Once institutions were up and running, the display of children became an integral part of the annual cycle, paralleling the charity-school processions inaugurated by the Society for Promoting Christian Knowledge from the early eighteenth century.[26] At the anniversary meeting of the London Asylum in 1800, pupils delivered a suitably unctuous poem that praised the 'bliss by your Asylum given' and expressed gratitude to their earthly and heavenly patrons.[27] Over time, it seems that the routine became more demanding, with mere rote learning being complemented by the interrogation of children before an audience of benefactors. Therefore, in its *Second Report* for 1828, the Exeter Institution noted with pleasure how

the interest of the public ... keeps pace with the improvement of the Establishment. At a Public Examination of the children, in September last, the largest apartment that could be procured for the purpose, was too confined to admit all the visitors who flocked to witness this gratifying exhibition, and no less than £51 was collected before the meeting dispersed.[28]

---

23 *Account of the General Institution Established in Birmingham for the Instruction of Deaf and Dumb Children* (Birmingham, 1814), pp. 3–6.

24 Fenton, *Brief View*, p. 16.

25 *The Welshman* (5 February 1847).

26 H. Cunningham, *The Children of the Poor: Representations of Childhood since the Seventeenth Century* (Oxford, 1991) pp. 38–49.

27 *Gentleman's Magazine*, 70 (12 May 1800): 436–7.

28 *Second Report of the West of England Institution*, p. 11. See also *Gentleman's Magazine*, 77 (January 1807): 36–8.

Visitors continued to be impressed, 'their approbation' at the progress made being 'a sufficient testimony of the success which is still attending ... efforts for the amelioration of deaf mutes'.[29]

Although there is some evidence that making a spectacle of deaf children became less popular with benefactors in the second half of the nineteenth century,[30] the public examination persisted. Inspectors who scrutinized the process were positive. On 24 January 1874, for instance, the *Cardiff Times* reported that the Llandaff Institution, founded in 1862, was 'free from tricks or finesse, and from the desire altogether to put children forward as prodigies'. Indeed, several pupils in the 'top' class, who had attended the school for up to five years, had given replies that 'evinced judgement and power of thought'.[31] Nevertheless, institutions did enforce relentless preparation. Writing in his *Reminiscences* of teaching at the London Asylum, Richard Elliott explained how 'the older children were to be paraded ... and their accomplishments exhibited' at the opening of a new school by the Prince of Wales in 1875. Staff 'in the schoolroom had spent much time in coaching them; but as we knew their capability or rather their want of it, we trembled for the result'. On this occasion, however, 'a mild outbreak of measles prevented their presence', providing 'a respite from unpleasant consequences which might have followed failure to show results'.[32]

For the Doncaster Institution, there was no lucky escape when the headmaster conducted a public examination at Halifax in 1897:

> Mr Howard had several of the boys and girls before him, whom he questioned, and got fairly audible answers ... Of course a question was not always gathered properly, and in reply to the question 'How tall am I?' came the answer, 'You are 53 years old.'

To the local reporter whose story appeared in the *British Deaf Monthly*, it was

> perfectly obvious ... that the exhibition was not a true criterion of the value of the oral method of teaching. How did the pupil know so well his master's age? Evidently because he was well drilled in it for exhibition purposes. Why did he give the master's height? Because he knew what he was going to be asked and had committed the answers to memory in a certain order, so that an accidental lapse of memory on the part of master or child inevitably brought confusion. It was not lip reading. It was parrot work.[33]

Irrespective of whether the performance unravelled, public examinations were stressful for deaf children. Placed centre-stage during the 'annual ordeal' at the Edinburgh Assembly Rooms in 1820, Alexander Atkinson 'felt sensitive to the gaze and scrutiny of the eyes and faces of nearly a thousand of mature aged persons'. He was allowed to return to his seat 'without any sensible embarrassment'.[34] However,

---

29   West of England Institution, *Report for the Year 1865*, p. 4.

30   A.J. Boyce, *The History of the Yorkshire Residential School for the Deaf, 1829–1979* (Doncaster, *c*. 1996), p. 29.

31   D. Woodford, *A Man and His School: The Story of Llandaff School for the Deaf and Dumb* (Cardiff, 1996), p. 9.

32   Beaver, *Tower*, p. 92.

33   Boyce, *History*, pp. 53–4.

34   Atkinson, *Memoirs*, p. 114.

the exhibitions in which he and other deaf pupils participated may have been no less humiliating than the intrusive medical examinations to which disabled children were subjected.[35]

Rhetoric: aims and methods

For the Abbé de l'Epée, the public appearance of deaf children in 'broad daylight' was an act of liberation, enabling them to be 'shown off with just as much confidence and pleasure as care had been taken … to keep them out of sight'.[36] But far from enhancing the status of deafness, its display exploited the 'otherness' of pupils, reducing them to 'a freak-show … that lured … spectators to come and watch … [them] perform tricks as if in a circus'.[37] As 'normal' human beings were able to hear, parading children who could not sustained a myth of 'wholeness' against which 'normalcy' could be calibrated.[38] Disability had been recognized as 'other' since the classical era,[39] but with the Enlightenment this difference was consolidated. From the sixteenth century, Christianity had been replacing its eschatological emphasis on death, judgement and destiny with a more earthly theology rooted in reason and natural morality. Eighteenth-century thinkers reinforced this emphasis, confident that man could be released from ignorance and superstition through rational knowledge and education. But whereas theology had stressed *a priori* reasoning, philosophy privileged experience. Therefore, from the 1750s, rationalists struggled to understand the intellectual functioning of a person without the senses that granted access to experience and hence formed the foundation for reasoning.[40]

At the same time, the precepts of the Enlightenment were themselves coming under the influence of the Romantic Movement and the Industrial Revolution,

---

35 D. Marks, *Disability: Controversial Debates and Psychosocial Perspectives* (London, 1999), pp. 67–9.

36 C.M. de l'Epée, *Institution des sourds-muets par la voie des signes méthodiques* (Paris, 1776), quoted in Z. Weygand, 'From Charity to Citizenship: Deaf-Mutes and the Blind in France, from the Middle Ages to the Legacy of the French Revolution', Enabling the Past: New Perspectives in the History of Disability, University of Manchester (17–19 June 2005).

37 Z. Weygand and C.J. Kudlick, 'Reflections on a Manuscript, a Life, and a World', in T.-A. Husson, *Reflections: The Life and Writings of a Young Blind Woman in Post-Revolutionary France*, translated with commentary by Z. Weygand and C.J. Kudlick (New York and London, 2001), pp. 113–4, 139–40.

38 N. Erevelles, 'Educating Unruly Bodies: Critical Pedagogy, Disability Studies, and the Politics of Schooling', *Educational* Theory, 50 (2000): 35. See also F. Armstrong, 'The Historical Development of Special Education: Humanitarian Rationality or "Wild Profusion of Entangled Events"', *History of Education*, 31 (2002): 454–5; P. Verstraete, 'The Taming of Disability: Phrenology and Bio-power on the Road to the Destruction of Otherness in France (1800–60)', *History of Education*, 34 (2005): 122.

39 C. Barnes, *Disabled People in Britain and Discrimination: A Case for Anti-Discrimination Legislation* (London, 1991), pp. 11–15.

40 H. Dunthorne, *The Enlightenment* (London, 1991), pp. 5–13; R. Porter, *The Enlightenment* (London, 1990), pp. 1–11; Verstraete, 'Taming of Disability': 119; Weygand, 'From Charity to Citizenship'; Weygand and Kudlick, 'Reflections', p. 76.

political radicalism, and the Evangelical Revival. The Romantic Movement bred the sentimentality that reached fever pitch with John Lashford, inspiring poetic depictions in works like Robert Browning's *Dramatis Personae*, which was still prefacing the 1930 *Annual Report* of the Cambrian Institution for the Deaf and Dumb in Swansea.[41] The Industrial Revolution – against which Romanticism was a backlash – also provoked unrest among the lower orders, dissatisfied with their economic conditions and their political disenfranchisement. Evangelicals, however, offered a solution to this disorder by exploiting moral self-reproach among the increasingly affluent middle class to generate social projects that aimed to rehabilitate the ungodly but retrievable poor.[42] Education for deaf children emerged in this post-Enlightenment ferment, their plight eliciting 'the great Christian virtue of charity'.[43] Institutional publicity, therefore, oozed compassion. Deafness was a 'distressing calamity'[44] which afflicted 'unfortunate objects'[45] who were 'doomed to a miserable existence' in which they suffered from a 'melancholy silence'.[46]

But compassionate benevolence was a double-edged sword. Supposedly, charity bound 'together all orders of men', illustrating 'the need we have of each other's help', and showing 'how that lesson of our Saviour ..., that we bear each other's burdens, might be carried out'.[47] For donors, there was social and moral status to be gained from good works.[48] 'The walls of the Committee-Room ... speak volumes for the liberality of English benevolence', wrote F.C. Fenton of the London Asylum in 1833; 'and the long list of subscribers, from all parts of the Kingdom, show the interest felt in the country for the deaf and dumb.'[49] For recipients, on the other hand, compassion was disempowering. In the first place, donors assumed responsibility for speaking on 'BEHALF OF THOSE TO WHOM PROVIDENCE HAS DENIED THE POWER OF PLEADING FOR THEMSELVES'.[50] Moreover, the institutions that they then constructed were not only financially reliant upon exposing recipients to the public gaze, but also subjected them to harsh regimes of living and learning, the rhetoric of which was incompatible with compassion.

---

41   Royal Cambrian Institution, *Annual Report: Eighty-Third Year 1929–30*. 'Only by Deafness may the vexed Love wreak/Its insuppressive sense on brow or cheek,/Only by Dumbness adequately speak/As favoured mouth could never through the eyes.'

42   D.W. Bebbington, *Evangelicalism in Modern Britain: A History from the 1730s to the 1980s* (London, 1989), pp. 70–71; M. Ignatieff, *A Just Measure of Pain: The Penitentiary in the Industrial Revolution* (Harmondsworth, 1978), pp. 148–9, 211.

43   Brighton Institution, *Seventh Report*, p. 32.

44   Fenton, *Brief View*, p. 9.

45   Asylum for Deaf and Dumb Children of the Poor, *Address*.

46   *Gentleman's Magazine*, 62 (August 1792): 696–7; *Gentleman's Magazine*, 65 (February 1795): 102.

47   Brighton Institution, *Seventh Report*, p. 32.

48   See, for example, A. Borsay, *Medicine and Charity in Georgian Bath: A Social History of the General Infirmary, c.1739–1830* (Aldershot, 1999), Ch. 8.

49   Fenton, *Brief View*, p. 18. See also *Account of the General Institution Established in Birmingham*, pp. 11–12; *A Report of the Purposes, Progress, and Present State of the Asylum for the Support and Education of Indigent Deaf and Dumb Children*, pp. 3–4.

50   Ibid., p. 15.

Although nineteenth-century missions represented deafness as a compensation for the commotion of modern life,[51] the dominant rhetoric used to fire deaf education stressed rescue from a state of savagery to a state of civilization. The 'child/savage analogy' attained increasing currency as it was taken on board by the natural and social sciences.[52] From an early stage, however, the 'uneducated deaf-mute' was seen as particularly 'dangerous to society', 'more resembling an animal than a human being, having ... all his faculties for mischief in full force but his sense of moral obligation unawakened and his passions unrestrained'.[53] Alert to the competitive environment in which they operated, charities maintained that deafness was 'one of the greatest evils to which flesh is heir': an evil worse than blindness, 'particularly if the affliction had existed from birth'.[54] 'Deprived of the power of communicating and recording his ideas, and of receiving the ideas of others, man never could have advanced beyond the boundaries of his own limited experience', argued W.R. Scott, Principal of the Exeter Institution in 1844.

> There might have existed in his soul the fountains of love, joy, and hope, but he never could have mingled these feelings with those of his race; he might have possessed a soul capable of admiring the beauties of Nature, but he never could have sympathized in such emotions with others.

But without language – 'the crowning gift of his benevolent Creator' – 'all his mighty gifts of intellect would have been but a painful burden'.[55] Blind people had access to this language. Deaf people did not. Uneducated, therefore, they were denied the means to express their humanity. As the *Gentleman's Magazine* had asked its readers way back in 1792: 'Is there in nature a more pitiable object than a rational being, incapable of communicating its ideas, of making known its wants, denied the use of speech, and devoted to a dreary melancholy life of silence and dejection?'[56]

---

51   N. Pemberton, 'The Privileged Other? The Deaf in Victorian England', Enabling the Past: New Perspectives in the History of Disability, University of Manchester (17–19 June 2005).

52   Cunningham, *Children*, p. 123.

53   B.St J. Ackers, *Deaf Not Dumb: A Lecture Delivered Oct. 12th, 1876, before the Gloucester Literary and Scientific Institution* (London, no date), p. 27. See also *Account of the General Institution Established in Birmingham*, p. 10; Boyce, *History*, p. 3; C.J. Kudlick, 'Disability History: Why We Need Another "Other"', *American Historical Review*, 108 (2003): 788–9.

54   Brighton Institution, *Seventh Report*, Appendix, 'Opening of the New Asylum, June 27 1848. From the *Brighton Gazette*', p. 27. See also Sleigh, *Voice*, p. 15; *Gentleman's Magazine*, 77 (January 1807): 36–8; National Institute for the Deaf, *The Problem of the Deaf: A Handbook of Information on Deafness, the Deaf and Dumb and the Deafened through Disease or Accident* (London, revised edn, 1929), p. 86.

55   W.R. Scott, *The Deaf and the Dumb: Their Position in Society, and the Principles of their Education, Considered* (London, 1844), pp. 9–10.

56   *Gentleman's Magazine*, 62 (7 February 1792): 134. See also *Gentleman's Magazine*, 92 (April 1822): 305–7.

The objective of deaf education was to engage with these rational beings by teaching them their duties towards God and man.[57] The religious agenda aimed to nurture a comprehension of Christianity.[58] Of course, God did not automatically condemn deaf people who died unacquainted with his scriptures through no fault of their own.[59] But, reflected the London Asylum in 1859, 'hundreds of these unfortunate beings must have passed to their graves ignorant of their God and Saviour, and uncheered by the consolation to be derived from his Holy Word'.[60] Rectifying this deficiency was demanding because the pupil arrived with no awareness of 'the existence of a God or of a soul or of a future state',[61] and at first appeared to be 'but a creature of flesh'. However, 'the constant daily events of domestic life gradually developed the power of the intellect', enabling staff to open minds to the knowledge of God, the 'salvation which Jesus Christ came on earth to make known to us', and the moral laws to be deduced from this theology.[62]

The interpenetration of religion and morality, which persisted into the twentieth century,[63] underwrote the secular agenda of the deaf institution: to prepare pupils for responsible adulthood by transforming them into independent workers, who were 'occupied in various trades, and usefully employed for the benefit of themselves and others'.[64] This work ethic embraced the entire institution. At Doncaster, for instance, children were 'instructed in everything useful in their situation in life, their time out of school hours being employed in gardening and other healthy employments'. Moreover, the girls – as well as learning 'the necessary duties of the household' – were taught to 'make clothing for poor people'. These goods were then purchased by visitors and the profits 'divided amongst the girls ... to encourage them in industrious habits'.[65] Patrons lauded the employability that was said to result from these policies, regarding it as a suitable reward for their labour. In the words of the Exeter Committee:

> [T]o see them afterwards employed in their several callings, to hear ... of the approval which their masters have given them and of their readiness to receive as many such apprentices as the Institution can send them; to see them settled down in towns and villages, ... occupied in various trades, and usefully employed for the benefit of themselves and others – this is indeed a result worthy of all philanthropy ...[66]

---

57   Boyce, *History*, p. 3.

58   Asylum for Deaf and Dumb Children of the Poor, *Address*.

59   Sleigh, *Voice*, pp. ii–iv.

60   *Report of the Purposes, Progress, and Present State of the Asylum for the Support and Education of Indigent Deaf and Dumb Children*, p. 3.

61   *The Welshman* (5 February 1847).

62   Brighton Institution, *Seventh Report*, Appendix, p. 28. See also *Account of the General Institution Established in Birmingham*, p. 13.

63   See, for example, Royal Institution for the Instruction of Deaf and Dumb Children, Edgbaston, Birmingham, *Annual Report, 1924/5* (Birmingham, no date) p. 40.

64   West of England Institution, *Report of the Year 1865*, pp. 8–9.

65   Fenton, *Brief View*, p. 17.

66   West of England Institution, *Report of the Year 1865*, pp. 8–9.

The economic rhetoric that infused deaf schooling was also instrumental in the general reform of education. Towards the end of the nineteenth century, Britain's deteriorating position in world markets was being attributed to an under-skilled workforce. In 1870, therefore, an Education Act for England and Wales required the establishment of elementary schools for children aged between five and 12 in areas where the voluntary or religious sector was delivering insufficient places. In Scotland, where legislation at the beginning of the century had already strengthened lay influence in parochial schools, obligatory attendance was introduced in 1872. Elsewhere, however, education did not become compulsory for pupils aged between five and ten until 1880.[67] With the application of 'Standards' to this enlarged school population, impairment was 'quickly exposed' by failure to pass the annual round of public examinations[68] and in 1885 a Royal Commission was set up to investigate the problem. Initially limited to blind children, its terms of reference were subsequently widened to include deaf children as well. Among the principal recommendations, published four years later, were the extension of the Education Acts to deaf children, their compulsory schooling between the ages of seven and 16, and the provision of technical instruction during those school years.[69] Under the Elementary Education (Blind and Deaf Children) Act of 1893, responsibility for the education of deaf children was duly transferred from the poor law authorities – previously empowered to support institutional placements – to local education authorities, which were required to grant-aid schools in the charitable sector and/or develop their own special schools, which were typically day rather than residential.[70]

Although renamed Royal Schools in 1897, the rhetorical devices deployed by deaf institutions were initially little affected by the new legislation. In tune with the economic motivation of education policy, they continued to focus on manual skills unaware of – or indifferent to – their role in reproducing the inequalities of class and gender that locked many deaf people into poorly paid occupations. Thus in 1924/5, the *Annual Report* of the Royal School for Deaf Children in Birmingham[71] devoted ten pages (half of them photographs) to 'trade training' in bootmaking, carpentry, tailoring, dressmaking and cookery: 'of great value in laying the foundations of a knowledge … which has enabled pupils on leaving to earn something towards their livelihood earlier than could have otherwise been the case'. In this way, they were able to 'take their places in the world as well-behaved, self-respecting citizens'.[72] By the mid 1930s, however, the kindergarten system of Friedrich Froebel was

---

67 D. Fraser, *The Evolution of the British Welfare State* (London, 1973), pp. 80–81; W.B. Stephens, *Education in Britain, 1750–1914* (Basingstoke, 1983), pp. 79–80; E. Topliss, *Provision for the Disabled* (Oxford and London, 1975), pp. 5–6.

68 Armstrong, 'Historical Development': 450–51.

69 *Report of the Royal Commission on the Blind, the Deaf and Dumb, and Others of the United Kingdom*, C. 5781 (London, HMSO, 1889) pp. xi, xc.

70 Elementary Education (Blind and Deaf Children) Act (1893), paras 2–5, 7.

71 This Royal School was formerly the General Institution for the Instruction of Deaf and Dumb Children.

72 Royal Institution for the Instruction of Deaf and Dumb Children, Edgbaston, Birmingham, *Annual Report, 1924/5*, pp. 5, 20–29.

gaining a modest foothold.[73] Though the Royal School still aimed to turn each pupil into 'a self-supporting member of the community', 'preparation for after-life' was delivered through handicraft, 'teaching ... said to produce "trained adaptability", so that on leaving school a child is able to take advantage of any suitable opening that offers'. Work was directly addressed only three months before the child was due to leave school, when the local education authority received 'a final report with ... recommendations about employment or further training'.[74]

The scaling down of job-related schooling coincided with the emergence of a more subtle economy of deafness. On 18 July 1879, when the *South Wales Daily News* praised the achievements of the Llandaff Institution, the measure of success was the reduction of pauperism. During the 17 years of its existence, '70 deaf-mutes ... [had] been taken from the streets or from very impoverished houses, fed, clothed, lodged and educated, and finally placed in some industrial employment whereby they were able afterwards to support themselves'. Therefore, the burden of poor relief had been considerably relieved.[75] By the late 1920s, the National Institute for the Deaf was quantifying the economic costs of deafness. Of course, producing 'an actual profit and loss account' was impossible. However, it was estimated that £7,000,000 of 'public money' was spent each year on education, health care and – most significantly – financial help for those 'deprived of their occupations' and hence dependent upon state benefits. Where deaf people were needlessly unemployed, the losses were 'twofold', the nation not only paying 'to enable them to exist' but also sacrificing 'the value of their contribution to its wealth'. Echoing John Bellers – the political arithmatician of the Enlightenment who lamented the economic waste of premature death – each deaf person denied a job could be 'counted as representing a loss of £150 a year to the community'.[76]

But such arguments cut little ice in inter-war Britain. Even prior to the Great Depression that struck during 1929, the economy was in recession and suffering from a surplus of labour rather than a surplus of jobs vacant for out-of-work deaf people to fill.[77] Furthermore, the reconfiguration of unemployment, which had happened from the late nineteenth century, was limited in its impact. In theory, being out of work had been stripped of moral culpability and attributed to the vagaries of markets and trade cycles. In practice, however, the past obsession with voluntary

---

73   The German philosopher Friedrich Froebel (1782–1852) advocated the combination of academic and manual skills as part of a programme of 'learning by doing' that stressed the educational value of play and the study of nature. See www.derby.ac.uk/telmie/documents/gloss.html; M. Jackson, *The Borderland of Imbecility: Medicine, Society and the Fabrication of the Feeble Mind in Late Victorian and Edwardian England* (Manchester, 2000), p. 170.

74   *The Education of a Deaf Child: An Explanatory Booklet issued by the Royal School for Deaf Children, Birmingham* (Birmingham, c.1935), pp. 15, 17.

75   Woodford, *Man*, p. 11.

76   National Institute for the Deaf, *The Problem of the Deaf*, p. 86. See also J. Bellers, 'An Essay Towards the Improvement of Physick', in G. Clarke (ed.), *John Bellers: His Life, Times and Writings* (London, 1987), pp. 179–80.

77   S. Howson, 'Slump and Unemployment', in R. Floud and D. McCloskey (eds), *The Economic History of Britain Since 1700: 2. 1860 to the 1970s* (Cambridge, 1981), pp. 265–85.

unemployment was slow to dissipate.[78] The net effect was a sharper differentiation between the 'respectable' poor – perceived as the victims of a volatile economy – and the underclass or 'residuum' – perceived as physically and mentally degenerate.[79] This bifurcation perpetuated ambivalence towards deafness. Nineteenth-century institutions had defined deaf children as 'helpless, and possibly dangerous, members of society', who had to be 'raised from their almost uncivilized state'; if education failed, they 'would be let loose … in all their vacant helplessness, blanks in their world and dangerous in their neighbourhood'.[80] That deafness ran in families was also noted.[81] However, it was twentieth-century eugenics that gave a scientific justification to irrational fears of all impairments, overlooking the diseases of poverty and the effects of inadequate health care in its bid to apply biological principles to the 'improvement' of the human race.[82]

Recipients: perspectives from experience

The harsh educational and institutional regimes that deaf children experienced – at odds with the idealized image of a caring community that the deaf institution manufactured for publicity purposes – were underwritten by this evolving discourse of danger. From the outset, deaf education was 'bedevilled' by an acrimonious dispute about teaching methods, which pitched oralists – who believed that all deaf children of 'normal' intelligence were capable of learning to lip-read and speak – against manualists – who believed that signing and finger spelling were 'essential tools in the learning process'.[83] At the first deaf institution in Edinburgh, Thomas Braidwood promoted an oral method, using a small silver rod – flat at one end and with a marble at the other – to position the tongue for the correct articulation of vowels and consonants.[84] But Braidwood's reputation as a pure oralist has been revised, given evidence that signs were increasingly used at his school.[85] Furthermore, after the London Institution opened in 1792, a combined method was evolved, in which speaking augmented 'writing, reading, and drawing and natural signs'. And even

78   I. Gazeley and P. Thane, 'Patterns of Visibility: Unemployment in Britain during the Nineteenth and Twentieth Centuries', in G. Lewis (ed.), *Forming Nation, Framing Nation* (London, 1998), pp. 184–8; L.H. Lees, *The Solidarities of Strangers: The English Poor Laws and the People, 1700–1948* (Cambridge, 1998), pp. 287–9.

79   G.S. Jones, *Outcast London: A Study in the Relationship Between Classes in Victorian Society* (Harmondsworth, 1971), pp. 281–314.

80   West of England Institution, *Report of the Year 1865*, pp. 8–9.

81   'Asylum for the Deaf and Dumb', *Gentleman's Magazine*, 92 (April 1822): 305–7; Fenton, *Brief View*, p. 14; *A Report of the Purposes, Progress, and Present State of the Asylum for the Support and Education of Indigent Deaf and Dumb Children, situated in the Kent Road, Surrey*, pp. 5–6.

82   Dimmock, *Cruel Legacy*, p. 25; Mold, *Derby Deaf*, pp. 35, 47, 67, 69.

83   Grant, *Deaf Advance*, pp. 6–7.

84   Dimmock, *Cruel Legacy*, p. 20; Rée, *I See*, p. 139.

85   Beaver, *Tower*, p. 33; Ladd, *Understanding Deaf Culture*, p. 319.

this approach proved too labour intensive for the growing number of pupils, leading to the majority of children being taught in sign language.[86]

By the middle of the nineteenth century, oralism was fighting back. In 1867, the Revd Thomas Arnold opened a pure oral school in Northampton and within four years two oral institutions had opened in London.[87] As early as 1839, however, the headmaster of the Doncaster Institution had visited Glasgow – where articulation was taught – following pressure from subscribers to consider whether pupils could learn to speak. Though experiments in articulation were discontinued in both institutions after 1845 on the grounds that the period of education was too short, oral instruction was reintroduced from 1875.[88] Such initiatives were consolidated by the First World Congress to Improve the Welfare of the Deaf and the Blind, which met in Milan in 1880. Essentially 'a brief rally conducted by hearing opponents of sign language',[89] the Congress resolved that since speech was 'incontestably superior to sign', only the oral method 'could fully restore deaf people to society'.[90] In Britain, this conclusion was reiterated by the Royal Commission, which recommended that state schools should use the oral method and permit the manual instruction – in segregated facilities – only where pupils had demonstrated their inability to cope with speech and lip-reading.[91]

Despite this endorsement, there was not the 'virtual unanimity of preference for oral teaching' that a *Times* editorial suggested on 28 September 1880.[92] The deaf press was protesting; 'international congresses of deaf people were established to resist the banishment of their language';[93] and anger at the recommendations of the Royal Commission provoked the formation of the British Deaf and Dumb Association.[94] Not all deaf institutions welcomed oralism either, and in October 1889 12 headmasters wrote to the *Deaf and Dumb Times* to complain that its fulsome coverage of the Commission's *Report* ignored the reservations of two commissioners who were more sympathetic towards sign language.[95] Therefore, the oral method was not uniformly taken up, and did not implant itself in Scotland and north-east England until the 1930s.[96] Nevertheless, the onslaught was relentless. At the time of the Milan Congress, a majority of deaf institutions had supported the manual above the oral or combined method.[97] But won over by arguments that sign language was

---

86　Beaver, *Tower*, pp. 47–8.

87　Rée, *I See*, p. 225.

88　Boyce, *History*, pp. 14–18, 38–41.

89　H. Lane, *The Mask of Benevolence: Disabling the Deaf Community* (New York, 1992), pp. 113–14.

90　*Report of the Royal Commission on the Blind, the Deaf and Dumb*, p. lxv.

91　Ibid., pp. lxxiii, xc.

92　Grant, *Deaf Advance*, p. 9.

93　Lane, *Mask*, pp. 117–18.

94　Grant, *Deaf Advance*, pp. 11, 21.

95　Woodford, *Man*, pp. 22–3. See also *Report of the Royal Commission on the Blind, the Deaf and Dumb*, pp. cxxv–cxxvii.

96　Ladd, *Understanding Deaf Culture*, pp. 135, 318.

97　J. Branson and D. Miller, 'From Myth to History: Maginn, Gallaudet and the Destruction of BSL-Based Manualism in Deaf Education in Britain', *Deaf History Journal*, 4

too crude for subtle, abstract expression and inimical to proper classroom control, they responded to calls for reform. New schools were also set up, often as day rather than residential facilities – especially after the 1893 Act – in a bid to maximize integration into the hearing community.[98] By 1929 the National Institute for the Deaf was thus able to declare that 'The oral method of teaching language is now most widely adopted'. Indeed, the Board of Education demanded that 'every child should have a fair and reasonable opportunity of acquiring speech and speech reading'.[99]

With the ascendancy of oralism came a medicalization of schooling. As Felicity Armstrong has argued, 'The development of special education ... was linked to ... the emergent and sometimes competing professionalism of teachers and doctors ... and a growth of official interest in the health of schoolchildren'.[100] Early deaf institutions had distanced themselves from doctors, the London Asylum insisting that since pupils were admitted 'only for the purposes of Instruction', they could not 'be subjected to any Medical Treatment whatever in regard to their Deafness'.[101] During the second half of the nineteenth century, educationalists began to organize to protect their professional interests and by 1878 the Society for Training Teachers of the Deaf was campaigning for oralist training to overcome 'dumbness ...caused by want of proper instruction, not from physical inability to speak'.[102] The medical profession – drawn into deaf education after 1907 by the state's new school medical service[103] – backed this oralism. There were two implications. First, political representation was narrowed by the creation of a 'medical-oralist establishment': a coalition that from 1924 operated through the National Institution for the Deaf, which 'brought Deaf people's own organizations under its aegis' and hence 'thwarted' their influence.[104] Second, the power and status of medicine relative to teaching enabled doctors to colonize schooling so that by the 1930s deaf institutions were using the metaphor of 'educational treatment'.[105] Under this medical model, deaf children were construed as 'patients' with a pathology. The job of deaf education was not to legitimize their difference through the use of signing, but to deliver a 'therapy' designed to bring them as close as possible to 'normality'.

The professionalization of deaf teachers may have been associated with the advent of a general science of childhood,[106] not to mention improvements in the

---

(August 2000): 15–25.

98   Lane, *Mask*, pp. 116–18, 125; Rée, *I See*, pp. 225–6, 230.

99   National Institute for the Deaf, *The Problem of the Deaf*, p. 27. See also National Institute for the Deaf, *All About the Deaf: How the Deaf are Helped and How they may Help Themselves: A Handbook of Information About Deafness, the Deaf and Dumb, and the Deafened by Disease* (London, revised edn, 1939), p. 47.

100 Armstrong, 'Historical Development': 445.

101 *Gentleman's Magazine*, 93 (July 1823): 9–11.

102 *First Annual Report of the Society for Training Teachers of the Deaf, and Diffusion of the 'German' System in the United Kingdom for the Year Ending December 31ˢᵗ 1878* (London, 1879), p. 5.

103 Dimmock, *Cruel Legacy*, p. 34.

104 Ladd, *Understanding Deaf Culture*, p. 140.

105 *Education of a Deaf Child*, p. 9.

106 Cunningham, *Children*, pp. 218–21.

educational environment as more staff gained qualifications, class sizes fell, and better equipment was made available. At the London Asylum, even blackboards were in short supply in the 1850s.[107] In addition, the approach to learning language may have become more 'intuitive' with less emphasis on 'individual speech sounds or the introduction of new forms'.[108] With such flexibility, institutions asserted that trained teachers could usually enable the deaf child 'to speak well enough for his [*sic*] friends and relatives to understand him: and teach him to understand what they say by reading their lips'. However, it was acknowledged that 'all this work was very difficult, very slow, and very tedious'.[109] That tedium was manifest in a harsh educational regime. In 1934, Billy Burt joined the Northern Counties School for the Deaf and Dumb in Newcastle, which had opened almost a century before, in 1839. Aged five, he was already fluent in sign language, but learning to speak was an ordeal:

> ... the teachers used different means such as a mirror or fingers pressing on my face and in my mouth. ... Sometimes I was kept in the school in the afternoons for speech lessons while all the other children went outside for games. The teacher would have a bowl of water with trace of disinfectant in it. She would dip her little finger in the bowl and then press down my tongue with it to try and help me make the correct speech sounds. After a session of this, I often became dizzy and tired. Once my mouth closed, trapping the teacher's finger between my teeth. The teacher was annoyed and slapped my arm with a ruler.[110]

Corporal punishment was also used to stamp out sign language. As Joyce Nicholson recalled of her period as a pupil at the Royal School for the Deaf and Dumb in Birmingham in the 1920s, 'we would get smacked on the hands and our arms would be tied by our sides ... just to stop us signing'. Children caught were called 'little monkeys'.[111]

The chastisement administered for linguistic misdemeanours was an integral part of the institutional regime. In his *Memoirs* of the Edinburgh Institution, Alexander Atkinson recalled how his tears on arrival – caused by the innocent stare of a fellow pupil – prompted the master to give this girl 'a sharp slap on her cheek'.[112] There were attempts to regulate the gratuitous resort to violence. At the Doncaster Institution in the 1830s, carelessness and idleness attracted the lesser penalty of extra school work. Flogging – to be inflicted only the headmaster – was reserved for lying, disobedience and theft.[113] Rules for the Birmingham Institution, pasted into the House Committee

---

107 Beaver, *Tower*, pp. 56, 63, 71, 74, 76.

108 Boyce, *History*, p. 73.

109 *Education of a Deaf Child*, p. 5.

110 . Hall, 'Keeping it in the Family: Five Generations of Deafness at the NCSD', *Deaf History Journal*, 3 (April 2000): 13–14.

111 S. Humphries and P. Gordon, *Out of Sight: The Experience of* Disability, 1900–1950 (Plymouth, 1992), p. 84. See also British Deaf Association, *Living Heritage of the Deaf Community*, video recording with transcript (Carlisle, 1993), pp. 1, 5; Mold, *Derby Deaf*, p. 62.

112 Atkinson, *Memoirs*, p. 11.

113 Boyce, *History*, p. 10.

Minute Book in the late 1880s, similarly banned classroom teachers from beating.[114] But even sanctioned punishments were brutal by our contemporary standards. Alexander Atkinson described savage thrashings for theft. Prior to expulsion, for instance, Charles Mackay, 'was severely scourged on his naked back in the presence of all the inmates' for breaking open a cash box. Moreover, in a separate incident, Alexander himself was 'severely ... whipped' for 'insolently' threatening to run away after his trunk was searched for stolen money. At the subsequent mock trial, those pupils drawn into the crime were put in the dock and sentenced to forty lashes, though only the offender actually 'underwent a severe punishment'.[115]

Although Alexander did not escape corporal punishment, his status as a 'parlour' pupil meant that he enjoyed better facilities than other pupils.[116] Such differentiation was not confined to Edinburgh. At Birmingham, too, the headmaster welcomed 'a few private deaf and dumb pupils into his family', where they received 'the benefit of a parental education';[117] while the Brighton Institution proudly announced when a new building opened in 1848 that 'arrangements are made for the reception of children of the higher classes, as parlour boarders, where they will have every advantage of a superior education, apart from the children of the poor'.[118] The extra income generated by these paying pupils was a valuable resource for deaf institutions plagued by economic insecurity. Poor law pupils were also admitted to boost funds after the Amendment Act of 1834 allowed guardians to support deaf (and blind) children in educational institutions: a responsibility that local education authorities assumed following the 1893 Act.

The balance between the different categories of pupil varied across institutions and over time. Not all immediately accepted children funded by the poor law or local authorities. For those who did, however, this source of funding – indicative of the evolving partnership between the statutory and voluntary sectors – accounted for a growing proportion of income. As the number of charity pupils declined, the electoral systems that had once chosen them were replaced by formal assessment procedures more consistent with professional aspirations.[119] But whether sponsored by philanthropy or the state, these children found their impairment compounded by poverty. Official reports exonerated institutional conditions. When the guardians of the Cardiff Union examined the Llandaff School in 1868, for instance, they concluded that it was 'in every respect adapted for the maintenance and education of its inmates', having been 'conducted by a most efficient and benevolent instructor with great success'.[120] Inspectors from the Board of Education were similarly impressed from 1893 after they took charge of an enhanced certification process that tied per capita

---

114 Birmingham City Archives, MS 1060/31, 'Rules for the Teachers', in Royal Deaf and Dumb Institution, Minutes of the House Committee, 1889–1901.

115 Atkinson, *Memoirs*, pp. 25, 57–8.

116 Atkinson, *Memoirs*, p. 13.

117 *Twenty-Fifth Report of the General Institution for the Instruction of Deaf and Dumb Children at Edgbaston, near Birmingham*, p. 78.

118 Brighton Institution, *Seventh Report*, p. 6. See also West of England Institution, *Report for the Year 1899*, p. 11.

119 Beaver, *Tower*, pp. 62–3, 140–41, 148–9; Boyce, *History*, pp. 71, 78.

120 Woodford, *Man*, p. 7.

grants to compliance with minimum standards.[121] Thus when the West of England Institution was visited in 1900, the 'tone and sympathy of the work' was found to be 'in every way in harmony with the natural surroundings'. Moreover, the children were 'excellently managed, ... happy, and intelligently taught' and members of staff 'spare[d] no pains to gladden ... [their] life ... and to ensure a useful future'.[122]

The narratives of deaf pupils suggest that these idealized images did not always accord with their experiences. Said especially to require a brand of 'discipline' combined with 'gentleness',[123] on occasions equated with the 'system' of the headmaster and the 'motherly care' of the matron,[124] they were subjected to a relentless routine of early rising and religion, instruction and drill, with comparatively little space for informal play before an equally early bedtime.[125] Allegedly, they thrived under this 'regularised life of healthy activity with proper hours of sleep and ... close attention ... to physical attention and diet'.[126] However, neither the physical conditions of the deaf institution nor the psychological conditions that it perpetrated were consistent with this claim. After the London Asylum moved to new premises in 1809, a building designed for 120 children was soon holding over 200, condemning charity and poor law children to serious overcrowding.[127] Outside the capital physical conditions were also 'often grim and unhygienic'. At the Exeter Institution, for example, there was no piped water until the 1840s and hot water took another 40 years to materialize.[128] By the 1870s, diet at the Doncaster Institution was said to be of a higher quality. Undiluted milk with cream had replaced skimmed milk thinned with water, while adding soup three times a week and increasing the varieties of meat improved meals.[129] During the inter-war period, however, former pupils at the Derby Institution talked of eating 'mainly bread and dripping',[130] while children at Newcastle were so hungry that they ate toothpaste.[131]

The psychological dynamics of the deaf institution compounded its physical hardships. Overwhelmed by the 'awesome' building,[132] their hair cropped short on admission,[133] pupils found their personal identities further undermined by an institutional uniform that for girls additionally concealed their sexuality. Fear of the children's 'reproductive capabilities'[134] further dictated a policy of strict segregation,

---

121 Jackson, *Pictorial History*, p. 75.

122 West of England Institution, *Report for the Year 1899*, p. 8.

123 *First Annual Report of the Society for Training Teachers of the Deaf*, p. 12.

124 *Second Report of the West of England Institution*, p. 10.

125 Boyce, *History*, p. 9; Beaver, *Tower*, pp. 54–5.

126 Royal Cambrian Institution, *Annual Report: Eighty-Third Year 1929–30*, p. 13.

127 Beaver, *Tower*, pp. 43–5, 53, 80.

128 Jackson, *Pictorial History*, p. 75. See also Royal West of England Residential School for the Deaf, *Historical Survey, 1826–1976* (Exeter, no date), p. 9.

129 Boyce, *History*, p. 37.

130 Mold, *Derby Deaf*, p. 44.

131 British Deaf Association, *Living Heritage*, p. 2.

132 Beaver, *Tower*, p. 90.

133 West of England Institution, *Report for the Year 1865*, p. 24

134 L. Iinthicum, 'Disabled People's Dress and Dressing, 1904–2004', Enabling the Past: New Perspectives in the History of Disability, University of Manchester (17–19 June 2005).

which barred boys and girls from even conversing with one another to reduce the risk of them forming attachments, marrying and producing deaf offspring.[135] In many respects, the teachers charged with policing this contrived social environment shared with pupils a common alienation from mainstream society. To some extent, the logistics of controlling large numbers of children single-handed militated against close relationships. Equally corrosive, however, was the demoralization brought about by low wages, long hours, cramped living quarters and Spartan food. Richard Elliott was therefore optimistic in insisting that at the London Asylum 'the old stand-offishness' had disappeared by the 1870s and 'attachment – even affection – between teacher and pupil' had become 'the ruling principle'.[136] As Erving Goffman observed of institutional life, staff and inmates occupied two different 'worlds', 'jogging alongside each other with points of official contact but little mutual penetration'.[137]

The benevolent culture that underpinned this dysfunctional regime was paternalist in nature, investing the protection of inmates in their charitable patrons. Some mechanisms were proactive, like the 'Committee of Ladies' at Exeter tasked with inspecting 'the House and Children' on a monthly basis and 'from time to time' preparing written recommendations 'expedient for the benefit of the establishment'.[138] For the most part, however, responses were reactive. In January 1846, the Minute Book for the Doncaster Institution expressed 'the utmost concern and regret ... that a charge of neglect and inattention had been brought' by the parish officers responsible for John Richmond. After 'the most patient investigation', which not only involved two staff but also an assessment by the headmaster of the Newcastle Institution, the Committee 'unanimously came to the resolution' that the charge was 'entirely without foundation'.[139]

Strenuous efforts were also made to prevent complaints. In April 1889, the House Committee of the Birmingham Institution learned from the matron that 'a boy had met with an accident in the gymnasium resulting in a broken arm and dislocation of the elbow'. It was resolved that any future accident would be immediately reported to the Chairman of the Committee. Two months later, when William Carr fell and fractured his thigh in the gymnasium, the Committee was persuaded that the cause was 'an attack of giddiness'. Greater caution was shown in February 1890 after two more boys were injured during gymnastics, one breaking his collar bone and the other spraining an arm. Though satisfied that 'the occurrences were purely accidental and that no means could have been taken to prevent them', the Committee nevertheless requested an examination of 'the ropes used in the apparatus' and a report as to whether they were 'sound'.[140]

These paternalistic devices – more a defence against scandal than a meaningful channel of communication – worked on the assumption that pupils were passive victims

---

135 Ackers, *Deaf Not Dumb*, p. 7.

136 Beaver, *Tower*, pp. 71–3, 98–9. See also N. Erevelles, 'Disability and the Dialectics of Difference', *Disability and Society*, 11/4 (1996): 529–32.

137 E. Goffman, *Asylums: Essays on the Social Situation of Mental Patients and Other Inmates* (1st pub. 1961; Harmondsworth, 1968), p. 20.

138 'Rules' in West of England Institution, *Report for the Year 1899*, p. 10.

139 Boyce, *History*, pp. 19–20.

140 Birmingham City Archives, MS 1060/31, Royal Deaf and Dumb Institution, Minutes of the House Committee, 1889–1901, 10 April 1889, 17 June 1889, 12 Feb. 1890.

of deafness rather than active agents with the right to influence their own fate.[141] Like blind institutions,[142] deaf institutions nurtured a shared identity in which the endurance of oppression played a major part. Dennis Boucher recollected how at the inter-war Doncaster Institution prefects organized night raids on the adjoining orchard for apples and pears to supplement meagre rations.[143] Furthermore, with the imposition of oral method, sign language became a subversive force that denied 'total control of their classrooms' to teachers unfamiliar with manualism.[144] However, it is vital not to exaggerate the significance of such opportunities. Deaf pupils managed to disrupt the 'smooth' operation of their institutions, but they were not engaging in 'transformative practices'. Acts of resistance were incapable of overthrowing the 'dominant structures' that determined their schooling.[145]

Conclusion

In this chapter, we have explored how institutions for the deaf in Britain managed their pupils during the nineteenth and early twentieth centuries. Our main point of entry has been the documentation, both published and manuscript, that these institutions fabricated. Needless to say, this in-house material is no substitute for the testimonies of deaf pupils. However, a critical reading does permit us to unpick the use of spectacle and rhetoric, and contrast their benevolent pretensions with the conditions of living and learning to which child inmates were exposed. The comparison is sobering. In the name of religious reclamation and economic productivity, the deaf institution subjected pupils to abrasive teaching methods in circumstances that were materially poor and psychologically threatening. Theoretically, the Education Act of 1944 sounded the death knell for segregation by suggesting that 'the most acceptable place for educating disabled children was in ordinary schools'.[146] But, in practice, the Act supported 'a huge infrastructure' of special education[147] and by 1972 the number of children attending special schools had almost trebled from 38,499 to 106,367.[148] The legacy of the deaf institution was longstanding.

---

141 Kudlick, 'Disability History': 781, 783.

142 Weygand and Kudlick, 'Reflections', p. 116.

143 Humphries and Gordon, *Out of Sight*, pp. 92–6.

144 Ladd, *Understanding Deaf Culture*, p. 122.

145 Erevelles, 'Educating Unruly Bodies': p. 46.

146 J. Campbell and M. Oliver, *Disability Politics: Understanding Our Past, Changing Our Future* (London, 1996) p. 28.

147 M. Oliver, *Understanding Disability: From Theory to Practice* (Basingstoke, 1996) pp. 68, 79–80.

148 S. Tomlinson, *The Sociology of Special Education* (London, 1982) pp. 49–52; Topliss, *Provision for the Disabled*, p. 30, Table II.

CHAPTER SIX

Joseph Townend and the Manchester Infirmary: a plebeian patient in the Industrial Revolution[1]

Stuart Hogarth

There is a powerful historiographical orthodoxy in the social history of medicine which suggests that the birth of modern clinical medicine in the late eighteenth and early nineteenth centuries transformed not simply medical knowledge but the social standing of the medical profession and with it the relationship between doctor and patient. As Andrew Wear has summarized this view,

> Historians have argued that in Europe the power of doctors over patients began ... in the early nineteenth century ... At the same time, the social status of doctors increased, and their occupation transformed itself into a profession with a monopoly and a large degree of self-regulation.[2]

In the early modern period, it is argued, the patient was powerful and doctors were weak, but this dynamic was reversed in the nineteenth century when medical theory and practice became forms of social control, part of a wider disciplinary system for the control of docile and passive bodies.[3]

This chapter examines the doctor–patient relationship at the beginning of the nineteenth century through the close reading of a single autobiographical source. But first it is important to explain the changing context of medical knowledge and power.

---

1   An early version of this chapter was presented as a paper at the 'British History in the Long 18th century' seminar series at the Institute of Historical Research. I am indebted to the seminar, my intellectual home as a postgraduate, for their comments, which have been most helpful in developing my argument. Special thanks to Penny Corfield, one of the conveners, who was unable to attend the seminar but took the time to read and critique the paper.

2   A. Wear, 'Introduction', in Y. Kawakita-Sakai *et al.* (eds), *History of the Doctor-Patient Relationship* (Tokyo: Ishikayu EuroAmerica, 1995), p. xiii.

3   The classic account of the new regime is M. Foucault, *Discipline and Punish: The Birth of the Prison* (London, 1979). For its application to the history of medicine, see, for instance, D. Armstrong, *The Political Anatomy of the Body: Medical Knowledge in Britain in the Twentieth Century* (Cambridge, 1983) and C. Lawrence, 'Disciplining disease: scurvy, the navy and imperial expansion 1750–1825', in D. Miller and P. Reill (eds), *Visions of Empire, Voyages, Botany and Representations of Nature* (Cambridge, 1996).

Medical knowledge and power

The early modern doctor–patient relationship was a more equal one for a variety of reasons.[4] Doctors practised alongside a plethora of orthodox and non-orthodox practitioners, all competing for the business of the sick in a diverse medical marketplace relatively free of state regulation.[5] Much primary care, moreover, was provided by friends and family in a society in which lay people both understood many of the basic aspects of medical theory, such as the humoral system, and supplemented this with different kinds of folk medicine. Medical hegemony was further undermined by the continuing power of religion; ill health was a spiritual, as well as a physical, crisis and clerical intervention might be as important as – or more important than – medical treatment.[6] Perhaps most importantly, prior to the nineteenth century medical knowledge was premised on a holistic vision which saw sickness as a deviation from a person's unique natural state; thus the individual patient, not an abstract disease concept, was at the heart of medical theory and practice.

All these factors led to clinical encounters in which the patient's voice was of primary importance in diagnosis and where even therapy was a matter of negotiation. But by the end of the eighteenth century, things were beginning to change. Medicine ceased to be a holistic investigation of the sick, based on their own account of their illness and medical history; the rise of pathological anatomy turned medical attention away from the words of the patient and towards the inner workings of the body. Diagnosis became a technical and scientific matter based on the use of new instruments such as stethoscopes and thermometers. Treating large numbers of patients with the same symptoms, doctors working in hospitals ceased to think of illness as a disruption of an individual's unique constitution and instead began to generalize about the common characteristics of the same disease in different people. The 'sick man', previously the focus of attention, was now simply 'the accident of his disease, the transitory object upon which it happens to have seized'.[7] Medical knowledge became esoteric, and a widening gulf developed between the lay understanding of sickness and the doctors' clinical disease theories. And with this change in medical theory and practice came a change in social relations; the sick were beginning to lose some of their authority. As Michael Neve has put it, 'patients slowly turned from commercially powerful consumers to nineteenth-century servile acceptors of medical orthodoxy'.[8]

4　N.D. Jewson, 'The disappearance of the sick man from medical cosmology', *Sociology*, X (1976); N.D. Jewson, 'Medical knowledge and the patronage system in eighteenth-century England', *Sociology*, VII (1974); D. Porter and R. Porter, *Patient's Progress: Doctors and Doctoring in Eighteenth Century England* (Cambridge, 1989).

5　See, for instance, Porter and Porter, *Patient's Progress*.

6　See, for instance, A. Wear, 'Puritan perceptions of illness in seventeenth-century England', in R. Porter (ed.), *Patients and Practitioners: Lay Perceptions of Medicine in Pre-Industrial Society* (Cambridge, 1985).

7　M. Foucault, *The Birth of the Clinic: An Archaeology of Medical Perception* (London, 1973).

8　M. Neve, 'Orthodoxy and fringe: medicine in late Georgian Bristol', in W. Bynum and R. Porter, *Medical Fringe and Medical Orthodoxy 1750–1850* (London, 1987), p. 44.

In *Medicine in the Making of Modern Britain,* Chris Lawrence draws on a wide range of research to create a powerful argument which is perhaps a useful indication of the current historiography. The rising power of doctors is an important theme: Lawrence describes doctors gaining 'a measure of authority and control' in a range of Foucaultian disciplinary institutions in the late eighteenth century, and helping to set the terms of important political debates in the late nineteenth century by providing naturalistic accounts of social problems.[9] Yet Lawrence's account is highly nuanced: medical authority was far from hegemonic; the authority of the doctor was continually called into question by the patient. The position of the working-class patients within this picture is complex: Lawrence argues that as hospital patients they were experimental objects for doctors practising new diagnostic techniques; but outside the hospital their patronage of 'local druggists and chemists' and their tendency to self-medication added to the precarious position of the general practitioner.[10] Similar revisions have been suggested by the work of Warner and Digby, who have stressed not only the slow diffusion of new medical ideas generally associated with medicalization, but also the continuing power of the patient in the clinical encounter, especially in general practice.[11] Yet despite these revisions, much work still repeats the orthodox account outlined. Thus Todd Savitt has argued that in nineteenth-century America the tradition of medical self-reliance declined and patients became more dependent on their doctors.[12]

As is made explicit in Lawrence's work, fundamental to this historiographical narrative is a desire to chart the relationship between the origins of modern society and the emergence of modern medicine. Thus the old-style egalitarian doctor–patient relationship reflected the low social status of medical men in a pre-industrial society dominated by the landed élite and with a small middle class.[13] The holistic style of medicine reflected the face-to-face social relations of a pre-industrial society based on patronage, paternalism and patriarchy in which personal bonds of fealty rested on a highly gendered social order in which the father, as head of household, was the model authority figure. And it is in the context of the creation of a three-class society, the rise of the professional middle classes and the growth of bureaucracies and of institutions such as the hospital, that doctors, as members of an emergent bourgeoisie, came to assert their authority. The modern medicine they practised reflected the new society, its generalizations about categories of persons and diseases being part of a wider attempt to create forms of knowledge which could be used in the management

---

9   C. Lawrence, *Medicine in the Making of Modern Britain 1700–1920* (London, 1994) pp. 22–5, 70–71.

10   Ibid., pp. 67–8.

11   J. Warner, *The Therapeutic Perspective: Medical Practice, Knowledge and Identity in America, 1820–1885* (Harvard, 1986) and A. Digby, *Making a Medical Living: Doctors and Patients in the English Market for Medicine, 1720–1911* (Cambridge, 1994).

12   T. Savitt, 'Self-reliance and the changing physician–patient relationship', in Kawakita *et al.* (eds), *History of the Doctor-Patient Relationship.*

13   This view of the size and role of both the middling sorts in general and the professional classes in particular seems outdated in the light of work published in the last decade or so of the twentieth century. See, for instance, L. Davidson *et al.* (eds), *Stilling the Grumbling Hive: the Response to Social and Economic Problems in England, 1689–1750* (Stroud, 1982).

of large bodies of men and women. Doctors, Lawrence argues, 'were working out a supervisory role for medicine, just as new disciplinary models were being elaborated in prisons and factories', and thus medicine emerged as 'one of the fundamental resources for the rational ordering of society'.[14]

The emergent rift between middle-class doctor and plebeian patient is thus understood as part of the wider social gulf developing between their respective classes. For instance, in Ruth Richardson's work *Death, Dissection and the Destitute*, the Anatomy Act is inseparable from that epitome of bourgeois political economy, the New Poor Law. The fear of dissection was just one more deterrent from becoming a burden on the parish, one more incentive to keep body and soul together outside the workhouse.[15] Just as the rise of the bourgeoisie in general was dependent on the exploitation of working-class bodies, so too the emergence of modern medicine expropriated the bodies of the poor to aid its progress. The rise of pathological anatomy was predicated on the theft of pauper corpses: 'No longer an object worthy of respect, the body ... became a token of exchange, subject to commercial dealing, and then to the final objectification of the dissection room.'[16]

While Richardson's detailed analysis of the relations between medicine and popular culture is unusual, her work is typical in identifying the site for the transformation in the social relations of medicine as the hospital. Waddington's account has been highly influential: the sick poor were low in status and could not afford to shop around for medical care, rendering them submissive and making them ideal clinical material. Doctors did not have to listen to poor patients; they could 'define the problems, and the manner in which they were to be solved, according to criteria established by the profession, not by the patient'.[17] This allowed doctors to move the focus of their attention from 'therapy ... of prime interest to the patient – to diagnosis and classification of disease', a shift which gave rise to therapeutic nihilism and experimental surgery. Hospitals also gave access to pauper corpses for pathological anatomy. Thus as clinical medicine helped to increase the prestige of doctors by linking their profession to modern scientific methods, so too it transformed the status of patients by turning them into objects of scientific scrutiny. Whether as dissected corpses or lying-in patients, the sick poor were clinical material for experimental surgery, pathological anatomy, and, as the hospital became the key site for medical education, training fodder for student doctors to practise their skills on.

Mary Fissell's work on medicine and the poor in eighteenth-century Bristol provides a specific local case study of this creeping medical hegemony. As lay governors retreated from involvement in the running of the hospital, relinquishing power to the medical men, the institution ceased to be a site for the philanthropic expression of the mutual rights and responsibilities which had connected the wealthy and the poor through a traditional and highly personalized paternalism. Authority was now exercised in a depersonalized, bureaucratic system of professional medical

---

14   Lawrence, *Medicine in the Making of Modern Britain*, pp. 25 and 33.

15   R. Richardson, *Death, Dissection and the Destitute* (London, 1989) p. 271.

16   Ibid., p. 72.

17   I. Waddington, 'The role of the hospital in the development of modern medicine: a sociological analysis', *Sociology*, VII (1973): 217.

power. Admissions had been controlled by the lay governors and subscribers; but the patrons' personal knowledge of patients was replaced by 'inspection and surveillance' by doctors as 'medical men came to reshape the Infirmary in their own interest'.[18] The advancement of these interests rested on the control of pauper bodies which came to medical men as they took over the running of hospitals:

> Infirmary surgeons granted the inmates of hospitals peculiarly opaque bodies, which only the powerful could read, and robbed the patient of his or her understanding of illness ... denying the poor ownership of themselves.[19]

For Fissell this was a fundamental form of disempowerment; losing the ability to interpret one's body and have this interpretation listened to was no different to other appropriations – 'the enclosure of common land ... [and] the denial of use rights'. Thus a Marxist critique of the era of primitive accumulation is linked to a Foucaultian analysis of the relationship between power and knowledge.[20]

This story in the history of medicine is part of a wider story about the institutional disciplining of the plebeian body; as Chris Lawrence puts it, there are 'obvious parallels ... [between] the growth of say prison, hospital, school and, most important, factory discipline'.[21] While many studies of such regimes have betrayed their Foucaultian roots by examining the institution from a top-down perspective, a 'history from below' approach has become more common. Broadly speaking we can identify two main approaches historians have adopted when they have studied such institutions from the perspective of their users or inmates: one is to analyse the conditions external to the institution which influenced people's contact with it; the other is to study daily life within the institution.

Thus, in the first contextualizing approach, historians and sociologists have studied the relationship between the resources available outside – care within the family and the community – and the decision to enter, or commit a family member to, an asylum, house of correction, workhouse or infirmary.[22] Such studies have shared similar assumptions and come to similar conclusions. The family is seen as the primary locus of care and it is the stresses which care within the family come under,

---

18 M. Fissell, *Patients, Power and the Poor in Eighteenth-Century Bristol* (Cambridge, 1991), pp. 123, 125, 199.

19 Ibid., p. 15.

20 For a recent critique, see P.J. Corfield, *Power and the Professions in Britain 1700–1850* (London, 1995).

21 Lawrence, 'Disciplining Disease'.

22 The general argument for this perspective was made by Michael Ignatieff in 'Total institutions and working classes: a review essay', *History Workshop Journal*, 15 (1983): 167–73. For a detailed study, see L. Mahood, *Policing Gender, Class and Family: Britain, 1850–1940* (London, 1995), esp. Ch. 7. On asylums, see, for instance, D. Wright, 'Getting out of the asylum: understanding the confinement of the insane in the nineteenth century', *Social History of Medicine*, 10 (1997): 137–55. C. Lis and H. Soly, *Disordered Lives: Eighteenth-Century Families and Their Unruly Relatives* (Cambridge, 1996) examines houses of correction, while various chapters in T. Hitchcock, P. King and P. Sharpe (eds), *Chronicling Poverty: the Voices and Strategies of the English Poor, 1640–1840* (Basingstoke, 1997) examines the workhouse from the perspective of the poor.

often related to social change in the context of industrialization – proletarianization, immizeration, migration, the breakdown of kinship ties and the family life-cycle of poverty – which lead to the use of institutional welfare. By placing greater emphasis on the continuing importance of the role of the family as primary carers, the influence of institutions is called into question. From this perspective such institutions are seen as resources strategically deployed by the poor, rather than oppressive regimes imposed on them.

The other approach is concerned with what happens once people enter institutions.[23] Here the assumption is that the operation of disciplinary regimes cannot be understood solely in terms of their rules, their architecture or their normative functions; these are only one set of factors which make up the life of an institution. Ranged alongside them are the attitudes and behaviour of the inmates or patients: the culture they construct, its codes and rules, and the complexities of their relationships with staff – the complicity in the relaxation of strict regimes which makes day-to-day life possible for both rulers and ruled, the petty acts of defiance, and the major outbreaks of disorder which set the limits of dominion. By placing the sick poor at the centre of historical attention, this chapter seeks to add to those revisions of historiographical orthodoxy which explore the agency of working-class people in their relations with institutionalized welfare.

The patient and his doctor

> My old doctor said, 'Well, Joe, thou's been a good patient, as patient as Job. Thou must go home to thy father and mother, and look at the green fields; and whatever else, don't let the doctors touch that hand, but keep it bound with the bandage, and go to Blackpool, and wash it in the salt water, and thou wilt see it will soon be well. It's a fine cure, my lad; but I'll never cut another case like thine.' With the tears running off my face, I gave him my left hand, but I could not speak; and even now, whilst I record that last interview, I am deeply affected. I called in at the neighbouring wards, bidding them all good-bye; and as I descended the great staircase, with my bundle in my hand, unable to wipe the tears as they fell upon the steps, Dr. Guest, the house-surgeon, turned away much moved. I entered that hospital with fourpence, had all my wants supplied, and received a perfect cure, and, with a pocket full of silver, was returning home. I, here on the 20th of January, 1852, in my study, Collingwood, Melbourne, Victoria, Australia, from the bottom of my heart, record my sincere thanks to Almighty God, and also to the subscribers and managers of that benevolent institution, for the kindness and care I therein received.[24]

Thus does the Reverend Joseph Townend conclude his autobiographical account of his time as a patient at the Manchester Infirmary. Townend was admitted to the Infirmary in the summer of 1827 at the age of 21 and remained there for several months, where he was treated for a wrist injury and, far more seriously, operated on to deal with the consequences of severe burns he had received as a child. His description of his time at the Infirmary takes up ten pages of his autobiography and

23   For an excellent example of this approach, see L. Zedner, *Women, Crime and Custody in Victorian England* (Oxford, 1991), esp. pp. 159–62 and 245–54.

24   J. Townend, *Autobiography* (London, 1869), p. 19.

is possibly the most detailed description of hospital life by a working-class patient in the nineteenth century now available to us. We shall use his account to consider how the view 'from below' might offer an alternative to some of the historiographical orthodoxies regarding the place of the plebeian patient in the early nineteenth-century hospital.

Before we consider his account of his time in Manchester Infirmary, some brief biographical details might be useful. Townend was born in 1806 in a rural village near Skipton, Yorkshire. His parents were Methodist shopkeepers. He went to work in a cotton factory at the age of seven, remaining a textile worker until his entry into the Manchester Infirmary in 1827. He later became a Methodist preacher and in 1851 he travelled to Australia as a missionary, returning to England 15 years later.

As a young child (the age is not clear, but somewhere between three and six), Townend was the victim of a domestic accident. Lifting the kettle from its pot-hook on the hearth, his apron caught fire. He was very badly burnt and the damage to his right arm and torso was so severe that the local doctor pronounced the injuries to be fatal. However, the young boy's mother insisted on treatment and so the doctor cut away the burnt flesh and for the next twelve months Townend was confined to bed and nursed by his mother. Eventually the burns healed but, as new skin grew, the right arm as far down as the elbow was attached to the side by a web of skin. It was this condition, as well as a more recent injury to the wrist on the same arm, which led Townend to seek treatment at the Manchester Infirmary.

The patient and his doctor

How did Townend come to be in the Infirmary? What can his entry to the institution tell us about Mary Fissell's argument that medical men came to dominate the admissions process? In fact he used the traditional route: personal recommendation. 'I made my case and desire known to my master, Thomas Kay, Esq., and he obtained from W. Townend, Esq., a recommendation to admit me as an in-patient.'[25] Whoever William Townend was (and Joseph Townend stated that he was not a relation), clearly it was through the intercession of his employer in the first instance that Townend came to be in the Infirmary. In the class-based industrial society of 1830s Manchester, the personal patronage ties of employers to their employees could still be important in the provision of medical care.[26]

Perhaps what is most striking about Townend's admission to the institution was the way he negotiated his status as an in-patient. Having gained initial admission, his house-surgeon had to decide whether to treat him in the hospital or as an out-patient:

---

25 Ibid., p. 9.

26 This process accords with the description of admissions to the Infirmary in J. Pickstone, *Medicine and Industrial Society – a History of Hospital Development in Manchester and its Region, 1752–1946* (Manchester, 1985), p. 11. A full discussion of the role of paternalism in Manchester's nineteenth-century industrial society can be found in P. Joyce, *Work, Society and Politics: the Culture of the Factory in Later Victorian England* (Brighton, 1980); see, for instance, pp. 135–7.

> On the first Sabbath morning, the house surgeon examined my wrist, probed it with his lancet, the mark of which I now see as I write; then he took down my card and said, 'You will be an out-patient, sir.' I reminded him of my arm grown to my side; and hanging up the card he said, 'Two birds with one stone: aye?' I said, 'Yes, sir.'[27]

It would appear that Townend was thus able to exert some influence over not only his resident status but also what was to be treated.

Once he was established as an in-patient, the Infirmary surgeons discussed Townend's treatment at length – separating the arm and torso was for these men a novel operation and they considered for some time whether surgery was feasible and how it should be carried out. Townend described himself as playing a decisive role in these meetings, which generally ended with the doctor turning to the patient. 'My old doctor used to conclude with, "Well, Joe, what's to be done?" My answer invariably being, "I should like to have it cut, sir"'.[28] This deference to the patient was not mere formality; the surgeons had grave concerns about performing a risky and untested surgical procedure and Townend's continued insistence on treatment would appear to have been crucial to the course of action taken. We can see then that in the nuts and bolts of identifying the problem and agreeing a treatment Townend was able to play the kind of active role normally associated with the more traditional kind of doctor–patient relationship. But these discussions also reveal another facet of the relations between medical staff and patients. Ultimately, there was an argument between Dr Ransom, the surgeon Townend had been assigned to, and another surgeon, Dr Thorpe. Townend described how Ransom concluded the argument thus:

> At length, the old gentleman, with his broad hat on, turned to me, and said, 'Joe, thou'rt my patient?' 'Yes, sir'. Then turning towards the other doctors, said, 'Gentlemen, you can go about your business; I will have my own way!'[29]

The dispute over treatment was resolved by the surgeon invoking a proprietary interest: Townend was Ransom's patient so he would do what he thought fit. This idea of a proprietorial relationship between doctor and patient can first be seen in Townend's description of the Infirmary's admissions process: 'the patients ... taken in *belonged to* and were *attended by* their surgeon [my italics]'.[30] The language suggests something beyond the merely contractual or bureaucratic. What was invoked was a feudal authority which granted powers but also bestowed responsibilities – the surgeons' proprietorial rights over their patients was predicated on, and balanced by, their duty to serve them. Such language raises questions about the relationship between the modern impersonal and bureaucratic forms of discipline which are normally understood as mediating doctor–patient relations in hospitals and more traditional and more personal forms of authority.

We discover more about the relationship between doctor and patient in Townend's description of the medical staff's bedside manner. After his operation Townend came

---

27 Townend, *Autobiography*, p. 11.
28 Ibid., p. 11.
29 Ibid., p. 11.
30 Ibid., p. 9.

under the care of Mr Waterhouse, a senior student of Dr Ransom, whose style of treatment Townend considered exemplary:

> He was easy, kind, careful, and communicative. Seating himself by my bed, he would place his hat carefully upon the bed, stroke his hair, turn his cuffs, all the while talking freely; and, if in no particular hurry, he would take up one of my books, and read me half a page.[31]

In this passage Townend used his Infirmary experiences to generalize about the importance of the sympathetic bond of trust between doctor and patient, citing the example of a woman whom he had read of who had received excellent medical care but who refused further treatment and would 'rather languish beneath excruciating pain … because [the surgeon] showed an utter insensibility to her sufferings'.[32] Doctors, then, must treat hearts and minds, as well as bodies. The importance of the affective relationship between patient and doctor is reinforced in Townend's description of the attention and care he received during his time at the Infirmary:

> …. my good brother Thomas … my true friend and companion, Mr. Thomas Howarth … and other friends, came a long way to sympathise in my distress … those unmistakeable tokens of real kindness I shall never forget. My good old doctor treated me with fatherly affection; and the house-surgeon for six weeks dressed my sores with the greatest tenderness and regularity.[33]

There is no distinction in this roll-call of Good Samaritans between friends, family and the medical staff of the hospital, and we see in the idea of 'fatherly affection' how the affective aspect of the doctor–patient relationship was expressed through a traditional familial form of authority. But this familial relationship was not always a cosy one; at times the assertion of medical paternalism was rather more brutal. Townend recounts how after his operation he was visited by his house-doctor in preparation for the first dressing of the wound. Waterhouse, so tender and attentive at other times, dragged him out of bed and into the centre of the room:

> I leaned to my left side, and holding up my right foot, I tried to keep up my poor arm. With violence he struck at the same moment with one fist the knee, and with the other the elbow, sternly exclaiming – '*Stand up, man*; you have not your mother for your doctor now!'[34]

The doctor's words were suggestive. Only in one passage of the account of his time at the Infirmary did Townend mention women; he had entered a masculine domain. And, as his doctor told him, while his care at home was the responsibility of his mother, he was now in the hands of men. Townend recalled another incident with Waterhouse during his post-operation recovery:

31 Ibid., pp. 16–17.
32 Ibid., pp. 16–17.
33 Ibid., p. 16.
34 Ibid., p. 13.

> On one occasion I had partaken rather freely of port wine, which a friend had poured into my tin. When the wound was dressed next morning, it was very much inflamed. Mr. Waterhouse said, 'What hast thou been doing? thou hast been out of bed?' He was very much grieved; and he suddenly jerked up my shoulder, which made me sweat with pain, and it cracked like the firing of a pistol.[35]

The doctor's brute control of the patient's body made plain the authority that the medical man could assert in the therapeutic encounter, yet the tone of the description was equally significant. Rules had been broken, the authority of the regime had been challenged but the reaction was described in terms of personal affect: Mr Waterhouse was 'very much grieved'. What had been breached was not simply the institutional system of authority but Townend's personal bond of trust with Waterhouse.

'A strong sympathy between fellow-sufferers'

While the doctor–patient relationship is the conventional focus of attention when thinking about the social relations of hospital medicine, Townend's account of his time at the Infirmary gives us an insight into the relations between patients. It is a fundamental aspect of the interactionist perspective in medical sociology that treatment – whether at home or in hospital – is a negotiated order. Part of that order is a search for independence; the sick 'organise their lives in a way allowing for as good a reconciliation between incapacity and autonomy as they can muster'.[36] As part of a wider patient community, Townend both participated in and resisted the official life of the Infirmary.

Early in his autobiography Townend wrote that as a child 'my besetting sin was levity and mirth ... I could not suppress a hearty laugh; and there was a vein of humour in my nature ...'.[37] This side of his character found expression in the Infirmary:

> On the Friday morning after the final consultation on my case, being in a humorous mood, with the long brush handle in my hand by way of staff, and followed by another patient, I was proceeding from ward to ward, inquiring if the patients had any complaints to lodge, as to their general treatment, diet, &c.[38]

Here in a carnivalesque spirit the established order had been turned on its head. Now it was the patients, not the doctors, who walked the wards and it was the behaviour of the medical staff, not the progress of the sick, which was under scrutiny. This event seems to have been a one-off but there were other, more established, floutings of convention:

> It was the business of the night-nurse to prepare gruel, and bring it round between one and two in the morning ... For half an hour, when supplied with gruel, all was life and stir.

---

35   Ibid., p. 16.

36   U. Gerhardt, *Ideas About Illness – an Intellectual History of Medical Sociology* (Basingstoke, 1989), p. 127.

37   Townend, *Autobiography*, p. 7.

38   Ibid., p. 9.

Smoking, snuffing, bartering with each other, and treating each other – especially after Thursday, when friends were admitted – fruits, gingerbread, toffies, wines, &c., which lay concealed from the doctors, all came out then.[39]

Again the patients' midnight feast invokes the Rabelaisian spirit of carnival, a hedonistic alternative to the Lenten gruel served by the night-nurse. The sharing of food might appear trivial, but control of diet was one the central planks of hospital regimes. However, it would be wrong to suggest that relations between patients simply revolved around challenges to the hospital regime. Patients who were fit enough participated in the day-to-day running of the Infirmary, as Townend did prior to his operation:

It was five weeks before I had to keep to my bed, so that I had an opportunity of making myself generally useful, which was of great service to me afterwards ... I now felt myself at home in the infirmary; I could dress wounds, make plasters, administer medicines, and frequently ventured to read with and talk to the sick and dying.[40]

This was an echo of an earlier passage in the autobiography in which Townend recounted the slow death of his brother, Benjamin, from consumption: 'I was, during his illness, his almost constant attendant.'[41] Townend made himself 'at home' by making himself useful. The tenderness and sympathy offered by medical staff was also to be found in the assistance given by one patient to another. As Townend explained: 'There is generally a strong sympathy between fellow-sufferers; but especially so in a large establishment like the Manchester Infirmary.'[42] These affective bonds were made clear in his description of his relationship with the other men in his ward:

After having been full three months in bed, I began to walk about, and make myself useful to the other patients. At this time, my two companions in the ward were elderly men, both dreadfully afflicted with stricture; the elder of the two, a recruiting sergeant, had a double rupture as well. Poor fellow! he would brush up, and walk as if nothing ailed him. I was very fond of him, waited on him as well as I could, making his bed, and keeping the door, when it was inconvenient for persons to enter, for which I was beloved and handsomely rewarded. It was understood that if he died suddenly, I was to run directly to the Castle Inn, Dean's Gate, and inform his wife; as he had a perfect horror of being examined by the doctors after his death. The other poor man I have seen literally dance with agony, as the sweat rolled off his face upon the floor. He made me a beautiful straw hat, which I wore when I went home.[43]

One could over-idealize this fellow-feeling; life in the patient community was not always so generous. For instance, Townend described how, after the brief entry and departure of a noisy and clearly very disturbed patient who was removed to a lunatic asylum, the other patients gathered together to congratulate themselves on having been relieved of a troublesome companion. Townend himself, when contemplating

---

39 Ibid., p. 14.
40 Ibid., pp. 10–11.
41 Ibid., p. 6.
42 Ibid., p. 14.
43 Ibid., pp. 18–19.

the state of his own soul, passed judgement on his fellow patients: 'it grieved me to see such deep depravity and crime in the patients'.[44] Thus we can see that the community of suffering created by the sick was one defined not only by processes of inclusion but also of exclusion.

Nevertheless, the overall impression Townend gave was one of compassion and solidarity. Alongside the official life of the Infirmary – the care provided by the medical staff and the rules and regulations of the institution – there was the social world created by the patients; a community of the suffering, in which fears were shared, gifts were exchanged and promises made.

The religious patient – sickness and salvation

Townend's active service ministering to patients around the Infirmary was unsurprising given his religious background. As a member of a dedicated Methodist family, Townend came from a tradition with a strong commitment to good works, where spiritual counselling was a responsibility shared by the whole religious community and where an egalitarian approach to religious authority and hierarchy stressed the value of independence.[45] Unsurprisingly, perhaps, the one aspect of Infirmary life which Townend criticized strongly was the pastoral care:

> Some of the ministers, all of whom were of the Established Church, preached and visited like men of God; but the majority were like mere talking-machines. One case I shall never forget. Hearing that a clergyman was going into one of the large wards to visit a dying man, I followed, and sat at a distance, so as to observe what passed. The minister said to the dying man, 'Do you believe the Articles of the Christian faith?' The patient replied, 'I do.' The minister then said to the man, 'Then you must say after me.' The Articles were read, and the dying man repeated after the minister as well as he could. Several collects of prayers were read, amongst the rest, one for the king, both Houses of Parliament, the Lord's Prayer, &c; then the sacrament was administered, and the minister took his leave. The next morning the poor man was dead. Alas! how many thousands have been thus officially packed up in ignorance, and sent in to the presence of Him who hath said, 'Verily, verily, I say unto thee, except a man be born again, he cannot see the kingdom of God.'[46]

We see here an echo of Townend's attitudes to medical care. It was not enough to go through the motions of care, no matter how efficiently. One must attend to the sufferings of the individual; there must be a meeting of minds and hearts. What upset Townend was the perfunctory nature of the care offered and the lack of engagement with the dying man. In the rote repetition of the sacraments, the patient was essentially passive. For Townend, this was unacceptable; patients and penitents had to be active participants in their physical and spiritual salvation.

---

44   Ibid., p. 13.

45   J. Obelkevich, 'Religion', in F.M.L. Thompson (ed.), *Cambridge Social History of Britain 1750–1950*, Vol.3 (Cambridge, 1990).

46   Townend, *Autobiography*, p. 11.

Townend's account of his time in the Infirmary can only be understood in the context of his religion. Sickness and death had long been powerful themes in spiritual autobiographies and Methodist narratives were no different. The stirrings of the soul were often expressed through the sufferings of the body. Strong religious feelings might induce fainting, weeping or complete physical collapse. Conversely, the sufferings of the body always had spiritual significance: the sickroom and the deathbed were sanctified spaces within which grace was displayed by the afflicted and good works were carried out by friends and family. Townend devoted so much space in his autobiography to his time in the Infirmary because of the importance of this period to his spiritual development. As we have seen, once he became a patient he lost no time in devoting himself to good works. But alongside these outward actions, his inner world was changing.

In order to understand this spiritual journey inside the hospital, we need to set it in the context of his life outside; he described his circumstances immediately prior to his entry to the Infirmary thus:

> With all my domestic, social, and religious privileges, I was not happy. I had for years resisted the strivings of the Holy Spirit; I had too much light not to see and feel my wretchedness; and I was too poor in circumstances, and too much under parental and restraining influence, to run headlong into open sin. Yet I was a poor factory lad, with no prospect of ever rising in the mill, my right arm grown to my side, sternly prevented that; and how in the world to get out of the factory, I could not conceive.[47]

In this lament, Townend linked his physical disability to his spiritual and material poverty. A cure had to be found for all these ills and the site for the cure was the hospital. We can understand his time in the Infirmary as a rite of passage which transformed him both physically and spiritually.

To put this in its proper context, we should note that fundamental to the narrative arc of many spiritual autobiographies such as Townend's is that they begin with a detailed account of the wretched nature of the subject's life of sin prior to conversion. In this respect Townend's own life was sadly lacking in great incident, although he did find one occasion of drunkenness to illustrate his sinful past. In the absence of further evidence of a debauched past, Townend focused instead on the dangers surrounding him in a community full of sinful behaviour and on his one persistent failing – his sense of humour. As noted earlier, he described how as a child his 'besetting sin was levity and mirth'; he went on to state that he felt that this 'vein of humour' in his nature 'needed to be subdued and chastened by severe discipline and divine grace'.[48] His period in the Manchester Infirmary is, I would suggest, the time when he was finally subject to both severe discipline and divine grace.

Earlier we described how Townend had patrolled the hospital in a mock round of the wards. This took place on the day that surgery was to be performed on Townend, and his satirical performance was interrupted by the male nurse Joseph, who called him away.

---

47   Ibid., pp. 8–9.
48   Ibid., p. 7.

Having just pulled the quilt off an ill-tempered man who was confined to bed, he having hurled the Bible at me ... just at that moment, the voice of the man-nurse was heard calling – 'Joseph Townend!' and he, perceiving that I was about , said, 'Come this way, sir; let's try to cure you of your larking!'[49]

The cure for his levity was nothing less than the surgery for which Townend had entered the Infirmary. Leading him away to another ward, the nurse blindfolded him and guided him into the operating theatre, where he was restrained and the cut was made to separate his arm from his side: 'the progress of the instrument I distinctly heard, and the pain was most extreme'. When the blindfold was removed, 'On the floor were Drs. Ransom and Wilson, in oil dresses, attended by the house-surgeon and Joseph, the man-nurse; and the gallery of medical and surgical students'.[50]

At this moment, Townend had become the subject of experimental surgery and, with the students looking on from the gallery, an object of medical knowledge. But alongside this medicalization, something else was going on. After the cut was made, he said he thought of 'home, and friends being distant', and, describing his wound, he 'felt the weight of the web which for fifteen years had been accumulating'. The physical cut separating arm from side was thus accompanied by two other separations – the isolation from friends and family, and a distancing from a past life of sin. The 'weight of the web' was not simply the physical weight of the skin which had joined arm to torso, but the weight of all that had gone before; the past life which Townend was now ready to move beyond. The exuberant youth had been subjected to the severe discipline of the surgeon's knife; now, in recovery, he was to experience divine grace. Townend described his first impression when he awoke in the operating theatre thus: 'The room was like a little chapel.' After the operation he was returned to his bed where he meditated on his situation:

> ... having swallowed a dose of aperient medicine, I was left to reflect on my past life, present position, and future prospects. I felt ashamed and grieved at my past neglect and wickedness in resisting the Holy Spirit. I thought of the chapel and school – I wept bitterly.[51]

Townend spent three months in bed recovering from the operation; he was tended by the medical staff and visited by friends and family. On Sunday mornings, he watched the crowds as they travelled to worship: 'I used to relieve my mind by weeping, and looking forward to the time when my feet again would stand within the gates of Zion.'[52] He spent his time reading religious works: 'my Bible and hymn-book, Pollok's "Course of Time", Milton's "Paradise Lost", Young's "Night Thoughts"'.[53] Patients came to visit him at his bedside and he returned their kindness by offering

---

49   Ibid., p. 12.
50   Ibid., p. 12.
51   Ibid., p. 13.
52   Ibid., p. 17.
53   Ibid., p. 18.

religious guidance: 'I was very cheerful, generally, and often gave out hymns, and explained portions of Scripture, especially historical parts.'[54]

Townend's internal journey did not go unnoticed. He became a kind of spiritual beacon, a talisman with special powers. During a thunderstorm, people flocked to his room for protection: 'It was an awful night. My room was filled with patients, and female servants, who seemed to think themselves secure here, for they thought me very religious.' Townend did not dismiss their behaviour as in any way superstitious; it was a recognition of his internal spiritual progress: 'I was the subject of restraining and constraining grace, and I thought my mind fully made up to be the Lord's when I should return home.'[55] As is often the case in conversion narratives, we later discover that this was something of a false dawn. Nevertheless, a religious awakening had begun.

It was when he left the Infirmary that the full transformation in his status and condition became clear. Medically, his 'perfect cure' was completed with a visit to the sea to bathe his wounds in salt water. Spiritually, his progress culminated in a full conversion experience some months later. Materially, his situation improved when he obtained a warehouse job with his old employer: 'I got a new suit; and things began to look up in the world.' Finally, his personal life was transformed when he married, his physical cure and improved prospects having increased his standing with his sweetheart: 'My Sarah, who had never turned her back upon me, but often secretly provided me with money, would now *openly* take a walk with me.'[56] The spiritual, emotional and material crisis with which he entered the Infirmary had been solved, he had entered the Infirmary as a troubled youth, but he left it ready for manly independence.

There is an important sense in which the hospital served as a liminal space, in which Townend underwent a rite of passage, shedding his previous identity and emerging with a new one. This was in large part a religious transformation, but it was also a highly gendered one. The masculine nature of this liminal space, with its separation from the influence of his mother, was perhaps an important aspect of this transformation. Tellingly, when Townend eventually returned home, his mother looked him over and asked: 'Is it my lad?'

Conclusion

Clearly, there were many ways in which the Manchester Infirmary fitted the archetype of a modern disciplinary regime. It was governed by a set of written rules and run to a strict timetable, all designed to give control of the minutiae of patients' lives – cleanliness, diet, movement within and outside the institution. It was, moreover, for some patients a place of horror, where the fear that their final end might be as another specimen in the dissecting room was ever-present. Clearly, too, Townend did in some senses become clinical material when he entered the Infirmary: the object of experimental surgery; an interesting case displayed to visiting doctors, and

---

54   Ibid., p. 17.

55   Ibid., p. 18.

56   Ibid., p. 22.

someone on whom medical students could practise their skills. Moreover, in so far as the surgeons' main concern was to treat the wrist injury Townend had received at the mill, his cure typified the Infirmary's socio-economic function, treating the victims of industrial accidents so that they could return to their roles as economically productive members of society.[57]

So far, so conventional. Yet there is much in Townend's account which does not square neatly with this picture. Inevitably, the institution looked different from the patient's perspective. We might read Townend's account in a number of ways. Firstly, his involvement in nursing duties cannot be seen simply as a passive acceptance of the rules of the Infirmary. We must also place this behaviour in the context of the long-standing tradition of lay medical care. Patients were involved in the running of the hospital precisely because there was no clear dividing line between the sick and their attendants; all could participate in the processes of healing. This suggests that it is to the professionalization of nursing and to the history not just of the doctor–patient relationship but also of the nurse–patient relationship that we must look for a chronology of patient disempowerment.

Secondly, in examining the doctor–patient relationship, what we have uncovered are powerful continuities. In Townend's active participation in the decision-making process which led to his surgery, in the style of bedside manner adopted by Mr Waterhouse, and in Townend's attitude to it, we can see a continuity with long-standing traditions in medical practice which were respectful to, rather than dismissive of, the patient. This would seem to support Chris Lawrence's argument that in many ways Victorian medicine remained a gentlemanly art based on trust and intuition, and recent work on general practice which argues that by and large the clinical encounter between GP and patient saw no sudden transformation in medical practice.[58]

One of the central questions here is the relationship between a modern impersonal disciplinary power and an older personal and familial power. In 'total institutions' the former is supposed to have replaced the latter; as Goffman argued, in such spaces one finds 'the staging of a grim social distance ... between two constructed categories of persons'.[59] Townend's account of his relations with his medical attendants emphasizes familial paternalism rather than a more modern bureaucratic discipline. This would seem to fit in with other studies of Victorian institutions. For instance, in her study of Victorian penal institutions for women, Luca Zedner suggests that the social distance between staff and inmates was constantly breaking down. Although in theory the two parties were forbidden from any unnecessary conversation, in

---

57 See Pickstone *Medicine and Industrial Society*, p. 49.

58 C. Lawrence, 'Incommunicable knowledge: science, technology and the clinical art in Britain, 1850–1914', *Journal of Contemporary History* 20 (1985): 503–20; C. Lawrence, 'The meaning of histories', *Bulletin of the History of Medicine*, 66 (1992): 643, and Digby, *Making a Medical Living*, pp. 98–103.

59 E. Goffman, *Asylums. Essays on the Social Situation of Mental Patients and Other Inmates* (1961; London, 1991).

practice their relations ranged from animosity and antagonism to emotional and even sexual intimacy.[60]

Perhaps we can help to explain this by turning to the historiography of the factory. The hospital has been understood as one example of a new kind of institution of which the factory has often served as paradigm. We might suggest that the weakness of such arguments are that they are predicated on outdated chronologies of the Industrial Revolution. Thus the shift from relatively informal systems of production centred on workshop or domestic manufacture to large-scale production in highly mechanized and highly disciplined factories has provided the model for understanding how the hospital became part of a wider disciplinary society.

However, not only is it now generally accepted that factory production was less important for the transformation of the British economy than was thought, but even where factories were important, they were often smaller than the traditional model.[61] Even large factories were often collections of small workshops in which production relied on traditional craft skills, rather than monolithic institutions based on deskilled, mechanized labour. This reliance on skill meant that control of production was rarely wrested entirely from the hands of workers. Indeed, factory owners often delegated the process by subcontracting production to working-class foremen who would hire, fire and supervise workers. It was these traditional forms of social relations which predominated in the bulk of factories: the scientific management of labour chronicled by the economic historian Sydney Pollard developed in the *late* nineteenth century; it was an afterthought to Britain's Industrial Revolution rather than something on which it was based. As Craig Littler argues, 'Pollard exaggerates and misinterprets the modernity of work relationships in the early nineteenth century, and correspondingly neglects the continuities of traditional relationships.[62] The same, we might suggest, has been true of historians of medicine charting the doctor–patient relationship.

Thirdly, there is the importance of the patient community. When historians of medicine have hypothesized about the fate of the hospital patient, they have generally thought about a lone individual pitted against a system. Townend's account of what he termed 'the strong sympathy between fellow-sufferers' belies this picture. The life of the sick was a collective one; sufferings were shared, as were pleasures. Studying hospital life without charting the relations between patients, we might argue, is akin to studying factory life without examining the role of trade unions.

Of course, it was not just with patients that Townend was linked by strong sympathy. As we have seen, there was a strong affective aspect to his relations with the medical staff. For Townend, power was always personal; the relationship between doctor and patient was one based as much on the idiosyncrasies of individual temperament as on institutional authority: 'How much of pleasure or pain is experienced in the aggregate of human life, arising out of tempers, dispositions, and habits of persons with whom

---

60   Zedner, *Women, Crime and Custody*, pp. 159–65.

61   N. Crafts, 'The new economic history and the Industrial Revolution', in P. Mathias and J. Davis (eds), *The First Industrial Revolutions* (Oxford, 1989), p. 39.

62   C. Littler, *The Development of the Labour Process in Capitalist Societies* (London, 1982), pp. 70–71.

we have to do, and most especially with the sensitive invalid!'[63] Townend's account suggests that we should not chart the doctor–patient relationship simply in terms of power. To take seriously our ability to invest affection in each other does not mean we should replace an interest in power with an interest in emotion: the two are both linked emergent processes in any given relationship. However, what we must avoid is the temptation to explain the affective aspects of social relations as simply an epiphenomenon of the more central issue of power.

Of course, emotional attachment cannot be treated ahistorically; a social history of the emotions must seek to locate the cultural origins of expressions of feeling. We might wish to draw on Miriam Bailin's work on fictional and nonfictional representations of the sickroom in late Georgian culture. She argues that the healing process was a powerful emotional signifier:

> Nursing the sick, was for both men and women, as sanctified an act as suffering itself. As long as it was not for hire, nursing was repeatedly invoked to verify in a way no other activity apparently could the genuineness of one's affections, the essential goodness of one's character.[64]

In the case of Townend we might also invoke what Patrick Joyce, writing about another Manchester autobiographer, Edwin Waugh, has called 'the cult of the heart', a plebeian valorization of 'the sincerity of unalloyed human feeling'.[65] In understanding such a cult and Townend's account, we might return to the quotation with which we began: his description of his departure from the Infirmary – his uncontrollable tears; the kind words of the doctor; the house-surgeon who 'turned away much moved' as he left, and his gratitude at the care he had received. There is something in this, and in much else of his account, which brings to mind in its intense emotionalism, the melodramatic mode so popular in Victorian culture. Its social uses have been analysed by Elaine Hadley:

> In the face of rapid industrialization, private capital accumulation, and bureaucratization, the melodramatic mode's distinctive theatricality insisted on the continued vitality of traditionally public, social formations, especially patriarchal status hierarchies, which constituted identity in terms of familial and communal relationships.[66]

And we cannot understand this affective aspect of the clinical encounter without turning to the final issue – the question of religion. If medicalization was part of a broader secularizing trend in society, then Townend would suggest it was being vigorously resisted at the end of the long eighteenth century. The competing discourses of medicine and religion left the patient's body a contested terrain over

---

63   Townend, *Autobiography*, pp. 16–17.

64   M. Bailin, *The Sickroom in Victorian Fiction: the Art of being Ill* (Cambridge, 1994), p. 11.

65   P. Joyce, *Democratic Subjects: The Self and the Social in Nineteenth-Century England* (Cambridge, 1994), p. 46.

66   E. Hadley, *Melodramatic Tactics: Theatricalized Dissent in the English Marketplace, 1800–1885* (Stanford, 1995), p. 4.

which no single power or authority had total hegemony.[67] Even here we can see continuities: the close relationship between Evangelical reform and medical charity was part of a much longer history of the hospital as house of God, which in Western civilization it can be traced at least as far back as the early Christians.

As part of a spiritual autobiography, it is perhaps inevitable that it is the religious reading of Townend's account which is the most powerful. All the elements we have already discussed can be interpreted as stemming in part from Townend's Methodism: the passionate language which he used to describe his relations with both staff and patients; the good works he carried out in the hospital; the independence of spirit and strength of mind which allowed him to insist against the doubts of the surgeons that his operation be performed. Even his willing acceptance of occasional harsh treatment from his medical attendants can be seen as part of a Methodist style of tough love, just as Townend's eventual conversion experience came only after stern words from his pastor – so physical cure required strong measures.

In our search for continuities, we might argue that even his conversion was a result of institutionalization, an expression of the persistence of the older non-medical foundations of the Infirmary. As Mary Fissell has argued: 'the *ancien régime* institution, often old, almost always multifunctional, looks back to a tradition of moral reform and local patronage and piety'.[68] There is no doubt that Townend was moved by the experience of life in the Infirmary, that the kindness of the medical staff provided some kind of moral example. But his was an independent, rather than an institutional, moral reformation; his condemnation of the Church of England clergy who attended the Infirmary makes this clear.

Furthermore, we cannot simply think of the institution acting on the patient. Townend entered into the life of the Infirmary, becoming an active member of the patient community and establishing emotional bonds with the medical staff. All this activity requires us also to think about the effect that Townend had on the life of the institution and the lives of its staff. This final point might encourage us to generalize about the relationship between early nineteenth-century institutions and their inmates. One would not want to dismiss the idea that such regimes did in part help construct the modern self, changing what it meant to be human by bringing habit, obedience, regularity and order – in short, discipline – to a more central place in the human psyche. But equally true is the insight that these institutions were themselves transformed through the experience of being lived in and worked in by human beings who were never reduced to the status of cogs in a machine. The people in these institutions broke and bent the rules as much as the rules broke and bent the people. Processes of reformation and transformation were not one-way.

---

67 See Corfield, *Power and the Professions*.

68 Fissell, *Patients, Power and the Poor*, pp. 13–14. Pickstone discusses the influence of reforming Anglican and Methodists on the expansion of the Infirmary at the end of the eighteenth century: see Pickstone, *Medicine and Industrial Society*, pp. 18–19.

CHAPTER SEVEN

Investigating the 'deserving' poor: charity and the voluntary hospitals in nineteenth-century Birmingham

Jonathan Reinarz

As elsewhere in England, patients entering Birmingham's voluntary hospitals were a carefully selected group. This is perhaps most evident in the first regulations of the town's General Hospital. Like those of many other provincial institutions, the General's 32-page list comprising nearly a hundred rules indicates that the medical charity was established specifically for members of the 'deserving' poor, and definitely not for the patient 'who can subsist himself, and pay for medicines'.[1] The actual criteria used by staff and subscribers in the selection of hospital patients are less evident in archival sources. Since some patients at all Birmingham's voluntary hospitals came from distant parishes, and were even preferred over local cases if free beds were limited,[2] individuals were often relatively unknown to everyone but a single empathetic subscriber. Moreover, despite the efforts some subscribers undoubtedly made to determine patients' financial circumstances before distributing letters of recommendation or tickets of admission, hospitals were not always attracting a narrow category of 'deserving' poor, especially as many quickly became familiar with the rules governing voluntary hospitals and especially their admissions policies. After a single visit to hospital, for example, the average patient would have become very proficient at depicting themselves as a deserving case. More commonly, despite some efforts to uncover details concerning patients' circumstances, their histories usually unfolded only after gaining admission to hospital wards. As often, even before interaction with staff and other patients encouraged personal details to emerge, others were ejected from these charitable institutions for breaking one of many hospital rules. Consequently, most nineteenth-century annual reports and minute books urged hospital subscribers and staff to inquire more effectively into the suitability of those candidates who were appearing in hospital entrance halls and waiting rooms. As one might expect, therefore, over the remainder of the nineteenth century, knowledge concerning patients' backgrounds appears to have improved considerably. Perhaps more unusually, these efforts to investigate the identities of patients more effectively were introduced precisely at a time when hospital medicine is said to have become progressively more depersonalized due to the simultaneous

---

1   Statutes and Rules of the General Hospital, Birmingham (hereafter GHB), 1779, Birmingham Central Library Archive (hereafter BCLA), GH/1/4/510.
2   Ibid.

rise of pathological anatomy and the medical gaze.[3] Looked at from the perspective of those charged with investigating patients' financial circumstances, the opposite appears to have been the case.

This chapter is an attempt to explore the relationship between patients, the intended beneficiaries of medical charities, and those who controlled entrance to the voluntary hospital, whether subscribers or staff, in greater detail than has been the case in the majority of hospital histories.[4] In particular, it compares the experiences of patients at five very different voluntary hospitals in Birmingham (two general and three specialist) and illustrates various efforts that were introduced in the nineteenth century to discover more about the recipients of charity at these local medical institutions. Though at times comparative, this particular approach cannot always be sustained as these hospitals themselves were founded over the century between 1779 and 1871, and their administration has been re-created using divergent sources. However, the examples very effectively illustrate changes in admission procedures throughout this period. Primarily, it will be argued that, as much as patients' backgrounds clearly concerned staff at a number of hospitals in Birmingham, the ability, or even desire, of medical staff and administrators to 'know' the recipients of health care in these years varied for a number of reasons, including the particular organization of a hospital and gradual changes in the type of subscribers and patients these institutions attracted, not to mention the ever-fluctuating state of hospital finances.

The General Hospital

Nationally, Birmingham was relatively slow to construct its first voluntary hospital. The first provincial centres to found such charitable institutions were Winchester and Bristol, both communities having established hospitals in 1737.[5] By the end of the eighteenth century, another two dozen towns, of which Birmingham was one of the last, established similar medical charities.[6] Although a booming, unregulated (and therefore hazardous) industrial region, Birmingham established a general hospital only in 1779. Like most charities preceding it, the 40-bed hospital in Birmingham was supported largely by voluntary philanthropy, comprising primarily annual subscriptions, which averaged a guinea. In exchange for monetary support, subscribers to the town's premier medical charity were permitted to recommend 'deserving' patients, namely those unable to pay for private medical treatment.

3   M. Foucault, *The Birth of the Clinic: An Archaeology of Medical Perception* (New York, 1973), pp. ix–xiv; N.D. Jewson, 'The disappearance of the sick man from medical cosmology, 1770–1870', *Sociology*, 10 (1976): 238.

4   Among the most critical of studies concerning charity is P. Mandler (ed.), *The Uses of Charity: The Poor on Relief in the Nineteenth-Century Metropolis* (Philadelphia, 1990).

5   R. Porter, 'The gift relation: philanthropy and provincial hospitals in eighteenth-century England', in L. Granshaw and R. Porter (eds), *The Hospital in History* (London, 1989), p. 150.

6   A. Wilson, 'Conflict, Consensus and Charity: Politics and the Provincial Voluntary Hospitals in the Eighteenth Century', *English Historical Review*, CXI, 442 (1996): 601.

Its founder especially identified those individuals employed in local industries who originated from parishes outside of Birmingham, as these were not entitled to existing forms of parochial relief.[7] Those excluded from attending the charity from the outset were the destitute, who – as in most other provincial towns – were to be sent to a workhouse infirmary, which had existed in Birmingham since 1727. Other undesirables included children, pregnant women and the mentally ill, though policies varied between individual hospitals.[8] Though such exclusion clauses are to be found in most hospital regulations, the earliest hospital sources provide considerable information concerning the charity's subscribers and shed far less light on the patient population.

Though the printed regulations of Birmingham's first medical charity specified those patients the institution did and did not serve, individuals who managed to gain access to hospital wards were often very different from those whom governors initially aimed to assist. For example, although Dr John Ash, the General Hospital's founder and its principal physician, suggested the hospital was intended primarily for those without legal settlement in Birmingham, the majority of early patients came from within the immediate town boundary.[9] As such, many would have been known to staff at the institution, doctors and clergyman having regularly visited the homes of the labouring poor in these years.[10] Such regular contact with all sectors of the community would also have made it easier for staff to assess the suitability of candidates that subscribers recommended. Nevertheless, though rules expressly prohibited children (an even easier group to identify) from admission to Birmingham's first general hospital, the charity's earliest patient registers reveal their presence. Included among the first 127 patients admitted to the institution during its first three months of operation were six children under the age of ten, all such patients having resided in the women's wards.[11] Rules were similarly breached at other general hospitals in these years.[12] Though few in number, these notable exceptions suggest that hospital regulations, despite their definitive appearance, and being hung in hospital wards, did not always accurately reflect hospital policy or the composition of its wards.[13]

While the transgression of hospital rules by staff might introduce some variety, the ejection of patients from hospitals was a regular occurrence and was an effective means of re-establishing order on the wards (Table 7.1). During its first ten years, staff and governors at the General Hospital discharged nearly as many patients as died in hospital for certain 'irregularities', which, among a host of offences, usually

7   *Aris's Gazette* (18 November 1765).

8   Statutes and Rules of the General Hospital, Birmingham, 1779, BCLA, GH/1/4/510.

9   J. Reinarz, *The Birth of a Provincial Hospital: The Early Years of the General Hospital, Birmingham, 1765–1790* (Stratford, 2003), p. 3.

10 J. Pickstone, *Medicine and Industrial Society: A History of Hospital Development in Manchester and its Region, 1752–1946* (Manchester, 1985) p. 110.

11 Patient Register, GHB, 1779–1788, BCLA, GH/4/2/560.

12 G. Risse, *Hospital Life in Enlightenment Scotland: Care and teaching at the Royal Infirmary of Edinburgh* (Cambridge, 1986), p. 86.

13 G.M. Smith, *A History of the Bristol Royal Infirmary* (Bristol, 1917), p. 28.

implied smoking, drinking and swearing.[14] For example, in 1790, 15 patients were discharged for irregularities or judged as improper recipients of charity, similar rates having been reported at other general hospitals.[15] According to hospital annual reports issued between the years 1781 and 1820, approximately 3 per cent of in-patients were discharged for similar reasons.[16] In other words, such acts of disorder occurred with sufficient frequency to be observed by nearly every inmate at the institution, given that most patients on average occupied their beds for longer than a month.[17]

Table 7.1   General Hospital, Birmingham: Patients discharged for irregularities or deemed improper objects of charity 1781-1789, 1800-1820

Year	1781	1782	1783	1784	1785	1786	1787	1788	1789	1800
Number discharged	6	13	8	11	5	16	17	19	17	26
Irregularity	6	8	6	2	5	16	10	13	12	12
Not proper		5	2	9			7	6	5	14
Year	1801	1802	1803	1804	1805	1806	1807	1808	1809	1810
Number discharged	26	34	25	24	30	40	25	32	31	32
Irregularity	15	22	17	20	19	32	10	14	20	30
Not proper	11	12	8	4	11	8	15	18	11	2
Year	1811	1812	1813	1814	1815	1816	1817	1818	1819	1820
Number discharged	22	29	34	22	19	21	27	30	18	38
Irregularity	20	22	26	10	12	6	7	9	7	17
Not proper	2	7	8	12	7	15	20	21	11	21

Source: Annual Reports, General Hospital, Birmingham, 1781–1820, BCLA, MS 1921/414.

While Such figures appear to suggest that hospitals dealt with insubordination very seriously, rules, as was suggested earlier, were occasionally broken. One particularly informative example of this involved Henry Bellamy, a surgical patient of George Kennedy in 1780. By repeatedly disobeying the directions of his surgeon, Bellamy was seen to be delaying a cure and setting a bad example to the other patients. If discharged, Bellamy, like other patients who were expelled from hospital, would

14   Rules of the General Hospital, Birmingham, 1779, BCLA, GH/1/4/510; Annual Reports of the General Hospital, Birmingham, 1779–1800, BCLA, GH/1/3/1.

15   Annual Report, GHB, 1790, Birmingham Central Library, Local Studies (hereafter BCLLS), GH/1/3/1; Risse, *Hospital Life in Enlightenment Scotland*, p. 238.

16   Annual Report, GHB, 1790, BCLLS, GH/1/3/1.

17   Patient Register, GHB, 1779-1788, BCLA, GH/4/2/560.

never be accepted as a patient again, a letter detailing the infraction being sent to the sponsor. On this occasion, however, rules were rendered more pliable. Kennedy pleaded on his patient's behalf, claiming that a cure could be had within two weeks, whereas an early discharge would only guarantee that the man would remain 'a cripple for life'.[18] Set on the road to full recovery, Bellamy's behaviour was reported as being 'orderly' the following week by the hospital's visitors and he was discharged 'cured' shortly afterwards.[19]

As this episode appears to indicate, much of the disorder that characterized early hospital wards was easily masked by members of staff, who usually tolerated a degree of disruption. Moreover, some patients may have formed close relationships with staff, or, on even rarer occasions, medical staff may even have become patient advocates. However, this is not to imply that they knew their patients any better, as is demonstrated by another incident from the hospital's early minute books. On 20 March 1790, another surgeon, Thomas Tomlinson, reported to the general committee that one of his patients, John Jones, a poor boy apprentice, who had both his legs amputated, may have been abused by his master, a Mr Clark of Bittel Farm in Alvechurch.[20] In response, the board agreed to summon the overseers of the Worcestershire parish where Jones and Clark resided, with the view to an indictment being presented against the boy's master. Three months later, it was determined that the overseers of the village should proceed against Clark to advertise his cruelty publicly, unless he agreed to provide the boy with an annuity of ten pounds. Should the overseers have been unwilling to proceed with the case, the medical staff were prepared to support the boy. However, following an investigation, it was discovered that the boy's accusation against Clark was wholly without foundation and the case was dropped.

Though this marked the end of the episode for hospital staff, the story appears to suggest more than Jones's predilection to invent untruths. The events surrounding the story after all took place during a period that predates the introduction of legislation intended to protect apprentices from the abuses of their masters.[21] Additionally, in the context of this chapter, the tale demonstrates the hospital's inexperience when it came to gathering information about its patients. To begin with, medical staff, including Tomlinson, usually attended their patients once a week. Consequently, most would have required a lengthy period of time to acquaint themselves with their patients. In the case of the General Hospital, in-patients on average remained in hospital a month, during which time they would have met with a doctor or surgeon on merely four occasions. In contrast, relations with the house apothecary, matron and nurses would have been more regular, and, not surprisingly, most patient ejections were instigated by evidence provided by the matron or nurses. Moreover, recruited from local working families, nurses and cleaning staff would have been familiar with many patients and their families. As Jones came from Alvechurch, near Redditch, however, he was relatively unknown to all involved. As a result, he attempted to use

---

18 General Committee Minutes, GHB, 1766–84, BCLA, GH/1/2/4.

19 Ibid.

20 Ibid.

21 J. Lane, *Apprenticeship in England, 1600–1914* (London, 1996), pp. 5–6.

his anonymity advantageously in order to get even with a master whom he clearly no longer respected. While historians of apprenticeship have regularly catalogued such hostile relations between apprentices and masters,[22] this episode did not conclude well for Jones, who, despite being discharged as 'cured', otherwise received no compensation for his injuries.[23] Hospital staff, on the other hand, had learned the importance of carefully investigating their patients' backgrounds before taking similar action in future.

The Eye Hospital

While the professional disease of blocked promotion is said to have created many specialist hospitals throughout the country in the nineteenth century, epidemics or a particular concentration of eye ailments, as could be found in most industrial regions, also encouraged the establishment of the nation's first eye hospitals.[24] In this respect, the Birmingham Eye Hospital was well suited to the needs of the regional economy, eye injuries having become prevalent in the town's numerous workshops over the preceding century. From its foundation in 1823, the Eye Hospital served the region's industrial base and especially the metal and glass trades. Moreover, with its foundation, another medical institution opened its doors to the region's 'deserving' poor. In its first year, the charity treated more than 1,700 men and women at a time when staff at the General Hospital were treating approximately 4,000 patients annually.[25] The regional appeal of the hospital was apparent from its first appearance, its governors, like those of other specialist hospitals, having added 'Midland' to the name of their institution in 1853 to better represent the community it served.[26] However, the Eye Hospital seems to have appealed more widely than did all other specialist hospitals in these years, its patient registers and subscription lists recording individuals and businesses from a very broad catchment area. As one might expect, this also determined relations between staff and patients.

Unlike the General Hospital, the Eye Hospital initially opened as a dispensary in the centre of Birmingham. Perhaps for this reason, its governors also appeared less concerned with detecting cases of hospital abuse, given that they were able to treat a great number of patients at very little expense. Providing a form of specialist care that had previously been offered by unqualified and itinerant practitioners, the hospital's medical staff, unlike that at the General, were less concerned that they were treating individuals who might ordinarily have attended the private practices of

---

22 Ibid., pp. 187–227.

23 Patient Register, GHB, 1788–94, BCLA, GH/4/2/561.

24 L. Granshaw, '"Fame and fortune by means of bricks and mortar": the medical profession and specialist hospitals in Britain, 1800–1948', in Granshaw and Porter (eds), *The Hospital in History*, p. 204.

25 General Committee Minutes, Birmingham Eye Hospital, 1823–57, BCLA, MS 1919; Annual Report, GHB, 1823, BCLLS, GH/1/3/1.

26 Ibid.

other local practitioners.[27] The hospital's own medical officers, however, were still determined that the institution would be compensated for its services. As a result, in most cases staff enquiries into the backgrounds of patients began and ended with the name of their employers. As soon as this information had been acquired, hospital administrators spent the majority of their time canvassing the local tradesmen and businesses who sent them their sick and injured labourers in an effort to cover the charity's costs. In the hospital's earliest years, this highly focused approach to hospital fund-raising led to greater than usual business donations, including a £10 donation from the Tipton Moat Colliery Company.[28] Additional generous support came from the branches of friendly societies, such as the local Oddfellows, while subsequent donations from former patients, including a single donation of £5 in 1849, suggest the hospital had never treated just the 'deserving' poor.[29] As a result, hospital governors easily managed to cover their costs and, four years later, they were even able to purchase a failed polytechnic institution for £1,900 and open a 15-bed eye hospital.[30]

With the provision of in-patient facilities and the subsequent increase in the cost of treatment, one would have expected staff to begin inquiring more carefully into patients' backgrounds. Besides noting the number of patients treated at the hospital each week, however, the institution's minute books do not mention patients again until February 1855, when governors were asked to prepare a lithographic note in order to assist individuals in obtaining notes of admission from subscribers.[31] Though the form was stamped with the words 'not to be used for begging', most patients appear to have been in full employment, the majority coming to the hospital from iron and coal districts near Birmingham.[32] Despite these efforts to improve access to the charity, however, by May 1856, the majority of its beds remained vacant. In general this was due to the fact that patients, many of whom came from outside Birmingham, found it difficult to locate subscribers, who tended to be local. As at other specialist hospitals, medical staff did have some control over cases admitted to the institution, both surgeons having been permitted to admit three patients without notes, but their numbers were limited. As a result, it was suggested that employers be made more responsible for their workers and, in March 1857, the iron and coal masters were again canvassed as successfully as in previous years. Two months later, the hospital received a bequest totalling £1,000 from John Crowther of Wednesbury to be invested in the 'Crowther Fund' and used for 'the relief of poor persons afflicted with Diseases of the Eye'.[33]

As a result of this and other donations, the governors opened eight additional beds and, by 1861, the hospital was expanded yet again when the governors purchased

27   R. Middlemore, *A Treatise on the Diseases of the Eye and its Appendages*, Vol. 1 (London, 1835), p. 7.

28   General Committee Minutes, Birmingham Eye Hospital (hereafter BEH), 1823–57, BCLA, MS 1919.

29   Ibid.

30   Ibid.

31   Ibid.

32   Ibid.

33   Ibid.

Dee's Royal Hotel, strategically located between the town's two rail stations. By the end of the year, staff had treated 4,000 out-patients, yet only 277 were admitted to the wards.[34] To rectify this situation, the charity began to offer admission tickets to patients for 2s. 6d. each, but the problem of excess space was only really solved when the charity let a portion of the hospital to the local ear dispensary, a less successful specialist institution.[35] This in turn further improved the hospital's financial state. Though spectacles were dispensed to some patients, the expenses associated with treatment remained low. The majority of patients came to the hospital to be bled and have their eyes rinsed in order to counter inflammations or to collect medicines, all prescriptions being dispensed in bottles that patients themselves were required to provide.[36] Friends and families of in-patients were also responsible for all meals until the last years of the nineteenth century.[37] Not surprisingly, the hospital continued to report a healthy balance for the remainder of the century. Unlike other institutions, subscribers' benefits were even increased, though at the expense of the surgeons, who had been increased to three in number and were now permitted to admit only two free cases each.[38] While two-guinea subscribers in the past had been entitled to recommend an in-patient and eight out-patients, by the 1880s, they were permitted to admit an additional in-patient, at no extra cost.

Instead of focusing on the patient, governors at the Eye Hospital developed an ever greater interest in the subscriber. With an increase in specialist hospitals, such as the eye hospital in Wolverhampton, subscriber numbers declined noticeably. As a result, the hospital secretary began to organize subscribers more carefully by region.[39] More rigorous financial methods were necessary in order to fund a very popular charity, which, by 1883, had replaced its old 44-bed institution with a new, purpose-built 70-bed eye hospital. In contrast, the local ear charity, no longer the eye hospital's tenants, continued to occupy rented accommodation for another decade.[40] Until more subscribers could be attracted, however, only 55 of these beds were in use. As such, the majority of cases by far were out-patients, whose treatment still cost little more than 2s. each, compared with more than £2 for in-patients.[41] By enforcing the ticket system more carefully, however, staff ensured that all patients receiving treatment had been paid for in some way. Unlike at other hospitals, most serious cases were seen only twice without a ticket, all patients having been forced to obtain a ticket to undergo further treatment. So strictly was entrance to the institution managed, that the belief soon began to spread that the hospital did not treat accidents.[42] All voluntary hospitals admitted accident cases without admissions tickets. On the other hand, not all of the voluntary hospitals, as this case demonstrates, were concerned about hospital abuse, or even inquired carefully into patients' backgrounds.

---

34 Annual Report, BEH, 1861, BCLLS.
35 Ibid., 1869.
36 Ibid., 1880.
37 Ibid., 1883.
38 Ibid.
39 Ibid., 1882.
40 Annual Report, Birmingham Ear Infirmary, 1894, BCLLS.
41 Annual Report, BEH, 1861, BCLLS, 1880–83.
42 Medical Committee Minutes, BEH, 1884–1900, BCLA, uncatalogued.

The Children's Hospital

Like the Eye Hospital, a medical institution for children was easily justified, and not only in Birmingham. The sheer number of children in society at this time appeared to justify the establishment of such hospitals, more than a third of the population of Victorian England being under the age of 14.[43] As a result, several such specialist institutions were founded across Britain in these years, children's hospitals being constructed in Dublin (1822), Liverpool (1851), London (1852) and Manchester (1853).[44] The fact that children were not always treated in general hospitals, given the likelihood of their transmitting fevers into these institutions, further justified the construction of separate children's hospitals. In general, many children were being treated by druggists or at home by their families, circumstances that were used by many nineteenth-century observers to explain the nation's very high infant mortality rate;[45] between one quarter and one half of all registered deaths were those of children.[46] These figures were used to justify the establishment of such an institution in Birmingham. Interestingly, it was the old eye infirmary at Steelhouse Lane that a local physician, Thomas Heslop, acquired in 1861 and transformed into a 16-bed hospital for children.[47]

Although described as a specialist hospital, the children's hospital was special in more ways than simply treating the town's youngest inhabitants. From the outset, control over administrative matters at the hospital was placed firmly in the hands of the institution's lay administrators.[48] The rules of the hospital also specified that all medical appointments came with restricted tenures in order that sought-after openings would regularly appear, and thereby allow more than a select group of medical practitioners the benefit of the hospital's clinical material.[49] It was also the town's first free hospital, patients desiring admission being expected to bring only a certificate signed by two local householders. The collection of certificates was ended a few years later in favour of a small regular fee, which was introduced in order to discourage trivial cases from daily filling the charity's waiting room and beds. Finally, as a result of such changes, it was also the first hospital in Birmingham to introduce systematic enquiries into the status of patients' families.

---

43   J. Walvin, *A Child's World: A Social History of English Childhood, 1800–1914* (Harmondsworth, 1982), p. 11.

44   E. Seidler, 'An historical survey of children's hospitals', in Granshaw and Porter (eds), *The Hospital in History*, p. 185; E.M.R. Lomax, *Small and Special: The Development of Hospitals for Children in Victorian Britain* (London, 1996), p. 15.

45   T.P. Heslop, *The Realities of Medical Attendance on the Sick Children of the Poor in Large Towns* (London, 1869).

46   Walvin, *A Child's World*, pp. 20–21; Pickstone, *Medicine and Industrial Society*, p. 54.

47   General Minutes, Birmingham Children's Hospital, 1861, BCLA, HC/BCH/1/2/1; R. Waterhouse, *Children in Hospital: a Hundred Years of Child Care in Birmingham* (London, 1962), pp. 24–5.

48   Waterhouse, *Children in Hospital*, pp. 26–7.

49   General Minutes, Birmingham Children's Hospital (hereafter BCH), 1861–70, BCLA, HC/BCH/1/2/1.

Compared with all other early specialist hospitals, the growth of the Children's Hospital was impressive. Though some local practitioners doubted the need for such an institution, by 1863, staff were treating almost 8,000 children annually, most coming from Birmingham and its adjoining neighbourhoods. Most individuals were treated as out-patients, some as in-patients and others in their homes.[50] As a result, a considerable amount of work was carried out at an institution that had only 22 beds in 1865, a tenth of the number found at the General in this year.[51] Unlike the Eye Hospital, these beds were almost always full. According to its governors, the numbers of patients staff treated was 'unparalleled in the history of any British Hospital, either for adults or children'.[52] In 1868, numbers were set to expand with the construction of a new out-patient building at Steelhouse Lane, in- and out-patient facilities having been separated in order to prevent the spread of infectious diseases.[53] Two years later, this partition was reinforced when a new 40-bed hospital for in-patients was opened on Broad Street, in a building that had previously been a lying-in hospital until the late 1860s.[54] A year later, in 1871, following additional expansion, beds numbered 55.[55] Though late to appear, the institution had become the town's third largest hospital in terms of patient numbers by 1873.

Much of this growth was due to the adoption of the free principle, which, despite improving access to the charity, threw up many unexpected obstacles. To begin with, in order to cope with excess demand, patient numbers were initially restricted to 30 a day. Based on the distribution of notes from householders, this system broke down almost immediately as persons of every class in the vicinity of the hospital signed notes for anyone who presented them. According to hospital managers, a '[w]ant of trustfulness of individuals in this stratum of society renders it impossible to frame any regulations that can be effective for their exclusion'.[56] As a result, precautions were instituted to ensure that only the deserving poor gained treatment at the hospital. Given that paupers generally could not afford a charge, this now involved detecting only those patients able to pay for treatment.

Originally intended to last six months, the precautions – which involved the dispenser enquiring into the incomes of patients' parents – proved so effective that investigations were continued indefinitely.[57] Though figures of hospital abuse were not immediately conveyed by governors in annual reports, a single anecdote concerning such enquiries was included in the hospital's publicity material in 1864. In this instance, the chair of the annual meeting recounted observing a woman who regularly accompanied her child to hospital, on one occasion arriving in a cab. When he told her this was wrong, the woman 'seemed astonished, and implored him not to mention it to the surgeon'.[58]

---

50 Annual Report, BCH, 1863, BCLA, HC/BCH/1/14/1.
51 Ibid., 1863; Annual Report, GHB, 1865, GHB 419.
52 Annual Report, BCH, 1863, BCLA, HC/BCH/1/14/1.
53 Ibid., 1868, BCLA, HC/BCH/1/14/2.
54 Ibid., 1870, BCLA, HC/BCH/1/14/2.
55 Ibid., 1871, BCLA, HC/BCH/1/14/2.
56 General Minutes, BCH, 1861–70, BCLA, HC/BCH/1/2/1.
57 Ibid.
58 Annual Report, BCH, 1864, BCLA, HC/BCH/1/14/1.

Though this account was intended to imply that the hospital's administrators had uncovered considerable evidence of abuse, the information collected by hospital staff soon began to shed more light on patients' backgrounds and dispelled such simplistic notions. Instead of abuse, figures reveal much poverty and neglect among local families. For example, of 215 children brought to the institution in 1862, 101 had never previously applied to the hospital, while 76 had only obtained the services of a druggist.[59] Far more surprisingly, only 15 had ever seen a medical man before coming to the hospital, two having seen both a surgeon and druggist. Of the remaining children, ten had been to a workhouse or dispensary, while another ten had attended similar public institutions, as well as a medical man; the remaining child had been to a public institution and a druggist. A further survey conducted in 1866 reveals that these trends changed only slowly. Of another 100 children brought to the Children's Hospital in this year, 90 had never before received medical attendance.[60]

Previous to the introduction of such inquiries, however, opportunities for staff members to familiarize themselves with patients' circumstances had existed. For example, from the charity's launch, the hospital's governors had introduced a system of home visiting, which was deemed essential by the charity's founder to uncover the reasons for childhood disease.[61] Besides providing opportunities to inspect patients' homes and neighbourhoods, home visits were ideal opportunities for house surgeons to investigate patients' financial circumstances. For example, in 1862, the house surgeon visited 47 patients a number of times in the first three months of the year. During the next two quarters he repeatedly visited another 94 patients.[62] While many children were visited at home when suffering from infectious ailments, others were visited when the hospital did not have any free beds or if parents refused to leave their children at the hospital. On average, numbers of domiciliary cases tended to decline in the summer months.

In the last quarter of 1866, home patients had increased dramatically, reaching 348, more than seven times the figure recorded four years earlier; in general, each case was visited five times by medical staff.[63] Cases continued to escalate in 1869, especially when a house surgeon, unfamiliar with his duties, visited far more children at home, leading in-patient numbers for some months to decline.[64] By 1874, however, the hospital had become so crowded that home visits were many patients' only option for obtaining care.[65] Four years later, a registrar was appointed to take over full responsibility of patient records, as well as home visits.[66] A similar appointment had been made at the Manchester Children's Hospital, where home patients surpassed 1,000.[67] A year after the creation of this post in Birmingham, however, the officer

59   Medical Committee Minutes, BCH, 1861–68, BCLA, HC/BCH/1/4/1.
60   Ibid.
61   General Minutes, BCH, 1861–70, BCLA, HC/BCH/1/2/1.
62   Annual Report, BCH, 1862, BCLA, HC/BCH/1/14/1.
63   Ibid., 1865.
64   Ibid., 1869, BCLA, HC/BCH/1/14/2.
65   Ibid., 1874.
66   Ibid., 1878, BCLA, HC/BCH/1/14/3.
67   Lomax, *Small and Special*, p. 92.

had made only a single visit, and, in 1888, home visits numbered only 44.[68] Reaching 72 in 1889, domiciliary cases again declined to 22 in 1890.[69] In the last decade of the century, hospital annual reports recorded only 12 more home visits before the practice was terminated.[70] Generally, most children's hospitals in these years gave up home visiting because of the expenses involved, as well as opposition from hospital and general physicians, who believed it interfered with private practice.[71]

There were, of course, other ways of obtaining information about patients. Some information regarding patients' backgrounds had always been acquired by nurses, whose greater numbers at children's hospitals often permitted them to become more familiar with patients.[72] However, many more nurses at all local hospitals were coming to Birmingham from outside the region and were, consequently, far less familiar with the local families they nursed than had been the case in previous years.[73] Other links with patients were strengthened through the establishment of a Samaritan Fund, which in the case of the Children's Hospital had been helping needy patients buy surgical instruments and appliances since 1875.[74] Each year, the fund relieved between 30 and 90 patients, though the majority were simply provided with transport to convalescent homes in these years, in which case their homes were never visited. Nevertheless, one of the Fund's reports in 1913, following visits to 93 homes, claimed that many parents could provide little more than a 'bed without bed clothes, and a soap box for the baby'. Perhaps this encouraged medical staff at the Children's Hospital to resume home visits in 1917.[75]

Despite the obvious need for medical care locally, inquiries throughout the late nineteenth century reveal that a number of children continued to be turned away from the hospital each year for various reasons, including the family's ability to pay for treatment Table 7.2. This alone appears to suggest that the hospital initially served more than just the 'deserving' poor. [76] In 1885, all such cases accounted for more than 10 per cent of inpatients, compared with figures at the General, which remained between 1 and 2 per cent.[77] However, while many patients at the Children's Hospital were being rejected for reasons related to family income, many more were not admitted to hospital for other reasons. For example, many children were simply too old, regulations having specified that no one over the age of ten was to be admitted to the hospital, though here, too, exceptions were often made.[78] Many parents refused to admit their children to hospital, while other children were simply 'rejected' with no

68   Annual Report, BCH, 1879, BCLA, HC/BCH/1/14/3.
69   Ibid., 1889–90, BCLA, HC/BCH/1/14/5.
70   Ibid., 1900, BCLA, HC/BCH/1/14/7.
71   Lomax, *Small and Special*, p. 12.
72   Ibid., p. 20.
73   S. Wildman, 'Fitness for practice, fitness for purpose: the changing nature of hospital nursing in the West Midlands, 1841–1914', in J. Reinarz (ed.), *Medicine and Society in the Midlands, 1750–1950* (forthcoming).
74   Annual Report, BCH, 1875, BCLA, HC/BCH/1/14/3.
75   Ibid., 1913, BCLA, HC/BCH/1/14/8.
76   Ibid.
77   Ibid.
78   Lomax, *Small and Special*, p. 43.

other details relating to the case being recorded. More often, parents sought medical attention for their children, but only as out-patients, refusing doctors' suggestions that their children be admitted as in-patients. In addition, very few children ever came to the hospital from outside Birmingham. Unlike the Eye Hospital, the Children's Hospital had always treated primarily local children. Nevertheless, as at the General, rules appear to have been flexible. Post-mortem records, for example, demonstrate that children older than ten were on occasion admitted to hospital.[79] At other times, however, staff refused to compromise. This was always the case when investigations uncovered children suffering from contagious fevers, which could spread to the rest of inmates and threaten an entire institution with closure. As a result, in the last years of the nineteenth century, the contagious nature of a case – as opposed to its deserving nature – more often determined whether a child would or would not be admitted to a children's hospital. Nevertheless, the numbers of children refused treatment at all children's hospitals in these years became insignificant in comparison to the numbers that were being admitted.[80]

Table 7.2 Children's Hospital, Birmingham: Patients rejected 1885–1900

Year	Patients rejected	Too old	Could pay	Contagious	Children not brought	Refused advice	Other
1885	92	34	34	3	4		17
1886	114	30	55				29
1887	67	7	28	14			18
1888	84	19	34	8			23
1889	114	16	33	26			39
1890	84	11	27	10			36
1891	68	9	32	2		7	18
1892	97	15	44	15			23
1893	68	8	15	38			7
1894	57	12	19	10			16
1895	88	38	19	14			17
1896	289	48	18	183			40
1897	99	18	25	25			31
1898	66	14	11	22			19
1899	60	6	10	26			18
1900	112	37	8	49			18

Source: BCLA, Children's Hospital, Annual Reports, 1885–1900, HC/BCH/1/14/5–7.

---

79 Post-mortem Report Book, BCH, 1862–1878, BCLA, HC/BCH/3/6/1.
80 Lomax, *Small and Special*, p. 50.

The Women's Hospital

Founded only a decade after the Children's Hospital, the Women's Hospital was Birmingham's sixth specialist institution.[81] Like the Eye Hospital, it started as a small dispensary in the middle of Birmingham in 1871. But unlike this institution, its governors were quicker to establish in-patient facilities, providing four free and four paying beds at the charity's launch for the use of women suffering from diseases of the pelvic organs.[82] In general, pelvic surgery was rarely attempted at any voluntary hospitals at this time. When an ovariotomy was attempted at the General in the early 1850s, its necessity was questioned and the incident developed into a scandal.[83] As a result, in subsequent years, the town's general hospitals tended to confine themselves to maternity cases. Had they not done so, their death rates would inevitably have escalated, which in turn would have affected subscription levels. At the Women's Hospital, however, such cases were regularly treated, often with little success. The death rate for ovariotomy cases between 1871 and 1877, for example, ranged between 30 and 100 per cent annually.[84] Though one might have expected the charity's popularity to have suffered, the staff's openness with even their poorest results, not to mention the desperate state of their patients, helped them retain a certain amount of public support and allowed surgeons, in time, to break new ground in their respective field.

Despite initially reporting poor results, the hospital's board soon acquired the funds from a local benefactress, Louisa Ryland, to extend the charity and purchased another, larger, building at Sparkhill, a few miles outside the town centre. In 1878, an enlarged hospital with 21 beds was opened, while out-patients attended a clinic in Upper Priory, erected in the same year. A year later, its medical officers at Sparkhill treated 162 patients, and the number rose to 236 in 1880.[85] Unlike the town's other medical charities, the Women's Hospital would not establish its reputation as a result of the numbers of patients cured or relieved. Its status was based entirely on other achievements. As at the original institution, sheds were erected in the new hospital's garden where the charity's surgeons, Lawson Tait and Thomas Savage, continued to perform and perfect ovariotomies.[86] Whereas mortality was high for early operations due to poor hygiene, death rates following the risky procedure rapidly dropped from 20 per cent in the late 1870s to 9 per cent in 1881;[87] the latter figure remained

---

81   These were, with the years in which they were founded, the Orthopaedic (1817), Eye (1823), Ear (1844), Dental (1858), Children's (1861) and Women's (1871) hospitals.

82   Governors' Minutes, Birmingham Women's Hospital (hereafter BWH), 1871–92, BCLA, HC/WH/1/1/1.

83   T. Gutteridge, *The Crisis: another warning addressed to the governors* [General Hospital, Birmingham], (Birmingham: privately printed, 1851).

84   Medical Board Minutes, BWH, 1871–1892, BCLA, HC/WH/1/5/1.

85   Ibid.

86   Ibid.

87   Annual Report, BWH, 1881, BCLA, HC/WH/1/10/3. Difficulties were creating an aseptic environment as opposed to an antiseptic one. Medical staff at the Women's did not use carbolic spray as suggested by Lister, but relied on a perfectly sanitary environment, as well as short incisions. Sometimes the hospital and equipment were not clean, other times their hands

the hospital's average death rate in these years, with staff performing more than 120 abdominal sections annually. Largely as a result of this very positive recovery rate, Tait went on to acquire an international reputation over the next decade, and desperate patients began to travel to the hospital from great distances. Meanwhile, the hospital's death rate continued to decline, reaching 1.4 per cent in 1892.[88]

Compared with the town's other medical charities, the Women's Hospital served a broader class base. While other voluntary hospitals catered for the 'deserving' poor, the Women's Hospital was intended for the wives and daughters of artisans and semi-skilled workers, as well as women who supported themselves, usually as governesses or servants.[89] Such women, it was thought, while often unable to afford private treatment, were far more reluctant to seek advice from a general hospital for reasons of delicacy, not to mention respectability. A similar view was expressed by one of the hospital's founders, Arthur Chamberlain, who claimed that 'women labouring under special maladies are particularly reticent and prefer to suffer, perhaps for years, rather than seek advice when they are exposed so publicly as in the waiting room and consulting room of a general hospital'.[90] Clearly, to overcome such attitudes, staff at the Women's Hospital had to cultivate a different environment from other voluntary hospitals. For example, in order to encourage women's attendance it was decided to dispense with the usual practice whereby subscribers were given 'tickets' to distribute among 'proper' subjects of relief, a system that was regarded as distasteful by the hospital's governors.[91] By abandoning such policies, governors hoped to spare women 'the labour and pain of a journey around the town'. In particular, it was deemed undesirable that women should have to explain their complaints to anyone but a medical gentleman.[92] As a result, a policy of open access to the out-patient department was adopted, whilst patients seeking admission to the hospital were to be selected by medical staff on the basis of clinical need.

The staff's success at attracting pelvic cases was equally due to the atmosphere on the hospital wards.[93] Visitors to the institution regularly spoke of the comfortable arrangements they found, one male visitor adding that 'one of the most pleasing features in connection with it was that ladies had a share of the management'.[94] Those who visited the wards noted that 'such was their comfort that they scarcely conveyed the idea of a hospital. The walls were decorated with pictures, there were white dainty curtains for the beds, and sofas for the convalescents ... everything reminded

---

were not quite clean, occasionally nurses were working in other wards and also assisting at operations and brought germs into the operating room. Eventually, everything was cleaned more carefully and assistants at operations did nothing but prepare the operating theatre and clean.

88 Ibid., 1892, BCLA, HC/WH/1/10/4.

89 Governors' Minutes, BWH, 1871–92, BCLA, HC/WH/1/1/1.

90 Annual Report, BWH, 1872, BCLA, HC/WH 1/10/1.

91 Ibid.

92 Ibid., Appendix 1.

93 For more on the hospital's work, see J. Lockhart, '"Truly, a hospital for women": the Birmingham and Midland Hospital for Women, 1871–1901' in Reinarz (ed.), *Medicine and Society in the Midlands*.

94 Annual Report, BWH, 1872, BCLA, HC/WH 1/10/1.

rather of the comforts of home'.[95] A further departure from the model of earlier voluntary hospitals was the comparatively relaxed disciplinary regime, visitors finding little evidence of the strict code of behaviour imposed at some institutions. Neither did they encounter a desire to combine physical healing with moral guidance, as was evident at the Hospital for Women, Soho Square, London, where patients were subjected to 'a disciplinary regime that bore a striking resemblance to the training of repenting prostitutes in Magdalen Institutions'.[96] Nor would one expect to discover such conditions at an institution that aimed to attract artisans', as opposed to labourers', wives.

In any event, the hospital proved very successful at attracting women in great numbers from all social backgrounds. Unlike the Eye Hospital, however, it had only a few – albeit influential – subscribers. Consequently, in the charity's first year, the governors already reported that expenditure on drugs and medical appliances exceeded available resources.[97] Initially, they had introduced a policy of free consultation and treatment in the out-patient department, but, to ease the financial pressure, a decision was made to introduce a fee of a shilling on a patient's first visit. As at other hospitals, this was intended to discourage both the 'pauper classes for whom satisfactory provision is made' and those who 'from their position ... ought to apply for assistance at private consulting rooms'.[98] This had the desired effect of reducing some of the 'abuses', notably the number of women attending the hospital whose complaints were not of a gynaecological nature. But the hospital's finances failed to improve. As a result, a paying ward, much as had existed at Chelsea Hospital for Women since 1869, was advertised as early as September 1873.[99] In the remaining three months of the year, 13 private patients were treated at the institution, and another 30 the following year.[100]

Patients were also screened more carefully by staff in order to determine their financial status. However, the ladies charged with drawing up guidelines, most of whom, unlike staff at other institutions, were the wives of middle-class, male subscribers, pointed to the difficulties of conducting such investigations. They argued that a 'patient's earnings had to be considered in relation to her general circumstances, the length of time she had been ill, the acuteness or reverse of her disorder, the number of children etc'.[101] Thus, each case required careful consideration, for it was impossible to lay down hard and fast rules, even for the labouring poor. For example, 'a pauper woman – a widow for instance – might be obliged from the fact of her illness to receive out-door relief while unwilling to go into a poor-house for treatment – or her parish doctor might certify that she required a more careful regime and

---

95   Ibid.

96   O. Moscucci, *The Science of Women: Gynaecology and Gender in England, 1800–1929* (Cambridge, 1990), p. 88.

97   Governors' Minutes, BWH, 1871–92, BCLA, HC/WH/1/1/1.

98   Annual Report, BWH, 1872, BCLA, HC/WH/1/10/1.

99   Moscucci, *The Science of Woman*, p. 93. The new wing at Chelsea was the first pay block in the British Isles.

100 Annual Report, BWH, 1873, BCLA, HC/WH/1/10/1.

101 Ibid.

nursing and more special appliances than he could ensure her'.[102] Initially carried out by surgeons, such enquiries were assigned to a female dispenser in 1879. By 1882, enquiries were being undertaken by the managing committee.[103] Rejections peaked at 667 in 1873, but soon averaged 7 per cent of annual admissions. Meanwhile, the division between paying and charity cases was reinforced in 1890, when the registration fee was raised to 2s. 6d.

While discouraging improper cases from attending the charity, hospital staff put as much energy into encouraging patients to attend regularly at the institution, given the ground-breaking work they were undertaking. In the charity's first decades, however, staff found this a particularly difficult task – a reminder that patients, and not only staff, exercised considerable control over hospital use in these years. For example, of 400 outpatients seen in 1872, 46 attended only once, and 42 twice only.[104] As a result, in the opinion of the hospital surgeons, 88 women 'failed to become patients in reality'.[105] In such cases, the time spent on such patients had been 'utterly wasted'. For the remainder of the century, the surgeon Tait regularly pleaded with governors to follow up patients after their release from hospital, as occurred at other institutions in London and Manchester. However, such measures were expensive and hard to organize, as many patients needed two or three years fully to recover and staff easily lost track of women in this age of high mobility. With little improvement in hospital finances during these years, Tait regretfully conceded that information concerning patients could never be complete. Clearly, the establishment of measures to investigate patients, while intended to protect charitable funds, equally entailed the expenditure of vital resources, something many smaller specialist institutions, such as the Women's Hospital, were reluctant to do. Consequently, it would be in one of the town's larger, well-funded general hospitals that such experiments would be taken furthest.

The Queen's Hospital

Throughout the nineteenth century, medical students had regularly walked the wards of local hospitals in order to supplement the lessons learned during very practical periods of apprenticeship. If not actually attending local hospitals, most pupils in Birmingham continued to travel to London for the purposes of obtaining additional clinical training and qualifications, even after the foundation of a local medical school in 1825. Like that of its medical students, the success of Birmingham's medical school depended on access to clinical cases and on financial support; the latter was provided by a particularly generous donor, albeit with strings attached, in 1838.[106] Clinical cases, on the other hand, became available when the Queen's Hospital opened its 70 beds to patients in 1841. It has been suggested that it was the

102 Ibid.

103 Ibid., 1882, HC/WH/1/10/3.

104 Ibid., 1872, BCLA, HC/WH/1/10/1.

105 Ibid.

106 J. Reinarz, 'Healthcare and the Second City: the development of the Birmingham teaching hospitals in the nineteenth century', *Birmingham Historian*, 26 (2004): 16–27.

first purpose-built teaching hospital in England.[107] More certain is that it was the first hospital in Birmingham dedicated to medical instruction. It was also very different from the town's other hospitals, with the exception of the General, in that it did not operate out of a building that was originally constructed for non-medical purposes.

It also grew more quickly than the town's other voluntary hospitals. In 1845, it received its first significant addition when a 28-bed fever ward was added to the building.[108] While this enhanced the charity's services to the community considerably, its central location also ensured the hospital received a disproportionate number of accident cases. Unlike other medical institutions, it, and the medical school with which it was associated, was run like a private business, many of its rules and regulations being flaunted by the hospital's primary consulting surgeon, William Sands Cox. Initially, this did not appear to hinder its development. By 1852, the number of beds at the institution had more than doubled, reaching 150, approximately 100 less than were found at the General.[109]

Over the next few years, however, the reputation of Cox's medical school did begin to decline as the surgeon and his allies attempted to transform the institution into what resembled an Anglican college. By 1864, members of the public actively intervened in the project's management and the relationship between Queen's College and its teaching hospital was finally dissolved following an investigation by the Charity Commissioners, who condemned the way in which both school and hospital were run. Moreover, in 1868, following additional investigations and negotiations, the hospital and medical school were legally separated, while the town's two medical schools merged, signalling the start of a new, dynamic period for medical education in Birmingham.[110]

Change was apparent from the outset. Records at hospital and school were finally properly kept and both institutions were run according to rules and regulations rather than the whims of founders and key donors. Moreover, meetings, formerly private affairs, were now held at the Council House and thrown open to the public. As a result of this inclusive policy, besides regaining the confidence of Birmingham's dissenting community, the school became more popular with both students and the public. The hospital, in turn, remained very popular with the town's labourers as it continued to treat many workplace accidents. In appreciation of this work, an Artisan's Fund had been founded as early as 1846 by a Mr S. Bradley, local workers donating nearly £1,000 to the institution the following year.[111] Thereafter, in the eyes of Birmingham's workmen, it became the town's premier voluntary hospital. Over the next two decades, one third of all patients treated at the institution were accident cases. When a finance committee was established in 1869, it also informed staff that two-thirds of patients were admitted to hospital free of charge and additional funds

---

107 V. Thomas, *An address upon laying the foundation-stone of the Queen's Hospital, Birmingham, June 18, 1840* (Oxford: W. Baxter, 1840), pp. 21–22.

108 Annual Report, Queen's Hospital, Birmingham (hereafter QHB), 1852, BCLLS.

109 Ibid.; Annual Report, GHB, 1852, BCLLS.

110 J.T.J. Morrison, *William Sands Cox and the Birmingham Medical School* (Birmingham, 1926), pp. 119–33.

111 Annual Report, QHB, 1853–4, BCLLS.

were required for further expansion.[112] With the help of certain influential inhabitants, including one of the hospital's surgeons, Sampson Gamgee, the Artisan's Fund was developed into the Hospital Saturday Fund, which initially paid for an additional wing at the Queen's Hospital in 1873 and thereafter financed many important developments at local hospitals.[113] In appreciation of this significant financial contribution, 20 working men were appointed life governors to the institution.[114]

Perhaps inspired by the Children's Hospital, in February 1873 the managing committee at the Queen's Hospital first expressed a desire more accurately to determine how many of the hospital's patients could pay for medical treatment.[115] Instead of adding to their secretary's duties, however, the governors invited the aid of the local Mendicity Society to investigate patients. While serious accidents and acute cases would continue to be admitted with no enquiry into the social fitness of patients, the admission of all other individuals was determined by their income and the size of their family.[116] In June 1873, after a few months of careful investigation, the Society presented its report to the hospital's finance committee. In its summary, only two of the 365 cases inquired into were said to have refused information; 33 gave false addresses; six received parish relief; 62 cases were judged 'obviously unsuitable', and several others were of 'less obvious unfitness', leaving 253 legitimate cases, or 69 per cent of the sample.[117] Satisfied with the report, which had armed the committee with much useful knowledge, and convinced that abuse could be managed, the Queen's Hospital's house committee advised the introduction of a free system, which took effect in January 1876. Enquiries were to continue, but would now be carried out by hospital almoners in an office in the out-patient department. As predicted, a decline in subscriptions followed, given that the hospital no longer offered subscribers the right to recommend patients, but this amounted to less than £40, while registration fees brought in approximately £400 annually.[118] As importantly, medical officers had gained greater control over the admissions procedure.

In the following years, it was argued that a small registration fee, alongside careful interviews on admission, was enough to discourage trivial cases from filling the hospital's waiting room (Table 7.3). As evidence, the governors commissioned another study, this time managed by the Charity Organisation Society (COS), to determine the existence of non-charity cases. Of the total number of patients coming to the hospital in 1877, 2.3 per cent had been refused admission.[119] A decade later, this had declined to little more than 0.8 per cent, which remained the rejection rate

112 Ibid., 1869.

113 Ibid., 1873.

114 General Committee Minutes, QHB, 1870–72, BCLA, HC/QU/1/1/1.

115 Ibid., 1873, BCLA, HC/QU/1/1/2.

116 House Committee Minutes, QHB, 1874–6, BCLA, HC/QU/1/2/6.

117 General Committee Minutes, Queen's Hospital, Birmingham, 1872–6, BCLA, HC/QU/1/1/2; see also R. Humphreys, *Sin, Organised Charity and the Poor Law in Victorian England* (London, 1995), p. 95.

118 Annual Report, QHB, 1873, BCLLS.

119 House Committee Minutes, QHB, 1876–9, BCLA, HC/QU/1/2/7.

Table 7. 3 Queen's Hospital, Birmingham: Patients rejected 1877–1900

Year	Patients rejected	Able to pay	Medically unfit	Parishes cases	Refused treatment
1877	378	236	81	55	6
1878	778	390	342	44	2
1879	671	438	207	21	5
1880	660	409	225	23	3
1881	332	215	90	27	
1882	239	175	49	15	
1883	111	76	23	12	
1884	79	31	22	26	
1885	170	71	75	24	
1886	200	89	96	15	
1887	226	113	95	18	
1888	286	136	124	26	
1889	291	113	168	10	
1890	252	109	126	17	
1891	190	100	85	5	
1892	247	132	104	11	
1893	303	174	120	9	
1894	312	165	141	6	
1895	243	106	134	3	
1896	342	188	154		
1897	307	181	126		
1898	240	111	129		
1899	179	70	109		
1900	246	119	97		30

Source: Annual Reports, Queen's Hospital, Birmingham, 1877–1900, BCLLS.

until the end of the century.[120] Nevertheless, 46 per cent of out-patients were still received free of charge for fear of turning away any urgent cases. Hospital staff were equally concerned not to turn away any labourers who contributed to the Hospital Saturday Fund, which had become the main source of the hospital's finance. As at a number of other provincial hospitals, the Queen's Hospital had progressively become a form of providential institution, where workmen were treated as of right.[121] Not surprisingly, governors claimed the registration system at the hospital was in no way 'inquisitorial'. Questions were put in a 'kindly and delicate way', for fear of offending the hospital's key donors.[122] Though the institution's annual

120 Ibid., 1887–93, BCLA, HC/QU/1/2/10.

121 Pickstone, *Medicine and Industrial Society*, p. 144.

122 Annual Report, QHB, 1882, BCLLS.

report in 1883 claimed no dishonesty was possible without certain detection given the institution's new regime, staff appeared to be referring only to the detection of paupers, rather than patients who could pay for medical treatment. Most patients were paying towards the cost of treatment, which not only contributed to Hospital Saturday's financial stability, but led to the inauguration of several similar schemes across the country.[123] Interestingly, systematic enquiry into the social circumstances of patients at the General Hospital commenced in 1898.[124] However, given the cost of such thorough investigations, not to mention a dislike of outside interference from organizations like the COS,[125] these methods were not introduced to many small specialist hospitals in these years.

Conclusion

Compared with the Queen's Hospital in the late Victorian period, staff at the General Hospital in the early nineteenth century were relatively unfamiliar with the financial status of their patients. To begin with, many patients initially came from outside Birmingham and were unknown to both medical officers and nurses. As such, most medical officers got to know in-patients only after they were admitted to the hospital's wards. Though each subscriber's mode of enquiry remains obscure, it is fair to assume that methods varied in the extreme. While this occasionally led hospitals to admit poorly screened patients, these were often subsequently ejected, usually after breaking one of many hospital rules. In most cases medical officers, given their infrequent appearance on hospital wards, would have required considerable time to familiarize themselves with patients.

At the town's first specialist institution, medical officers at the Eye Hospital were no more familiar with patients, as most tended to be out-patients until the 1850s. As most patients contributed to the already low costs of treatment, incentives to investigate any existing abuse did not exist, especially as the charity's main competition was regarded to comprise unqualified oculists. Incentives further declined as hospital funds grew more quickly than patients throughout the century. Instead, governors concentrated on the identities of patients' employers, in order to canvass potential subscribers more effectively. In this way, however, staff at many eye hospitals developed the skills of enquiry that would eventually be used to investigate patients in the twentieth century.[126]

Not all specialist hospitals, however, were so slow to enquire into the status of their patients, especially those founded in the years when 'compassion withered

123 S. Cherry, 'Hospital Saturday, Workplace Collections and Issues in late Nineteenth-Century Hospital Funding', Medical History, 44, 4 (2000): 461–88.

124 Annual Report, GHB, 1898, BCLA, GHB 432.

125 Lomax, Small and Special, pp. 10, 55; Humphreys, Sin, Organised Charity and the Poor Law, p. 115.

126 E.T. Collins, The History & Traditions of the Moorfields Eye Hospital: One hundred years of ophthalmic discovery & development (London, 1929), p. 179.

away with thoughts of charitable abuse'.[127] At the Children's Hospital, for example, hospital staff enquired into the financial status of patients soon after the institution's foundation in 1861. Though unfeasible at other institutions, this was easier when the majority of patients came from the town in which the hospital was located, few parents at this time sending their children to distant hospitals. Medical staff were therefore more familiar with those benefiting from their charity, especially as their work often involved visiting patients in their homes. To some extent, knowledge of patients had always been satisfactory here, given the greater proportion of nurses to patients at all children's hospitals.[128] However, as a rapid increase in patient numbers and shorter lengths of stay in the late nineteenth century made such tasks more difficult, staff became more reliant on systematic enquiries into patients' circumstances.

The Women's Hospital offers yet another very different model. Although individuals, as at the Eye Hospital, came from outside the Birmingham region in order to access the medical services of this particular institution's renowned staff, patients at many women's hospitals were not drawn exclusively from the labouring poor. Unlike other specialist hospitals, the Women's Hospital offered a particularly specialized form of care, unavailable at private practices, let alone many other voluntary hospitals. Consequently, in order to satisfy the needs of desperate women suffering from life-threatening conditions such as ovarian cancer, staff welcomed paying patients far earlier than at the town's other hospitals. Though this decision, among other things, improved information concerning patients, influenced the hospital environment and led staff to dispense with the harsh disciplinary regime found at other institutions, staff continued to face earlier difficulties, especially when it came to monitoring the progress of cases, as patients here, as elsewhere, came and went as they pleased. Collecting the personal details of patients, especially when widely distributed, cost money, which many small specialist hospitals often could not spare.

Though charitable abuse no doubt existed at all of Birmingham's hospitals, staff at the Queen's Hospital were less hesitant to invest in the investigation of patients. In all cases, however, saving money through the introduction of such measures meant spending it first. As one would expect, much abuse was found, though rarely did rejections surpass 2 per cent of admissions, a figure that would have pleased donors. Perhaps convincing staff at other hospitals that charitable abuse was not as widespread as some members of the community originally believed, such figures may have further delayed systematic investigation at Birmingham's other medical charities. Over the last three decades of the nineteenth century, however, Birmingham's labouring classes also became the hospital's primary donors. Consequently, the charity's governors found it increasingly difficult to enquire into the backgrounds of labouring patients, leading staff to concentrate on the elimination of pauper patients instead. Denying care to all those who could afford it had become almost impossible, as the Hospital Saturday Fund continued to evolve into a provident scheme, whereby members' contributions entitled them to medical care. Moreover, once members of

---

127 M. Simey, *Charity Rediscovered: a Study of Charitable Effort in Nineteenth-century Liverpool* (Liverpool, 1992), p. 83.

128 Lomax, *Small and Special*, p. 20.

the working class were granted representation on the hospital's board of governors, they finally acquired a voice in hospital matters.

As this should suggest, the ability of administrators to 'know' their patients did not necessarily improve their ability to control them. As a result, historians are right to doubt the existence of simple models of philanthropy which depict patients as little more than the passive recipients of charity.[129] By the end of the period with which this chapter is concerned, the lines between donor and recipient had begun to blur as donations from Birmingham's working community grew more quickly than all other sources. Perhaps there is more truth in a model that depicts voluntary hospitals as institutions run by passive donors, at least in their earliest years. Over the nineteenth century, however, as donors and staff became more active in the affairs of hospitals, either as committee members or as hospital visitors, their enquiries began to shed more light on patients, who, in Birmingham, if not the rest of England, had always actively shaped their experiences of health care.

---

129 P. Mandler, 'Poverty and Charity in the Nineteenth-Century Metropolis: An Introduction', in Mandler (ed.), *The Uses of Charity*, pp. 1–2.

CHAPTER EIGHT

Choice and the children's hospital: Great Ormond Street Hospital patients and their families 1855–1900

Andrea Tanner

Medical historians currently concerned about the patient's perspective on medical care have, by and large, ignored the child as institutionalized patient. This chapter addresses a hitherto neglected subject by looking at the relationship between the families of patients at a Victorian children's hospital, and the management and medical staff of the institution. In early Victorian Britain, the concept of establishing a special hospital for children found little favour among the charitable élite, as it directly challenged parental prerogative and responsibilities.[1] At the beginning of the twenty-first century, state and medical experts once more attest to the view that home and the family environment is preferable to a separate institution for the sick child.[2] Children's hospitals have given way to children's wards in general hospitals, and parents once more assert their rights to refuse state intervention in the health of their children, most notably with regard to vaccination.[3] In between, hospitalized children, removed from their domestic environment for considerable periods of time, and subject to increasingly technical treatment regimes, became a notable feature of medical life in Britain.

Childhood, poverty and sickness are familiar themes in Victorian historiography, but the three rarely appear together, except in the case of infectious disease.[4] While demographers have recently carved out a sub-discipline in examining infant mortality, the child who endured sickness but not premature death is found infrequently in anything but the unfashionable realm of institutional histories. And yet child disease was a preoccupation of the Victorians, and many of the Herculean efforts made in cities (and most especially in London) by the local authority departments of the Medical Officers of Health, by charities and by an increasingly sophisticated network of hospitals, were made precisely to ensure that sick children survived into adulthood. Equally, historians of poverty and charity have become preoccupied with

---

1   B. Abel-Smith, *The Hospitals 1800–1948* (London, 1964); E.M.R. Lomax, *Small and Special: the Development of Hospitals for Children in Victorian Britain* (Medical History Supplement no. 16, Wellcome Institute for the History of Medicine, London 1996).

2   A. Digby and J. Stewart, *Gender, Health and Welfare* (London, 1996).

3   J. Lewis, 'Gender and Welfare in the late 19th and early 20th centuries', in Digby and Stewart, *Gender, Health and Welfare*; B. Mayall, *Negotiating Health: Children at Home and Primary School* (London, 1994).

4   A. Hardy, *The Epidemic Streets: Infectious Disease and the Rise of Preventative Medicine, 1856–1900* (Oxford, 1993).

what might be termed the client base of the huge number of philanthropic agencies that operated in Britain.[5] Studies of the attitude of recipients of charity and Poor Law relief have in recent years rewritten the simplistic view that the relationship between benefactor and beneficiary was merely that of passive suppliant and controlling almsgiver. To date, however, little has been done on what Sandra Cavallo termed the 'gift relation' in the world of the Victorian voluntary hospital.[6]

Part of the great explosion in health and welfare in Victorian Britain was the creation of 31 children's hospitals for the offspring of the poor between 1852 and 1894.[7] The in-patients of these institutions received the best care that the funds of the hospital and the skills of the clinicians and nurses could give. They might also have had the opportunity to convalesce in the hospital's country branch before being returned to the domestic circumstances that were, by and large, the root cause of their illness in the first place.[8] The patients were the beneficiaries of a changing attitude towards the needs of children, and indeed towards childhood itself. According to Philippe Aries's thesis,[9] this is the time when childhood was recognized as a separate phase of existence, essentially different from adulthood. This 'discovery' has been identified with the Romantic view of childhood as promulgated in the works (a generation and more earlier) of Wordsworth and Blake, which was exploited by social reformers as an important vehicle for social protest and social change.[10] This theory has been challenged by Linda Pollock in her work on family relationships over three centuries, although she does concede that child welfare became increasingly a concern for state and philanthropic agencies in the late eighteenth and nineteenth centuries.[11] More recently, Carolyn Steedman has argued that in the early nineteenth century, childhood was a category of dependence, a term that defined certain relationships of powerlessness, submission and bodily inferiority or weakness. By 1900, childhood had become categorized as a definite time-span, and was increasingly becoming a legitimate area for state intervention and control.[12]

Children's hospitals in the United Kingdom in part developed from this growing concern for the child as a worthy recipient of attention in his or her own right, and

---

5   For example, T. Hitchcock, P. King and P. Sharpe (eds), *Chronicling Poverty: the Voices and Strategies of the English Poor, 1640–1840* (Basingstoke, 1997).

6   S. Cavallo, 'Charity, Power and patronage in eighteenth century Italian hospitals: the case of Turin', in L. Granshaw and R. Porter (eds), *The Hospital in History* (London, 1989), pp. 93–122.

7   Lomax, *Small and Special*, Table One, p. 178.

8   Convalescent homes became increasingly popular with children's health institutions; by 1890 there were nearly fifty such institutions in England and Wales. *The Charity Register and Digest: Convalescent Section* (London, 1890).

9   P. Aries, *Centuries of Childhood: A Social History of Family Life* (English edition, Harmondsworth, 1962).

10   P. Brown, *The Captured World: the Child and Childhood in 19th century Women's Writing in England* (London, 1993).

11   L. Pollock, *Forgotten Children: Parent-Child Relationships from 1500 to 1900* (Cambridge, 1983).

12   C. Steedman, *Strange Dislocations: Childhood and the Idea of Human Interiority 1780–1930* (London, 1995).

from the attendant sentimentalization of children, whether sick or well.[13] They benefited from increasing state intervention in the lives of its youngest citizens; by the date of their foundation in the 1850s and 1860s, children were being excluded from industrial environments by law; and London had seen the creation of several large pauper children's schools, where children were reared by the state, apart from their parents.[14] Children's bodies were now liable to surveillance through the school authorities, and childhood (at least, working-class childhood) was increasingly seen as a distinct period in the life of the individual during which both the state and medicine had the legitimate right of close observation and control.[15]

The process of acceptance of the child's world as being separate from the adult's, and the view that it was desirable to create specific structures to accommodate them, had already begun by the early 1850s.[16] Within a few years of the hospital's foundation in 1852, compulsory vaccination against smallpox and compulsory elementary education had been introduced. For its own good, the child's world was being separated from that of the adult, and what was more indicative of this separation than a hospital exclusively for children?

Thus it has been argued that the introduction of child-labour laws and compulsory education transformed the wage-earning 'non-child' of the labouring poor into the category of economically worthless child-scholar.[17] For the first time, the majority of children came to be appropriated into a neo-romantic middle-class ideal of childhood in which the child became economically useless and emotionally priceless – not just to their families, but to the state. In this argument, the development of the children's hospital, and of paediatric medicine, might be seen to be a consequence of western society's changing attitudes to the preservation and protection of the working-class child.[18] Those who created and ran the children's hospitals were convinced that

---

13   Keir Waddington has pointed out that the hospital exploited that attitude to childhood in its fundraising, *Charity and the London Hospitals, 1850–1898* (Woodbridge, 2000).

14   F. Duke, 'Pauper Education', in D. Fraser (ed.), *The New Poor Law in the Nineteenth Century* (London, 1976). For an extended consideration of the development of childhood as a separate state and time-span, see J. Walvin, *A Child's World: A Social History of English Childhood 1800–1914* (Harmondsworth, 1982).

15   D. Armstrong, *Political Anatomy of the Body: Medical Knowledge in Britain in the Twentieth Century* (Cambridge, 1983), pp. 13–14.

16   Pat Thane has argued that it began long before that, with the reduction in legally permissible hours of work for pauper children in 1802. See P. Thane, 'Childhood in History', in M. King (ed.), *Childhood, Welfare and Justice: a critical examination of children in the legal and childcare systems* (London, 1981), pp. 6–26.

17   V. Zelizer, *Pricing the Priceless Child* (New York, 1985). This argument does not take into account the fact that the vast majority of working-class parents chose to send their children to school for at least some of the time in the 80 years before compulsory elementary education. See T.W. Laqueur, 'Working-Class Demand and the Growth of English Elementary Education, 1750–1850', in L. Stone (ed.), *Schooling and Society: Studies in the History of Education* (Baltimore, 1976), pp. 193–200.

18   The studies to date focus on the 'medicalization' of childhood, principally through the medical services of the post-1872 universal elementary education system. Especially significant here is B. Harris, *The Health of the Schoolchild; a History of the School Medical Service in England and Wales* (Buckingham, 1995), as is Harry Hendrick's study of the

physical removal from the impure domestic environment, in which everything from the water and air to the bedding and language was polluted, would not only cure them, but would enable them become better citizens.[19] It might be imagined that the environment was attractive to a sick child, that poor parents would have been more than willing to leave their offspring there for as long as possible, and that return to the cramped and dirty conditions of home life would be unwelcome.[20] In exchange, perhaps parents and children would be bound to respectful obedience, or, at least, compliance, to the dictums of the medical professionals, who determined the length and nature of the child's hospitalization. However, a study of children removed prematurely from one children's hospital indicates that the families and friends of young patients did exercise choice and control over both the duration of their time in hospital and the nature of the treatment given to them.

Great Ormond Street Hospital

The material for this study comes from the Hospital for Sick Children, Great Ormond Street (GOSH), in London, the first successful paediatric hospital in Britain. As with many specialist hospitals, it owed its existence to the vision and ambition of a single physician, Charles West, who had trained in London, France and Germany, and who had been associated with the Children's Dispensary in Waterloo Road for ten years.[21] When he could not persuade the governors of that institution to open up wards for in-patients, he resigned his post and spent several years visiting children's hospitals in Europe and recruiting both medical and philanthropic support for his projected hospital.[22] Charles West's trump card when arguing for the necessity for establishing a children's hospital was the appalling mortality among children between the ages of two and 15. In 1850, while only 3 per cent of hospital in-patients were children, over 50 per cent of the deaths in London were among the under 15s.[23]

The stated objects of the institution in 1852 were threefold. The primary aim was the medical and surgical treatment of poor children, with medical advice offered

---

development of child welfare services after the Education Act; see H. Hendrick, 'Child labour, medical capital and the school medical service c.1890–1918', in R. Cooter, *Child Welfare, England 1872–1989* (London, 1994).

19   J. Golden (ed.), *Infant Asylums and Children's Hospitals: Medical Dilemmas and Developments 1850–1920* (New York and London, 1989), Introduction.

20   Hospital fundraisers stressed the appalling domestic squalor of the patients' normal environment in fundraising. 'Report of 16th Anniversary Festival' (1868) Great Ormond Street Hospital (hereafter GOSH) Archive, GOS/14/1. For Charles West's career, see N.G. Coley, 'Charles West 1816–1898', *Oxford Dictionary of National Biography* (Oxford, 2004) doi:10.1093/ref:odnb/29077.

21   L. Granshaw, '"Fame and Fortune by Means of Bricks and Mortar": the Medical Profession and Specialist Hospitals in Britain, 1800–1948', in Granshaw and Porter (eds), *The Hospital in History*.

22   J. Kosky, *Mutual Friends: Charles Dickens and Great Ormond Street Hospital* (London, 1989), pp. 30–55.

23   *Appeal to the Public in Behalf of A Hospital for Sick Children*, 1851, GOS/8/1 and GOS/14/1.

to those not admitted to the institution. The second object was the attainment and diffusion of knowledge regarding the diseases of children and the improvement of teaching with regard to childhood diseases. Lastly, the hospital's founders sought to train nurses for sick children, and to educate all classes in the management of sick children.[24] Although inspired by European institutions, it was a very English establishment; small in size, open only to the children of the poor, and supported entirely by voluntary contributions. Its primary purpose was to treat the sick children of the poor, and not – as in continental Europe – to provide research facilities for clinicians.[25] The rules of the hospital demanded good behaviour from the patients and imposed strictly limited visiting hours on their families (although not on wealthy supporters), which might imply that patients and their parents were passive recipients of the hospital's attention and were expected to conform to a rigid set of standards in return for free treatment.[26] Failure to conform to the hospital's rules was punished by withdrawal of treatment and removal from the wards of what was (for a short time) the only children's hospital in Britain.[27] However, the use that the Victorian poor made of the hospital suggests that patients exploited the institution in a more sophisticated way than was acknowledged by the authorities.

Admission to the hospital was probably not the goal of most parents who brought their children to Great Ormond Street. Charles West himself recounted the reluctance of poor parents to leave their children behind in the hospital when it was first opened in 1852, and the time and effort that it took to convince them that the hospital ward was the best place for their sick child. During its first month, only 24 children were brought as out-patients, and mothers generally refused to allow their children to be taken into the ward. As he commented, 'The Hospital had its character to make among the poor'.[28]

Parental suspicion of the motives of philanthropists with regard to their families was not new. A charity schoolmaster had noted this several years before:

---

24 Minutes of the Provisional Committee of the Hospital for Sick Children, GOS/1/2/1.

25 Lomax, *Small and Special*.

26 Parents were allowed to visit their children twice a week for an hour. Visitors were banned when infection broke out in the institution.

27 Rules set out in the 1860s give some flavour of the expectations of the hospital:

'1st. You are to attend as punctually as possible, and to remember that NO PATIENTS ARE ADMITTED AFTER 10 O'CLOCK

2nd. You are to keep this letter clean, and under cover, and to bring with you clean Bottles, with Corks, and Cups, for your Medicine

3rd. If you stay away for 10 days, you will be discharged

4th. You are to conform in all respects to the Rules laid down for your conduct, and failing to do so, you will be at once discharged.' GOS/8/1.

28 *First Annual Report of the Hospital for Sick Children* (1853), pp. 8–9. Great Ormond Street Hospital was known officially in the period as The Hospital for Sick Children, the street name being added after 1948.

... [T]he uneducated poor speculate upon the motives of those who take upon themselves any office which is professedly for their good, much more than they are generally supposed to do, and ... the result of our exertions depends in a great measure upon the motives they ascribe to us.[29]

Within six years (when it was doubled in size), the hospital was well established, and, judging by the out-patient figures, seemingly popular among poor metropolitan families. However, admission to hospital of one member of a family was not something to be taken lightly. It involved not just the separation of the child from its loved ones, but constituted an interruption to the household routine, inconvenience to both parents on visiting days, and some considerable expense. Children were given a robe and slippers when they were admitted, but parents were expected to present children in unragged and clean clothing, and to do their child's laundry. Surviving photographs of parents and children indicate that the expectation that the children would be brought to the hospital in a clean and tidy condition was realized in most instances, with both mothers and children seemingly in their best clothes (or the best that the family and neighbours could supply) for their visits to the hospital.[30] This would imply that parents (and especially mothers) had weighed the costs of hospital treatment in terms of economics and disruption to family life against the benefits that their children would derive, and had – by and large – decided that it was worth acceding to the rules and regulations of the institution.[31] This contrasts with the metropolitan poor parents' attitude to the requirements attendant on free schooling (as opposed to free medical treatment), as shown in the evidence of the Secretary of the National Society for the Education of the Poor in the Principles of the Established Church to the Select Committee on the Education of the Poorer Classes:

> The parents, will, in their ignorance, not value the schools according to the kind of instruction they give, but they will take into account whether they are allowed to break the rules or not. They resist the discipline of our schools to a surprising extent; they do not like the obligation of attending at fixed hours, and conforming to rules, having clean dress and short or tidy hair.[32]

Compulsory education was one thing, but taking a sick child to a voluntary hospital implied another relationship altogether, and not one in which the state had much say. Part of the hospital's 'mission statement' was to imbue middle-class values into the families of the patients. It is possible, however, that the mothers, at least, had already had a taste of these in their pre-marital working lives. At a time when one in three women in England worked in domestic service at some point in their

---

29   T. and E. Kelly (eds), 'A Schoolmaster's Notebooks', in *Remains Historical and Literary Connected with the Relative Counties of Lancaster and Chester*, vol. 8, 3rd ser. (Manchester, 1957), p. 24.

30   Great Ormond Street Hospital Photograph Collection, B-INT 00834D.

31   For a study of the attitude of poor metropolitan mothers to philanthropic agencies, see E. Ross, 'Hungry Children: Housewives and London Charity 1870–1918', in P. Mandler (ed.), *The Uses of Charity: The Poor on Relief in the Nineteenth Century Metropolis* (Philadelphia, 1990), pp. 161–96.

32   Quoted in Laqueur, 'Working-Class Demand', p. 199.

lives, the experience of a Victorian housemaid turned working-class mother might be said to have given her expectations of cleanliness and order beyond her station and means. This somewhat transitional occupation could arguably have been crucial in determining the housewifely and maternal skills of the mothers who brought their children to the hospital.[33] At the moment, it is not possible to determine whether the mothers of the patients had paid employment at the time of their children's admission to hospital, or whether they had been in domestic service prior to their marriages.[34] The view of the hospital management and the journalists who visited the hospital, however, was nothing if not clichéd as regards the domestic circumstances of the patients, and the effect that a spell in hospital would have on the whole family,

> ... [T]he untutored little Bohemian becomes transformed into a civilised and well-behaved member of society ... The child goes back into its native wilds and becomes an example to other children, a lasting illustration of an excellent lesson to parents!..[35]

The hospital supporters present at the Annual General Meeting (which was the main fund-raising event of the year) were left in no doubt by one distinguished speaker as to the civilizing role of the institution:

> No doubt it may be said that those children found in the Hospital a vast improvement on their own poor squalid homes of dirt and disorder; but I believe that when they leave the Hospital, they go away not only with their diseases cured, but with the moral frame of their minds improved and invigorated, and there is no telling how far the discipline to which they have been subjected in the Hospital, the kindly gentle influences to which they have been exposed bear fruit in the comfort and happiness of those squalid homes to which they often return.[36]

In spite of the extolling of the virtues of spending time on the wards, the small numbers of beds available for in-patient treatment, the length of time that a child admitted to the wards was retained, the fear of infectious disease, and the limited range of treatments open to the physicians and surgeons meant that over 90 per cent of Great Ormond Street's clients were out-patients.[37]

---

33   The under-recording of women's occupations in census returns has been ably covered in the work of E. Higgs, *Making Sense of the Census Revisited: Census records for England and Wales 1801–1901* (London, 2005). For the importance of domestic service in the development of working-class housewifery, see L. Davidoff, 'Mastered for Life: Servant and Wife in Victorian and Edwardian England', *Journal of Social History*, VII (Summer, 1974): 406–8.

34   This may be addressed (at least in part) in future; as this chapter goes to press, two volumes of admissions for the patients of Dr West and Dr William Jenner have been found in the GOSH Archive that give the occupations of both parents.

35   *The Day* (April 1867).

36   Rt Hon. the Earl of Carnarvon , 'Report of the Anniversary Festival February 21st 1877', GOSH Archive, GOS/8/1, p. 3.

37   Hospital for Sick Children, *Annual Reports*, 1855–1901.

From the hospital's point of view, out-patients were cheaper to treat, and spread the influence of the hospital more quickly to the homes of the poor.[38] For parents there were advantages, too. Although all-day waits for parent and child were not unusual at the institution, the disruption caused by regular out-patient appointments was less than that occasioned by having a child on the wards for weeks or months. Nursing could be shared with friends and other family members, and could take place away from the supervision (and possible disapproval) of the hospital nursing staff.

Unlike the metropolitan voluntary hospitals for adults, subscribers to the children's hospital did not have priority in determining who would be seen. Thirty four per cent of the admissions on the database were based on governors' letters, 22.5 per cent have no name attached, nearly 21 per cent were admitted on the authority of the medical officers, 15 per cent per cent were admitted on the authority of the assistant physicians, less than 6 per cent by the assistant surgeon, and just over 3 per cent were brought into the hospital on tickets that the hospital had in its own name, thanks to anonymous benefactors.[39] The predominance of the medical staff in deciding who was to be admitted on to the wards might in some way explain why Great Ormond Street appears to confirm Lindsay Granshaw's judgement that medical staff held sway in specialist hospitals, but is the exception to her rule that specialist hospitals were not welcomed by the medical establishment, and were viewed as parasites on the general hospitals. The children's hospital did not tread on the toes of its larger neighbours, who, by and large, did not treat patients under the age of 14 until the turn of the century. It accepted patients referred by other institutions, and its medical staff published a steady stream of observations and treatment results that were of benefit to their colleagues in their private practice.[40]

Most parents presented their children for examination because they were willing to surrender the temporary care of their offspring to the hospital. While clinical need, as judged by the doctors, decided who would, and who would not, be admitted to the hospital ward, it was the parents who decided whether their child came under the scrutiny of the hospital in the first place. The composition of the patient population was thus as much in the hands of the children's families as of the medical staff. As has been indicated, parents were allowed to visit for just two hours each week (one

---

38   Out-patients were in general far more significant statistically in Britain's voluntary-sector hospitals in the nineteenth and early twentieth centuries; in Wakefield Infirmary, for example, the ratio of in- to out-patients was 1 to 53. See H. Marland, *Medicine and Society in Wakefield and Huddersfield 1780–1870* (Cambridge, 1987), p. 101. In 1887, London's 4 million inhabitants accounted for 1.5 million out-patient attendances at metropolitan hospitals. See D.G. Green, *Working Class Patients and the Medical Establishment; Self-help in Britain from the mid 19th Century to 1948* (Aldershot, 1985), p. 91.

39   The Medical Committee recommended the abandonment of the letters for in-patients in early 1891, highlighting that few patients admitted actually had a letter at this date. It also stated that it was impractical for a mother of sick child to go searching for one; that often those with letters were not as sick as those without, and that the hospital's imminent expansion should enable GOSH to announce 'that henceforth ours is to be a Free Hospital for Children'. Medical Committee 4 February 1891, GOSH Archive, GOS/1/6/11.

40   Charles West told his students in the 1840s that one-third of their patients would be the children of middle-class parents.

hour on a Wednesday and one hour on a Sunday, which was known as 'father's hour'), which was substantially less than the time on the wards granted to well-heeled benefactors.[41] This was not unique to the London, or even British, hospitals; in the 1870s and 1880s, Boston's Children's Hospital limited parental visits while encouraging 'the kind and cultivated' to call upon the patients.[42] Once a child was admitted, the environment created by hospital management and staff was designed to improve not only their physical status, but also their morals and manners. Again, Great Ormond Street was not unusual in this; the Children's Hospital in Philadelphia (developed along the same lines as the London institution from its foundation in 1869) had similar aims:

> Children admitted to the hospital found an environment structured by the hospital's trustees, who hoped that the young patients would, during their lengthy stay, learn the rules of health and by implication, the customs of middle class life. Upon returning home, the children would thus become agents of reform within their own families.[43]

During this period, sympathetic management of the interface between parents and the hospital left much to be desired. While grateful for the care taken of their children, those parents who were dissatisfied with the treatment received at the hospital were upset by what can only be called lack of courtesy and scant understanding of the impact of sickness on the poor family. It is likely that the hospital management did not always appreciate the sacrifice that submitting a child to their care – possibly for months – was to working-class families. In her study of family life, Linda Pollock concluded that acute parental anxiety accompanied a child's illness (especially in working-class families), given the possibility that childhood sickness could so easily have resulted in death. The parents she studied looked upon it as part of their responsibility to nurse their sick children and were reluctant to leave children who were ill, even for a short time.[44]

If her conclusion is correct, the distress to parents occasioned by sacrificing the duty of nursing a sick child to a strange institution – no matter how well intentioned – must have been acute. Keeping appointments and actually getting into the building presented their own problems to parents. One local resident complained of the difficulties mothers encountered in getting into the building to keep appointments. As late as the mid 1880s, posts at the entrance were so placed as to prevent the passing of a perambulator through the doors.

---

41 By the middle of the nineteenth century, restriction of visiting hours on the grounds of hygiene and order seems to have superseded the attitude of the eighteenth-century Edinburgh Infirmary physician William Blizard: 'Shall a parent be denied the satisfaction of seeing a child, more dear on account of its misfortune, and shall not the child receive parental comfort?' Quoted in G.B. Risse, *Hospital Life in Enlightenment Scotland* (Cambridge, 1986) p. 24.

42 Golden (ed.), *Infant Asylums*, p. 21.

43 Ibid., p. 17.

44 Pollock, *Forgotten Children*, pp. 131–3.

... [I]t is sometimes pitiable. In wet weather I have seen the child taken out and set aside on a wet step while the thing is got through, a wheel coming off in the effort and all with frantic haste to be at the Hospital in good time.[45]

After the opening of the new building in 1875, once through the door, parents were interviewed by a clerk, who enquired after their financial circumstances in order to screen those who could afford to pay for treatment. The interrogation was so exacting that many mothers left before the doctor saw their child. The length patients had to wait before seeing a doctor in out-patients became the stuff of legend and allegations that nurses demanded bribes to advance people up the queues abounded.[46] One husband wrote to complain of his wife's experience of waiting seven hours in vain to see a doctor for a pre-arranged appointment:

To take the wife of a working man away from her home for 6 or 7 hours, on such a fool's errand was really a somewhat discreditable proceeding on the part of the authorities of such a hospital as yours ... Doctors and other leading authorities preach very loudly about 'our duty to the nation's children', but you don't give much encouragement to those who do 'interpose' between the ignorant parent and the child.[47]

Where a child was prescribed medication or a specialist piece of equipment, the nursing staff could pass judgement on the financial circumstances of the family, thus causing deep offence.[48] Children waiting for ward admissions were frequently kept hanging around for many hours in overcrowded reception rooms, required to undress in front of strangers and compete for an inadequate number of dressing gowns, all of which added to the trauma of imminent parting from their mothers.[49] The management were aware of the sensitivities of parents and patients, and occasionally

---

45 Letter from William Lethaby, Medical Officer of Health for the City of London, dd. 17 July 1885, Great Ormond Street Hospital Archive, GOS/8/163.

46 Board of Management Committee Minutes 12 & 25 April 1870, GOSH Archive, GOS/1/5/1.

47 Letter from subscriber, 1 October 1910, GOSH Archive, GOS/8/163. Another angry husband, furious at the insolent treatment of his wife, wrote to the managers complaining of the gross incivility of the clerical staff: 'You ask for subscriptions for your institution from the public and apart from the doctors' and nurses who are in every case most civil, the parties attending are met with most insulting remarks ...' Letter from patient's father, 22 June 1904, GOSH Archive, GOS/8/163.

48 In 1894, Bertram Shepherd was prescribed a truss by the out-patient consultant. The nurse asked his mother how much his father earned, and told her to buy one, and not to beg for one from the hospital. The reconciliation of perceived medical need and the ability of parents to pay a physician for treatment was a source of constant anxiety to the hospital that even recruiting the Charity Organisation Society to assist in assessing parental income failed to solve. In 1876, the management committee decided that the upper limit of 30 shillings a week should be applied except in cases of acute medical necessity. Management Committee Minutes 24 February 1876, GOSH Archive, GOS/1/2/14.

49 It may be an exaggeration to say that a working-class child might have found the parting from his or her mother more traumatic than a middle- or upper-class child would have done, but Ellen Ross, for example, makes a powerful argument for the importance of the working-class mother as provider of material and emotional comfort in the lives of her

advised the medical staff on how to treat them, as in the following admonishment of a doctor in 1876:

> Although they are sure his patients receive good treatment, it is important for patients not only to receive it but to feel they are receiving it 'the patients should not only be well attended to, but should seem to be so attended; and it is better that some time both of the Medical Officer and of the patient should be wasted, than that the feeling of those in attendance upon the patients should constantly be wounded by what to them seems (even though unreasonably) carelessness or haste.[50]

It is perhaps not surprising that an out-patients department that saw up to 300 children daily, attended by anxious parents and siblings who could not be left at home, would become the focus of discontent. The very fact of an examination in public circumstances, and the distress that this could cause the patient was a notable feature of parental objections to medical interference with their children's bodies.[51] A patient's father who had attended from Bishop's Stortford in Hertfordshire, wrote to describe the mêlée in Out Patients, adding:

> I have almost hated writing this letter because amongst so much which was beautiful in the care and love given to my daughter, not to mention the very high standard of skill of surgeon and house staff, it seems ungrateful ... My little one has – once she was inside the ward – received every care and attention, and we are grateful ...

The appreciation expressed by this father of the kindness shown to his child is more typical of the surviving communications from patients' families; in the overwhelming majority of cases, they were thankful for the care that was taken of their children.[52] Obliged by the desire to have their children treated, most parents put up silently with rude admissions staff, the inquisitiveness of the almoner, long waits and infrequent sightings of their children. However, where treatment was perceived to be inadequate, or misguided, or where their children were unhappy, significant numbers of parents – in spite of warnings that re-admission would not be permitted – removed their children from the hospital.[53]

---

children. See E. Ross, *Love and Toil: Motherhood in Outcast London, 1870–1918* (New York, 1993).

50 Management Committee Minutes 26 Oct 1876, GOSH Archive, GOS/1/2/15.

51 This was reflected in parental attitudes to school medical examinations brought into being under child welfare legislation in the Edwardian era. See D. Hirst, 'The Early School Medical Services in Wales: Public Care or Private responsibility?', in A. Borsay (ed.), *Public Service or Private Commodity? Medicine in Wales c.1800–2000* (Cardiff, 2003), p. 68.

52 Hilary Marland has argued that the whole process of hospital admission, treatment and discharge was designed to inculcate feelings of gratitude and dependence in patients and their families. See Marland, *Medicine and Society in Wakefield and Huddersfield*, p. 146.

53 Parents' distress at the evident unhappiness of their child in hospital was a major reason for the removal of patients immediately after the first visiting hour at the Sophia Children's Hospital in Rotterdam. See Prof. Dr M.J. van Lieburg, *The History of the Sophia Children's Hospital in Rotterdam* (Rotterdam, 2004), p. 45.

An ongoing project creating a database of the in-patients at Great Ormond Street, using the admission registers from 1852 to 1899 as the primary source, has been studied to attempt some consideration of how the parents of the patients viewed and used the hospital. It is the nature of surviving archives that the hospital management's outlook is well represented through committee minutes, annual reports and correspondence, and that the voice of the patients and their families should be more muted. By looking at the choices made by families firstly in entrusting their sick children to the hospital, and then in their willingness to leave them on the wards until in-hospital treatment was completed, it is hoped that some picture of the attitude of poor parents to voluntary institutional provision for their children might be gauged.

Age and gender differentials

The age profile of the total in-patient population between 1852 and 1899 shows marked differences in admissions, with four- and five-year-olds making up one-third of all in-patients. It is at this age that children are able to articulate pain to parents, and that the after-effects of infectious disease make themselves more obvious. Consequently, their numerical significance is perhaps not surprising. Two-year-olds are the least numerous, at 3 per cent of all admissions. After the age of five, admissions drop gradually until the age of 12 (the maximum age allowed by the hospital management), when the numbers mirror those of the two-year-old patients. The rise in numbers that might have been expected from six to ten, showing the influence of infections caught or recognized at school, does not occur.

Of the 46,458 children on the Great Ormond Street Patient Database between 1852 and 1899, 1,654 have been identified as having left the hospital before treatment was completed.[54] The reasons for premature removal are as follows: 1,398 children acquired an infectious fever; 151 were deemed not suitable for treatment; 75 were discharged to other hospitals; four were discharged for disruptive behaviour, while 26 were removed when the hospital was emptied in 1875.

However, some 800 children have been identified as having been removed prematurely not at the wish of the hospital, but at the instigation of their parents or guardians.[55] It is these patients who will be the focus of this study.

Ten per cent more boys than girls were admitted to the hospital in the period under consideration, and so it might be expected that the ratio of early removals would reflect the gender bias of the intake.[56] To see if the sex of the patient had any significant impact on premature removal, the numbers of each sex admitted and removed were compared. When the ages of the children taken away are set next to the percentage of the children of their sex admitted, there is not an exact correlation between patients admitted and the proportion of each age group removed early.

---

54   Patients who contracted an infectious disease (notably scarlet fever) were discharged and seen at home by a Visiting Officer. GOSH Archive, GOS/1/6/5.

55   The ratio of self-discharged patients, while large, is not as large as that in the Huddersfield Infirmary in 1865–66, where 45 patients left at their own request and one was dismissed from the ward. See Marland, *Medicine and Society in Wakefield and Huddersfield*, pp. 157–8.

56   24,216 boys and 22,242 girls were treated as in-patients.

Figure 8.1 shows that the age profile of male in-patients removed by their families does not exactly mirror the intake of patients, with 22 per cent of the sample being two-year-old boys taken out prematurely. On the other hand, babies (boys under twelve months old) were more likely to remain in the hospital until treatment was completed than any other male group. The only group of premature leavers to shadow the percentage of the intake for age and sex was that of one-year-olds. It is possible that by the time patients were two years old, they had established strong emotional bonds with their families, and that separation was distressing for both parties. Those under twelve months arguably would not have had the same awareness of separation from family, and those being breast-fed had the daily contact with their nursing mothers.[57] The numbers relating to the other age groups do not offer sufficient difference to allow speculation as to whether the age of male patients was a determining factor in their early removal from the wards.

The early departure from the hospital among female patients has a different pattern, with those most likely to be removed being aged three, with four- and two-year-olds following behind (see Figure 8.2). Girls in metropolitan working-class families traditionally had an important part to play in terms of childcare, but it would be premature to posit the theory that these very young patients were taken home in order to resume childcare duties for a younger sibling, or because an older brother or sister wished to have them returned to their care.

The statistics in themselves pose several questions. The low instance of the early removal of babies might imply that parents were happy with their treatment, or that the close involvement of the mothers in the infants' care (many mothers visited daily in order to breast-feed their babies) satisfied the family as to the benefits of hospital treatment. It was stated hospital policy not to admit babies under two years old. Babies were deemed to be better off with their mothers, and did not, as a rule, thrive in hospital. However, from 1878, figures kept by the hospital reveal a steady increase in the number of babies on the wards. Elizabeth Lomax views this as being the natural result of the admitting medical staff being interested in the medical condition of the children, but it may also reflect the influence of infant welfare clinics, and a growing confidence in the hospital's ability to treat babies successfully. The hospital's expertise in treating very young children – and also the difficulties hospitalization posed for mothers – is intimated in the case of Georgiana Harding, aged 4 months, who was admitted with constipation. The baby was the youngest of ten children, and her mother had to take her out of the hospital after two days, as she found the hospital's requirement that she attend daily at intervals to breast-feed her child impossible to reconcile with caring for the rest of her family.[58]

---

57 It would appear that the percentage of working-class infants who were breast- (as opposed to bottle-) fed was 'fairly high' in England. D. Dwork, *War is Good for Babies and Other Young Children: a History of the Infant and Child Welfare Movement in England, 1898–1918* (London, 1987), p. 117.

58 Georgina (admitted 4 August, left 6 August 1870), whose family lived in Dowgate Hill in Cannon Street, City of London, had suffered from constipation for half of her short life. Great Ormond Street Historic Patient Database ref. GH0209/0176.

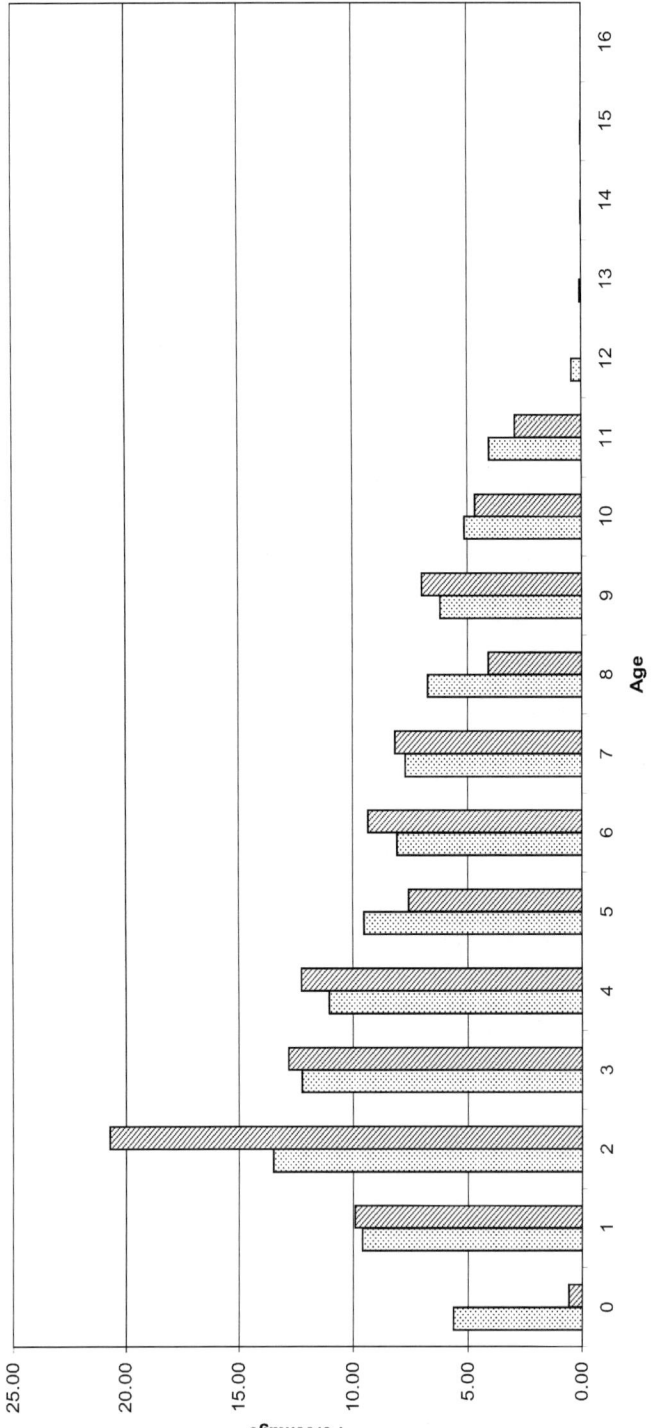

Figure 8.1 Great Ormond Street Hospital: male patients removed prematurely 1852–1899

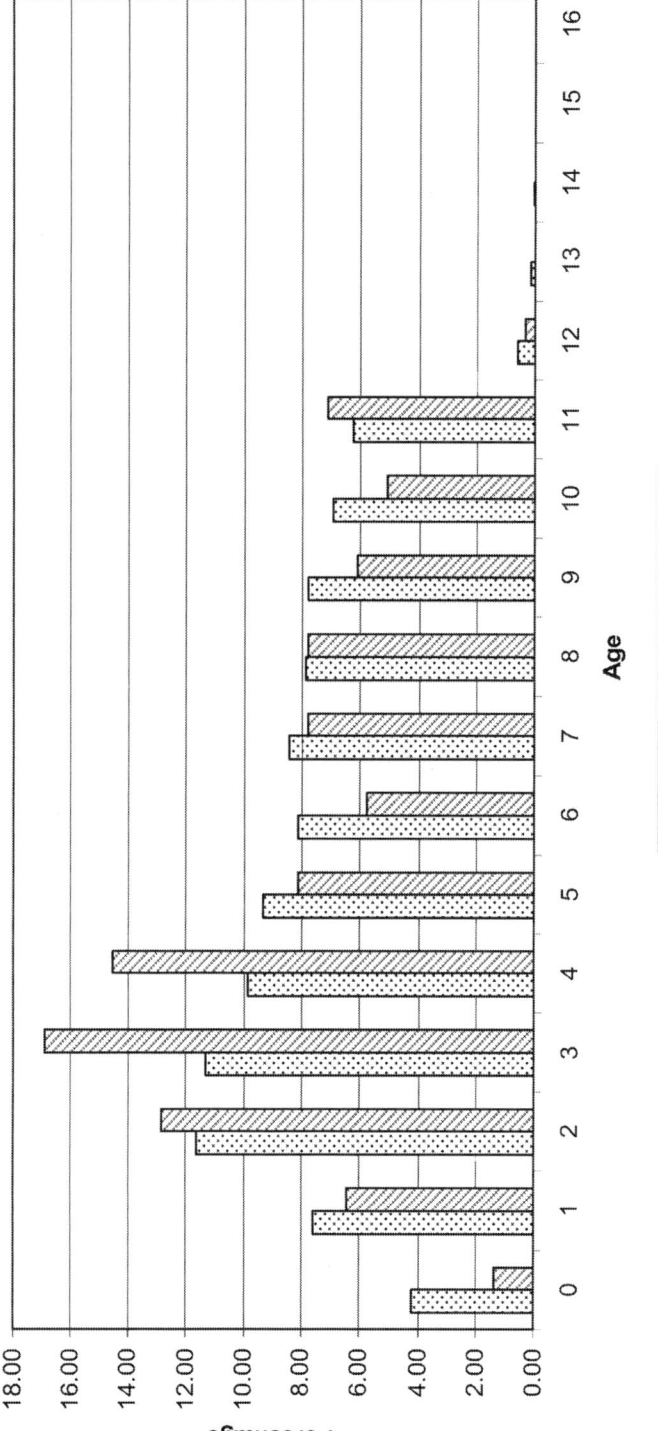

Figure 8.2 Great Ormond Street Hospital: female patients removed prematurely 1852–1899

Three days after she left, the child died, after medical staff at St Bartholomew's had punctured her bowel while trying to treat her.

The preponderance of two- to four-year-olds in the ranks of those taken away early might indicate the awareness of the child of separation from the family, and the emotional difficulties inherent in what might be lengthy periods in hospital. The dependence of toddlers on the proximity of their mothers is well documented, as is the crucial role of the working-class mother in the lives of very young children.[59] More so than her richer counterpart, who had a range of help available in bringing up her children, the poor mother was frequently the sole provider of security in the precarious world of the labouring family.[60] It is perhaps not surprising, therefore, that toddlers represent the highest percentage of children taken out early from the hospital wards.

The diseases of the patients

The disease profile of Great Ormond Street in-patients shows that the illnesses prompting the admission of the children were, by and large, the same conditions that were responsible for the early deaths of their parents, but they were not the infectious diseases that were to remain the focus of public-health attention for the rest of the century. The most significant diseases were those resulting from malnourishment, overcrowding and poverty, namely, tubercular diseases, heart and lung complaints and infectious fevers.[61] Diseased joints, probably mostly tubercular, are the single most important cause of admission, followed closely by respiratory disease. The preponderance of chronic hip and joint disease is a direct contradiction of the rules of the hospital.

> Many cases of rickets, hip joint disease or of scrofulous disease of the spine or of the joints are of necessity refused; either because they are quite incurable, or because they require nothing but rest for many months, or because good diet and fresh air for months or years are essential to improvement; and the reception of such cases would convert the hospital into an Asylum for Sickly Children, instead of a place for the treatment and cure of the Diseases of Childhood; such cases, therefore, can be received only on special medical certificate.[62]

The diseases given in the figures have been clustered to show the general site of the condition. For example, diseases of the digestive system include constipation, diarrhoea, Bright's disease and liver complaints. The class 'Joints, bones and

---

59   See J. Robertson, *Hospitals and Children: a Parent's-eye View; a Review of Letters from Parents to the Observer and the BBC* (London, 1962).

60   For a fuller consideration of this, see Ross, *Love and Toil*.

61   In the first two hospital buildings, 1852–75, infectious cases were either discharged home or looked after in a room at the top of the house with separate nursing staff. After 1875, infectious cases contracted at the hospital were cared for in a fever block. The hospital managers had proposed a separate hospital for children with infectious fevers, but the advent of the Metropolitan Asylums Board fever hospitals made this unnecessary. Management Committee Minutes, 1 April 1874, GOSH Archive, GOS/1/2/3.

62   *16th Annual Report of the Hospital for Sick Children*, 1869.

muscles' contains conditions from knock knees to necrosis of the jawbone. This form of simple classification is not without its problems, the greatest of which is where to place tubercular diseases. Diseases of the respiratory system undoubtedly include a great many instances of pulmonary tuberculosis (phthisis), but where the register does not state that the condition was tubercular or phthisical, the patient is given a classification of having a respiratory, and not a tubercular, disease. Similarly, joints, bones and muscles will contain many children with tubercular hip and joint disease, but – where it is not specifically stated in the register – such are given under the site, and not the suspected underlying tubercular condition. Violence is used where the patient has suffered an injury (by accident or not), and also contains many children who have swallowed foreign bodies. Figure 8.3 gives the distribution of all patients from 1852 to 1899, as classified by disease.

The diseases of the children who left the hospital prematurely in general mirror the trend of admissions (Figure 8.4). However, there are some significant deviations from the pattern that give some clues as to the likely outcome of the cases and the reasons why parents removed their children. Although diseased joints, bones and muscles account for the majority of admissions, it is respiratory disease that prompted the early removal of the patients under review. Joints, bones and muscle disease, although next in importance, accounts for less than half of those removed with respiratory conditions. Radical surgery and a therapeutic regime of exercise and rest could do a certain amount for a child with a diseased joint and, in general, such patients could be sent home (or to convalesce) after several weeks. Respiratory disease – especially if it was tubercular – did not enjoy the same 'success rate' as the amputation of necrosed limbs. Watching a small child (recalling the age pattern of admissions) fighting for breath, with little in the physician's cupboard to offer relief, might have been expected to prompt parents to take a child home to be nursed and perhaps to die. On the other hand, removals of patients suffering with nervous conditions reflect the admissions ratio. There was little that the physicians could do for patients with neurological conditions, apart from sedation. The exception to this was Sydenham's chorea (St Vitus' dance), which was a condition that almost guaranteed admission, and which – treated or not – tended to get better of its own accord, given time.

Results of treatment

Neither the age and sex of the children in themselves, nor their disease profile, are sufficient to indicate why the patients were removed early. It is possible that the results of treatment did not justify, in the parents' eyes, continued residence in the hospital. The hospital had four categories of result: recovered, relieved, not relieved, and died. In the main database, 41.24 per cent of the patients were cured, 35.51 per cent relieved, 9.24 per cent unrelieved and 13.01 per cent died. A further 0.4 per cent had no result recorded. One has to be suspicious of a high recovery rate at a time when limited therapeutics were available, and the term may not always have described a total recovery. Guenter Risse has pointed out that there was a tendency among British hospital clinicians to say that a patient was cured when he or she

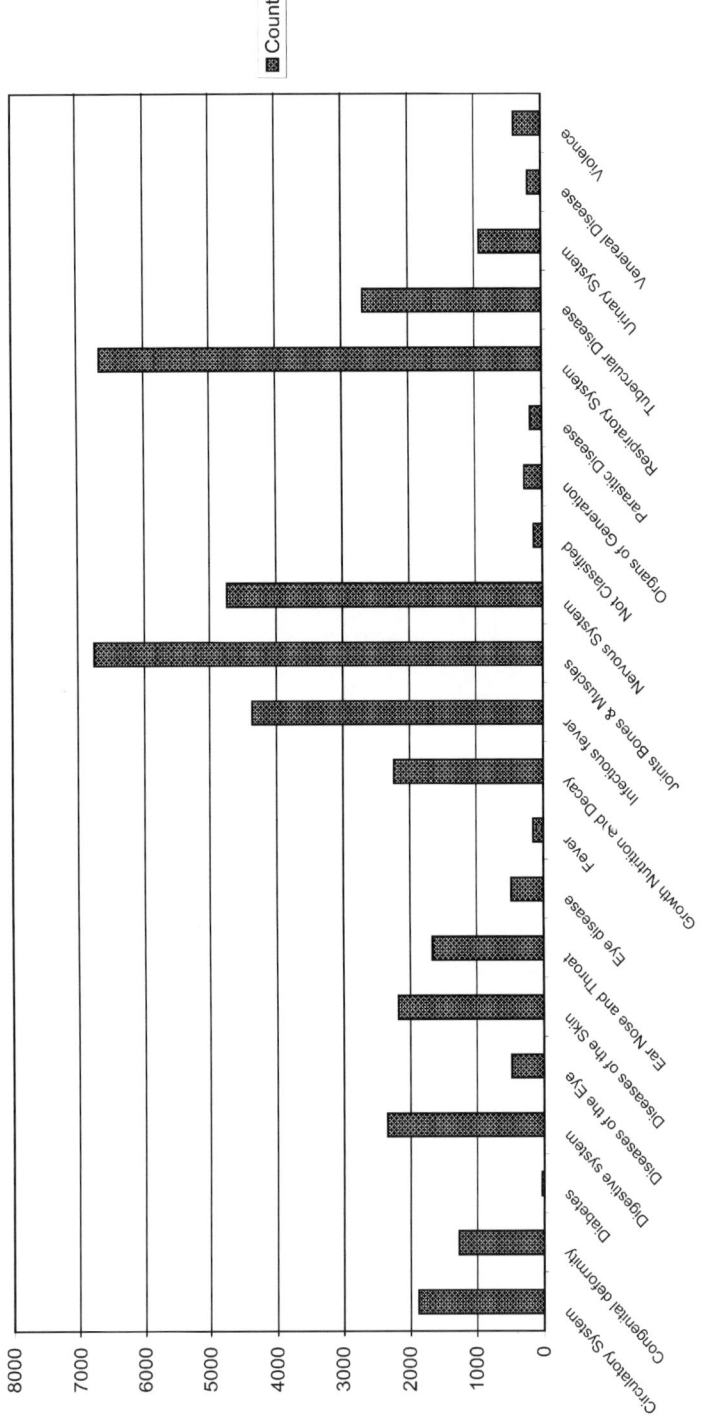

Figure 8.3   Great Ormond Street Hospital: simple disease classification: all patients 1852–1899

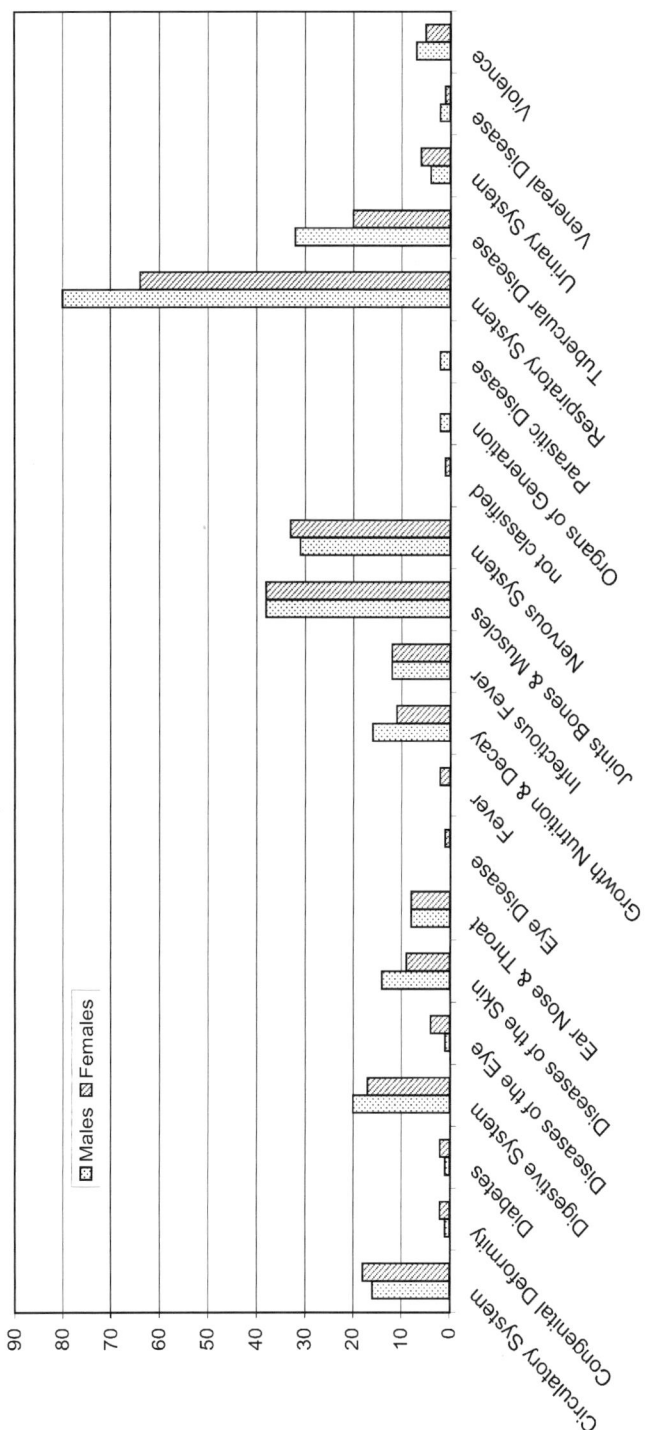

Figure 8.4 Great Ormond Street Hospital: diseases of children taken out: by gender 1852–1899

appeared to be on the mend, even if the recovery was not complete or clearly only temporary.[63] High recovery rates were important for the reputations and finances of hospitals in the voluntary sector, and a certain amount of wishful thinking was evident in nearly all hospital results tables.

As indicated, cases of Sydenham's chorea were notable in this respect. Since the progress of the condition was cyclical, the patient nearly always made a recovery sufficient to warrant discharge, whether the physicians had done anything or not. Children suffering from chorea were what Elizabeth Lomax has described as 'gratifying patients'.[64] They were interesting to study and invariably quietened down in the hospital, almost certainly as a result of being given considerable doses of sedatives, although these were discontinued if the patient's heart seemed to be affected as a result. Visitors liked to see the dramatic changes in the behaviour of such patients, and when they were sent home the ward clerk could put a large tick in the 'cured' column of the register.[65]

A comparison of the percentages of children removed early with the total intake of patients before 1900 shows that only 6.7 per cent of the former had recovered (as compared to 42.24 per cent of all in-patients), 30.6 per cent were relieved (compared to 35.51 per cent), and only 1.1 per cent died (against 13.01 per cent). The majority – some 61.2 per cent – of the early leavers were not relieved, but they were almost six times more likely to have this result recorded than the totality of patients, at 9.84 per cent. This implies that either the judgement of the parents and friends was sound, and hospital treatment produced no discernible benefit to their children, or that they did not remain in hospital long enough to derive any relief from professional medical and nursing care. What is perhaps more surprising is that those who were relieved account for nearly one-third of those taken out before treatment was completed. Thus – in the hospital's judgement – the time spent on the wards had a beneficial effect pro rata on almost as many prematurely removed patients as on those who were discharged after completing treatment.

What constitutes 'relieved' in these circumstances? The case notes examined give some clues. Michael Kelly, a three-year-old with a cranial hemiplegia, squint and partial paralysis, was taken home to Bow in east London by his mother after five weeks on the ward, 'walking more steadily than he did'.[66] The doctors did not state the cause of the patient's illness, and did not intervene in his removal. Experience would undoubtedly have told them that the child probably had a brain tumour, and would die in due course. From the point of view of the hospital, however, as his gait had improved slightly on discharge, he was therefore 'relieved'.

As indicated, the 'not relieved' percentage is considerably higher than the other categories among this cohort of early leavers, and almost in direct reversal of the relieved/not relieved experience of the total number of patients in the database. It may

63   Risse, *Hospital Life in Enlightenment Scotland*, p. 230.

64   Lomax, *Small and Special*, p. 97.

65   See D. Martino, A. Tanner, G. Defazio, A.J. Church, K.P. Bhatia, G. Giovannoni and R.C. Dale, 'Tracing Sydenham's chorea – historical documents from a British Paediatric Hospital', *Archives of the Diseases of Childhood* 90: 5 (May 2005): 507–11.

66   GOSH Archive, GOS/10/14/205–207.

be that the stay in hospital ended before any discernible improvement was noted. It is also possible that death was seen as inevitable in some cases, and the patients were removed to spend their last days surrounded by family and friends. Hospital was not the best place in which to experience a 'happy death', and high mortality statistics did not look well in the Annual Reports of an institution that was meant to cure children. In these circumstances, it is not difficult to imagine a consensus between medical staff and parents that the child should go home. Additionally, a death at home would avoid the inevitable request from the doctors to perform a post-mortem on the child, an event that could easily have compounded the family's grief.

The evidence from case notes

The bald statistics from the database so far pose more questions than they answer, but the admission registers and annual reports are not the only source available. Case notes survive for approximately 5 per cent of the in-patients, and give a much more sophisticated picture of the patient experience of the hospital than the registers. In order to test the validity of the tentative conclusions from the admission register database, the case notes of a small sample of 25 of the patients removed early have been examined for evidence of influences on the parents' decision to take the child away from the institution.[67]

Of this small sample, 16 lived within a mile of the hospital, and all but two of the patients resided in London. Of the two country patients, only one was truly from some distance (her address was Harpenden, Hertfordshire); the other, a boy from Three Bridges in Sussex, had a father working for the railways and living in central London. The age range is shown in Figure 8.5.

This reflects the ages of the total taken out early, with two-year-olds being the largest single group. Their diseases are primarily tubercular, with tubercular peritonitis being particularly marked.[68] Non-tubercular lung, liver and kidney disease also feature. While an infectious disease is given as the primary cause of admission in only one case, the notes make it clear that failure to thrive after contracting an infectious disease (notably measles and whooping cough) served as the catalyst for persuading the parents to take the child to the hospital in the first instance.

Although most display the effects of growing up in poverty and in overcrowded conditions, only one child is described in the notes as having been neglected or malnourished. Given the intended patient constituency, this is rather surprising. George Ryan, from Fulham, was admitted on 3 February 1865 with phthisis. He was

---

67   Case notes survive for about 5 per cent of the in-patients. The bound volumes were the property of the individual physicians and surgeons, and only those donated to the hospital survive. The case notes are not exactly representative of the in-patients. However, notes taken by Drs West, Barlow, Batten and Poynton are to be found in the collection. The sampled patients were all patients of either Dr Charles West or Dr Hillier, and their residence at the hospital covers the period 1855 to 1873.

68   By 1907, tuberculosis killed 15,000 children in England and Wales annually, and was the cause of death of one-third of children dying in hospital. G. Newman, *The Health of the State* (Social Service Handbooks no. 2., London, 1907), p. 139.

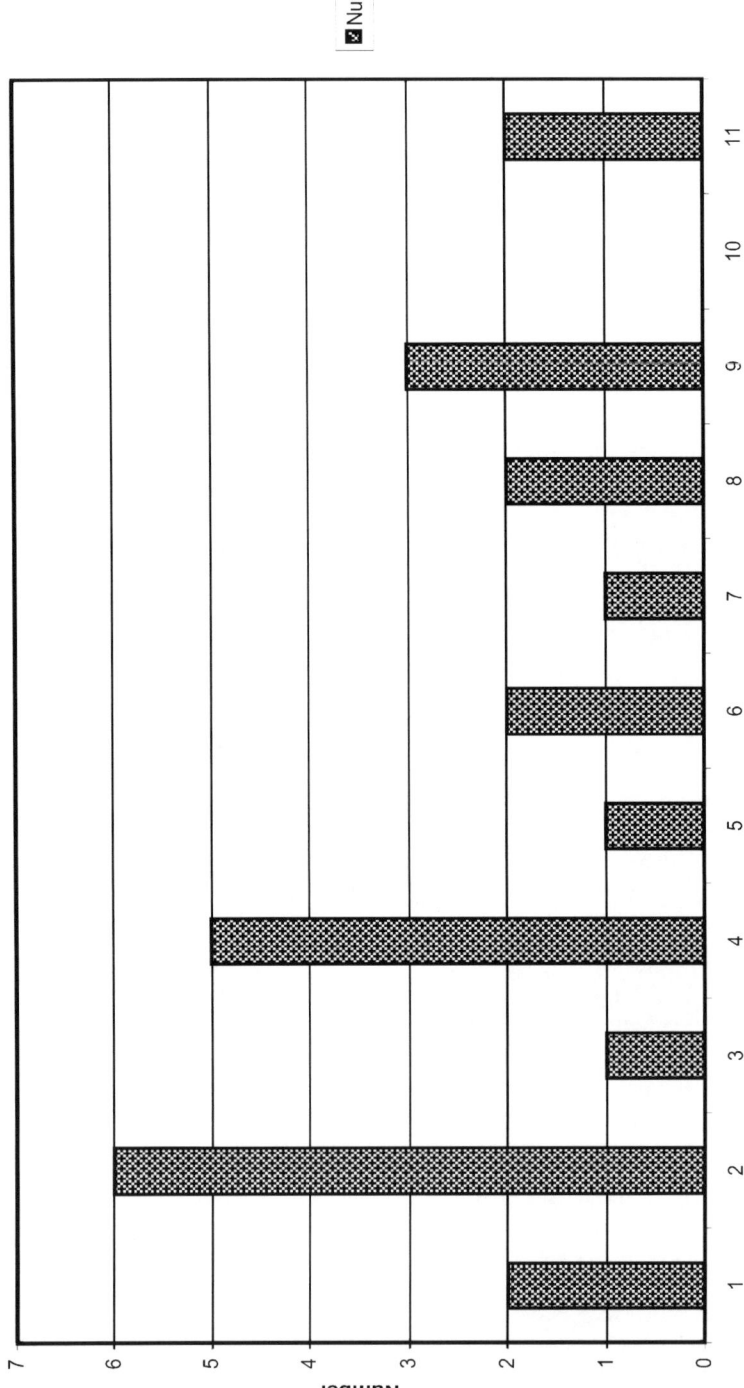

Figure 8.5   Great Ormond Street Hospital: age of patients in case notes removed prematurely 1852–1899

aged seven, and one of eight children of a father who was out of work and a mother who had been seriously ill with emphysema. She herself offered the view that the child had been sorely neglected during his parents' recent difficulties. He came into the hospital undernourished and covered in flea-bites, and was fetched after only three days by his mother, 'saying she could not do without the boy'.[69]

This expression was used in one other instance, where the doctors tried to keep the child in hospital. James Whittey of Drury Lane was nine years old when he was admitted with tubercular peritonitis. After three days, and little improvement, his mother took him home, as his father 'could not do without him'. The phrase is ambiguous. It might mean that the parents were missing the child too much, or – given that in both instances the patients were boys of an age when they would have been economically significant to the family – it is possible their stay at Great Ormond Street was costing too much money in terms of lost earnings.[70] A child working part-time (even one suffering from a tubercular condition) could mean the difference between survival and disaster for a poor family.[71]

Peter Laslett showed over 30 years ago that the children of the poor almost always worked to augment the family's income.[72] The importance of working-class children in child-minding or earning money is highlighted in several of the cases. Louisa Summers of Fitzroy Square was admitted at the age of six with heart pain, headaches and difficulty in walking. She was taken to the Blenheim Street Dispensary when her mother noticed that she was unable to hold the baby, the responsibility for whose nursing rested with the six-year-old, as she was the second of five children. Treatment for Sydenham's chorea proved useless, and so she was taken to the hospital. The child remained in hospital for eight days, but was taken home 'by her mother's desire', as she was needed there.[73] This case highlights the role in domestic chores that was played by daughters, and the dependence of mothers on the baby-minding skills of their older daughters.[74]

Although the parents and guardians took the decision to remove the children, in all but four of these cases, the doctors' notes imply that they did not oppose this course of action. The judgement of the parents that the child would gain no further benefit from remaining in hospital was corroborated by the doctors. Notes in ten

---

69 GOSH Archive, GOS/11/1/37.

70 In 1907, it was estimated that 200,000 juveniles worked in shops, street-trading, home industries and agriculture. See Newman, *The Health of the State,* p. 147.

71 This was not restricted to London, and is highlighted in a study of children's roles in the textile industry in Bradford. See K. Ittman, *Gender and Family in Victorian England* (London, 1995).

72 See also M. Abbott, *Family Ties: English Families 1540–1920* (London and New York, 1993), pp. 144–53, for a detailed consideration of working-class children's labour.

73 GOSH Archive, GOS/11/1/37. This is the only instance found to date of a child's being verminous. The picture of a generally clean and flea- and lice-free patient population contrasts starkly with George Newman's description of the town child as being frequently verminous. See Newman, *The Health of the State,* p. 141.

74 Anna Davin has shown that the London School Board inspectors tended to overlook absences of up to two days a week among girls with housekeeping duties at home. See A. Davin, *Growing Up Poor – Home, School and Street in London, 1870–1914* (London, 1996).

of the cases show that the doctors kept in touch with the family after discharge to track how the child was progressing. This would imply that the parting did not cause offence to the clinicians or the hospital management, and that early removal did not exclude the patient from further treatment, or – at least – continued interest on the part of the hospital.

The four patients removed against advice were all critically ill. George Shepherd, a nine-year-old from Clerkenwell, was admitted with typhoid fever and acute tuberculosis on 26 October 1855 and removed by his parents 20 days later. The day before his removal his pulse had been weak and he was still feverish, but he was taking nourishment in the form of beef tea. On his removal, Charles West commented:

> On this day his parents removed him during a dense fog and the thermometer being very low. He was rather better but his removal was a very wicked act. I do not know whether he survived it.[75]

'Wicked' is a very strong word for a physician to use. The patient was one of four surviving children of a family that was riddled with asthma and phthisis. The boy was of an age when he would have been expected to have given meaningful help to the family in the form of a part-time job, childcare or undertaking a number of household chores. The parents had managed without him for nearly three weeks, and perhaps the strain on the household arrangements was now too much to bear. If he was going to die, better the whole family be around him than that he meet his end among strangers. It begs the question whether this institution, designed to promote children's welfare, did not always appreciate the needs of the child's family, and was reliant on what one commentator has described as a 'self-generated version of what that welfare consists of'.[76]

Only two children appear to have taken an active part in their own departure from the wards. The female patient mentioned above from Hertfordshire was eleven and a half when she was admitted in May 1852 for an hysterical cough. After three days of cold showers, she wrote to her father asking him to take her away, '…as she did not like cold baths'.[77] The other was a two-year-old boy from Wardour Street, Soho, who had pleural effusion. He fretted so much that his family could not cope with his unhappiness and took him away after just three days.

Examples abound of patients, and their siblings, experiencing unbearable distress at long separation, and of parents relying on their own instincts as to what was better for their children, which included death at home rather than at the hospital. This was the case of five-year-old Thomas Downing of Drury Lane who spent just one day in hospital in October 1867, when it was clear that his lungs were fatally compromised

---

75   GOSH Archive, GOS/10/20/208.

76   M. King, *A Better World for Children? Explorations in Morality and Authority* (London, 1997), p. 61.

77   GOSH Archive, GOS/10/4104. The case note records that the family's general practitioner wrote to Dr West in November 1863 stating that the patient had recovered spontaneously by that date.

and the hospital could do little for him.[78] Of the 25 children examined in the case notes, 13 were either on the point of death, or were suffering from terminal illness, when the families took them out. Received wisdom has held until recently that parents in the past were not overly affected by the loss of a child, as so many died. Linda Pollock's work into parent and child relationships has refuted this, leading her to assert that, 'parents [in history] were grief stricken at the loss of a child'.[79]

The refusal to surrender the claim of the close family to medical expertise was often expressed strongly to the hospital, which had no sanction in such cases, in spite of the vocal disapprobation of the medical staff. The father of Olive Attwood, whose removal from the hospital angered the nursing staff, was not intimidated into silence or acquiescence, writing to the managers after his daughter's death:

> I may say it is no pleasure for me to think all this and can only regret that a Hospital with a noble purpose so Highly pratronised [sic] so popurlar [sic] should leave the slightest loophole for parents to get such impressions I have (viz) that I might have saved my child had I kept her home.[80]

It is worth noting the preponderance of fathers both as the catalyst in the removal of children from the hospital and in the correspondence concerning unsatisfactory treatment of wives and children. It is possible that mothers blamed absent husbands as the instigators of the decisions to take a child home, but one cannot deny that it was the fathers who took the initiative in complaining to the hospital about perceived slights and inadequate treatment. The significance of the male parent in determining the uptake of state and charity provision was particularly marked in the metropolis. For example, it was London fathers who were nearly always the objectors to compulsory vaccination of their babies, which had been introduced in 1853. Their motives were impugned by a witness to the Select Committee on the Vaccination Acts in 1867: 'The father would like the family as small as possible that he had to work for; I am afraid is at the bottom of it.'[81]

This harsh judgement would seem to be contradicted by the role that fathers took in decisions regarding the care of their hospitalized children at Great Ormond Street. It is also significant that fathers not infrequently offered services to the hospital (such as making and repairing toys, bringing allotment flowers to the wards and collecting money at their places of work). This does not fit easily with the picture given above of men glad to be rid of another mouth to feed.

Alongside what may be termed the clinical judgement of the parents were reasons that had more to do with the economic and physical burden that having a sick child in hospital placed on a poor family. Free treatment was all very well, but if it was not seen to be benefiting the child, and if the hospital's regime was adversely

---

78   GOSH Archive, GOS/10/8/193–4. The child had been ill for 14 months, or over half his life.

79   Pollock, *Forgotten Children*, p. 51.

80   22 July 1903. GOSH Archive, GOS/8/163.

81   James Furness Marson, resident surgeon at the Smallpox Hospital, *Select Committee on the Operation of the Vaccination Act* (1867) PP 1871; XII, QQ.4, pp. 174–6.

affecting the 'health' of the family unit (physical, emotional and economic), then it was rejected emphatically.

Conclusion

The documentary material for Great Ormond Street indicates that poor metropolitan patients and their families could exercise a choice with regard to the medical care offered by the institution, even at a time when there was only one children's hospital in London, and the admission process was apparently controlled by the professionals and hospital supporters. Treatment could be, and was, rejected by parents, whose reasons reflect their judgement of the best interests of the sick child and of the family as a whole. In contrast to the pathetic pictures of passive suffering and dependence, so effectively used in fundraising campaigns by the Victorian hospital administrators, the patients – through their families – did have a voice, exercised choice in accepting or rejecting treatment, and thereby influenced the nature of medical philanthropy.

While not wishing to diminish the autonomy of the hospital, it is possible that the family's attitude was of more relevance to the make-up and motivations of all in-patients, and not just those who left the institution before treatment was concluded. Mothers may not have wished to be parted from younger children, while those over the age of five may have been too valuable in terms of earning power to be spared for a four- to eight-week hospital stay. Institutions may also have had their part to play, with teachers alerting parents to the symptoms of illness.[82] Finally, perhaps the child's own experience was a factor. Having endured measles and several other infectious conditions, the insults to an under-nourished city body began to tell in other ways by the age of nine. Tubercular and rheumatic disorders, for instance, made themselves more obvious, and growth spurts made bone and joint disease more apparent. Disease thus became visible to adults for the first time, in changing symptoms, or in the failure of a child to recover from attacks as he or she once did.

The length of stay for the sampled children ranges from one day to 18 months. The hospital's stated policy was that children were not kept on the wards beyond one month, but an examination of the ratio of beds to patients taken from the *Annual Reports* from 1852 to 1900 shows that there was an average bed occupancy of 8.36 children per annum at the main hospital, and 5.57 at Cromwell House convalescent home. This suggests that a significant percentage of in-patients stayed considerably longer than the four weeks. Moreover, the onset of infectious disease, either among individual patients or throughout the hospital, resulted in rapid decamping of patients

---

82   Pupil numbers were significant even before the 1870 Education Act made elementary schooling compulsory. In 1851, two million English children (13 per cent of the population) were registered for elementary education, with a further 525,000 Sunday schools offering part-time instruction. See Laqueur, 'Working-Class Demand', p. 193. Schools themselves were not used to study child health until the early 1900s, when a survey in Dundee and Edinburgh showed that between 57 and 70 per cent of pupils were diseased. London's record was even worse, with 94 per cent of older pupils and 92 per cent of the infants at the Johanna Street School in Lambeth being judged below normal physical condition. See Newman, *The Health of the State*, pp. 135–8.

to fever hospitals and home. The percentage will probably therefore increase when these episodes are taken into account. The only year in which the ratio reached one patient per bed per month was 1866, which, from the metropolitan health viewpoint, was exceptional.[83] In 1889, the hospital managed only four children per bed, or three months per in-patient stay.

The children's hospital offered free treatment to the sick children of poor families on condition that the recipients of their charity submitted to the rules and regulations of the institution. Once the charity was well established, the targeted constituency of users generally accepted what was on offer, while acknowledging the evangelical nature of the service and their 'policing' (to use Donzilot's phrase) by the hospital management, staff and supporters. The acceptance of medical treatment was not done blindly, or in an unsophisticated manner, by the families, and – should what was on offer be deemed harmful to the individual child or the family as a whole – this acceptance was discontinued. In the words of one commentator:

> Every attempt to discipline family conduct – or, in the Victorian vernacular, to 'fortify family character' – required some sort of negotiation over the frontier between public and private needs ... Parents ... were often shrewd judges of the 'help' on offer.[84]

They were not only alert to the cost that accepting in-patient treatment for their children would have for their families, but also displayed the confidence that their judgement as to what was best for their sick children was the final one. In the Victorian age, in spite of encroaching state intervention and the number and influence of charitable organizations, parental prerogative remained a powerful control on what was – and was not – acceptable in terms of child medicine.

83   1866 was the year of the last significant outbreak of cholera in the East End, which was also adversely affected by the collapse of the Thames shipbuilding business.

84   G.K. Behlmer, *Friends of the Family, the English Home and Its Guardians, 1850–1940* (Stanford, 1998), p. 24.

CHAPTER NINE

Mental health care and charity for the middling sort: Holloway Sanatorium 1885–1900

Anne C. Shepherd

Holloway Sanatorium, Virginia Water, Surrey, was established by private bequest for the exclusive benefit of the insane middle classes. It was almost entirely reliant on a scheme whereby the fees of better-off patients subsidized those less affluent but deemed 'deserving' of assistance. Holloway Sanatorium allows observation of the world of the recipient of charitable mental health care during the latter years of the nineteenth century, and an examination of the nuances of psychiatric custodial care for this patient group in an environment created for their specific needs.

Occupying a 22-acre site and only 20 miles from London, the Sanatorium was conveniently accessible by rail, its proximity to the capital thus attesting to the importance of the metropolis as a source of potential patients. Considerable public interest was manifested in the Sanatorium for some years prior to its opening because of both its outstanding architecture and its intended clientele. While building was in progress, Thomas Holloway utilized the site's close proximity to the South-Western Railway by erecting a huge sign facing the railway bridge. For nine years this sign proclaimed the forthcoming opening of Holloway Sanatorium for the care of mental diseases in persons of the middle class.[1]

Increasingly, the middle classes were perceived as requiring their own medical facilities, particularly when it came to hospitals or other forms of custodial institution where association with paupers was deemed both inappropriate and potentially detrimental to recovery. Cost was also a prime consideration, and options were limited. This chapter will examine the increased demands for the treatment of the middle-class insane and the rationale behind the building of this elegant hospital before considering the founders' charitable intentions and the reality of their implementation for the patients. The uniqueness of this institution will be further illustrated by an overview of the environment and the patients, and by examining how they were provided for in terms of both comfort and entertainment. It is not intended to consider specific medical treatment within the confines of the chapter.[2]

---

1   Miscellaneous notes, anonymous, Surrey History centre (hereafter SHC) Acc. 2620.

2   For a discussion of this, see A. Shepherd, 'The Female Patient Experience in Two Late-Nineteenth-Century Surrey Asylums', in J. Andrews and A. Digby (eds), *Sex and Seclusion, Class and Custody. Perspectives on Gender and Class in the History of British and Irish Psychiatry* (Amsterdam and New York, 2004).

Caring for the insane

By the early nineteenth century, the state had become the principal provider of custodial care and treatment for the insane poor. The huge growth of 'asylumdom'[3] initially took place during a period of therapeutic optimism, which rapidly gave way to growing medical and lay concerns regarding the efficacy of these institutions. County asylums, in particular, swelled to accommodate ever-increasing numbers of poor and troubled individuals, many of whom had previously resided in workhouses or in rate-funded accommodation within licensed houses. Some county asylums made provision for a limited number of private patients, and subsequently some charitable private cases, but the take-up was slow and inherent prejudice against them persisted.[4] That county asylums became increasingly viewed almost as 'warehouses' for transient members of the lower classes did little to enhance their appeal for the prospective treatment of those classes who had no desire to see their relatives rubbing shoulders with former workhouse inmates, petty criminals and other undesirables.

Generally, there was some concern that the ongoing involvement of the courts in the certification processes of the private patient would lead to families avoiding sending their relatives to any institution at all. From the latter years of the eighteenth century, private care became increasingly within the financial reach of growing numbers of the population.[5] Many private establishments had received considerable bad publicity, but despite this, demands for private care continued and the numbers of private patients increased throughout the nineteenth century (although more slowly than for pauper patients, for whom large county asylums continued to be built) as more affluent families sought treatment for afflicted relatives. This corresponded with a growing awareness of the perceived relationship between insanity and hereditary disorder.[6] The middle and upper classes tended to favour registered hospitals and private accommodation in public asylums as opposed to licensed houses, which may, as Charlotte MacKenzie has suggested, have been due to the notoriety that such establishments had continued to receive throughout the century.[7]

Private asylums have been interpreted as 'institutions for private imprisonment' where, despite huge amounts of expenditure by the patient's relatives, there was no more likelihood of effecting a cure than in a public institution.[8] However, as MacKenzie has pointed out in her work on the Sussex private asylum at Ticehurst, most patients were not incarcerated for years on end, so that the discharge rates of patients within the private sector were not dissimilar to those seen in public institutions. The evidence at Holloway broadly endorses this, with one important

---

3   A. Scull, *Museums of Madness: The Social Organisation of Insanity in Nineteenth-Century England* (London, 1979).

4   L. Smith, 'The County Asylum in the Mixed Economy of Care, 1808–1845', in J. Melling and B. Forsythe (eds), *Insanity, Institutions and Society, A social history of madness in comparative perspective* (London, 1999), p. 38.

5   C. MacKenzie, *Psychiatry for the Rich, A History of Ticehurst Private Asylum* (London, 1992).

6   Ibid., p. 20.

7   Ibid., p. 20.

8   Scull, *Museums of Madness*, p. 204.

exception, in that single women formed a substantial proportion of the residual asylum population. MacKenzie has also suggested that accusations of social control are perhaps less appropriate with regard to the private institution than to the public sector, where there was a class difference between the incarcerated and their keepers.[9] At Holloway, the management was acutely aware that the class differentials between inmates and staff could be problematic when patients' carers were of an inferior social standing. This was particularly difficult in respect of voluntary patients and contributed to the management's decision to employ middle-class 'companions'.

Fear of impoverishment for middle-class families endeavouring to care for their sick relatives was not new. In 1750, the Trustees for St Luke's Hospital for Lunatics in London declared the rationale for their new asylum thus:

> From hence it appears that the expense necessarily attending the confinement and other means of cure are such as people born in middling circumstances cannot bear, it generally requiring several months, and often a whole year, before a cure is completed ...[10]

The founders recognized that the result was that often afflicted 'families without such assistance must sink under the expense'.[11] Partly as a response to their financial vulnerability, Holloway Sanatorium was specifically intended to benefit this patient group, which was considered as being largely excluded from access to appropriate, and affordable, institutional psychiatric care.

One option was mixed-class asylums. A few existed in England, but they were more common in Scotland, where alternative methods of caring for the insane were prevalent. Glasgow Lunatic Asylum, founded in 1814, was intended to be a mixed institution that accommodated both the wealthiest citizen and the lowly labourer, where the fees of the former supported the accommodation and care of the poor. This principle infiltrated the very design of the asylum, so that while unnecessary cost was avoided, the building was intended to '... enshrine a happy consensual medium...'.[12] However, as Andrews has pointed out, the needs of the pauper inmates were frequently subordinated to those of the private patients, and by 1897 no pauper patients remained.[13] In England, Bethlem, Europe's oldest psychiatric establishment, was observed to be increasing its middle-class admissions by the 1880s and – as Dr George Henry Savage (Resident Physician-Superintendent, 1878–88) proudly stated

---

9   C. MacKenzie, 'Social factors in the admission, discharge, and continuing stay of patients at Ticehurst Asylum, 1845–1917', in R. Porter, W.F. Bynum and M. Shepherd (eds), *The Anatomy of Madness*, vol. 2, *Institutions and Society* (London, 1985), p. 159.

10   C.N. French, *The Story of St Luke's Hospital* (London, 1951), p. 8.

11   Ibid., p. 8.

12   J. Andrews, 'Raising the tone of asylumdom. Maintaining and expelling pauper lunatics at the Glasgow Royal Asylum in the nineteenth century', in J. Melling and B. Forsythe (eds), *Insanity, Institutions and Society, 1800–1914* (London, 1999), p. 206.

13   J. Andrews, 'The Patient Population', in J. Andrews and I. Smith (eds), *'Let There be Light Again'. A History of Gartnavel Royal Hospital from its Beginning to the Present Day* (Glasgow, 1993), p. 106.

– this had been achieved by way of '… careful selection of cases on application'.[14] Mixed-class accommodation was one option for the middle classes, but possessing sufficient means to pay was usually essential for their admission.

Class definitions within the context of the asylum are fraught with ambiguities. The Dundee Royal Lunatic Asylum had a separate private patient facility between 1890 and 1903, before becoming exclusively private. Lorraine Walsh's work demonstrates that respectability and social propriety were important determinants in patient selection there.[15] This is mirrored to some extent at Holloway, where only those patients meeting the board's middle-class 'criteria' were considered worthy of charitable assistance. As the century drew to a close, there was an increase in the number of upper-class patients admitted so as to subsidize those of 'scanty means'.[16]

The middle-class insane

The emergence of separate facilities for the middle-class insane was in keeping with a growing recognition of the different types of mental illness and their subsequent categorization. This led to the development of new and specialized types of provision, such as the early institutions for the congenitally defective as opposed to those who were mentally ill.[17] Often these were the result of private philanthropy, as there were insufficient public resources to provide for these harmless and incurable patients. At the same time, the Poor Law increasingly emphasized segregation and specialized provision for the more difficult or dangerous lunatics.

Admission of one's relatives into an asylum was considered shameful, particularly for those middle classes who considered institutional care a last resort. Charitable institutions were one option for concerned families anxious to avoid financial ruin and minimize stigma, leading to the establishment of asylums such as The Lawn at Lincoln in 1818. Here, 'appropriate' care was offered to those who emanated from an educated background but who were of limited financial means.[18]

Likewise, St Luke's Hospital for Lunatics was originally intended to house just 25 patients. Specifically, these were to be those with families '… not rich enough to send their relations to a private institution and too proud to allow them to be classed as parish poor'.[19] Keen to emphasize itself as a hospital and not an asylum, St Luke's operated a system of 'disqualifying rules'.[20] Holloway Sanatorium followed

---

14   J. Andrews, A. Briggs, R. Porter, P. Tucker and K. Waddington, *The History of Bethlem* (London, 1997); *Bethlem Annual Report*, p. 519.

15   L. Walsh, 'A Class Apart? Admissions to the Dundee Royal Lunatic Asylum 1890–1910', in Andrews and Digby (eds), *Sex and Seclusion*, pp. 249–71.

16   Superintendent's Annual Report for 1891, SHC Acc. 2620/1/1.

17   Examples include the National Model Asylum for Idiots (later Royal Earlswood) and Normansfield Hospital. Both aimed to provide care for defective children from wealthy backgrounds.

18   H. Richardson (ed.), *English Hospitals 1660–1948, A Survey of their Architecture and Design* (Royal Commission on the Historical Monuments of England, 1998), p. 164.

19   French, *St Luke's*, p. 54, as quoted in *English Hospitals 1660–1948*, p. 155.

20   S. Low, *The Charities of London* (1867), p. 33.

suit, striving to ensure that it did not become a moribund custodial institution, while reliant on a scheme whereby the fees of the better-off patients subsidized those less affluent. Similarly, while The Retreat in York admitted relatively few non-Quaker patients from 1796 (especially as subsidized cases), it was acknowledged that high fee-paying non-Quaker inmates were a particularly important financial benefit. In 1841, Samuel Tuke reported that the lowest terms paid by these high-class patients stood at two and a half guineas a week. By 1910, some were paying as much as seven guineas a week, thus supplementing many Quaker patients being treated at less than economic cost.[21]

An 1859 Parliamentary Select Committee, to which Lord Shaftesbury (first chairman of the Commissioners in Lunacy) was the chief witness, publicly aired the issue of appropriate and affordable custodial care for the middle-class insane.[22] Shaftesbury had attempted unsuccessfully to raise funds for a middle-class asylum. Inspired by his efforts, Thomas Holloway (1800–83) began to consider the possibility of realizing this vision for an establishment in keeping with middle-class social status, irrespective of financial means. Shaftesbury had stated:

> Asylums where there are not a number of proprietors looking for profit present the very greatest advantages; and I find that patients are taken into them at a lower figure than at any private house, and the richer patients who go into these asylums, by the larger sum they pay, contribute from the overplus to alleviate the burdens upon the poorer inmates.[23]

Holloway's legacy

Major donations to support voluntary hospitals, or single philanthropic endeavours to establish a new hospital, were increasingly common as the nineteenth century progressed.[24] Holloway Sanatorium was described as '… the most grandiloquent of all nineteenth-century donations …' both in the actual size and scale of the building and in its lavish interior.[25] When the Sanatorium eventually opened, praise was heaped upon the superior accommodation. The *Surrey Advertiser* reported:

> For persons whose friends are opulent there are front rooms or suites of rooms, and for others less fortunate apartments in less prominent parts of the building. But for all, rich or poor, is provided the same bright surroundings, and everything calculated to create an interest in those of our fellow creatures who are inmates of the Sanatorium.[26]

---

21   A. Digby, *Madness, Morality and Medicine. A study of the York Retreat 1796–1914* (Cambridge, 1985), p. 181.

22   A.A. Cooper, 7th Earl of Shaftesbury, KG (1801–85), was concerned with the welfare of the insane for over 60 years.

23   The *Surrey Advertiser* (20 June 1885).

24   J. Taylor, *Hospital and Asylum Architecture in England 1840–1914. Building for Healthcare.* (London, 1991), p. 34.

25   Ibid., p. 35.

26   The *Surrey Advertiser* (20 June 1885).

Thomas Holloway was a wealthy patent-medicine manufacturer and philanthropist whose annual profits were reported to have been in excess of £50,000 by the 1870s.[27] Married but childless, and having amassed a considerable personal fortune, Holloway sought outlets for his money that would also constitute a permanent testimonial to his success, achieved, as it was, from humble origins. Thus he embarked on the two major projects which would ensure the continuation of his name: Holloway Sanatorium (1873–85) for the insane middle classes, and the nearby Royal Holloway College (1879–86) for the education of women.

Holloway often stated that 'charity demeans the recipient of charity'[28] – a view broadly in keeping with many political economists of the time who perceived charity as having created an unfortunate culture of dependence. Instead they advocated the employment of a more rational and scientific approach to philanthropy. Something of a recluse, leaving few surviving clues as to his personality, Holloway's broad philanthropic principle was that help should be given only to the deserving. By his definition, this meant those who had previously been imbued with the work ethic and had abandoned it only as a result of necessity or ill fortune. It has been suggested that Holloway possessed a London shopkeeper mentality together with a certain liberal radicalism that strove for better opportunities for the lower middle classes. He was certainly closely associated with some London radical reformers who assisted him in furthering these two ambitious projects.[29]

That the Sanatorium took so long to come to fruition is puzzling, but it appears that Holloway spent considerable time researching the idea of building an insane asylum for the middle classes within easy reach of London, a 'Model place'.[30] He visited several asylums, both abroad and in England, and corresponded with the Commissioners in Lunacy and with many architects, including George Godwin, who was also editor of *The Builder*.[31] Early in 1871, Holloway enlisted Godwin's help, and in a series of articles headed 'How to Spend Money for the Public Good',[32] he anonymously solicited public opinion regarding his plans to donate money for an institution for the benefit of the middle classes that would be '… for the greatest public good'.[33] Later that year, Holloway purchased the land at St Ann's Heath, Virginia Water, where he proposed building the first in what he hoped would be a series of hospitals for the afflicted middle classes.

---

27   J. Elliot, *Palaces, Patronage and Pills – Thomas Holloway: His Sanatorium, College and Picture Gallery* (Egham, 1996), p. 8

28   A. Harrison-Barbet, *Thomas Holloway, Victorian Philanthropist* (Royal Holloway College, University of London, Egham, 1994), p. 80.

29   James Beal, instrumental in the campaign for governmental reforms in the 1870s, acted as Holloway's public relations agent in matters concerning both the College and the Sanatorium. See A. Saint, 'Holloway Sanatorium: A Conservation Nightmare', *Victorian Society Annual* (1993): 19–34.

30   Elliot, *Palaces, Patronage and Pills*, p. 23.

31   Under his editorship (1844–83), George Godwin transformed *The Builder* into the most successful specialist paper of its kind, with a readership well beyond the world of architecture and building.

32   *The Builder* (23 March, 15 and 22 April 1871).

33   *The Builder* (25 March 1871), vol. xxix, 1468, p. 220.

In 1872, Holloway and Godwin organized a competition to select the architect from a final list of 13 designs. The judges included many who were familiar with asylum requirements, among them medical practitioners such as Dr Yellowlees and Dr Lockhart Robertson (of Haywards Heath Asylum), and the architect Thomas Henry Wyatt, co-designer of the county asylums for Wiltshire and Buckinghamshire. The panel finally chose 'Alpha' by William Henry Crossland (1834–1908).[34] The resultant building followed Flemish style, as exemplified by the Cloth Hall at Ypres.[35] But while Holloway strove to build an institution that would be a worthy and fitting testimony to his munificence, at the same time his thrifty disposition engendered many subtle alterations to the original plan. Numerous modifications resulted in a diminution of the Flemish style and less 'pure' Gothic, and it is fairly certain that the finished building differed greatly from the original competition plan, which unfortunately has not survived.[36] Holloway's concern to provide a luxurious environment with the most up-to-date equipment appears to have dominated to the extent that it overrode the more practical considerations of providing secure and legally compliant accommodation for the insane middle classes. Holloway himself must have been aware of potential pitfalls from the outset. *Building News*, while paying tribute to the competition entrants, baldly stated that their evident talent and style did not necessarily mean they were capable of designing an asylum,[37] and that the Commissioners in Lunacy would be unlikely to pass any one of the competition plans in their present format.[38] Clearly, these early warnings regarding the suitability of the accommodation for lunatics went largely unheeded, as in 1877 the Commissioners in Lunacy refused to grant a licence. An ongoing emphasis on aesthetics, combined with Holloway's declining health and other professional and personal preoccupations, meant that the final building encompassed many flaws.

The first brick was laid by Jane Holloway, Thomas's wife, in spring 1873 and the main contractors were on site by the summer of that year. By 1877 *The Builder* claimed that the Sanatorium was 'approaching completion'.[39] The Sanatorium was virtually finished by 1878, yet it was seven years before it was officially opened and the substantial time lapse caused costs to escalate to over £300,000. Holloway did not survive to see the completion of his ambitious projects, dying of lung congestion in December 1883. His businesses, including the Sanatorium, continued to be run by his two brothers-in-law, Henry Driver Holloway and George Martin Holloway, who, as his heirs, adopted the name Holloway by deed poll in 1884. They strove to enshrine the founder's ideals in the daily running of the hospital, which eventually opened to receive patients in June 1885.

---

34   Crossland's architectural practice centred on Huddersfield, Halifax and Leeds and was responsible for at least 58 designs, including Rochdale Town Hall, which served as a precursor for the Sanatorium. The largely obscure architect John Philpott Jones had, by Crossland's own admission, made a significant contribution to the winning design.

35   Saint, 'Holloway Sanatorium: A Conservation Nightmare'.

36   Ibid., p. 21.

37   *Building News* (2 August 1872) vol. xxiii, no. 916.

38   *Building News* (11 October 1872).

39   *The Builder* (14 July 1877).

The Sanatorium's architecture and environment

Sanatoriums were associated with other, physical (and arguably less shameful) illnesses, most usually tuberculosis. Evolving from the Latin *sanare* – to heal – sanatoriums were primarily for the reception and medical treatment of invalids or convalescents, who often underwent 'open-air treatment'. In the nineteenth century, the terms sanatorium and sanitarium were often used interchangeably, but the second has its origin in the Latin *sanitas*, meaning health. Thus it has been suggested that the former term implied active medical intervention, whereas the latter is associated with healthy living, as opposed to medical skill.[40] The nomenclature 'Holloway Sanatorium' certainly helped to preserve middle-class propriety: 'A father will feel terrible repugnance at committing his son to a mad-house, whereas the notion of sending him for a time to a sanatorium seems far less dreadful ... .'[41] Brochures advised prospective patients and their families that in correspondence there was no need to write anything on the envelope other than 'Dr. Rees Philips [*sic*], Virginia Water, Chertsey'.[42] This was in keeping with a general increased awareness of middle-class sensitivity with regard to psychiatric illness; from the 1880s, many adverts for private nursing homes, sanatoriums, inebriate asylums and hydropathic establishments could be found in the *Medical Directory*, for example. In the same spirit, yet other institutions altered their names; the licensed house West Malling Place, previously William Perfect's Madhouse, was seen to metamorphose into the Kent Sanatorium.[43] The basic principles that formed the bedrock of the treatment of tuberculosis in the nineteenth-century sanatoriums – fresh air, good diet and controlled exercise – were also much in evidence in the treatment of psychiatric patients.

When Holloway died in December 1883, the Sanatorium was furnished, equipped and insured, yet it remained unopened. The Trustees, headed by George Martin Holloway and Henry Driver Holloway, were anxious to complete the project and duly appointed the first medical superintendent, Dr Sutherland Reece Phillips, in 1884.[44] Despite the Sanatorium's impressive design, Reece Phillips was perturbed by various shortcomings in the Sanatorium's construction and immediately began to work with the trustees to ensure that the hospital would comply with current legislation. Upon his appointment, he observed that some 'prime requirements' were deficient. In particular:

> There were no corridors of communication in the portions of the building intended for occupation by the patients. The rooms opened into one another, so that there would have been no privacy for the patients, and great difficulty in administration. All meals for patients residing in the wings would have to be carried through several of the principal sitting rooms.[45]

---

40   T. Dormandy, *The White Death. A History of Tuberculosis* (London, 1999), p. 147.

41   *The Builder* (7 January 1882).

42   Rules for the Admission, Visiting and Discharge of Patients, 1886, SHC Acc. 2620.

43   MacKenzie, 'Ticehurst', p. 207.

44   Formerly Superintendent of Wonford House Hospital, Exeter.

45   Superintendent's First Annual Report (1 February 1887), p. 5.

Anticipating the class of inmate, expansive suites of rooms had been built across the front of the patient accommodation, with access via staircases at the rear for their personal servants. This contravened fire regulations, while difficulties regarding the excessively narrow design of the corridors had been identified as far back as 1872.[46] At short notice, Charles Dorman, architect to St Andrew's Hospital, Northampton, was engaged and thus Crossland's design was updated to incorporate domestic innovations and legislative changes that had evolved since the project had begun several years previously. These included the aforementioned corridors, the addition of storerooms and pantries connected to patient galleries, extra staircases to act as fire escapes, and the removal of some partitions to admit more light into patient accommodation. Sanitary arrangements and the water supply were completely overhauled, new gas works were built in the grounds, electric light installed, the superintendent's accommodation extended and improved, and paths and roads laid out. On the women's side, a walled garden for the exercise of 'troublesome' female patients and two padded rooms were constructed.[47] A chapel had not been included in the original plans (Holloway himself was a Nonconformist), but as this requirement had since been stipulated by law, the Sanatorium had started building one in 1882.

At last the Commissioners in Lunacy were able to certify the Sanatorium as suitable for the receipt of 200 prospective patients, just three days before the official opening on 15 June 1885. The ceremony was presided over by the Prince of Wales, who travelled over from Ascot during the racing season with his retinue. The occasion was reported at some length by the local press, which praised the deceased Holloway and his charitable intention '... to provide a home for persons temporarily deprived of their reason, at charges suited to their means'.[48] Thus those families unable to afford private care were relieved of the burden of having to place their relatives in a pauper asylum, 'which must have proved particularly loathsome'.[49]

Built of red brick and Portland stone, the Sanatorium was designed in the popular 'block and corridor' layout. A three-storey main building comprised a central portion that focused on a seven-bay high-roofed hall, flanked by subordinate sections of 19-bay apartment ranges on each side, one for female patients and one for males. An impressive 530-foot terrace ran across the front and a formidable central tower 145 feet high dominated the whole area.

Spacious public rooms including an enormous high-ceilinged recreation hall measuring 80 by 40 feet. This featured a 60-foot high hammerbeam roof, elaborate gilding and numerous portraits of distinguished figures, both contemporary and historical, including Thomas and Jane Holloway. A statue of Thomas Holloway originally stood in the lavish entrance hall, in addition to the 'striking portrait'[50] in the recreation hall. Monograms of the Holloway initials with their adopted coat of arms can still be seen today in the ceilings and at numerous points throughout the restored building. Holloway himself wished thus to ensure that patients and visitors

46 *Building News* (2 August 1872), vol. xxiii, no. 916.
47 Superintendent's First Annual Report (1 February 1887), p. 5.
48 The *Surrey Advertiser* (20 June 1885).
49 Ibid.
50 Ibid.

to the Sanatorium would not forget who had built the hospital. In addition, he clearly wished to differentiate his asylum stylistically from other institutions. Contemporary commentary suggests that he more than achieved this.

Holloway's dining and recreation halls were sumptuously decorated, seemingly to provide cheerfulness and distraction to troubled minds; '... cold and grey columns and walls, even if enlivened by sculpture would, it was considered, sit heavily on a mind diseased'.[51] The lavish interior had caused *The Builder* in 1882, three years prior to opening, to exclaim: 'Such a combination of rich colouring and gilding is not to be found in any modern building in this country, except the House of Lords.'[52] Not everyone was quite so complimentary regarding the décor; the young designer and architect Charles Ashbee, visiting the Sanatorium in 1885, observed in his journals that 'The decoration of the asylum is very garish and ghastly but appropriate.'[53] The decorative scheme, particularly extravagant around the entrance to the reception hall and the chapel, was said to be surpassed only by that of Great Ormond Street Children's Hospital, suggesting that high decoration was considered suitable for both the childish and the mad.

From a therapeutic perspective, the comfort and elegance available to patients was designed to ease their adjustment to changed circumstances, and the 'normality' of a homely but luxurious environment was believed beneficial to recovery. This concern to preserve 'normality' continued to be an ongoing consideration for the Medical Superintendent and the Governors over the years, contributing to both medical and administrative policy. As the century progressed, seaside trips became part of many families' itinerary and, partially in keeping with this, and also in acknowledgement of the reputed therapeutic value of sea air, the management rented coastal properties for the ease and comfort of their patients during the summer months. Eventually, in 1892, the Sanatorium's management purchased their own small property, Hove Villas, near Brighton (which was sold in 1909).[54] This was predominantly run by Mrs Reece Phillips, listed in local trade directories as the female superintendent. She appears to have taken a particular pride in this branch, rejoicing that there she actually lived among the patients and oversaw every detail herself, as opposed to occupying separate quarters.[55] A considerably larger 13-acre site at Canford Cliffs in Dorset was purchased and here the dedicated seaside branch known as St Ann's Hospital opened in 1903. Designed by Weir Schultz, it could accommodate up to 40 patients at any one time.[56]

---

51   *Building News* (16 September 1881).

52   *The Builder* (7 January 1882).

53   Ashbee Journals, quoted in Saint, 'Holloway Sanatorium: A Conservation Nightmare': 25.

54   Local trade directories for the area show that from *c.*1915–68 this property operated as the convalescent branch of Camberwell House.

55   'An Asylum and an Elysium', *Woman* (31 August 1892).

56   SHC Acc. 2620.

Management and charitable assistance

Holloway's brother-in-law George Martin Holloway chaired a board of 26 trustees, and in addition, an annually elected General Committee of between eight and 26 persons was established. This comprised ex-officio members that included the trustees, the Lord Lieutenant of Surrey, the Lord Bishop of Winchester, the Lord Mayor of London, the Chairman of the Surrey Quarter Sessions and all the Surrey Justices of the Peace who served as House Committee members of one of the Surrey Asylums. Such a high-profile committee of Surrey dignitaries helped the Sanatorium become an integral part of the local community, while lending gravitas and increasing the possibility of charitable donations. Meetings were twice yearly, although 'Special Meetings' could be instigated at any time if deemed appropriate by the Chairman. This Committee was responsible for the senior staff appointments, accounts and the implementation of the Sanatorium's rules and regulations in accordance with lunacy legislation.

The day-to-day asylum management came under the scrutiny of the House Committee, which met monthly and dealt with matters such as the regulation of ordinary expenditure, tenders, contracts, the overseeing of general and medical administration, and staff issues. Members inspected the Sanatorium fortnightly, examining the condition and treatment of the patients and listening to any complaints. The Committee paid particular attention to new admissions to ensure that they were correctly classified and comfortable in their new surroundings. In common with other institutions, the resident Medical Superintendent was responsible for the patients' medical treatment and had the 'entire direction of the Institution, subject only to the control of the General and the House Committee'.[57] Buttressed by two Assistant Medical Officers, the Superintendent was responsible for the appointment, engagement, regulation and dismissal of all other asylum employees, from the Head Attendants to the lowest of the servants.

An interesting addition to the staffing at Holloway was the employment of male and female 'companions', initially two on each side, although the numbers increased to between six and nine in subsequent years. These accomplished employees, the female companions distinguished by their white caps, were engaged to live among the patients to encourage normal behaviour and conversation, and were reported to be '... of the greatest use in promoting occupation and amusement'.[58] Companions' daily duties included eating with the patients, ensuring they were appropriately dressed, accompanying them on walks and participating alongside them in various recreational amusements such as embroidery, bagatelle or cards. They were required to possess particular social skills, such as singing or playing a musical instrument, and they were also required to assist the Superintendent and his officers in the planning and execution of the Sanatorium's busy and varied entertainment schedule. This was always an important feature of asylum life, but at Holloway it was given a particular emphasis by the management, as – given the social background of many of the patients – physical labour was seldom an appropriate therapy. Overall, these

---

57 Regulations for the Holloway Sanatorium 1886, SHC Acc. 2620.
58 Superintendent's First Annual Report, p. 10.

companions were seen as a valuable asset to the re-socialization and training of the patients. However, things did not always run smoothly, and in common with other asylum employees, they too fell foul of the management when they transgressed the rules. For example, 'Mr M.', one of the male companions, was promptly removed from his post following a bout of intemperance at the end of 1886.[59]

Patients' admissions

Originally intended to house 200 patients, the Sanatorium was popular from the outset and received many more applications for financially assisted places than was anticipated. Six months after opening in June 1885 there were 70 resident patients, eight of these being voluntary boarders – that is, patients admitted without certification. During the course of 1886, 89 certified patients were admitted in addition to 17 boarders. By the end of the year, 110 patients and nine boarders remained. In the Superintendent's *First Annual Report*, Dr Reece Phillips observed that '… several hundreds of applications were received, the greater number expecting to be admitted gratuitously or at a low rate of board'.[60] As the hospital was still in its infancy, there was some consternation and it was agreed that such admissions had to be restricted. In 1886, therefore, despite sufficient patient income, the General Committee expressed their intention to limit admissions of highly subsidized cases to ensure the hospital's financial well-being. In addition, it was hoped that this approach would help limit the admission of incurable cases. Yet despite this declaration and a number of costly building improvements undertaken that year, the Committee strove to remain mindful of the Sanatorium's original philanthropic intentions and was able to admit 68 patients at reduced rates. 'The benevolent object with which the Institution was founded has not been lost sight of. Several patients, including one kept gratuitously, have been maintained at low weekly rates. … Indirect aid has also been given to certain patients in the shape of clothing and other extras.'[61]

Applications for reduced rates were usually made by relatives and friends of the patients and, occasionally, by the patients themselves, particularly in the case of voluntary boarders. Such applications were duly discussed and agreed at General Committee meetings, with personal recommendations from Committee members more favourably received, as were applications from former members of the armed forces, diplomatic services, medical professions and clergy. The patient's familial, social and occupational status were considered by the Committee, whose members wished to be assured that the applicants were 'of the middling sort'. How they ultimately arrived at their decisions is unclear from the records and there is no evidence of consistent criteria being applied in order to determine appropriate social status and financial requirements.[62] The Hospital Rules for the Admission and Visiting

---

59   Minutes of the House Committee, 3 January 1887, p. 17, SHC Acc. 2620/2/1.

60   Superintendent's First Annual Report, p. 9.

61   Minutes of the Annual & Ordinary Meetings of the General Committee, 15th November 1887 SHC Acc. 2620/1/1.

62   The surviving Minutes of the General Committee provide details only of those that the hospital has actually admitted, not those who have applied and perhaps been refused.

of Patients and Boarders in 1889 stated that terms of admission varied from £2 2s. to £3 3s. per week and that reductions for special cases were '*entirely at the discretion of the Committee*'.[63] Patients and their representatives could also make a personal, as opposed to written, appeal to the Committee. As Wright has also illustrated in his work on the Poor Law Asylum in Buckinghamshire, the confinement process here was clearly a decision arrived at by way of a collaboration between patients' families and the hospital management, with the Superintendent playing a contributory as opposed to a pivotal role in the admissions process.[64]

Prior to opening, there appears to have been an understanding that the Sanatorium would have patients resident for a maximum of only one year, creating the impression of the institution as a temporary refuge for the afflicted members of the impoverished middle classes.[65] These rules were similar in some respects to those initially issued by St Luke's, but both institutions were obliged to relax their approach over time.[66] At Holloway cases such as that of 'Eva A.' were by no means unique. Religious and identity delusions beset this 21-year-old Hampstead woman, and in 1898, following a brief stay at a private licensed house in Hendon, she was admitted to Holloway as a voluntary boarder. She remained as such for six months before being discharged as recovered in July 1899. Over the next five years, she was admitted to Holloway on five other occasions, in most cases initially as a voluntary boarder, but often being certified within days. She was finally discharged as recovered in October 1905, but at no point in her records were there any apparent difficulties regarding her many re-admissions.[67]

Re-admissions and prolonged periods of residence were particularly evident when it came to Holloway's voluntary boarders. Annual reports bear frequent testimony that medical staff firmly believed the voluntary-boarder system assisted patient well-being and the efficacy of any ensuing treatments. Non-certification minimized stigma and as such removed a perceived hindrance to the recovery process. Many of these patients were subsequently certified, but this was by no means always the case. Their admission provided additional income for the Sanatorium and the system also allowed other patients with less serious conditions to be admitted for respite care.

'Helen W.' was first admitted in August 1891 at the request of her mother. A young, single, epileptic woman, she was described as being 'weak-minded'. However: '... she answers questions rationally, recognises money value, understands the chief political events of the day, and appears to have a good memory. Though unable to earn her living does not appear a suitable subject for certification'.[68] During the

---

Some details are included of those cases where payment arrears have occurred and their subsequent removal.

63   Copy of the Hospital Rules for the Admission and Visiting of Patients, p. 50, Third Annual Report of Holloway Sanatorium, 1888, WLM28 BE574.

64   D. Wright, 'Getting out of the Asylum: Understanding the Confinement of the Insane in the Nineteenth Century', *Social History of Medicine*, 10, 1 (1997): 137–55.

65   *The Builder* (7 January 1882).

66   Within a few years of opening, St Luke's was re-admitting incurable or uncured patients at a slightly higher weekly charge. French, *St Luke's*, p. 16.

67   'Eva A.', Holloway Female Casebooks SHC Acc. 3473/3/1, 6, 7, 29.

68   Holloway Sanatorium Casebook – Voluntary Boarders, SHC Acc. 3473/3/28.

following 14 months, she was admitted under voluntary status on five occasions, notably when suffering so many fits a day that her family were unable to cope. This admissions pattern was repeated several times during the following eight years.

The Regulations of 1886 stated that three categories of patients were essentially admissible to the Sanatorium, whether they were certified or boarders. These were those curable patients who were unable to pay at all; patients either curable or incurable who could not afford full payment; and patients whether curable or incurable whose circumstances did allow for full payment.[69] First-class rates were set at £2 2s. (two guineas) and upward, and second-class at between £1 5s. and £2 2s. Rates of payment for both the third-class and urgent second-class cases were determined by the Medical Superintendent, but were also subject to subsequent House Committee approval. Gratuitous admissions and maintenance cases, whether boarder or patient, had to be approved by the House Committee in the first instance, and were intended only for those patients deemed to have a high probability of being cured.[70]

In 1889, the hospital registered as a charity, and thereafter a minimum of 50 per cent of admissions were to be admitted at a weekly inclusive rate not exceeding two guineas, and a further quarter of all admissions at a rate of 25 shillings or less.[71] By 1891, 28 per cent of patients occupied the first-class and more substantial accommodation at the front of the institution, paying over 42 shillings per week. Here they enjoyed private rooms, often with special attendants, or if their relatives preferred they could be accommodated in a private cottage in the grounds. The majority of patients – 45 per cent – were 'second class', paying between 42 and 25 shillings per week, with the remaining 27 per cent of third-class patients on rates of 25 shillings or less.[72] By 1891, the total amount of charitable aid given by the hospital had risen to over £4,000 and was '... mainly bestowed on patients of good social position but scanty means, who could not obtain equal comforts in private asylums, except at greatly increased cost'.[73] At the request of the hospital's management, charitable assistance was extended to include the much-favoured voluntary boarders.

Holloway's management also worked with the After Care Association, taking some 20 or more discharged asylum patients into their care on a yearly basis.[74] These men and women were provided with money, food, clothing, medical attention and accommodation while they adjusted to the 'outside world'. In his sermon at St Mary's, Oxford, in January 1884, the Association's founder, the Revd Hawkins, while acknowledging the predominantly lower-class origin of most of its members, drew the attention of the congregation to those afflicted middle-class patients that it strove to help. Thus the Sanatorium and the After Care Association were united

---

69 Regulations for the Holloway Sanatorium Hospital for the Insane, 1886, SHC Acc. 2620.

70 Rules for the Admission, 1886, SHC Acc. 2620.

71 Charity Commission Deed, 29 January 1889, SHC Acc. 2620.

72 Ibid.

73 Superintendent's Annual Report for 1891, SHC Acc. 2620/1/1.

74 Originally known as the Aftercare Association for Poor and Friendless Female Convalescents on Leaving Asylums for the Insane, this charitable organization was started in 1879 on the initiative of the Revd Henry Hawkins. Lord Shaftesbury was the first president.

in their concern for the plight of those '… members of professions and literary vocations, teachers male and female, and others who, from their position in society, have sunk, and so are most to be pitied, to a low estate'.[75] Once at the Sanatorium, distinctions were made by the management and those deemed middle-class were permitted to associate with the patients, while the others were accommodated with the servants. Members of the After Care Association, while not counting strictly as admissions, were still active participants in Sanatorium life and, as many originated from different social backgrounds, this further indicates the fluidity of 'class' as defined within Holloway's admissions policy.

The social and medical character of patients

Since defining 'middle-class' was problematic for the asylum's management, the term must have retained some variability. It is clear that the middling sort formed the core of the patients, but it was financially expedient, for example, that a proportion of high-rank and therefore (usually) higher-paying patients was also admitted, either voluntarily or under certification. Some chancery lunatics[76] were also resident, and with a guaranteed income from the trustees of their estates, they were likely to have been a welcome addition to help balance the asylum's books. A very small number of criminal lunatics was also admitted, usually those who had been incarcerated for relatively petty offences and had served their time.

The type of patient expected included overworked students, barristers or clergymen and those '… whose minds are "filled with illusions" on account of domestic troubles or bereavements'.[77] While these occupations were indeed represented, most patients had no occupation or were of private means. In his 1887 Annual Report Dr Reece Phillips stated that 'All forms of insanity were freely admitted' and that 'The mental condition of those admitted and not the actual amount of money paid for their maintenance, was the criterion by which they were classified and treated'.[78] Applications for reduced rates were agreed at General Committee meetings, with member's personal recommendations favourably considered, as were most former members of the armed forces, diplomatic services, medical professions and clergy. However, 'George C.', previously a servant (an unusual occupation among Holloway's patients) from Piccadilly, London, was admitted at a reduced rate of two guineas set by the House Committee in November 1891. Aged 65, he had been suffering from GPI (General Paralysis of the Insane) for some 18 months, and his sister was also insane. On admission, he had difficulty walking without aid, was tremulous, incoherent and confused. He deteriorated rapidly and died the following January. His case – one of obvious incurability – was not unusual among

---

75   'An Extract from a Sermon by Revd H. Hawkins, at St Mary's Oxford, 29th January 1884', *Journal of Mental Science*, April 1884, vol. 30.

76   Chancery lunatics were those who were of considerable financial means whose estates were placed under statutory supervision.

77   *The Builder* (7 January 1882).

78   Superintendent's Annual Report 1887, in Minutes of the General Committee, SHC Acc. 2620/1/1.

the charitable patients that the hospital accepted. General Paralysis accounted for 90 per cent of deaths at Holloway during the opening 18 months, and the death rate stood at 7 per cent for several years, attributed by the Superintendent to the poor condition of many admissions.

The 1886 rules and regulations stated that no patient or boarder was to be admitted '... unless in the opinion of the House Committee, he or she has held such a respectable position in society as unfits him or her for association with paupers'.[79] The fees of the upper classes supplemented the charitable cases as predicted, and these patients, whether certified or voluntary, were often able to live as if in the 'outside world' and enjoyed additional privileges. 'Margaret C.', certified and then transferred to boarder status, was noted throughout her two-year stay as 'being an excellent horsewoman'. Allowed to keep her own horse for riding daily, she even participated regularly in the local hunt.[80] Keenly aware of the status of some of his patients, the Superintendent frequently requested improved social facilities, among them more carriages and stabling, Turkish baths for male patients, and a London property so that patients might avail themselves of theatres and exhibitions, so sadly lacking in the provinces.

Admissions (including boarders) rose to 292 by 1890 and in some years up to 35 per cent were voluntary boarders. Of these, it was not unusual for over 20 per cent to be certified and transferred to the patients' list. In 1890, recoveries on all admissions stood at 40.6 per cent, rising to 59.4 per cent in 1891, a high recovery rate partially attributed to the high number of voluntary borders admitted. Women dominated the admissions in all classes (although this was not the case with regard to the county asylums)[81] and were considered by the Superintendent as more likely to recover because they usually suffered from 'merely functional disturbances' and were less likely to suffer from GPI. Medical staff believed the voluntary boarder system assisted patient recovery: non-certification meant no stigma, and accordingly patients were kept on this status for as long as possible without coming into conflict with the Commissioners in Lunacy. The admission of voluntary patients also had the potential for generating additional income and for allowing others with less serious conditions to be admitted for periods of respite care.

The medical and social concerns of families caring for their relatives can often be glimpsed within the evidence provided on admission of the patients, who could be prone to embarrassing and dangerous behaviour, whether in public or in private. A concerned mother felt it necessary to bring both her daughters to be cared for at the Sanatorium and so 'the W. sisters' were frequent inmates over many years, both as certified patients and as voluntary boarders. (This directly contravened the Founder's original intentions.) Mrs W. first brought her elder spinster daughter Edith from Teddington to Holloway in August 1887. Certified at the age of 32, and provided with an assisted place, she was described as suffering from acute mania. Her mother testified that her daughter was prone to giving away money to strangers,

79   Regulations for the Holloway Sanatorium, Hospital for the Insane, St. Ann's Heath, Virginia Water, 1886, SHC Acc. 2620.

80   Holloway Sanatorium Casebook, Voluntary Boarders, SHC Acc. 3473/3/28.

81   Ibid.

embracing them, and generally behaving indecently. Her early days at Holloway were punctuated by reports of her exposing herself 'at every opportunity', having dirty habits and attacking members of staff. Eight months later she was sufficiently recovered to be discharged.[82] Edith was re-admitted eight times as either voluntary boarder or certified patient between 1887 and 1902, when she stayed for 22 years. During this last and lengthy stay at the Sanatorium, Edith was diagnosed as suffering from a thyroid disorder which was easily rectified, so that 12 months later she was discharged recovered, perhaps finally cured, at the age of 66.[83]

Edith's sister Florence was first admitted as a voluntary boarder in 1894. Also in her mid 30s and single, her 'mild melancholia' rapidly deteriorated during her three-month stay, so that she too was diagnosed as suffering from acute mania and duly certified. She stayed for five months, exhibiting similar symptoms to Edith, who was regarded as a contributory factor to Florence's condition, as was allegedly the girl's father, reported by Mrs W. to be hypochondriac.[84] Three years later, Florence was re-admitted with acute mania and upon arrival was immediately placed in a padded room for her own safety. She was routinely treated with hypnotics to quieten her during the following month. She was discharged recovered three months later to the care of her mother, now residing in a more rural location.[85] She did not return to the asylum.

Many patients resided for lengthy periods of time, such as 'Ada H.', 22, from Winchmore Hill, petitioned by her father in December 1887. Having caused much disruption within the family home, she had eventually been diagnosed as suffering from mania two years previously. This was allegedly due to hereditary causes – an uncle had died in an asylum and a young sister had died as an infant from hydrocephalus. Her family testified that she had been increasingly difficult for them to manage and her behaviour was both irrational and embarrassing. Her certificates stated that she 'Laughs & cries continually without evident reason: at times sullen refusing to answer any questions. Refuses to swallow. At times retained food in mouth in large quantities', and that 'Selina H. her mother states that there has been a change in her disposition for more than a year, that she is becoming worse & has recently struck her on several occasions'.[86] When Ada was admitted to the Sanatorium, she was pale and anaemic due to her refusal to eat and possibly due to her experience of care within the family. She spent 15 years at Holloway, on a reduced rate, and was transferred to another private establishment in 1902.

Entertainment and culture

Entertainment was an important component of Holloway's therapeutic regime and the patients were able to participate in a full and varied programme of activities and social events. Many of Holloway's middle- and upper-class patients would have

---

82 Holloway Female Casebook, SHC Acc. 3473/3/1.
83 Holloway Female Casebook, SHC Acc. 3473/3/4.
84 Holloway Female Casebook, SHC Acc. 3473/3/3.
85 Holloway Female Casebook, SHC Acc. 3473/3/4.
86 Holloway Female Casebook, SHC Acc.3473/3/1.

been unused to manual work and so it was particularly vital that they should be kept as fully occupied as possible. As part of the therapeutic regime, patients were encouraged to follow the middle-class lifestyle that they were presumed to have enjoyed prior to admission. George Martin Holloway, writing a draft of the life of his illustrious relative, stated that the intention was to provide '... all the elegancies of a refined House ...'.[87] Tennis courts (flooded in the winter for skating), billiards rooms, a cricket and football pitch and a swimming pool in the summer months were all available for the patients' use. Archery, golf and croquet were regularly played, and by 1894 a gym was available for male patients who were being trained in Swedish drill.[88]

Every suitable recreational facility imaginable was made available to the patients. There was a well-stocked library; classes were held in oils and water-colours, drawing, photography and needlework, and the results of many patients' endeavours were proudly displayed in exhibitions such as that held on 16 December 1899. In 1894, *St Ann's*, a magazine for the patients, written by the patients themselves, was started. Within its pages articles, poems and anecdotes jostled with proud reports of annual billiards and tennis tournaments and of cricket and/or football matches. An Annual Athletics Sports Day was held; and in 1896 the magazine listed the many events participated in by both patients and staff, ranging from 'Throwing the cricket ball' to long-jump and the egg-and-spoon race. Spectators included, of course, all those not participating, but also 'numerous friends from the outside', thus indicating the centrality and status of the Sanatorium within the local community as many events such as these were open to the public.[89] Further interaction was seen by way of competing with other local institutions (sometimes, but not exclusively, hospitals) and visits to the asylum from brass bands, choirs and theatrical groups. The Sanatorium had its own choir and string band that also made public appearances in the locality, further establishing the relationship with the surrounding county.

The dizzy list of activities was outlined in the Superintendent's *Annual Reports*. For example, in 1887 there was a varied selection that included picnics, cricket matches, garden parties, outdoor fêtes, dances, theatricals, music and dinner parties and excursions to the seaside or London, as well as shopping trips. The Sanatorium's management particularly valued the social skills of doctors, attendants, and companions. Musical ability was seen as especially advantageous, with many staff regularly participating in the Sanatorium's theatrical or musical evenings. Smoking concerts were a regular feature, as were the winter Sunday afternoon concerts held weekly from November onwards. According to Reece Phillips, most facilities were available to voluntary and certified patients alike, regardless of their financial or charitable status, always provided they were not maniacal. For the lower middle-class patients, it must be supposed that many experienced a far better lifestyle in every sense than they had prior to admission. Little wonder, then, that it was not unusual for medically discharged patients to elect to stay at Holloway on a voluntary

---

87   Royal Holloway College Archives, the Papers of George Martin Holloway, ref. GB131/11/1.

88   Superintendent's Annual Report for 1894, p. 100.

89   *St Ann's Magazine*, Christmas 1896, SHC Acc. 2620/6/23.

basis. Thus we see the evolution of the Sanatorium's secondary role – as that of a genteel convalescent home.

Some of the wealthier patients appear to have been keen attenders at all the local noteworthy events such as Henley Regatta, and took regular trips on the river to Windsor, Marlow or Taplow Woods for picnics. Dr Reece Phillips pointed out that the Sanatorium's rural location necessitated sufficient horses and carriages, not only for general excursions, but also for those particularly infirm patients for whom a carriage ride was the only form of outdoor amusement.[90] Some of the more affluent and able patients were entrusted to organize their own independent social life, assisted by their private servants. Many of these maintained their own carriage and pair, necessitating extended stabling. They enjoyed a comparative amount of freedom, and by and large, the Superintendent saw no reason to alter the asylum's approach, which he described as ensuring that '… the utmost liberty, consistent with safety, is permitted'.[91] He steadfastly maintained this policy, despite the occasional abuses of the Sanatorium management's trust. It also allowed for some patients to continue with their destructive habits. For example, 'Mrs T.', admitted in November 1891 (at a reduced rate of £2 12s. per week) consumed a large bottle of chlorodyne and several cigars on a daily basis. She remained for only five weeks as a voluntary boarder, during this time refusing all examinations and restrictions on her movements, so that every day she visited the town alone and purchased her drugs and cigars.[92] Yet other patients visited the local public houses, where they frequently became a nuisance and had to be forcibly removed by attendants. Some pre-agreed excursions lasted considerably longer than was permitted, and the records bear testimony to patients venturing beyond the regulatory three-mile radius of the hospital, often for days at a time. In one such incident, a gentleman boarder was eventually found wandering the Derby racecourse. This incurred the condemnation of the Commissioners regarding the care and control of the Sanatorium's voluntary patients.

Conclusion

The construction of the supremely elegant and highly decorative Holloway Sanatorium served as a memorial to the Holloway family and as a monument to their business success. Prior to opening, the publicity surrounding this elaborate scheme for the middle-class insane had caused admirers to remark:

> It is a noble and most generous benefaction to the nation at large, and must, we should think, be looked upon as a great blessing both to those who suffer from a temporary visitation from the most terrible of all maladies to which flesh is heir, and to the relations and guardians of those so afflicted.[93]

---

90   Superintendent's Annual Report for 1887, p. 21.
91   Rules for the Admission, 1886, SHC Acc. 2620.
92   Holloway Sanatorium Casebook, Voluntary Boarders, SHC Acc. 3473/3/28.
93   *The Builder* (7 January 1882).

Glorious in its elevation and environment, it took many years to complete, and was beset by tensions between the founder's desire to provide an incomparable institution for the custodial care of the afflicted middle classes, and the requirements of contemporary lunacy legislation. Intrinsic to policy was the provision of assisted places for 'deserving' middle-class patients whose illnesses might worsen if treated under pauper status. In a luxurious environment that would have been far superior to any that many patients had ever experienced, the concept of charitable provision for the middle-class insane in an enclave among their own sort overrode notions of patient curability and short periods of residence.

CHAPTER TEN

Urban tuberculosis patients and sanatorium treatment in the early twentieth century

Flurin Condrau

The writing of the history of tuberculosis has undergone considerable change since the 1970s, when a renewed interest in the 'role of medicine' and a more critical approach towards medicine launched the modern historiography of tuberculosis.[1] One largely demographic strand of research has subsequently used the disease in an attempt to explain the secular mortality decline, which, as part of the demographic transition, brought mortality rates from early modern peaks down to relatively constant low levels after World War II. This has led to a still unresolved controversy known as the McKeown debate, which concentrates on Thomas McKeown's hypothesis that tuberculosis, as the key disease of the general mortality transition, declined without any significant medical intervention.[2] While this rather general statement has been repeatedly challenged, virtually no one has advocated that therapeutic medical intervention played any role in the decline.[3] For the purpose of this chapter, the debate is interesting because it sets the stage for a surge in historiographical interest in tuberculosis, while emphasizing the important connection between specific disease and general mortality.[4]

The social history of tuberculosis, developing from McKeown's initial stance, has usually taken the form of case studies based on a single country. Most tuberculosis control programmes in western countries, which generally started in the 1890s,

---

1   I. Illich, *Medical Nemesis: The Expropriation of Health* (New York, 1976); T. McKeown, *The Role of Medicine: Dream, Mirage, or Nemesis?* (London, 1976).

2   T. McKeown and R.G. Brown, 'Medical Evidence Related to English Population Changes in the Eighteenth Century', *Population Studies* 9 (1955): 119–41; T. McKeown and R.G. Record, 'Reasons for the Decline of Mortality in England and Wales During the Nineteenth-Century', *Population Studies* 16 (1962): 94–122; T. McKeown, R.G. Record and R.D. Turner, 'An Interpretation of the Decline of Mortality in England and Wales during the Twentieth Century', *Population Studies* 29 (1975): 391–422.

3   S. Szreter, 'The Importance of Social Intervention in Britain's Mortality Decline 1850–1914. A Reinterpretation of the role of Public Health', *Social History of Medicine* 1 (1988): 1–38.

4   J. Colgrove, 'The McKeown Thesis: A Historical Controversy and Its Enduring Influence', *American Journal of Public Health* 92 (2002): 725–9.

have now been extensively studied. Sweden,[5] Britain,[6] France,[7] Germany,[8] and the USA,[9] as well as Japan[10] and South Africa,[11] are among the many countries for which specialist case studies are available. All these studies, following in the footsteps of the classic contribution by the Duboses,[12] agree on the importance of a social if not cultural analysis of medical concepts in tuberculosis control, while quite rightly rejecting simple medical positivism. The latter can occasionally be found in works more specifically concerned with the introduction of antibiotic treatment.[13]

Despite a degree of similarity in most case studies, their results reveal interesting differences between countries. Scholars interested in British history have extensively studied how the major public-health campaign against tuberculosis, initiated by the foundation of the National Association for the Prevention of Consumption in 1895, was structured by class relations and élitist, non-medical ideas about a healthy society.[14] Authors examining the close relation between ideas of social integration and social policy in Germany have successfully used tuberculosis as a case study to exemplify the notion that medical ideas followed, rather than determined, a

5   B.-I. Puranen, *Tuberkulos. En sjukdoms förekomst och dess orsaker, Sverige 1750–1980*, Umea Studies in Economic History, vol. 7 (Umea, 1984).

6   L. Bryder, *Below the Magic Mountain: A Social History of Tuberculosis in Twentieth-Century Britain* (Oxford, 1988); F.B. Smith, *The Retreat of Tuberculosis 1850–1950* (London, 1988); M. Worboys, 'The Sanatorium Treatment for Consumption in Britain, 1890–1914', in J.V. Pickstone (ed.), *Medical Innovations in Historical Perspective* (New York, 1992), pp. 47–71.

7   I. Grellet and C. Kruse, *Histoires de la Tuberculose: Les Fièvres de l'Ame, 1800–1940* (Paris, 1983); P. Guillaume, *Du Désespoir au Salut: les Tuberculeux aux 19e et 20e Siècles* (Paris, 1986); D. Dessertine and O. Faure, *Combattre la tuberculose, 1900–1940* (Lyon, 1988); D.S. Barnes, *The Making of a Social Disease: Tuberculosis in Nineteenth-Century France* (Berkeley, 1995).

8   G. Göckenjan, *Kurieren und Staat machen. Gesundheit und Medizin in der bürgerlichen Welt* (Frankfurt a.M., 1985); S. Hähner-Rombach, *Sozialgeschichte der Tuberkulose. Vom Kaiserreich bis zum Ende des Zweiten Weltkriegs unter besonderer Berücksichtigung Württembergs*, Medizin, Gesellschaft und Geschichte, suppl. 14 (Stuttgart, 2000); F. Condrau, *Lungenheilanstalt und Patientenschicksal. Sozialgeschichte der Tuberkulose in Deutschland und England im späten 19. und frühen 20. Jahrhundert*, Kritische Studien zur Geschichtswissenschaft, vol. 137 (Göttingen, 2000).

9   B. Bates, *Bargaining for Life: A Social History of Tuberculosis, 1876–1938* (Philadelphia, 1992); K. Ott, *Fevered Lives. Tuberculosis in American Culture since 1870* (Cambridge, 1996).

10   W. Johnston, *The Modern Epidemic: A History of Tuberculosis in Japan* (Harvard, 1995); M. Fukuda, *Kekkaku no Bunkashi* [Cultural History of Tuberculosis in Japan] (Nagoya, 1995).

11   R.M. Packard, *White Plague, Black Labor: Tuberculosis and the Political Economy of Health and Disease in South Africa* (Berkeley, 1989).

12   R. and J. Dubos, *The White Plague. Tuberculosis, Man and Society* (1952; New Brunswick, 1987).

13   F. Ryan, *Tuberculosis. The Greatest Story Never Told* (Bromsgrove, 1992).

14   For the clearest example of this, see Smith, *Retreat*.

social agenda.[15] And researchers looking at US anti-tuberculosis programmes have emphasized the extent to which issues of discipline and control became part of the medical agenda.[16] Despite these clear differences on a macro-historical level, comparative or even transnational studies of tuberculosis control have remained scarce indeed.[17]

Sanatoriums for tuberculosis

One of the main areas of historiographical interest has been the sanatorium – the only therapeutic institution available to patients with tuberculosis around 1900. The first sanatorium pioneer, the German physician and 1848 revolutionary activist Dr Hermann Brehmer, opened his sanatorium in Gorbersdorf, Silesia, in 1854 in an abandoned hydrotherapeutic sanatorium.[18] Over the course of the second half of the century, sanatorium treatment was developed in different ways. Germany opted for open-air rest treatments, where the emphasis was put on remaining outdoors in all weather conditions, coupled with a rich diet. Britain favoured the ideal model of occupational therapy led by Marcus Paterson, medical superintendent of the Brompton Hospital Sanatorium at Frimley in Surrey, which took the form of auto-inoculation through graduated labour. But many other models and mixtures of sanatorium treatment existed: for example, Dr Karl Turban founded the first high-altitude sanatorium in Davos, Switzerland. A systematic comparative study that takes into account a variety of historical contexts, looks at therapeutic regimes and considers patient experience would be eminently helpful.[19]

The historiography of the sanatorium does not entirely match that of tuberculosis in general as, interestingly, there was never a positivist perception that it was particularly successful as a treatment centre. Arthur Newsholme, one of the most influential policy advisors in England before World War I and Medical Officer of Health of the Local Government Board, argued that the decline of tuberculosis was largely due to isolation.[20] And even though this position was reiterated relatively recently, it has never really caught on as a justification for the sanatorium.[21] Debates

---

15   P. Weindling, 'Hygienepolitik als sozialintegrative Strategie im späten Deutschen Kaiserreich', in A. Labisch and R. Spree (eds), *Medizinische Deutungsmacht im sozialen Wandel des 19. und frühen 20. Jahrhunderts* (Bonn, 1989), pp. 37–56.

16   S.M. Rothman, *Living in the Shadow of Death. Tuberculosis and the Social Experience of Illness in American History* (New York, 1994).

17   Condrau, *Lungenheilanstalt und Patientenschicksal*.

18   I. Langerbeins, *Lungenheilanstalten in Deutschland von 1854–1945* (Köln, 1979).

19   F. Condrau, 'Lungenheilstätten im internationalen Vergleich. Zur Sozialgeschichte der Tuberkulose im 19. und frühen 20. Jahrhundert', *Historia Hospitalium* 19 (1993/1994): 220–34.

20   A. Newsholme, 'The Causes of the Past Decline of Tuberculosis and the Light Thrown by History on Preventive Measures for the Immediate Future', *6th International Congress on Tuberculosis* (A Series of Public Lectures, Suppl. to the Transactions: Philadelphia, 1908), pp. 80–109.

21   L.G. Wilson, 'The Historical Decline of Tuberculosis in Europe and America: Its Causes and Significance', *Journal of the History of Medicine* 45 (1990): 366–96.

about the merits of long treatment sojourns in these institutions started along with the sanatorium movements themselves; the idea that the sanatorium was an uncontested, indeed widely accepted, medical intervention probably owes more to fictional than to factual accounts of sanatoriums.[22] Far from celebrating its therapeutic value, orthodox historiography conceptualized the sanatorium as a stage in hospital development.[23] In particular, historians have recently pointed to the architecture of sanatoriums as symbols of modernism, an aspect that has recently attracted renewed interest.[24] While accepting the sanatorium's limited therapeutic value, some writers have emphasized its part in the 'requiem for a great killer' because of its contribution to medical science.[25] The abundance of fictional accounts, however, proves that there is more to the sanatorium than mere architectural interest or medical science. In fact, there was a time when the sanatorium novel was a highly fashionable genre, producing some intriguing books contributing to the cultural representation of the sanatorium, and by extension to that of tuberculosis treatment.[26]

For a long time sanatorium historiography thus presented two major thrusts: one focusing on its architecture, and the other on fictional accounts of upper-class sanatoriums in the Swiss Alps, which were assumed also to represent the sanatorium experience of the working classes.[27] This position was further underlined by Susan Sontag's *Illness as Metaphor*, in which she made a strong case for the romantic image of tuberculosis.[28] Strangely, Sontag's classification of the disease as romantic has never really been questioned, although every study of urban poor relief confirms that tuberculosis has always been closely associated with poverty. Roy Porter's widely read article on 'doing medical history from below' suggested a paradigm shift in the history of medical institutions.[29] At the intersection of social policy and medical treatment, the sanatorium has provided a prime example of this renewed interest in patients and a patient-driven narrative of health and illness. In two extraordinary studies, both Linda Bryder (for Britain) and Sheila Rothman (for the USA) have argued with the help of sophisticated accounts of patients' viewpoints that sanatorium treatment is

---

22   Worboys, *Sanatorium Treatment*.

23   A.H. Murken, 'Vom Heilpalast zum Sanatorium des Volkes', *Die Waage* 21 (1982): 64–72; A.H. Murken, 'Heilanstalten für Tuberkulöse. Zur Geschichte der Lungensanatorien und ihrer Therapiekonzeption im 19. Jahrhundert', in W. Göpfert and H.-H. Otten (eds), *Metanoeite. Wandelt euch durch neues Denken. Festschrift für Professor Hans Schadewaldt zur Vollendung des 60. Lebensjahres* (Düsseldorf, 1983), pp. 107–24.

24   M. Campbell, 'What Tuberculosis did for Modernism: The Influence of a Curative Environment on Modernist Design and Architecture', *Medical History* 49 (2005): 463–88.

25   J. H. Williams, *Requiem for a Great Killer: The Story of Tuberculosis* (London, 1973).

26   See the extremely helpful analysis of V. Pohland, *Das Sanatorium als literarischer Ort. Medizinische Institution und Krankheit als Medien der Gesellschaftskritik und Existenzanalyse* (Frankfurt a.M., 1984).

27   For the sanatorium novel as a source in French historiography, see Grellet and Kruse, *Histoires de la Tuberculose*, and Guillaume, *Du Désespoir au Salut*.

28   S. Sontag, *Illness as Metaphor* (New York, 1978).

29   R. Porter, 'The Patient's View. Doing Medical History from Below', *Theory and Society* 14 (1985): 175–98.

an ideal example of Erving Goffman's 'total institution'.[30] These studies start with a critique of the sanatorium's treatment success, emphasizing its ineffectiveness, if not exposing its inherently dangerous nature due to cross-infections. Once medicine is dispensed with as the main justification, the stage is set for a Goffmanesque analysis of the sanatorium, which highlights and ultimately criticizes the non-medical aspects of sanatorium treatment.[31] However, applying Goffman to the sanatorium brings its own problems. While the emphasis on patient identity suggests otherwise, the 'total institution' essentially denies any form of patient agency and thus limits the scope of the analysis.[32]

Sanatorium treatment and tuberculosis mortality

The ideas of Goffman, one of the most stimulating and influential writers in modern sociology, have unfortunately served as a strait-jacket, preventing essential debate about the nature of medical success. Using the term 'total institution' to analyse the sanatorium has undoubtedly contributed to a modern understanding of its being a social rather than a strictly medical institution. But it has also limited the range of perspectives in the historiography of the sanatorium by co-determining the results through the terms used.[33] For a long time one of the principal assumptions, perhaps even limitations, of the social history of medicine has been to treat medical knowledge itself as a given, rather than to question its own historicity.[34] Hence the interest in the sanatorium rather than, say, in specialist chest hospitals, because the sanatorium's treatment regime is more easily branded as, essentially, a waste of time. Indeed, writers have often argued that by means of cross-infection, the sanatorium actually contributed to the problem that it pretended to solve.[35] These statements, however, are often based on the benefit of hindsight offered by the experience of post-war antibiotics, rather than on actual historical evidence. But perhaps the problem goes deeper than merely pointing out the inefficacy of a past treatment: understanding success as an objective rather than a historically shaped category appears ultimately to be an ahistoric notion.[36]

---

30 Bryder, *Below the Magic Mountain*; Rothman, *Living in the Shadow of Death*.

31 E. Goffman, *Asylums. Essays on the Social Situation of Mental Patients and Other Inmates* (1961; London, 1991).

32 F. Condrau, 'Beyond the Total Institution: Erving Goffman and the History of Tuberculosis', in F. Condrau and M. Worboys (eds), *Tuberculosis then and now. Modern approaches in the history of tuberculosis*, Montreal (in press).

33 See the discussion on social theory and medical institutions in K. Jones and A.J. Fowles, *Ideas on Institutions. Analysing the Literature on Long-Term Care and Custody* (London, 1984).

34 R. Cooter, '"Framing" the End of the Social History of Medicine', in F. Huisman and J.H. Warner (eds), *Locating Medical History: the Stories and their Meanings* (Baltimore, 2004).

35 Worboys, *Sanatorium Treatment*.

36 F. Condrau, 'Behandlung ohne Heilung. Zur sozialen Konstruktion des Behandlungserfolgs bei Tuberkulose im frühen 20. Jahrhundert', *Medizin, Gesellschaft und Geschichte* XIX (Stuttgart, 2001): 71–93.

The analysis suggested here is to get beyond this assumption in two ways, firstly by offering a brief venture into the available quantitative data, and then by focusing on the changing nature of the terms used to analyse medical success itself. The first step thus has to be a review of the available data for sanatoriums to see what they offer in terms of explaining therapeutic success. Unfortunately, general mortality data, while clearly showing a general decline of tuberculosis since the latter half of the nineteenth century, does not offer much by way of an explanation for this decline. To this day, McKeown's graph of arrows of therapeutic innovation, pointing towards the declining mortality curve in order to undermine the notion of any correlation between medicine and mortality, remains one of the most widely used in the history of medicine. Using mortality data to get a first assessment of the role of the sanatorium requires an examination of age-specific mortality data by birth cohorts.[37] Studying epidemiologic data using birth cohorts is a relatively recent statistical method that developed during the transition from descriptive to more stochastic statistics. Interestingly enough, its first application was to tuberculosis mortality.[38] The key message of cohort analysis is that the decline of tuberculosis benefited every birth cohort in a linear way, rather than favouring specific age groups over others, as had previously been thought.[39] From the mid nineteenth century onwards, every generation was basically healthier than the previous one at the same age. Potentially, however, cohort analysis allows a more causal analysis to link specific innovations with shifts in the cohort pattern. A cohort analysis would show any event with clear implications for mortality at the same time point, hence affecting the various birth cohorts at different ages. The First World War is such an event, which can indeed be tracked through cohort analysis as it clearly leaves its mark in the mortality pattern for all generations. Similarly, evidence for specific medical interventions such as antibiotics shows for all generations at the same age point. If the sanatoriums had had a strong effect on tuberculosis mortality, it would have to be visible as a period effect from around the turn of the century, when the growth of sanatorium treatment became obvious. However, even accepting the limitations of English mortality statistics when the English sanatorium movement lagged slightly behind those of other countries, there is no visible impact – other than a general decline – before the arrival of streptomycin after World War II. Needless to say, this has to be taken as a preliminary analysis on the basis of national data, but the indications are that, quantitatively, sanatorium treatment was indeed rather limited in its impact on mortality data. This statement can be substantiated by a German study that looked at sanatorium survival and mortality statistics in more detail. Here,

37   J.J. Collins, 'The Contribution of Medical Measures to the Decline of Mortality from Respiratory Tuberculosis: An Age-Period-Cohort Model', *Demography* 19 (1982): 409–27.

38   W.H. Frost, 'The Age Selection of Mortality from Tuberculosis in Successive Decades', *American Journal of Hygiene* 30 (1939): 91–6.

39   V.H. Springett, 'A Comparative Study of Tuberculosis Mortality Rates', in D.W. Hastings and L.G. Berry (eds), *Cohort Analysis: A Collection of Interdisciplinary Readings* (Oxford, 1979), pp. 115–48.

too, the gist of a sophisticated enquiry is that any mortality benefits of sanatorium treatment are questionable at best.[40]

The nature of medical success

But is medical success always measured against the objective data of mortality statistics? Even a casual look at contemporary health-care policy reveals that this is not the case. Resources hardly ever go where they are most needed as measured by mortality statistics, but where the case for more resources is best made. The relation between the relative impact on population level of mortality patterns (or health indicators in general) on the one hand and specific medical interventions on the other is not clear at all. The notable exception seems to be modern vaccination policy with its huge success in the story of smallpox control.[41] But with vaccinations, the issues can be unclear, as is exemplified by the introduction of BCG vaccination against tuberculosis. As Bryder has conclusively shown, there is no relation between the introduction of BCG and the decline of tuberculosis in France, Britain or the USA.[42]

The obvious historical question is whether sanatorium treatment was at all successful in treating and curing this major threat to people's health. An equally important question is what kind of success it aspired to have. The very nature of the treatment makes it obvious that a comparison with the clinical efficacy of modern antibiotics might not be particularly useful, but one wonders whether it offered any benefits to the patients at all. Not being a specific cure, and with tuberculosis a chronic disease, sanatorium treatment was different from, say, surgery, where survival and recovery tended to occur over a measurable period of time. Moreover, the definition of what was supposed to be called a success was in itself controversial: since most doctors and funding bodies clearly knew that the patients were not *clinically* healed, so-called success involved a prognosis based on clinical change whose relation to the disease process was always contestable. The stages of tuberculosis, a basic classification scheme to group patients on entry and discharge, proved very problematic in practice as it applied a qualitative definition of the stages themselves, while also relying on practitioners on location to diagnose the relevant stage.[43] Medical success, therefore, is a difficult area for the historian, a fact

---

40 R. Spree, 'Zu den Veränderungen der Volksgesundheit zwischen 1870 und 1913 und ihren Determinanten in Deutschland (vor allem in Preußen)', in W. Conze and U. Engelhardt (eds), *Arbeiterexistenz im 19. Jahrhundert. Lebensstandard und Lebensgestaltung deutscher Arbeiter und Handwerker* (Stuttgart, 1981), pp. 235–92.

41 P. Razzell, *The Conquest of Smallpox. The Impact of Inoculation on Smallpox Mortality in 18th Century Britain* (Firle, 1977); C. Huerkamp, 'The History of Smallpox Vaccination in Germany. A First Step in the Medicalization of the General Public', *Journal of Contemporary History* 20 (1985): 617–35.

42 L. Bryder, '"We shall not find salvation in inoculation': BCG vaccination in Scandinavia, Britain and the USA, 1921–1960', *Social Science and Medicine* 49/9 (1999): 1157–67.

43 L. Teleky, 'Die Bekämpfung der Tuberkulose', in A. Gottstein *et al.* (eds), *Handbuch der sozialen Hygiene und Gesundheitsfürsorge*, vol. 3 (Berlin, 1926), pp. 207–341.

further highlighted by often-used key terms such as 'healed' or 'cured', which have meant different things at different times and in different places. Basically, 'cure' and 'healing' should be seen as historically bound categories that have not always carried the meaning they do today.[44]

Having thus thrown the concept of success into question, the focus shifts to the sanatorium's contribution to understanding medical efficacy. Here the main achievement was to reframe medical success through hitherto unknown mass empirical studies. The world looked to Germany at the time in all areas of social security, since it was the first country to start a comprehensive scheme of social insurance. Applying these principles favoured economic rather than clinical considerations in the assessment of medical success. All sanatorium treatment was deemed successful as long as it prolonged the ability to work for an appreciable period of time. The idea was simple: by extending the working life of the patients, their disability pension claims, which formed part of their insurance, could be postponed.[45] Whether or not the patient survived in the long term was not seen as important *per se*, because from the insurer's point of view long-term disability would have been as bad as – if not worse than – a speedy death. While that stark rationale was never expressed in writing, it was an obvious underlying assumption. The key was to delay serious illness as measured by a person's inability to work. This economic interpretation of medical success produced an estimate that – from an insurance perspective – roughly two years of working ability were necessary to justify sanatorium treatment of three months.[46]

This debate about the relative merits of sanatorium treatment was hugely influential in Britain. One commentator wrote in 1904: 'This, to my mind, is the most eloquent testimony as to follow the good example of Germany.'[47] The economic rationale behind health insurance and sanatorium treatment was considered as a typically German and very un-British concept which had to be rejected. In fact, while admiration for the German sanatorium-building scheme was widely shared, representatives of the Friendly Societies argued that their best interest, from an economic point of view, would be served by complete therapeutic inactivity, as any postponement of death would only increase the total cost caused by prolonging a patient's survival. Hence they had no motivation to encourage sanatorium building.[48] While damning elements of the economic principle, British studies of sanatorium success nevertheless engaged in a similar discourse about the costs of treatment as measured against the benefits for the patient after discharge – substituting for ability to work the notion of survival after treatment. Interestingly, this did not

---

44   Condrau, *Behandlung ohne Heilung*.

45   H. Gebhardt, 'Ausbreitung der Tuberkulose unter der versicherungspflichtigen Bevölkerung', *Bericht über den Kongress zur Bekämpfung der Tuberkulose als Volkskrankheit* (Berlin, 1899), pp. 80–92.

46   For more details on this, see Teleky, *Bekämpfung*; Condrau, *Lungenheilanstalt und Patientenschicksal*.

47   N. Raw, 'The Value of the Sanatorium in the Prevention of Consumption', *Tuberculosis* 3 (1904/1906): 267–72.

48   E.W. Brabrook, 'The Attitude of Friendly Societies Towards Sanatoria', *Transactions of the British Congress on Tuberculosis for the Prevention of Consumption*, July 22–26 1901 (London, 1902), vol. 2, pp. 333–6.

lead the British to collect similar data, even after the National Insurance Act of 1911 had guaranteed a 'sanatorium benefit'. Clearly, the advantage of the German insurance system was to be seen in its accounting, whereas the tax-funded system in Britain was pragmatic – a tradition that has beset the British health-care system and its historiography throughout the twentieth century.[49] While the German health-insurance bodies engaged in a systematic review of quantitative material from all types of sanatoriums as part of their reporting to the Imperial Insurance Office in Berlin, nothing comparable was done in Britain. Supported by the Medical Research Council, two substantial special reports compiled figures from two carefully chosen sanatoriums, the King Edward VII Sanatorium in Midhurst and the Brompton Hospital Sanatorium at Frimley.[50] Notably these were two élite institutions, originally led by Noel Bardswell and Marcus Paterson, both well-established medical doctors who had served as experts on the Astor Committee implementing the sanatorium benefit as part of the National Insurance Act.[51] The Frimley sanatorium additionally benefited from having all its patients sent from the Brompton Hospital, which selected candidates according to their suitability for sanatorium treatment. Interestingly, German and British sanatoriums, despite using different medical criteria, reported well-matched success ratios. Both countries reported a 50 per cent cohort survival (ability to work in the German case) of all sanatorium patients after five years.[52] This implied, as was rather explicitly pointed out in German insurance documentation, that success could not be guaranteed on an individual level but had more to do with probability and the selection of appropriate patients for treatment.[53] With hindsight, these empirical studies without control groups have to be regarded as very limited in value. Would as many patients have survived with no treatment at all? That is, of course, impossible to determine. Though the survival rate of 50 per cent after five years was not very impressive, commentators argued at the time that this was better than nothing and they were probably right. And taking into comparison contemporary figures for cancer treatment, 50 per cent seems to be a pretty reasonable result for unspecific treatment.[54]

---

49   Reporting under the National Insurance Act was very limited. For some ideas about the extent of sanatorium benefit, see National Insurance (Health) Acts, 1911–1918; Return as to the Administration of Sanatorium Benefit, in: Parliamentary Papers: House of Commons, HMSO (1913–1918). On the context of the legislation, see B.B. Gilbert, *The Evolution of National Insurance in Great Britain. The Origins of the Welfare State* (London, 1966).

50   Medical Research Council (MRC): 'Pulmonary Tuberculosis. Mortality After Sanatorium Treatment', *Special Report Series* 33 (HMSO, London, 1919); MRC: 'An Inquiry into the After-Histories of Patients Treated at the Brompton Hospital Sanatorium at Frimley, During the Years 1905–1914', *Special Report Series* 85 (HMSO, London, 1924).

51   Departmental Committee on Tuberculosis, Final Report of the Departmental Committee on Tuberculosis, 2 vols (HMSO Cd. 6641/6654, London, 1913).

52   'Statistik der Heilbehandlungen bei den Versicherungsanstalten', *Beihefte zu den Amtlichen Nachrichten des Reichsversicherungsamtes* (Berlin, 1897–1914).

53   Spree, *Veränderungen*.

54   See Cancer Survival: England and Wales, 1991–2001, four major cancers, Office for National Statistics publication, Cancer Survival Trends, http://www.statistics.gov.uk/statbase/ssdataset.asp?vlnk=7091 (2.2.2006).

Social policy and the body politics of tuberculosis

In order to understand the specific relationship between medical treatment, the sanatorium, and body politics, it is useful to explore the history of the sanatorium in a little more depth. We have seen that before antibiotic treatment and its easily observable results became available after World War II, ascertaining success was a complex matter, not only for insurance bodies or the Medical Research Council, but for doctors as well. While diagnosis could utilize powerful tools such as bacteriologic analysis or X-ray technology, the treatment arsenal essentially relied on supporting the self-healing properties of the patients' own bodies through rest treatment, food and 'auto-inoculation' with graduated labour therapy. These therapies did little to underpin professional medical authority as the doctors' expertise was not beyond lay people's grasp.[55] However much medical superintendents tried to invoke special competence, it was never enough to silence critics.

One of the major innovations in tuberculosis treatment was chest surgery. It fulfilled the expectations of the medical world in the search for a treatment for tuberculosis, as surgery was the leading medical specialism at the time. Rather than feeding patients and exposing them to fresh air and a good day's work, this intervention offered a sophisticated operating technique, complex technical setups and real medical expertise. Interestingly, it hinged on the idea of rest treatment, no less, as the procedure aimed at collapsing the lung to allow it to recover from tuberculosis. Pioneered by the Italian surgeon Carlo Forlanini in 1892, chest surgery became popular as a field of medical research before World War I, and attracted a particularly strong interest in German universities.[56] The long-term effects of chest surgery were, however, not at all clear. Most surgeons considered the intervention to be successful enough if the patient survived the operation without severe complications.[57] Neither clinical control studies in the modern sense, nor comparable large-scale evaluations or data sets, were made available. Chest surgery, it appears, contributed to a shift in the meaning of medical success from the statistical probability of survival to the immediate clinical recovery of individual cases. While little different from unspecific treatment, it was performed by widely respected medical specialists, who could basically set their own targets.

Doctors, and in particular surgeons, saw these operations as somehow honourable for the patient. Dr Fred Holmes, a US surgeon, wrote in 1935 that chest surgery

---

55   E. Freidson, *Profession of Medicine. A Study of the Sociology of Applied Knowledge* (New York, 1970); M.S. Larson, *The Rise of Professionalism. A Sociological Analysis* (Berkeley, 1977).

56   M. Oury, 'Die Geschichte der Tuberkulose', in: R. Toellner (ed.), *Illustrierte Geschichte der Medizin*, (1978; Erlangen, 1992), pp. 2735–56.

57   Chest surgery remains a strangely under-researched episode of tuberculosis medicine. It is probably telling that modern approaches of cultural history tend to focus much more on diagnostic than therapeutic medicine. Good examples are the extremely interesting study by J. Lachmund, *Der abgehorchte Körper. Zur historischen Soziologie der medizinischen Untersuchung* (Opladen, 1997), and B. Pasveer, *Shadows of Knowledge: Making a representing practice in medicine. X-Ray Pictures and Pulmonary Tuberculosis, 1890–1930* (Amsterdam, 1992).

resulted in a 'medal to be pinned on the battle-scarred veteran after a bloody campaign'.[58] For the patient, however, these operations were usually very painful experiences. Jack, a working-class Swiss patient at the Zurich alpine sanatorium in Davos-Clavadel, wrote in a letter to his sister:

> Thursday morning, at 11 o'clock, I was prepared to get my nerves squeezed. Normally this procedure takes up half an hour. Well, I was comfortable in my beddings and covered from head to toe, only my throat was free. Before getting covered, I had seen the doctors, all dressed in white with only the eyes uncovered. The narcotics started to have an effect and I didn't feel much of all the butchery until some complications occurred. After that, I had to feel exactly how many nerves there are in me. I'd rather go to the dentist to have three nerves extracted than endure another operation of my chest.[59]

Like so many other patients of chest surgery, Jack died within a fortnight of the operation. Chest surgery was widely used as a treatment for 'hopeless' – or, in medical terminology, 'far advanced' – cases.[60] One of the reasons for the considerable spread of this operative technique was the fact that it was easy to perform and required only simple equipment available at most sanatoriums. For the doctors it was routine; for patients it was usually the first experience of surgery, and for the sanatoriums it was an important step in the quest to reinvent themselves as modern hospitals during the inter-war period.

Interestingly, chest surgery led to the end of any serious attempt to measure medical success statistically, replacing it with clinical analysis of individual cases.[61] Insurance bodies were happy to support this intervention for advanced cases because it allowed them either to keep patients in hospital or to send them to rehabilitation from surgery. While the take-up of chest surgery in Britain was markedly lower than elsewhere, here, too, it contributed to the transition of the sanatorium from a treatment to a rehabilitation institution.[62]

But doctors and patients – and not least insurance companies, local authorities and voluntary donors required to cover the costs of often lengthy treatment – quite legitimately asked for more immediate results. The discourse in medical practice came to place more emphasis on the shorter term. This soon produced a set of divergent interpretations of therapeutic success that coexisted side by side. A large proportion of sanatorium patients were discharged as 'healed' or 'improved', probably more or less regardless of their physical condition, as practising doctors must have known the questionability of these results. When patients who were discharged as 'healed' were found to have died within 24 to 48 hours of leaving a sanatorium, heated exchanges

---

58   F. Holmes, *Tuberculosis: A Book for the Patient* (New York, 1935), pp. 283ff.

59   Jack, letter to his sister, made available to me by Dr Iris Ritzmann, University of Zurich. See her excellent case study in I. Ritzmann, *Hausordnung und Liegekur. Vom Volkssanatorium zur Spezialklinik. 100 Jahre Zürcher Höhenklinik Wald* (Zürich, 1998).

60   Ritzmann, *Hausordnung*.

61   H. Liebe, 'Kritischer Bericht über 104 Pneumothoraxfälle', *Beiträge zur Klinik der Tuberkulose* 49 (1921): 125–37.

62   Bryder, *Below the Magic Mountain*, pp. 157–98.

about the merits of the sanatorium and its doctors were bound to arise.[63] But, seen in context, these coexistent interpretations of healing are unsurprising as expressions of the tension between an effective professional ability and the claims for therapeutic competence made by medical doctors. Also, patients were clearly less interested in a statistical probability of survival of five years than in a rather more specific prognosis. The doctor–patient encounter, particularly during the final meeting before discharge, led to a dynamic that ignored essential medical knowledge through a consensus on both sides, as it looked towards short-term health indicators to decide whether or not to discharge; the probability of survival was not taken into account at this point.

Among the patients and probably among the general public as well, cases which were discharged as healed only to die within a week added to a sense of suspicion about the disease (and about medicine in general). This anxiety about hidden medical secrets is one of the common stories in the history of infectious diseases: conspiracy theories about the 'real' reasons for epidemics go back to medieval plagues.[64] But since tuberculosis was a chronic rather than an acute disease, these suspicions never developed into fully fledged social or cultural unrest; rather, they played a part in the way individuals coped with the disease. Essentially, the issue of conflicting evidence and interpretation has to be seen as a case of asymmetric information. This concept of health economics has never really been taken up by historians, despite its clear potential for explaining the situation.[65] Medical doctors involved in the diagnostic process usually know or suspect more than they care to tell their patients; the latter, while being told details about their medical condition, are not necessarily fully in the picture. The consensus between doctors and patients to regard success and imminent discharge as synonymous was, therefore, particularly compelling. To justify these discharges, doctors installed a system of numerical measurements of relative health status. Erich Stern, a medical psychologist who was once a sanatorium patient himself, observed that the patients actually helped the doctors establish these scales by constantly debating the results of the 'fever curve' and their body weight.[66] Everything came together neatly: a treatment regime emphasizing food and exercise; a food intake with an unsurprisingly positive influence on the working-class patient's weight; and the importance of body weight for the perception of health. During the First World War, patient complaints about food were rejected by the authorities, who used weight gains as proof of the obvious quality of the food provided. A similarly neat scale of relative health was at the heart of graduated labour treatment in Britain.

---

63 A. Grotjahn, 'Die Krisis in der Lungenheilstättenbewegung', *Medizinische Reform* 15 (1907): 219–23; C.W. Wilkinson, 'Tuberculin and Tuberculin Dispensaries', *British Medical Journal* (1911): 403 and 656ff.

64 C.J. Kudlick, *Cholera in Post-Revolutionary Paris. A Cultural History* (Berkeley, 1996).

65 K.J. Arrow, 'Uncertainty and the Welfare Economics of Medical Care', *American Economic Review* 53 (1963): 941–73; C.E. Phelps, *Health Economics* (New York, 1992), pp. 281–6; C.S. Lee, 'Optimal Medical Treatment under Asymmetric Information', *Journal of Health Economics* 14 (1995): 419–41.

66 E. Stern, *Die Psyche des Lungenkranken. Der Einfluß der Lungentuberkulose und des Sanatoriumslebens* (Halle, 1925).

Of course, labour treatment was full of class stereotypes; however, the ability to work longer hours and perform harder tasks was not merely an outcome of medical discipline, but also served to highlight the patient's progress to health and thus discharge from the sanatorium.

It has been argued that the importance attached to these elements of sanatorium treatment has to be understood more as part of a lay medical culture than as part of a specific medical regime.[67] But differentiating between lay medical culture and professional medical knowledge seems arbitrary, given the recent historiographical emphasis on the cultural formation of medical knowledge. Recent investigations of the history of tuberculosis emphasize that the borderlines between medical and patient knowledge as well as social and cultural perception of the disease were blurred.[68]

This can easily be highlighted by a look at the way sanatorium treatment was sold to the wider medical public. In a most revealing article in *The Lancet*, Marcus Paterson, first medical superintendent of the Brompton Hospital Sanatorium, elaborated the merits of graduated labour therapy, which he had developed in order to take over his post at Frimley:

> First, it would do much to meet the objection that members of the working classes are liable to have their energy sapped, and to acquire lazy habits by such treatment; secondly, it would make them more resistant to the disease, by improving their physical condition; and thirdly, it would enable them by its effect upon their muscles to return to their work immediately after their discharge.[69]

It is interesting to note that only one of the three arguments presented is a medical one; rather, class stereotypes are obvious in the reference to needing muscle strength in order to be able to go back to work as well as in the point about acquiring lazy habits during the sanatorium cure. For the British medical élite, it seemed unwise to advocate open-air *rest* treatment for working-class patients, as the whole field of social policy and tuberculosis control was bound up with ideas of class difference. Indeed, it is perhaps possible to hypothesize that the English sanatorium owed as much to the Chadwickian workhouse of the nineteenth century as it did to modern tuberculosis treatment.[70] Both shared a strong moralistic element and were based on the 'healing' powers of a good day's work, while being similarly unpopular among the working classes.

This ties in with the doctor's role in the sanatorium, which was only partly to exert medical expertise, but involved a substantial responsibility in controlling the patients as social groups. There was also considerable difference between the various

---

67   M. Martin, 'Bedeutung und Funktion des medizinischen Messens in geschlossenen Patienten-Kollektiven. Das Beispiel der Lungensanatorien', in V. Hess (ed.), *Normierung der Gesundheit. Messende Verfahren der Medizin als kulturelle Praktik um 1900*, Abhandlungen zur Geschichte der Medizin und Naturwissenschaften, 82 (Husum, 1997): 145–64.

68   Ott, *Fevered Lives*.

69   M.S. Paterson, 'Graduated Labour in Pulmonary Tuberculosis', *The Lancet* 86 (1908: I): 216–20.

70   R.G. Hodgkinson, *The Origins of the National Health Service. The Medical Services of the New Poor Law, 1834–1871* (London, 1967).

sanatoriums: the ones connected to voluntary hospitals were the most respected, while the local-authority institutions and provincial sanatoriums were less well regarded, both within the medical community and among patients. Indeed, it seems that British patients typically went through a number of tuberculosis institutions in what I have elsewhere called 'the institutional career of tuberculosis'.[71] Many patients who were discharged from esteemed voluntary sanatoriums subsequently entered a Poor Law sanatorium before ending up in a Poor Law infirmary, where care was provided more for the dying than as a healing treatment. British patients, therefore, experienced a parallel decline in their health and their social status according to the institution to which they were sent.

Peter Dettweiler, one of the leading international experts on open-air rest therapy at the turn of the century, accepted that therapeutic success in the sense of a clinical improvement was impossible to achieve.[72] This was a surprisingly straightforward acknowledgement in the light of raised expectations through bacteriology. Sanatorium treatment seemed indeed to be over when Robert Koch announced successful attempts to treat tuberculosis with tuberculin in 1891.[73] It soon became clear, however, that Koch's claims were overly optimistic and after a short while, tuberculin turned out to be ineffective in the treatment of tuberculosis. This failure of a bacteriological solution made it possible for Dettweiler and others to achieve international recognition for a treatment that could have been carried out two centuries earlier without any change at all.[74] Despite the limited aim of treatment, Dettweiler and other sanatorium pioneers emphasized the importance of an *individualistic* scheme of rest and plentiful food aimed at putting the patient on the path to recovery. This fitted well into the rising individualism prevalent in medical practice at the time; Virchow's famous statement that 'medicine is a social science' no longer seemed valid.[75] Individualistic treatment regimes of whatever provenance fitted in well with a general move to explain the disease through the logic of bacteriology. Tuberculosis facilitated this coexistence of treatment and medical science, while still rooted in two entirely different traditions of dietetics and bacteriology. Individualistic explanations highlighting infection were at the basis of a public-health campaign that focused to a large extent on the prevention of infection. In essence this led to the belief that the individual behaviour of the victims of tuberculosis was to blame.[76] With their rhetoric about individualistic treatment, sanatoriums contributed to this shift towards individual responsibility. With this in

---

71   F. Condrau, 'The Institutional Career of Tuberculosis Patients in Britain and Germany', in J. Henderson *et al.* (eds), *The Impact of Hospitals in Europe, 1000–2002: People, Landscapes, Symbols*, Clio Medica Series in the History of Medicine (in press).

72   P. Dettweiler, 'Einige Bemerkungen zur sogenannten Ruhe- und Luftliegekur bei Schwindsüchtigen', *Zeitschrift für Tuberkulose und Heilstättenwesen* 1 (1900): 96–100, 180–87.

73   C. Gradmann, 'A Harmony of Illusions: Clinical and Experimental Testing of Robert Koch's Tuberculin 1890–1900', *Studies in History and Philosophy of Biological and Biomedical Sciences*, 34c (2003): 465–81.

74   C. Gradmann, 'Robert Koch and the Pressures of Scientific Research: Tuberculosis and Tuberculin', *Medical History* 45 (2001): 1–32.

75   R. Virchow, 'Der Armenarzt', *Die medicinische Reform* XVIII (1848): 125.

76   Göckenjan, *Kurieren*.

mind, it becomes clear that diagnostic assessments of 'healed' that succumbed to tuberculosis only shortly afterwards owed as much to patient expectation as to setting the patient up to fail where the institution had to guard its own name. Countless sources indicate that patients were discharged with a moral obligation to pursue a hygienic lifestyle which, taking into account the reality of their circumstances, was impossible to achieve.[77] Rather than questioning medical factors, deteriorating cases were often seen as cases of dubious moral quality. In fact, rather than blaming lack of therapeutic success, the sanatorium exponents often preferred to blame the patients themselves. This blame game has continued wherever therapeutic competence is limited and is probably not confined to the history of infectious diseases.

Spatial effects of sanatorium treatment

The location of the sanatorium and the time spent there has always fascinated patients, doctors and literary writers as well as exponents of social and health policy. The basic facts indicate that rural locations, in Britain usually set amid pine woods, were preferred places to build sanatoriums.[78] But location had wider implications for doctors and patients alike. A good starting point for trying to understand the importance of location for the sanatorium is the tuberculosis novel.[79] In Thomas Mann's *The Magic Mountain* and in Joseph Kessel's *Les Captifs*, the journey to the remote sanatorium in the Swiss Alps is of utmost importance to the narrative as it represents the distance the characters are putting between themselves and their regular social environment.[80] By the time Mann got to see Davos at first hand in 1912 (he visited again in 1921), it had already become perhaps the world's most famous resort, a place where ski tourism, alpinism and health treatments of all kinds were flourishing.[81] During the inter-war period, Davos and other locations in the Alps housed several well-known international sanatoriums as well as institutions run by various Swiss cantons. For most patients in Britain and elsewhere, however, sanatoriums were a lot closer, and treatment did not routinely require international travel. Indeed, quite often the sanatoriums were, in today's terms, part of the extended suburbs of regional or national centres. Frimley in Surrey was only about 40 miles from central London and other sanatoriums were similarly close to their constituents. For urban working-class patients, the experience was not of travelling to a distant place like Davos, but of taking the train from London to Frimley or catching a tram from Sheffield city centre to Lodge Moor, a site just a few miles away, bordering on the Peak District.[82]

77   Condrau, *Lungenheilanstalt und Patientenschicksal*, pp. 255–69.

78   Bryder, *Below the Magic Mountain*, pp. 46–9.

79   Pohland, *Sanatorium*.

80   T. Mann, *The Magic Mountain* (New York, 1927); J. Kessel, *Les Captifs* (Paris, 1926).

81   J. Ferdmann, *Der Aufstieg des Kurortes Davos* (Davos, 1947).

82   T. Willis, 'Vaccination: politics, the press and public health', *Wellcome History* 21 (2002): 2–4.

Initially, though, the sanatorium was supposed to follow a stricter spatial agenda as part of its medical merits. The first German institutions were built under the advocacy of Hermann Brehmer, a medical pioneer who claimed that tuberculosis in the early stages could always be healed. In fact, his medical ideas were largely based on the notion of immune locations. Thus, he refuted the idea of going to Swiss alpine resorts such as Davos and favoured geographical regions where tuberculosis mortality rates were either close to zero or at least clearly below the average. But Brehmer's assumptions about immune locations never really caught on; the more tuberculosis was seen as an infectious disease, the less appealing localized conceptualizations of it became.[83] And as the need to build more institutions for a wider range of patients was articulated, the ideal location for tuberculosis treatment became an economic issue, because building sanatoriums for working-class patients far away from the target population was considered much too expensive. Given that transporting the masses to the sanatorium was deemed impossible, it was the sanatorium that had to be positioned closer to the cities from which the patients were supposed to come. Dettweiler, himself an important advocate of the working-class sanatorium, opened his first such sanatorium in Falkenstein, some 25 km north-west of Frankfurt, where most patients subsequently originated. Interestingly, the erection of a sanatorium often jump-started other regional infrastructure by putting a village or small town on the map and requiring railway connections. The most notable example, as we have seen, was Davos, where Alexander Spengler developed alpine tuberculosis treatment in hotels and guesthouses from the 1850s. Karl Turban developed this further with the erection of the first sanatorium in Davos in 1889, which soon expanded to be the major European health resort for tuberculosis.

Conflicts with the hosting villages, probably somewhat exaggerated in secondary literature, were often resolved either by increasing the touristic value of the locality or through providing jobs for the local building trade and support infrastructure. In fact, sanatorium doctors were often called 'doctors who are no more than business-minded hoteliers' because the establishment of a sanatorium was often followed by a healthy growth in tourism, while the institution itself gained a questionable track record of medical success.[84]

A specifically British issue involved considering the most suitable climate for patients. Even though British travellers contributed substantially to the rise of luxury tourism on the Continent from the mid nineteenth century, cross-channel facilities to transport large numbers of patients were probably not available before the inter-war years.[85] That said, however, the main argument against sending patients to the Continent was more to do with keeping British workers on British soil. When workers had to be kept working through labour therapy in order to facilitate reintegration into the labour market, it was only common sense to keep them in the country regardless of its climate. A certain amount of territorial proximity between the sanatorium and patients' homes was therefore seen as desirable even if it potentially compromised

83   See P. Baldwin, *Contagion and the State in Europe, 1830–1930* (Cambridge, 1999).

84   F. Wehmer, 'Rückblick auf Brehmers Lebensarbeit', *Beiträge zur Klinik der Tuberkulose* 31 (1914): 460.

85   M. Morgan, *National Identities and Travel in Victorian Britain* (Basingstoke, 2001).

the therapeutic value of open-air treatment – an issue that became obvious in the industrial centres of the North, where sanatoriums often had to be built relatively close to polluted areas. While in many other countries the medical merits of the Swiss Alps were keenly debated, this provoked little discussion in Britain, even though the better-off Britons often travelled to expensive private sanatoriums in Scotland or Switzerland.

Fictional accounts and secondary literature have suggested that the social isolation of the patients in the sanatorium was directly proportional to the length of the journey to the sanatorium. That, however, assumes that distance is an objective, rather than a subjective, measurement. How distant a location felt to a patient did not necessarily reflect the distance actually measured in miles. For working-class patients, shorter geographical stretches implied no less social distance from their peers; in fact, it can be argued that the alienating experience was felt more strongly by working-class patients on the outskirts of cities than by middle-class patients enjoying themselves in Scotland or the Alps. Indeed, travelling from London to Frimley in Surrey had all the ingredients of journeying to a foreign land for working-class patients who had never before been out of London.[86] And certainly before the mass-trespassing uprising of the 1930s, working-class families tended to be unfamiliar with the countryside.[87] Similarly, travelling from Frankfurt to Falkenstein or even the 20 km from Munich to Planegg was as important a distance for German working-class patients as Hamburg–Davos must have been for the better-off as portrayed in *The Magic Mountain*.

In addition to the experience of travelling a hitherto unknown distance, the sanatorium treatment provided an experience of nature previously not commonly shared by patients. Most sanatorium accounts are full of praise for the exposure to the natural environment in the countryside, and a sojourn in the clean and healthy sanatorium did much to accentuate the sense of dirt and of the inappropriateness of their living conditions after patients' return home.[88]

For urban tuberculosis patients visiting the countryside for the first time, the experience of nature was among the prime long-term effects of sanatorium treatment and did much to ignite a discussion of leisure activities and the open-air school movements. Dettweiler was the most outspoken about this, referring to his patients as potential 'hygienic apostles' whose task it was to bring the good news about hygiene, fresh air and health to their families.[89] Given the unpleasant industrial landscape and polluted environment, the emphasis on this hygienic education lay more in experiencing nature and taking healthy walks in the park than with leaving the windows open to admit so-called fresh air.

---

86   G.A. Cook, *A Hackney Memory Chest* (London, 1983).

87   B. Rothman, *1932 Kinder Trespass: Personal View of the Kinder Scout Mass Trespass* (1982).

88   Condrau, *Lungenheilanstalt und Patientenschicksal*, pp. 236ff.

89   O. Roepke, 'Tuberkulose und Heilstätte', *Beiträge zur Klinik der Tuberkulose* 3 (1904): 15.

Timing the treatment

Ever since the introduction of sanatorium treatment, its recommended duration was a contentious issue. Historiography, fiction and collective memory has it that the patients stayed for a very long time together in the sanatorium. Certainly, there existed patients who remained for years, or who stayed on because they were recruited by the sanatorium to become nurses. From the point of view of the treating doctors, the ideal duration would potentially be unlimited. It is difficult, of course, to disentangle vested interests from medical expertise, but it is not surprising that an unspecific treatment regime aimed at keeping patients for a very long period. How achievable that was in practice depended both on the financial set-up of the institution and on the social class of the patient.

Sanatoriums for private patients could cater for long-term patients simply because they paid the necessary fees. But even in financially favourable circumstances, sanatoriums were under some pressure to return patients as healed; it must have been difficult to argue that a sanatorium with no patient turnover was particularly successful. Also, since tuberculosis was a deadly disease, keeping the patients for an unlimited time would have involved facing difficult success statistics. In general, sanatoriums – particularly the more prestigious ones – went out of their way to avoid institutional mortality, which made it necessary to discharge any patients whose health did not improve while in residence. And the funding regime had a direct influence on patients' length of stay, too. This is clearly obvious with insurance-funded patients, whose average length of stay had to be around the minimum that was seen as medically viable; anything longer would have been regarded as excessive by the insurance bodies. But even in the case of English voluntary sanatoriums, with a relatively small number of beds, the length of stay had to be limited in order to justify attracting donations. This limited provision led to the development of tuberculosis colonies that became well known in Britain during the inter-war years. The most famous of these, Papworth Village, founded by Sir Pendrill Varrier-Jones in 1917, housed around 200 such ex-patients and their families, who all contributed to a tuberculosis village economy.[90]

The historiographical emphasis on a stable and static patient collective does not seem particularly convincing in the light of actual admission data based on sanatorium case studies.[91] In general, those institutions connected to a specialist hospital achieved higher average stays. Patients of the Brompton Hospital Sanatorium, for example, achieved an average length of stay of over five months in 1920, while even the minimum stay exceeded a month and the maximum was very nearly two full years.[92] An institution of similar social structure in Greifenstein in the Harz differed dramatically from this. Patients treated there stayed a minimum of two days, and averaged about ten weeks (which was actually less than the twelve weeks medically

90 L. Bryder, 'Papworth Village Settlement: A Unique Experiment in the Treatment and Care of Tuberculosis?', *Medical History* 28 (1984): 372–90.

91 Condrau, *Lungenheilanstalt und Patientenschicksal*, pp. 165–212.

92 Brompton Hospital Sanatorium at Frimley, Patient clinical notes, 1920, in University of London: Imperial College archives.

understood to be the minimum), while the longest-staying patient was resident for about six months.[93] This means in practice that the institutional context was crucial to determine lengths of stay. For patient cohorts, however, there was quite a bit of 'traffic' in the sanatorium; the coming and going of inmates was an everyday experience which affected the whole social and cultural situation in the sanatorium.

While exceeding real-life institutions dramatically in length of stay, literary sanatoriums essentially existed to show the character's development over a substantial period. Those who went to a literary sanatorium came back with changed personalities. They were transformed as much by the institutional treatment as by the disease. Long stays in luxury sanatoriums provided the opportunity to return from the treatment looking healthy and nicely tanned; literary and private sanatorium patients notoriously returned looking well, regardless of their actual physical condition.

The issue of duration of stay raises different questions in relation to working-class patients. One implication of going for sanatorium treatment was concern for those who were left at home. This clearly applied in particular to married patients with an established family life. While the National Insurance Act in Britain did not provide for families at all, the German health insurance system entered an agreement with the Imperial Insurance Office that it would provide for the family members of sanatorium patients treated under the invalid insurance.[94] However, while this indicates a willingness to accept the problem, it does not show its solution, as living standards of family members declined when income-producing relatives had to stay in a sanatorium for any length of time. In short, sanatorium treatment might have been perfectly respectable, but it often meant that the family had to apply for poor relief.[95] The biggest worry for Moritz Bromme, a patient of the sanatorium Charlottenhöhe near Stuttgart, was how his wife and five children were to subsist. Every time he went to the sanatorium, his family faced extreme poverty. Obliged to look after five young children in the absence of a wage earner, his wife suffered as much from the immediate consequences of tuberculosis as Moritz himself. Indeed, he often blamed himself for leaving his family alone to cope, saying: 'How can I enjoy full pots of meat knowing that my wife and our five children have to lead their daily life on 5.25 Marks?'[96]

The second problem related to the length of a sanatorium stay is no less important. Historical studies of urban mobility show that roughly one-third of the urban working class changed address each year.[97] During several months of treatment in a sanatorium, therefore, not only might friends leave the area, but even the patient's family might move home. The loss of social life due to prolonged treatment might

---

93 Dr Liebe's Heilstätte für den Mittelstand, Aufnahmebuch, Archiv der Pneumologischen Klinik Waldhof-Elgershausen.

94 Telcky, *Bekämpfung.*

95 Hähner-Rombach, *Sozialgeschichte der Tuberkulose,* p. 186.

96 M.W.T. Bromme, *Lebensgeschichte eines modernen Fabrikarbeiters* (Jena, 1905), p. 295.

97 S. Bleek, 'Mobilität und Seßhaftigkeit in deutschen Großstädten während der Urbanisierung', *Geschichte und Gesellschaft* 15 (1989): 5–33.

also particularly strike relatively young and unmarried patients. One ex-patient, who was treated in Frimley sanatorium near London before World War II, remembered:

> My main interest was of course the cinema, of which I had always been fond, but became increasingly addicted to for it was indeed a lonely time for me. We had moved house while I had been away and I had again completely lost touch with my friends.[98]

A German industrial worker in the politically turbulent times before World War I, Moritz Bromme was welcomed back both by his family and by Social-democratic Party colleagues, who immediately plunged him into intense party propaganda activities. Even though he did not get his old job back at the time of his discharge, he found work soon enough in another industrial factory, and noted:

> But what now? That was the big question. I finally ended up in an industrial factory again, that was the sad end of all my treatment. After one month, I had contracted a bad influenza and had to call in sick. My foreman asked me 'How long this time? – I bet you end up in the Castle of the Coughers within a year!'[99]

In this example, the likelihood of repeated prolonged absences is at the basis of lay knowledge about tuberculosis and its incurability. The industrial labour market in Germany at this time was such that Bromme could find work relatively easily, but the regular treatments in the sanatorium kept him from social mobility, his aspirations for leaving the factory job being thwarted by his disease. Not only was his job likely to be at least partly to blame for his chest problems, but because of the nature of the disease he could not get away from the work, which in turn kept him in the vicious cycle of going back and forth between sanatorium and factory.

Patients treated with chest surgery at a sanatorium fared no better. All available accounts of chest surgery speak at length of its disabling effects. Those who had a thoracic operation had experienced nothing like it. While within the sanatorium, the endurance of physical disability may have been a bonus, life after the sanatorium was bound to be very difficult. Alan, an English middle-class patient treated in a sanatorium during World War II, reported of his life after chest surgery:

> Another of my difficulties was the problem of women standing in buses and trains. If I remained seated I felt uncomfortable and loutish, and if I stood I suffered real pain as the vehicle rattled and jolted. ... What I did was to travel a little later when the buses and trains were less crowded. ... I have evolved countless ways of keeping myself out of difficulty.[100]

His strategy, thus, was to avoid most social contacts because he felt his body was inadequate to participate as a normal man. It is remarkable to note that his worst feelings had to do with general courtesy to women, which of course was particularly important for bachelors. It is a common misconception that sanatorium treatment was mostly provided for married people. In reality not everybody came home to a

---

98 Cook, *Hackney*, p. 68.
99 Bromme, *Lebensgeschichte*, p. 342.
100 Ibid., pp. 129ff.

family to be looked after. In Alan's case he was fortunate to have enough money and a job to go back to. All this certainly helped overcome some of the long-term effects of his treatment. But for those who lived long enough, life after the sanatorium was often a lonely one. George, a working-class English patient, described the immediate problems:

> My doctor was in no hurry for me to go back to work and I was content not to do so, for I had developed a giant-sized inferiority complex. I had all the usual youthful desires, but felt I was a social outcast as far as girls were concerned. So, it was the heroines of the Cinema I courted, rescuing them from impossible situations and seducing them in their eternal gratitude of my heroic exploits.[101]

Obviously, the sanatorium cure itself was comparably agreeable for most patients, particularly where the nutritional intake and accommodation were a substantial improvement compared to 'civilian' life. But the real problems started after discharge. Joan, who was treated in an English sanatorium directly after World War II, noted that 'Actually coping with every day tasks with a collapsed lung was a trial, but it was a joy to be away from the suffocating atmosphere of the sanatorium'.[102] She also noted how much her former social contact withdrew from her, thinking that she was still a threat to their health. But, again, medical treatment had physical consequences:

> Rehabilitation to normal life, including overcoming social prejudices, was prolonged, pride enabled me to persevere with the painful exercises needed to restore my now deformed right side to some degree of normality but it was many years before I was brave enough to wear a swimsuit.[103]

Obviously a strong-minded character, Joan later became a teacher for the Welsh Amateur Swimming Association. But her story points to an important element in the history of chest surgery, which is medical intimidation. Reading patients' accounts together with the absence of any regulated medical quality control demonstrates how operations could become instruments of power for the surgeons involved. Patients often did realize this at a later stage in their lives and started to refuse this particular treatment. In fact, chest surgery often led to prolonged medical problems which were a direct outcome of the treatment, rather than of the initial tuberculosis.

Conclusion

Around 1900, after several decades of sanatorium treatment for rich tuberculosis patients, anti-tuberculosis campaigns in the western world started to build institutions specifically for the treatment of urban working-class patients. Fighting the most important single cause of death among adults, the sanatorium was strategically

---

101 Ibid.

102 J.M. McCarthy, '"Tuberculosis" before and after Waksman' (unpublished bachelor's thesis, Chester College, 1986), p. 44.

103 Ibid., p. 45.

placed within a complex system of social insurance, Poor Law and public-health campaigns. The therapeutic ideas behind the sanatorium were comparably simple, consisting of either a self-strengthening of the body by complete rest (in the German model) or an auto-inoculation of the body through graduated labour (in the British model). Doctors in the sanatorium reflected the fact that their treatment did not offer a specific cure; rather, they could only assist the sick body in its fight against tuberculosis. This also implied the importance of psychological stimulation, which in practice implied a broadly understood hygienic education of the patient.

During the early stages of medical professionalization, and while specialist forms of medicine became dominant in many fields of medicine, an old-fashioned system of treatment was adopted and sold to the general public as the best way to combat tuberculosis. Of course, sanatorium treatment existed only because all reasonable alternatives failed; in that sense, it symbolized the prolonged failure of specialist medicine to treat tuberculosis. Most doctors agreed that the sanatorium offered a marginally increased likelihood of survival, and virtually none argued for any guaranteed effect from treatment.

All this changed in the 1950s. Large-scale clinical trials had showed the efficacy of streptomycin, and the administration of a three-drug cocktail of streptomycin, Isoniazid and PAS led to the transformation of tuberculosis into a chronic yet perfectly treatable disease. There was no need for sanatoriums any more, as antibiotics provided the necessary treatment irrespective of the patient's circumstances.[104] The arrival of antibiotic drugs also had a fundamental influence on the writing of the history of tuberculosis. Medical historians, dazzled by the efficacy of antibiotic treatment, tended to dismiss the sanatoriums as futile. Social historians usually discarded sanatorium treatment as completely ineffective, if not ultimately dangerous, claiming that treatment success was neither achieved nor really intended. From their point of view, it served as a façade behind which discipline, order and militaristic concepts of hygiene were used to control working-class sufferers. Both these positions are unsatisfactory. It is doing the past a disservice to see it as a mere step on the way to today's world. The brief analysis of changing ideas about medical success underlines the fact that all treatment regimes – conventional sanatorium treatment, tuberculin and chest surgery – were only possible under specific historical circumstances. This means that from a historian's point of view, notions of success are far from being objectively set in stone. Instead, the conceptualization of medical success was often adjusted to what could ideally be achieved by any therapeutic regime.

Nor does it help to understand the sanatorium as an institution of discipline rather than medicine. This position ultimately leads to a conspiracy theory blaming doctors for exploiting their position in society. While the briefest of looks at modern health-care systems confirms that medicine does indeed command an impressive economic and political power, a simple conspiracy theory does not even begin to do justice to the complex and multi-dimensional position of medicine in society. But the main problem this position poses is the fact that it negates any agency on the side of the patients. Patients sometimes ask for treatment, they have hopes and fears, and they

104 S. Amrith, 'In Search of a Magic Bullet for Tuberculosis: South India and Beyond, 1955–1965', *Social History of Medicine* 17 (2004): 113–30.

want help. Whether it is always the best advice to seek this from medicine is another matter, but this chapter suggests that both the hope for successful treatment and the capacity to deliver it have to be judged within a historical context. That is not to say that contemporary issues bear no relevance for the past or vice versa. It could be said, for instance, that even the problematic success statistics for sanatorium treatment are comparable to success ratios in modern cancer treatment. Only with the benefit of hindsight, namely with knowledge of the power of antibiotics, can we discard earlier tuberculosis treatments as pointless.

Analysing the long-term effects of sanatorium treatment is, consequently, not simply a matter of measuring cohort survival rates. Indeed, it seems advisable to assess a multi-functional institution using a multi-dimensional approach. One important lesson to learn from the history of the sanatorium is the existence of conflicting terms for medical success. To be discharged as 'healed' could mean anything for the survival chances of a patient, with length of life ranging from 24 hours to years and decades. This may be confusing, but it follows from the historical context of medical success. The sanatorium needed discharges and good success statistics, therefore it provided just those. On the other hand, governing bodies of sanatoriums (whether local government, health insurance or voluntary institutions) required long-term survival in order to legitimize the treatment. Again, the numbers were provided, with 50 per cent of patients surviving for more than five years. Whether or not all these patients really suffered from tuberculosis is, of course, impossible to say; cases of mis-diagnosis must have been widespread and the evidence does indeed point to the fact that many patients in sanatoriums received preventive treatment: they were in danger of developing tuberculosis, from which only treatment could save them.

From the point of view of the patients, obviously, survival mattered. One of the pitfalls of taking into account the patient's view in medical history is that the patients whose stories we know were usually long-term survivors. Those who died in the sanatorium or shortly after discharge tended not to leave much in the way of diaries or letters describing their experience. That does not make the accounts by survivors invalid, but it shapes a historical context in which they need to be understood. The experience of sanatorium treatment was for many patients a period of prolonged worry, coupled with exposure to a totally unfamiliar environment. It is hard for contemporary observers to understand what a trip into the countryside meant at a time when workers usually did not leave the town where they were living. In that sense, the sanatorium provided an early example of health tourism, not because Davos developed splendidly after Alexander Spengler started to treat affluent tuberculosis patients there, but because a trip to Frimley or Falkenstein allowed workers for the first time to experience nature and the open countryside. Sanatorium accounts might therefore be as useful as part of the history of the environment as they are for the history of medicine. All this leaves us with a multi-faceted answer to the question about the long-term effects of tuberculosis treatment. A lot depends on proper contextualization but, in general, sanatorium treatment remained a fixture in the biographies of the survivors. That, more than any objective medical merit, makes it an interesting subject for historical enquiry.

CHAPTER ELEVEN

Power and accountability in the voluntary hospitals of Middlesbrough 1900–1948[1]

Barry Doyle

Until recently, the history of pre-National Health Service (NHS) hospital provision was dominated by pessimistic accounts which drew attention to the undemocratic, patronizing and financially precarious nature of the voluntary sector and the growing desire of local populations for a system free from the stigma of charity or poor relief.[2] However, since around 1990 an increasing body of work has emerged which challenges these perspectives and provides a more optimistic account of the early twentieth-century hospital system, especially the way in which hospitals were financed and the impact this had on access and power within institutions.[3] Recent work by Cherry has provided an important corrective to the pessimistic case showing that many voluntary hospitals did adapt after the temporary crisis of 1921, and as the subscriber system declined a substantial number found new sources of income with the development of contributory schemes.[4] Furthermore, he and Mohan, Powell and Gorsky have demonstrated that contributory schemes based on central collection (like those in London and East Anglia), Saturday and Sunday Funds or a workplace-based system had spread to many parts of the country by the late 1930s, providing millions of people with hospital cover.[5] Workplace collection predominated in heavy

1   The research for this paper was conducted with financial support from the Wellcome Trust Grant no. 060540. I am indebted to Robina Weeds for carrying out the research with such assiduousness, imagination and enthusiasm. I am also grateful to the editors for their helpful comments and patience.

2   For standard pessimist accounts, see B. Abel-Smith, *The Hospitals, 1800–1948: a Study in Social Administration in England and Wales* (London, 1964); C. Webster, *The National Health Service: A Political History* (new ed., Oxford, 2002). Contemporary evidence such as Ministry of Health [H. Lett and A.E. Quine], *Hospital Survey: The Hospital Services of the North-Eastern Area* (London, 1946) was very important in shaping these ideas.

3   S. Cherry, *Medical Services and the Hospitals in Britain, 1860–1939* (Cambridge, 1996); S. Cherry, 'Accountability, Entitlement and Control Issues and Voluntary Hospital Funding, c.1860–1939', *Social History of Medicine* 9/2 (1996): 215–33 are key, as is the work of John Mohan, Martin Powell, Martin Gorsky and Tim Willis cited below.

4   Cherry, *Medical Services*, Ch. 6; S. Cherry, 'Beyond National Health Insurance. The Voluntary Hospitals and Hospital Contributory Schemes: A Regional Study', *Social History of Medicine*, 5/3 (1992): 455–82. See also M. Gorsky, M. Powell and J. Mohan, 'British Voluntary Hospitals and the Public Sphere: Contribution and Participation before the National Health Service', in S. Sturdy (ed.), *Medicine, Health and the Public Sphere in Britain, 1600–2000* (London, 2002), pp. 123–44.

5   M. Gorsky, J. Mohan and M. Powell, 'British Voluntary Hospitals, 1871–1938: The Geography of Provision and Utilization', *Journal of Historical Geography*, 25/4 (1999):

industrial areas like Teesside, with Middlesbrough funding two hospitals by the end of the 1860s – the North Ormesby Hospital (NOH) and the North Riding Infirmary (NRI).[6] Admittedly, coverage of these schemes was patchy and they could not always provide a full and consistent service, yet they do suggest a very different picture of the financial health of the voluntary sector from the traditional view and raise important questions about who had access to hospital provision and on what terms.

Access, democracy and power

Recognition of the more nuanced state of hospital finance has encouraged closer scrutiny of the issue of access. Despite changing understanding of the funding regimes in voluntary hospitals, there remains a belief that the inter-war system was not working,[7] and in particular that access remained restricted either by patronage or ability to pay at the point of delivery.[8] It is probable that such conditions remained into the 1920s and 1930s, especially in rural areas, and that in London direct charging became more prevalent,[9] but clearly many patients were joining schemes which allowed them to bypass the charitable gate-keeper and access a hospital bed on purely medical grounds.[10] Yet it is not clear what impact these contributors and their representatives had on the management of these institutions and the relationship

---

463–82; Cherry, 'Beyond National Health Insurance'; S. Cherry, 'Change and Continuity in the Cottage Hospitals c.1859–1948: The Experience of East Anglia', *Medical History*, 36/3 (1992): 271–89; S. Cherry, 'Hospital Saturday, Workplace Collections and Issues in Late Nineteenth-Century Hospital Funding', *Medical History* 44/4 (2000): 461–88; Martin Gorsky and John Mohan, 'London's Voluntary Hospitals in the Inter-War Period: Growth, Transformation or Crisis?', *Nonprofit and Voluntary Sector Quarterly* 30/2 (2001); B. Doyle and R. Nixon, 'Voluntary hospital finance in North-east England: the case of North Ormesby Hospital, Middlesbrough, 1900–1947', *Cleveland History*, 80 (2001): 5–19.

6   B. Doyle, *A History of Hospitals in Middlesbrough* (Middlesbrough, 2002); J.E. Croker, 'Early Hospital Provision in Middlesbrough, 1860–1880' (unpublished master's dissertation, Teesside Polytechnic, 1982); M. Yasumoto, 'Medical Care for Industrial Accidents in a Late Nineteenth Century British Voluntary Hospital: Self Help, Patronage, or Contributory Insurance?' (unpublished paper presented to *Health between the Private and Public: EAHMH Conference*, Oslo, 2003).

7   See especially J. Mohan, *Planning, Markets and Hospitals* (2002) for perceived failure in the north-east of England.

8   For an extreme example, see N. Timmins, *The Five Giants: A Biography of the Welfare State* (London, 1995), p. 104.

9   G. Rivett, *The Development of the London Hospital System, 1823–1982* (London, 1986); Gorsky, Mohan and Powell, 'British Voluntary Hospitals', p. 133.

10   M. Gorsky, J. Mohan and M. Powell, 'The Financial Health of Voluntary Hospitals in Inter-War Britain', *Economic History Review*, LV (2002): 533–57; J. Pickstone, *Medicine and Industrial Society: A History of Hospital Development in Manchester and its Region, 1752–1946* (Manchester, 1985); Cherry, 'Beyond National Health Insurance'; M. Daunton, 'Payment and Participation: Welfare and State-formation in Britain, 1900–1951', *Past and Present, 150* (1996): 169–216.

between payment and participation. Did the democratization of payment and access lead to a change in power relations within voluntary hospitals?

Historians of the nineteenth century have highlighted the importance of the development of urban voluntary institutions and their subscriber democracies,[11] Morris suggesting that hospitals could serve as a key focus for uniting the middle class through the egalitarian subscription[12] – although this optimistic account has been questioned by Gorsky.[13] Historians of twentieth-century institutions, however, have tended to overlook these socio-political aspects, either arguing that voluntarism – and with it subscriber democracy – largely disappeared in the run up to the First World War,[14] or asserting a rigid class division within institutional provision.[15] Thus Martin Daunton concludes that hospitals were of limited importance either as vehicles for middle-class identity (the subscriber-democracy model) or for pan-class negotiation,[16] and that the rise of contributory schemes further distanced activists from management and ownership of the hospitals.[17] The assumption overall is that the nineteenth-century model of the subscriber democracy was not viable in the twentieth century and that for universal, fair and democratic welfare services to be provided, some sort of state-administered and -financed system was required and demanded by the population at large. This view informs assessments of the politics of hospital care in the first half of the twentieth century, which have been dominated by discussions of the emergence of the NHS[18] along with some examination of local municipal provision, but with little attention paid to power relations in the voluntary

---

11   R.J. Morris, *Class, Sect and Party: The Making of the British Middle Class, Leeds 1820–1850* (Manchester, 1990); R.J. Morris, 'The Middle Class and British Towns and Cities of the Industrial Revolution, 1780–1870', in D. Fraser and A. Sutcliffe (eds), *The Pursuit of Urban History* (London, 1983); M.J.D. Roberts, *Making English Morals: Voluntary Association and Moral Reform in England, 1787–1886* (Cambridge, 2004); the 'Civil Society' special issue of *Urban History* 25 (1998).

12   R.J. Morris, 'A year in the public life of the British bourgeoisie', in R. Colls and R. Rodger (eds), *Cities of Ideas: Civil Society and Urban Governance in Britain 1800–2000. Essays in Honour of David Reeder* (Aldershot, 2004), pp. 129–30.

13   M. Gorsky, *Patterns of Philanthropy: Charity and Society in Nineteenth-Century Bristol* (Woodbridge, 1999), p. 152.

14   For example, S. Yeo, *Religion and Voluntary Organisations in Crisis* (London, 1976). For a recent reflection on the decline of voluntarism shaped by Jurgen Habermas's public sphere, see Gorsky, Powell and Mohan, 'British Voluntary Hospitals and the Public Sphere'.

15   M. Savage and A. Miles, *The Remaking of the British Working Class, 1840–1940* (London, 1994).

16   Daunton, 'Payment and Participation': 188–91.

17   This view is shared by Gorsky, Powell and Mohan, 'Voluntary Hospitals and the Public Sphere', pp. 139–40. Daunton, 'Payment and Participation': 191.

18   D. Fox, *Health Policies, Health Politics: The British and American Experience* (Princeton, 1986); D. Fox, 'The National Health Service and the Second World War: The Elaboration of Consensus', in H.L. Smith (ed.), *War and Social Change* (Manchester, 1986); C. Webster, 'Conflict and Consensus: Explaining the British Health Service', *Twentieth Century British History*, 1/2 (1990): 115–51; H. Jones, *Health and Society in Twentieth-Century Britain* (1994); John Stewart, '"For a Healthy London": the Socialist Medical Association and the London County Council in the 1930s', *Medical History*, 41/4 (1997): 417–36; John

sector.[19] Such an approach both overlooks the possibility that voluntary institutions could and did continue to develop in democratic directions between the wars and that there were many seats of power and contests for power within the inter-war voluntary hospital.[20]

As eighteenth- and nineteenth-century historians have recognized, issues of power, and especially subscriber power, were central to the operation of the urban voluntary hospital.[21] However, such issues have been less prominent in discussions of the early twentieth century. This is unusual, as the number of arenas for the exercise of power grew in this period, moving beyond the hospital and its patient to encompass the contest between contributor and hospital, governors and contributors, governors and doctors, governors and administrators, doctors and patients, and doctors and nurses.[22] These relationships are seen largely within a modernization/professionalization model in which the interests and involvement of patients, subscribers and contributors were superseded by those of doctors, administrators and the institution.[23] Certainly in many places it would seem that the growth of contributory schemes and joint bodies took power from subscribers and groups of contributors and concentrated it in the hands of a few élite members.[24] Equally, the growing professional standing of surgeons, along with their honorary status, made doctors difficult to control while their demand for improved technology and resources became paramount.[25] Finally, there is evidence to suggest that the secretary-superintendent was in the

---

Stewart, 'The Battle for Health': a Political History of the Socialist Medical Association, 1930–1951, (Aldershot, 1999).

19   J. Welshman, Municipal Medicine: Public Health in Twentieth-Century Britain (Bern, 2000); T. Willis, 'Politics, Ideology and the Governance of Health Care in Sheffield before the NHS', in R.J. Morris and R.H. Trainor (eds), Urban Governance: Britain and Beyond since 1750 (Aldershot, 2000), pp. 128–49; S. Thompson, 'A Proletarian Public Sphere: Working-Class Provision of Medical Services and Care in South Wales, c.1900–1948', in A. Borsay (ed.), Medicine in Wales, c.1800–2000: Public Service or Private Commodity? (Cardiff, 2003), pp. 86–107.

20   This possibility is addressed by Gorsky, Powell and Mohan, 'British Voluntary Hospitals and the Public Sphere', pp. 133–9, though their conclusions are ambiguous.

21   Gorsky, Patterns of Philanthropy, Ch. 8.

22   This issue forms the core of Keir Waddington's work on the late nineteenth-century London voluntary hospitals and features in some of Cherry's material. K. Waddington, Charity and the London Hospitals (Woodbridge, 2000); K. Waddington, '"Grasping Gratitude": Charity and Hospital Finance in Late-Victorian London', in M. Daunton (ed.), Charity, Self-interest and Welfare in the English Past (1996), pp. 181–202; K. Waddington, 'Subscribing to a Democracy? Management and the Voluntary Ideology of the London Hospitals, 1850–1900', English Historical Review cxviii (2003): 357–79; Cherry, 'Accountability, Entitlement and Control': 225–8.

23   Gorsky, Powell and Mohan, 'British Voluntary Hospitals and the Public Sphere', pp. 126–7 and 139–40.

24   This would seem to be the case in both Sheffield and Norwich, where area contributory schemes were usually managed by a small group with limited worker representation. Willis, 'Governance of Health Care in Sheffield'; Cherry, 'Beyond National Health Insurance'.

25   Gorsky, Powell and Mohan, 'British Voluntary Hospitals and the Public Sphere', p. 127.

process of acquiring almost monopolistic power, given his command of resources, growing staffs and day-to-day administration of the institution.[26] Yet this process was probably not as seamless, complete or uncontested as has been suggested, nor as straightforward at the local level.

Local studies of voluntary hospital provision in the first half of the twentieth century are rare, with many based on London.[27] This chapter will examine contests for power in voluntary hospitals in one northern industrial town in the half-century before the inauguration of the NHS. It will explore three inter-linked themes: how the hospitals were financed; what effect the system of finance had on access to treatment, and what its impact on management structure was. In particular, it will investigate the extent to which patients, through their workers' representatives and the broader labour movement, were able to challenge the power of traditional and new professional élites. The chapter will explore these ideas through an investigation of North Ormesby Hospital and the North Riding Infirmary, Middlesbrough's two voluntary institutions, paying particular attention to finance, access, management and power. Accessing patient views (except for letters in the press) or identifying ways in which individual patients could influence hospital power structures is extremely difficult. For this reason the views and actions of the contributor representatives have been taken as a proxy for those of the patient. This is problematic, as the type of activist willing to spend time on the work of the hospital may have followed an agenda at variance with the wishes of the bulk of contributors, but in the absence of a consistent alternative source this is felt to provide an entrée to patient views and the ways they could influence decision making and policy.

The health of Middlesbrough

The nature and politics of hospital provision in Middlesbrough were closely related to the development of the town itself. Established in 1835 as a planned community of 5,000 people, by the middle of the 1850s Middlesbrough was the focus of a booming iron industry based on local iron ore deposits, the population increasing to 100,000 inhabitants by 1910.[28] Both the rapid population growth and the iron

---

26 S. Sturdy and R. Cooter, 'Science, Scientific Management, and the Transformation of Medicine in Britain, c.1870–1950', *History of Science*, 36/4 (1998): 421–66.

27   Rivett, *London Hospital System*; Waddington, *Charity and the London Hospitals*; Gorsky and Mohan, 'London's Voluntary Hospitals'; Cherry, 'Beyond National Health Insurance'; Cherry, 'Change and Continuity'; Pickstone, *Medicine and Industrial Society*; Mohan, *Planning, Markets and Hospitals*; Thompson, 'Proletarian Public Sphere'; Doyle, *Hospitals in Middlesbrough*; M. Gorsky, '"Threshold of a New Era": The Development of an Integrated Hospital System in North-East Scotland, 1900–39', *Social History of Medicine*, 17/2 (2004): 247–67.

28 A.J. Pollard (ed.), *Middlesbrough: Town and Community, 1830–1950* (Stroud, 1996); W. Lillie, *The History of Middlesbrough: An Illustration of the Evolution of English Industry* (Middlesbrough, 1968); A. Briggs, 'Middlesbrough: The Growth of a New Community', in *Victorian Cities* (Harmondsworth, 1963).

and steel industries created severe environmental and health problems,[29] the demand for housing in the nineteenth century leading to rapidly declining standards,[30] while the emissions from the iron- and steelworks' chimneys produced huge smogs as late as 1945.[31] Furthermore, the working conditions, and the dangers attached to the processes of metal-making, impinged directly on the workers' health with accidents (especially burns and crushings) commonplace.[32] Added to these dangers was the unemployment and poverty of the inter-war period, which left death rates, especially infant mortality, stubbornly high in the poorest areas.[33]

Middlesbrough's late development, small middle class and high levels of occupational risk combined with environmental factors to shape voluntary institutions in the town.[34] Its nineteenth-century origins meant the town had no old urban élite to fund voluntary organizations such as those in Leeds or Bristol,[35] while the new élite could initiate but not control such activities.[36] The workers, on the other hand, were well paid and generally prosperous (at least before the 1920s),[37] but both cyclical depression and the very dangerous nature of work in the town's staple industry meant that the need for mutual welfare provision was high. Workers paid into sick clubs, friendly societies and insurance providers as well as contributing substantially to the running of the town's voluntary hospitals,[38] while employers recognized the need for emergency and medium-term hospital provision.[39] Together workers and bosses joined forces to meet an important need, reflecting the generally good

---

29   M. Lock (ed.), *Middlesbrough Survey and Plan* (1946); A.-K. Woebse, 'The environmental history of Middlesbrough', *Cleveland History* 69 (1995): 2–19.

30   L. Polley, 'Housing the Community, 1830–1914' and J.W. Leonard, '"The City Beautiful": Planning the Future in Mid-twentieth Century Middlesbrough' in Pollard (ed.), *Middlesbrough*, pp. 153–92; J. Albery, 'Housing', in Lock (ed.), *Survey and Plan*.

31   J. Blanco-White, 'Atmospheric Pollution in the County Borough of Middlesbrough', in Lock (ed.), *Survey and Plan*.

32   L. Bell, *At the Works: A Study of a Manufacturing Town* with a new introduction by Jim Turner (1st pub. 1907; repub. 1997), especially pp. 90–91.

33   K. Nicholas, *Social Effects of Unemployment on Teesside, 1919–1939* (Manchester, 1986); and G. Rowntree, 'Health Services in Middlesbrough', in Lock (ed.), *Survey and Plan*.

34   Lillie, *History of Middlesbrough*.

35   Morris, *Class, Sect and Party*; H. Meller, *Leisure and the Changing City, 1870–1914* (London, 1976); Gorsky, *Patterns of Philanthropy*.

36   G. Stout, *History of North Ormesby Hospital* (Stokesley, 1989) pp. 13–35; Croker, 'Early Hospital Provision'. For background on the political élite at this time, D.W. Hadfield, 'Political and Social Attitudes in Middlesbrough, 1852–1889, with Special Reference to the Role of the Middlesbrough Ironmasters' (unpublished doctoral thesis, Teesside Polytechnic, 1981).

37   Bell, *At the Works*, pp. 48–9; Nicholas, *Social Effects*, pp. 43–69. But see also A.A. Hall, 'Wages, earnings and real earnings in Teesside: a reassessment of the ameliorist interpretation of living standards in Britain, 1870–1914', *International Review of Social History* 26/2 (1981): 202–19.

38   J.J. Turner, 'The Frontier Revisited: Thrift and Fellowship in the New Industrial Town, *c.*1840–1914', in Pollard (ed.), *Middlesbrough*, pp. 81–102; Yasumoto, 'Medical Care for Industrial Accidents'.

39   Stout, *North Ormesby*, pp. 13–15; Croker, 'Early Hospital Provision'.

relations between capital and labour in the town.[40] The form hospital provision took in Middlesbrough was thus profoundly influenced by its unusual urban development and the attendant economic and social structures that it shaped.[41]

The emergence of a hospital system in Middlesbrough

The development of a hospital service in Middlesbrough was stimulated by a serious ironworks accident in 1858 which saw 17 men killed or severely injured. Yet following a number of meetings of the town's élite to discuss the opening of a Middlesbrough Infirmary, a split appeared among the promoters, with religion, politics, location, medical professionalism and urban versus rural interests all at issue. The result was two hospitals – one in North Ormesby (1861), to the east of the town, beyond the borough boundary, and the other, North Riding Infirmary (1864) on the west side of the town adjacent to the Ironmaster's Quarter.[42] Middlesbrough was undoubtedly unusual in having two voluntary institutions in a town of its size, and all attempts to merge the two institutions foundered. The 1870s saw public developments with an isolation hospital (1872) and a Workhouse Infirmary in 1878. Three further public hospitals were built during the 1890s, while at North Ormesby a 15-bed 'Workmen's Wing' was completed in 1892 with the assistance of over £700 collected by the workers of the town. The 1920s were characterized by developments in the voluntary sector, including the opening of the Carter Bequest Hospital, while the 1930s saw considerable expansion of the services provided by Middlesbrough Borough Council, which 'appropriated' the Workhouse Infirmary in 1930, remodelling and modernizing it over the next ten years. The inter-war period also saw the development of a more unified approach to the delivery of hospital services and the emergence of a nascent hospital system. A Liaison Committee between the various hospitals began to meet regularly and by 1937 NRI, North Ormesby and the General had agreed a reciprocal arrangement for admitting each other's patients.[43] Thus, on the eve of the NHS, Middlesbrough, a town of around 140,000 people, had ten hospitals (including three voluntary institutions) with 1,945 beds. It was within this context of high environmental health risks and extensive but small-scale institutional provision that the politics of the two key voluntary institutions was played out.

---

40   M. Chase, 'The implantation of working-class organisation on Teesside, 1830–74', *Tijdschrift voor Sociale Geschiedenis* 18/2-3 (1992): 191–211; R. Lewis, 'The Evolution of a Political Culture: Middlesbrough, 1850–1950', in Pollard (ed.), *Middlesbrough*, pp. 103–26.

41   For a similar situation in Cardiff, see N. Evans, '"The First Charity in Wales": Cardiff Infirmary and South Wales Society, 1837–1914', *Welsh History Review*, 9 (1979): 319–46.

42   For the sequence of events see Stout, *North Ormesby*, pp. 13–31; Croker, 'Early Hospital Provision'.

43   Doyle, *Hospitals in Middlesbrough*, pp. 8–11; J. Mansfield, 'From Competition to Co-Operation: Co-Ordination of Acute Hospital Services in Middlesbrough, 1920–1950' (unpublished master's dissertation, Teesside Polytechnic, 1991), pp. 43–7. This mixed economy of hospital provision is explored in detail in B.M. Doyle, 'Searching for a System: Relations between Public and Private Hospitals in Inter-war Middlesbrough' (forthcoming, 2007).

Finance

Central to understanding the rights, entitlements and power of the patients of the town's voluntary hospitals were the sources of day-to-day finance. NOH and NRI largely comprised self-financing 'accident and emergency' facilities established to ensure treatment for those injured in the workplace. By 1900, however, they were beginning to change and widen their mission to that of general community hospitals, with a broad patient base including the wives and children of the predominantly male heavy industrial workforce. Although both hospitals relied to some extent on traditional charitable subscribers, donations, collections and fairly significant employer contributions, a substantial and growing part of the income was drawn from workers' contributions collected at the workplace.[44] Initially dominated by iron- and steelworks, railway yards and dock and shipping concerns, new sectors like chemicals, retailing and services were increasingly represented as the number of works' collections for NOH rose from around 90 in 1900 to 420 in 1946.[45] Coverage was extensive. In 1914, North Ormesby claimed to represent 30,000 employees in Middlesbrough and Cleveland, rising to over 50,000 paying members by the 1940s, while NRI had over 25,000 members in 1930.[46] Although the hospitals set the entitlements by statutes, members voted on how much to pay into the scheme per week, contributions rising from one penny a week in 1900 to 2d. per week by the mid 1920s, which would ensure treatment for worker and family.[47] Thus, for an increasing proportion of the population of Middlesbrough and Cleveland, access to hospital treatment was based on their medical condition, membership of a scheme and availability of beds, rather than 'charity', a situation which changed the traditional relations between hospital and patient.

Workers' contributions proved vitally important to the income of both institutions, accounting for over half of NOH and almost two-thirds of NRI's ordinary income in 1900, while by 1930 they were the source of 70 per cent of funds at both hospitals.[48] The growth of contributions was at the expense of more traditional forms of income,

---

44   *The Forty-Second Annual Report of the Cottage Hospital, North Ormesby, Middlesbrough, 1900* (hereafter *NOH Annual Report* followed by year), p. 6.

45   *NOH Annual Report 1900*, pp. 23–8. G.A. North, *Teesside's Economic Heritage* (Middlesbrough, 1975); *NOH Annual Report 1946*, pp. 29–52 including £428 9s. 8d. from ICI Billingham and £2,253 15s. 8d. from ICI Billingham Works Hospital Fund. *Annual Report of North Riding Infirmary 1934* (hereafter *NRI Annual Report* followed by year) includes 15 separate Dorman Long schemes contributing over £3,000, plus £500 from the management as an employer contribution.

46   NOH Council Minutes, 'Resume of Minutes of House Committee Meeting', 14/5/1914, Teesside Archives (hereafter TA) H/NOR 1/10.

47   *Bye-Laws of the North Ormesby Hospital, Middlesbrough: Revised 1926* (Middlesbrough, 1926), para. 182, p. 23.

48   *NOH Annual Report 1900* and *1930*. The income and expenditure pages were unpaginated at the end of the report. *NRI Annual Report 1908*, p. 36 and *1930*, p. 38. See also Doyle and Nixon, 'Voluntary Hospital Finance'; Mansfield 'Competition to Co-operation', Appendix B2, p. 95, and compare proportions of funding with Gorsky, Powell and Mohan, 'British Voluntary Hospitals and the Public Sphere', p. 128.

such as individual subscriptions, community fundraising or personal benefactions, although these did remain important in capital projects.[49] The Depression reduced the dominance of workers' contributions, especially at NRI, in favour of government and institutional grants, but on the eve of the NHS they were still responsible for 61 per cent of NOH and 40 per cent of NRI income, while subscribers and private patients were relatively unimportant.[50] This financial basis had the potential to confer privileges for the members in three areas – access to beds and treatment; entry into the management structure of the hospitals; and, most contentiously, greater power for patients over the traditional élite, the administrators and the medical staff.

Access

Undoubtedly patients benefited from this financial regime, with a substantial proportion of the population of Teesside enjoying wider access to provision than was normal in an industrial town.[51] Admittedly, access was restricted to members of works' schemes and their families, or to those recommended by subscribers and fundraisers, while conditions such as infectious diseases, cancer and maternity cases and those who could not be 'materially improved' were excluded.[52] Yet despite these restrictions, both hospitals saw a phenomenal rise in admissions, with in-patient numbers at NOH increasing 500 per cent, and those at NRI by over two and a half times between 1900 and 1946.[53] Furthermore, the type of patient treated also changed. In 1900 the majority of patients were male, many the result of accidents at work, with crushing, burns, eye injuries, fractures and general orthopaedics the

---

49   For example, the Sir Bernard Samuelson Memorial Wing at North Riding Infirmary, a major extension of the hospital completed in 1907 and funded entirely by the Samuelson family. South Tees-side Hospital Management Committee, *Commemoration of the Centenary of the North Riding Infirmary, 1864–1964: Official Opening of the Staff Canteen* (Middlesbrough, 1965). Similarly, North Ormesby acquired the Elizabeth Caroline Brown Wing in 1909 with the assistance of a bequest of £4,000 and a subscription list which raised a further £8,000. Stout, *North Ormesby*, pp. 93–4. See also Stout, *North Ormesby*, p. 122 for discussion of Councillor Edwin Turner's £10,000 mayoral fundraising drive for the town's hospitals in 1925 and *NOH Annual Report 1930*, pp. 13–15 and North Ormesby Hospital, *Official Handbook of Bazaar* (Middlesbrough, 1930).

50   Doyle and Nixon, 'Voluntary Hospital Finance'; Mansfield, 'Competition to Co-operation', Appendix B1, p. 93.

51   Gorsky, Mohan and Powell, 'British Voluntary Hospitals', Table 4: 472 and 473–4.

52   *NOH Annual Report 1933*, p. 54; *Statutes and Rules for the Government of the Infirmary, Middlesbrough for the North Riding of the County of York: Revised 1902* (Middlesbrough, 1902), pp. 17–18. These restrictions were common, see Cherry, *Medical Services*, p. 45.

53   *NOH Annual Report 1900*, p. 8 and *NOH Annual Report 1946*, p. 20. *NRI Annual Report 1908*, p. 8 and *NRI Annual Report 1946*, p. 17. There are extensive patient records available for North Ormesby Hospital for most of this period. These have been analysed in a preliminary form in R. Lewis, R. Nixon and B. Doyle, 'Health Services in Middlesbrough: North Ormesby Hospital 1900–1948' (unpublished report, Centre for Local Historical Research, Middlesbrough, 1999).

most common ailments.[54] As this suggests, most patients were surgical, with both hospitals eschewing medical cases. As North Riding explained in the late nineteenth century:

> It should be remembered that as a rule it is only medical cases of some moment that are admitted. Many of them are hopeless cases to begin with, but though so are yet very worthy of great attention and interest not admitting of cure in the ordinary sense of the word, but still such as should be cured or cared for in the highest sense of the term.[55]

However, the age and gender profile of admissions began to change during the Edwardian period, with the number of children in particular increasing, possibly as a result of school inspections.[56] By the 1940s the age and gender profile at North Ormesby saw fairly equal numbers of men (37 per cent of admissions) women (34 per cent) and children under 12 (29 per cent) treated, including a significant number of children admitted for routine operations like tonsils, adenoids and circumcisions, and overall there were ten times as many women admitted in 1946 as there had been in 1900. The number of male admissions increased fourfold during the same period.[57] Access to these voluntary hospitals was increasingly perceived to be 'by right', as shown by the reminiscence of one NOH patient who recalled that 'everybody could come in North Ormesby that paid in to it'.[58] Another explained:

> We paid a penny a week to the NRI and a penny a week to NOH. Then if you wanted a ticket there used to be a lady called Bella Russon at Port Clarence where I first worked. She issued you with a ticket to go to one of these places to get your interview. What ever they decided to do with you, you'd have a bed.[59]

However, this relatively open access could lead to problems, especially long waiting lists (which were characteristic of most of the inter-war period),[60] mistakes by overworked staff (see below) and conflicts over the right of access for women and children. The sources of finance and the extensive patient access also had an impact on the management structure and the relationship between works schemes' representatives and patients on the one hand and hospital management and doctors on the other.

---

54   For a list of the ailments treated at North Riding Infirmary in 1908, see *NRI Annual Report 1908*, pp. 8–10. For a more detailed analysis of ailments at North Ormesby in 1900, 1928 and 1946, see Lewis, Nixon and Doyle, 'Health Services in Middlesbrough', pp. 25–30.

55   *Middlesbrough News and Cleveland Advertiser* (2 April 1875).

56   'Report on Children of School Age admitted into the North Ormesby Hospital during the years 1908, 1909 and 1910', NOH Council Minutes, May 1911, TA H/NOR 11/7.

57   Lewis, Nixon and Doyle, 'Health Services in Middlesbrough', pp. 20–31. Women's access to hospital treatment has received limited coverage, but see A. Digby, 'Poverty, Health, and the Politics of Gender in Britain 1870–1948', in A. Digby and J. Stewart (eds), *Gender, Health and Welfare* (London, 1996), pp. 67–90.

58   Teesside Archives Oral Testimony Collection, Accession 381, pp. 21–2.

59   Teesside Archives Oral Testimony Collection, Accession 80, p. 14.

60   Lewis, Nixon and Doyle, 'Health Services in Middlesbrough', pp. 32–41.

Management

Gorsky, Powell and Mohan have asked whether 'the new citizenship of contribution [brought] with it genuine participation'?[61] The evidence from Middlesbrough suggests that financial power gave patients, through their works' representatives, a visible presence in the running of the hospitals, with both NOH and NRI providing places on House Committees to worker representatives from firms donating more than £20 per annum.[62] However, the degree of power differed. Initially NRI had a Board of Governors composed mostly of people (including women) who owed their place to financial donations or honorific appeal (though medical staff were represented).[63] However, managerial power lay with the House Committee, consisting of equal numbers of governors and workmen's representatives, which was transformed into the General Board in the mid 1930s, with a majority of employees' representatives.[64] On the other hand, in 1900 NOH was run by a Council of 14 members and a House Committee (responsible for the day-to-day running of the hospital, especially the fabric and admissions) with 66 members, the vast majority of whom were workers.[65] Real power lay with the Council, which jealously guarded access to its membership. Doctors were admitted only in 1903, while up until the First World War, representation from the House Committee was restricted to the Chairman and Vice Chairman, who could speak but not vote. However, after the First World War, NOH was democratized as the Council expanded to 38 members, including representatives of the medical staff and House Committee, which itself had swollen to 76 including trades-council and trade-union representatives. Although women made up a growing proportion of patients, they were slow to break into the management structures of NOH. The Linen Guild, formed in mid 1913 under the leadership of Mrs Charles Dorman, the wife of a leading steel manufacturer, provided an entrée, but women had to wait until the late 1920s, when Mrs Dorman became a Vice President, to begin to access real power.[66] It has been suggested that this expansion was 'to serve the purpose of fundraising

---

61   Gorsky, Powell and Mohan, 'British Voluntary Hospitals and the Public Sphere', p. 134. The phrase is from G. Finlayson, *Citizen, State and Social Welfare in Britain, 1830-1990* (Oxford, 1994), p. 9.

62   *Statutes and Rules, North Riding, 1902*, p. 9; *Statutes of the North Ormesby Hospital, Middlesbrough: Revised 1924* (Middlesbrough, 1924), p. 5.

63   See, for example, *NRI Annual Report 1908* for membership of Board of Governors. For similar discussion of the composition of boards of management in the nineteenth century, see Waddington, *Charity and London Hospitals*, Ch. 5 and Gorsky, *Patterns of Philanthropy*, pp. 180–81.

64   *NRI Annual Report 1934*, p. 48 for a summary of the new structure and entitlements to committee membership, and pp. 3 and 4 for the actual membership of the various bodies.

65   Stout, *North Ormesby*, p. 127; *NOH Annual Report 1900*, pp. 3–5. The functions of the Council and the House Committee are set out in the bye-laws and can be followed in the minutes. *North Ormesby Bye-Laws, 1926*, pp. 3–6. NOH House Committee Minutes TA H/NOR 1/28 for Edwardian period.

66   Audrey, wife of Arthur Charles Dorman, leading steel manufacturer and director of Dorman Long. I. Stubbs, 'Some Brief Biographical Notes about Members of the Dorman Family', *Cleveland History*, 86 (2004): 43.

– to reach as wide an audience of subscribers as possible'.[67] However, it can also be seen as the democratization of the hospital, as previously excluded groups – the medical staff, workers and women – challenged the dominance of the middle- and upper-class males who had monopolized the management of the hospital for 50 years. The result in both institutions was a genuinely pan-class organization in which middle- and working-class groups shared responsibility and management functions to ensure the efficient running of the institution for the good of the patients and the community.[68] But whether such a democratization of role translated into a spreading of power is less certain.

Power, conflict and accountability

From a very early date workers were defined as both consumers and producers of the hospital services. The central importance of the worker/contributor was highlighted in the field of fundraising, where workers' representatives were incorporated into the efforts of the hospitals to increase income. Thus, while the workers voted on their contributions, the hospitals could attempt to influence them in the rates they set,[69] or make special appeals to deal with temporary crises.[70] Major capital fundraising could target the workers specifically, especially the 'Workers' Wing' at North Ormesby and the enormous amount contributed by ordinary Middlesbrough citizens during the 1930 Grand Bazaar, which raised £30,000. In fact, during the 1930s the focus for non-contributory fundraising shifted away from traditional subventions, collection days and bequests to more modern methods which increasingly involved women as well as men, such as North Riding Infirmary's 'Prettiest Girl in Middlesbrough' contest of 1933.[71]

In these cases the workers and their representatives were largely reactive, responding to appeals from the hospital management. However, they could also be more actively involved, working with employers in lobbying government in the interests of the hospitals, for example over the introduction of National Health Insurance from 1911,[72] or the proposals in 1914 to extend the Truck Acts to prevent employers from making any deductions from workers' wages for hospital subscriptions. The latter prompted a motion to local MPs stating:

---

67 Stout, *North Ormesby*, p. 127.

68 This interpretation supports that of R.H. Trainor, 'Urban Elites in Victorian Britain', *Urban History Yearbook* (1985): 1–17, and to a lesser extent Gorsky, Powell and Mohan, 'British Voluntary Hospitals and the Public Sphere', p. 139, rather than Savage and Miles, *Remaking of the British Working Class* or Daunton, 'Payment and Participation'.

69 NOH House Committee Minutes 14/12/1911 TA H/NOR 1/28.

70 NOH House Committee Minutes 13/3/1913 TA H/NOR 1/28.

71 Stout, *North Ormesby*, pp. 75–6; *North Eastern Daily Gazette* (hereafter *NEDG*) (30 August 1933). For fundraising at NRI in the 1930s see the Newscuttings book in the possession of the PR Department at James Cook Hospital, Marton Road, Middlesbrough.

72 .NRI House Committee Minutes, 2 and 9/1/1911, TA H/MI (2) 1/6 and NOH Council Minutes, 30/7/1912 and 19/12/1912, TA H/NOR 1/10.

That we, representing some 30,000 workmen and employees in Middlesbrough and Cleveland, and elected by them to represent them on the House Committee of the North Ormesby Hospital, Middlesbrough ... strongly disapprove of the Bill ... as ... the effect of any such legislation upon the income of this Hospital and kindred Institutions would be very serious ...[73]

Most significantly, workers could and did flex their muscles and challenge the management of the institution in the interests of patients, efficient hospital management and workers' rights. Prior to 1914, representatives of Anderston Foundry, sitting on the House Committee of both institutions, raised objections on a number of occasions, including opposing any increase in the salary of the NRI Secretary Superintendent in 1910. In the latter case, they also asserted 'that unless the committee would restore to them the privilege of admittance for any of the members of the workmen's families in addition to the workmen themselves, they would at once withdraw their subscriptions',[74] indicating that works' committees believed they had both rights and power when it came to 'their' hospital.

This power was exerted more fully through the Trades Council – which was represented on the NOH House Committee – including their unsuccessful complaint to the House Committee of NRI in 1920 about the length of wait experienced by patients on admittance to the institution,[75] and their effective lobbying of NOH in 1925 for the insertion of a 'Fair Wage Clause' in all future painting contracts. During the 1930s, with the growing political power of Labour locally,[76] the Trades Council was able to flex its muscle further. In 1936 it complained vociferously about the charging of voluntary hospital contributors admitted to the municipal hospital, setting up a 'Hospitals Vigilance Committee' to collect information and suggest improvements in the service. Although they were denied representation on the Hospital Advisory Joint Committee inaugurated in 1937, a reciprocal payment scheme was agreed between the voluntary and municipal hospitals in that year.[77] However, it was in the course of the three-year crisis at North Riding Infirmary – running from 1929 to 1932 – that the strength of patient power was really tested.

---

73 . NOH Council Minutes, 'Resume of Minutes of House Committee Meeting', 14/5/1914, TA H/NOR 1/10.

74   NRI House Committee Minutes, 27/10/1910 and 24/11/1910, TA H/MI (2) 1/6.

75   NRI House Committee Minutes, 26/1/1920, 18/3/1920 and 27/5/1920, TA H/MI (2) 1/7.

76   Lewis, 'Political Culture'. By 1936 Labour held around one-third of the seats on the borough council. *NEDG* (2 November 1936).

77   'Report of a Conference held between the Representatives of the North Ormesby Hospital, the North Riding Infirmary and the Hospitals Committee of the Middlesbrough Town Council, held at the Town Hall, on Thursday 19th November 1936',TA H/NOR 1/15; Hospitals Committee, Middlesbrough Council, 14 June 1938 and 5 July 1938, TA CB/M/C 2/233.

Crisis and authority

The crisis erupted in late 1929, when the local newspaper, the *North Eastern Daily Gazette*, reported under the headline 'Doctors get to blows – Sensational incidents at Infirmary' that the 'serious differences' between members of the honorary medical staff had erupted into violence during a meeting of the House Committee.[78] The incident, which involved an assault by an Honorary Surgeon on his junior, opened up four years of civil war within the institution, leading to changes in management structures, the dismissal of the Matron and the Secretary Superintendent, chaos in the medical staff and house committee, and ultimately financial ruin. Attempts by patients and their representatives to influence the outcome of these events, while very visible, had only limited effects in the long run.[79]

At the heart of the crisis was the question of power and accountability, and especially the accountability of the honorary medical staff. In 1929 the worker-dominated House Committee had made serious allegations against the honorary medical staff of neglect of patients – including non-attendance for long periods, non-attendance after serious operations and insufficient regulation of the activity of the house surgeons. Evidence 'of the long existence of strained relations between the Secretary Superintendent and the nursing staff, house surgeons and honorary medical staff' was also suggested.[80] The honorary medical staff questioned the right of the House Committee to investigate complaints against them and were subsequently exonerated by a sub-committee of the Board of Governors, chaired by the steel manufacturer, Francis Samuelson,[81] which admitted no more than that 'there may have been occasionally some lack of co-ordination between House Surgeon and members of the Honorary Staff and between senior members of the Honorary staff and the Assistants'.[82] Further accusations of incompetence emerged a year later when a contributor complained that his child, having been admitted to the Infirmary to have a piece of pencil removed from her ear, instead had her tonsils taken out. The alleged cavalier response of the honorary medical staff caused outrage, a trade unionist claiming that the Honorary Aurist and Laryngologist, Dr Keswick, had said that he would have done the same himself 'and that parents should have more confidence in the doctors and authorise them to do whatever they thought fit in the patient's interest', an accusation the consultant denied.[83] Moreover, February 1931

---

78   *NEDG* (30 November 1929).

79   For similar conflicts within medical societies in south Wales, see Thompson, 'Proletarian Public Sphere', p. 92.

80   *NEDG* (20 January 1930).

81   Samuelson was a prominent ironmaster whose family had been involved in the management of the Infirmary since the late nineteenth century. He was a President of the Infirmary and a member of the Board of Governors from the death of his father in 1907 until 1938.

82   'Report of the Committee Appointed by the Special Court of Governors Held on the 24th July 1929', NRI Court of Governors October 1929, TA H/MI (2) 1/1. It became known as the Samuelson Report.

83   *NEDG* (7 January 1931) included in NRI House Committee Minutes, TA H/NOR 1/21, p. 110.

saw the pre-emptory sacking of the Matron on the recommendation of the medical staff and without recourse to a hearing from the House Committee. Once again the issue was taken up by the press and local trade unionists and led to the resignation from the Linen Guild of Mrs Dorman, the withdrawal of some subscriptions and a one-day strike by most of the nurses.[84]

Each of these events suggests that patient interests were not necessarily being upheld by the senior management of the hospital and that the worker-dominated House Committee was insufficiently powerful to challenge either the medical staff or the Board of Governors. Honorary medical staff acted arrogantly, sweeping aside criticism, questioning the authority of their accusers and, it was claimed, engineering the dismissal of the matron after she had made complaints about them to the House Committee and trade unionists.[85] Furthermore, it was claimed that the presence of medical staff on the House Committee was often sufficient to sway decisions in their favour despite their relatively small numbers, especially in regard to the sacking of the Matron.[86] Given the weakness of the House Committee, especially after their defeat in October 1929 by both the Governors and the doctors,[87] and the apparent quiescence of the Board of Governors, campaigners for Infirmary reform were increasingly focusing on a constitutional change which would limit the power of the medical staff within the management of the hospital and deliver greater control to the contributor representatives. The campaign climaxed in May 1931 when the Trades Council, along with the workers' representatives, decided to hold their own enquiry which drew the support of the management of Dorman Long – the largest steel manufacturer in the town.[88] Clearly, long-running and worrying divisions existed at the North Riding Infirmary which severely compromised the patient experience and undermined the authority of the House Committee, the main site of contributor power. Thus, in order to challenge the authority of the medical staff and the traditional élite, patients and contributors had to look outside the management of the Infirmary.

Community mobilization and hospital reform

The campaign for Infirmary reform and the defence of patients' interests was increasingly led by local trade unionists, in particular the Middlesbrough Trades' Council and Thomas McKenna, National Secretary of the Blastfurnacemen's Union. From the start McKenna pushed the case for public enquiries and frequently asserted the rights of the subscribers to a larger voice in the running of the hospital.[89] He was a particular critic of the Secretary Superintendent, C.F. Postgate, but also of the doctors, condemning them as accusers and judges in the case of the Matron.[90] Undoubtedly,

84   *NEDG* (3, 4, 5 17, 25, 27, 28 February 1931; 2, 4, 5, 18, 19 March 1931).
85   Letter from Thomas McKenna, *NEDG* (5 March 1931).
86   *NEDG* (7 May 1931).
87   *NEDG* (20 January 1930).
88   *NEDG* (1 and 7 May 1931).
89   For example, *NEDG* (29 January, 19 February 1930; 14 January and 19 January 1931).
90   *NEDG* (5 March 1931).

as the leader of the largest union in the town, he was an important figure, though significantly he never instructed his union members to withdraw their subscriptions to NRI, preferring to use this as a threat. While McKenna moved quickly into action, the Trades and Labour Council – the wider voice of workers in Middlesbrough – was rather more considered in its response, though in every case it was ultimately the body which carried the most authority. In part this authority was justified by its membership of 23,000, most of whom subscribed to the Infirmary.[91] It was also aided by a very measured and steady attitude to the hospital which, though critical of the secretive stance often taken by the management, was invariably willing to meet and talk with the governors – often in secret.[92] Only in 1931 did it really flex its muscles, calling a conference of workers and allowing a much more radical critique of the hospital administration to take place, including calls to put the honorary medical staff on to salaries to discipline them – as had occurred in the medical societies of south Wales.[93] Like McKenna, the Trades Council did not employ the ultimate sanction of calling on its members to withdraw their subscriptions, choosing always to negotiate with the threat of withdrawal as a key bargaining counter.

But the labour movement also received extensive support and publicity from the *North Eastern Daily Gazette* along with slightly erratic backing from maverick doctors and members of the élite such as honorary surgeon William Dickie and the steel magnate Arthur Dorman.[94] The latter's support was particularly important, as workers at Dorman Long were responsible for over one-third of the hospital's income by the early 1930s, and his threat to suspend payment of contributions was a significant blow to the hospital management.[95] Thus the reform coalition encompassed all the main players in the management structure of the hospital; the driving force, however, following the early defeat of the House Committee, was undoubtedly the trade union movement, which was able to elicit substantial reform of the hospital. The labour movement was able to play such a prominent role in this period because the vast majority of the population of Middlesbrough were involved in the industrial sectors of the economy and were linked together through employment, union membership and hospital contributions – in 1931 it was noted that 'The Trades and Labour Council represented about 75 per cent of the Infirmary's subscribers. Of the £13,000 revenue of the institution, £9,000 was provided by workpeople who were represented on the council'. As such, the town's industrial structure gave legitimacy to the unions to act as the representatives of patients and citizens in this dispute in a way that would have been less likely in more diverse urban environments.[96]

As a result of this campaign, the hospital received a new constitution – leading to a much tighter management structure, more like that operating at NOH. On the face of it this gave greater power to the workers, who became the largest group on

---

91 *NEDG* (7 May 1931).
92 *NEDG* (1 May 1930).
93 *NEDG* (7 May 1931); Thompson, 'Proletarian Public Sphere', pp. 88–90.
94 Doyle, *Hospitals in Middlesbrough*, p. 42; Stubbs, 'Dorman Family'.
95 The employers still deducted and remitted the contributions for the workers.
96 *NEDG* (5 March 1931). Again, there are similarities with the situation in the smaller towns of south Wales; see Thompson, 'Proletarian Public Sphere'.

both the new General Board and Committee of Management, yet in reality their influence in the new Committee of Management was less than it had been in the old House Committee. In particular, they lost control of the chair in the Management Committee and all the important sub-committees, leading the Blastfurnacemen's Union to express misgivings about this new, more managerial structure. The Union noted that: 'such a change merits close and continuous scrutiny in the interests of the patients, for whose benefit alone the infirmary and its officers are maintained by the public'.[97] On the other hand, numerically both the doctors and the traditional honorific élite who had packed the governors had greatly reduced influence. Just 15 members of the general board of 43 and six of the management committee of 15 were drawn from subscribers and employers, while medical representation on the management committee was reduced to just two, suggesting that the onward march of the doctor could be halted, at least temporarily.[98] Yet ultimately, although the crisis weakened the power of the doctors, it did not deliver the NRI into the hands of the workers. Rather, as at North Ormesby, it strengthened the hand of the traditional élite who continued to run the institution up to nationalization in 1946 in alliance with the workers and the medical staff.

Conclusion

What does all this tell us about the relationship between financial structures, management and the patient experience in the hospitals of a medium-sized industrial town? Overall, these two hospitals created memberships and management structures which may have been unusual by the standards of the first half of the twentieth century.[99] The committees included working-class involvement in the management, with employers and employees serving together with (almost) equal power. This created a cross-class, community-based organization which swam against the general trend (at least as suggested in the historiography) of single-class organizations, spatial segregation, class politics and the decline of the public sphere.[100] Furthermore, the concept of community remained very strong and there was a genuine communitarian element involved – through representation, appeals/fundraising, and a strong sense of ownership of the hospitals by the local populations. Nor is it clear that the local labour movement was hostile to the system. Certainly they wanted an efficient service, and they wanted the voluntary hospitals to discharge their responsibilities to their contributors, but there is no evidence of hostility to the works'-funded 'voluntary' sector. Indeed, members of the Middlesbrough Labour movement did not

---

97   *NEDG* (10 March 1932).

98   For news coverage and the response of the unions to the reforms see *NEDG* (8 and 10 March 1932); for the structure of the new committees, *NRI Annual Report 1933* onwards.

99   Gorsky, Powell and Mohan, 'British Voluntary Hospitals and the Public Sphere'.

100 See M. Savage, 'Urban History and social class: two paradigms', *Urban History* 20/1 (1993): 61–77 and Daunton, 'Payment and Participation' for the pessimistic case; Gorsky, Powell and Mohan, 'British Voluntary Hospitals and the Public Sphere' for a neutral position, and Thompson, 'Proletarian Public Sphere' for an optimistic case which mirrors the findings in this study.

advocate municipalization of the hospitals, probably because the population of the town saw NRI and NOH as public institutions owned not by their Council or Court of Governors but by the workers who subscribed to them. Moreover, the attitude of the Trades Council in both the NRI crisis and other incidents suggests that organized labour believed it had a stake in the management of these hospitals, even if it was not always able to force its will.

Undoubtedly there were tensions and the balance of power shifted over time, but Middlesbrough's hospitals show that voluntary institutions were not moribund and that they could still both deliver services and act as a focus for a form of community politics. Patients were given a powerful public voice (through the unions and the press), which allowed their representatives to challenge the authority of the traditional élite, the medical profession and ultimately the Secretary Superintendent, and extract significant reform. Whether this was completely successful remains debatable, but the sovereignty of the contributors, and through them the patients, was acknowledged in the new constitution. This spread power more widely than is generally acknowledged to be the case in the pre-NHS hospital system and created the rather unusual situation in which workers were not only consumers but also producers of hospital services. This may have owed much to the late-developing and predominantly heavy industrial structure of Middlesbrough, which demanded a heavy investment in self-generated welfare provision among the workforce, a situation also apparent in south Wales. Middlesbrough's was thus a voluntary hospital system which offered extensive patient access by right, and levels of payment and participation, which question Daunton's pessimism about workers' faith in voluntary and mutual welfare provision before Bevan.

CHAPTER TWELVE

The Co-operative Men's Guild, citizenship and the limits of mutual aid 1911–1960

Peter Shapely

Mutual aid as a form of collective self help emerged from the eighteenth century with a series of informal networks.[1] They became an integral part of the relief network for working-class communities. The Co-operative Movement provided an invaluable contribution to this network of self-help support organizations, especially in urban areas. The Co-op was also the biggest consumer organization providing a wide range of goods and services for its customers in Britain. This is not a contradiction. Mutual-aid groups were distinct consumer organizations. Members paid a fee and they expected a 'return', including sickness benefits, burial expenses or the promotion of civil rights. In short, they existed to promote the interests of their members. This chapter will look at one such group, the Men's Guild. Its aim was to educate and politicize its working-class members, to mobilize working-class men, to make them active members of society and to promote their rights and interests through the political system. This was part of a wider involvement in politics by the Co-operative Movement during the inter-war period. Like its successful counterpart, the Women's Guild, it attempted to establish local branches across the country to advance notions of citizenship for working-class men. Membership rose steadily throughout the inter-war years. A national network of groups was successfully established.

However, this exercise in mutual aid and citizenship enjoyed only limited success. It was never entirely clear why men joined the organization. They paid their fees, but many simply enjoyed the opportunities offered by the numerous social events provided by the Guild. The attraction was restricted, highlighted by the relatively small membership. After the war, the Guild's membership plummeted. The hierarchy constantly struggled to re-ignite interest. The Guild was, in effect, a glorified vehicle for recreational activities. There was a constant need to provide social facilities to attract and keep members. Yet the purpose of the Guild was meant to be education and political action, to promote members' rights through mutual aid and within the context of Co-operative ideology. This is important in what it suggests about the limits, not only of the Men's Guild, but also of mutual-aid organizations in general. Members were paying customers; the organization was only useful if the service

---

1   The importance of mutual aid as a central part of the aid network from the late eighteenth century and throughout the nineteenth century was underlined by A.J. Kidd, *State, Society and the Poor* (Basingstoke, 1999), pp. 109–59.

offered was perceived to be of real benefit to the recipients, the working-class members who supported it. People did not go along with mutual-aid organizations for the sake of it. As a type of consumer organization, mutual-aid groups had to engage with their target groups in a meaningful way. Failure to attract enough members to their form of mutual aid could only lead to decline and collapse.

The Co-operative Movement, consumerism and mutual aid

Any history of non-governmental support systems is incomplete if it fails to consider mutual aid. Besides informal neighbourhood networks, formal mutual aid took three basic forms, the trade unions, the friendly societies and the Co-operative societies.[2] In all three instances, mutual aid was not simply based on providing welfare support for paying members. Organizations became involved in a range of social, economic and political activities, each designed to secure more fundamental improvements in the lives of their members and even of the working-classes and the poor as a whole.[3]

In the nineteenth century mutual-aid networks were an important feature of working-class life. Female friendly societies allowed women to have a positive degree of control over their finances and have even been seen as providing a model for future state welfare.[4] Societies helped to support class and neighbourhood solidarities, though they were also limited in averting the physical and economic risks that threatened many working-class communities. Social exclusion and division also continued to exist.[5] Nevertheless, they were democratic organizations, formed by the working-classes for the benefit of their members. This clearly differentiates them from voluntary charities that had a subscriber-recipient relationship at the centre of their structure and activities. Mutual aid was based on equitable social relations within the organization, while charities had a dominant power relationship between those who provided the benefits and those who received aid. Finance, management and organization came from within their own membership. This is not to deny the broad similarities between charity and mutual aid. Each is associated with notions of kindness and altruism, while in both instances recipients expect to receive some type of benefit, such as material assistance.[6] This is as far as it goes. In mutual-

---

2   See, for example, M. van der Linden (ed.), *Social Security: The Comparative History of Mutual Aid* (Berne, 1996); E. Hopkins, *Working-class Self-help in Nineteenth Century England: Responses to Industrialization* (New York, 1995), p. 3.

3   Hopkins, *Working-class Self-help*, pp. 224–5.

4   E. Lord, 'Communities of Common Interest: The Social Landscape of South-East Surrey 1750–1850', in C. Phythian-Adams (ed.), *Societies, Culture and Kinship 1580-1850: Cultural Provinces and English Local History* (Leicester, 1993), pp. 131-200.

5   M. Gorsky, 'Mutual Aid and Civil Society: Friendly Societies in Nineteenth-Century Bristol', *Urban History*, 25/3 (1998): 302–22; M. Gorsky, *Patterns of Philanthropy: Charity and Society in Nineteenth-century Bristol* (Woodbridge, 1999).

6   A.J. Kidd, 'Philanthropy and the Social History paradigm', *Social History*, 21/2 (1996): 180–92; P. Shapely, 'Charitable responses to the Cotton Famine', *Urban History*, 28/1 (2001): 46–64.

aid organizations, the recipients expected to make gains from their involvement. They were a type of consumer association, promoting the cause and protecting the rights of their members. The general principle is underlined by the Co-operative Movement. When people joined their local Co-op it was with the promise of the dividend, a share of the profits. Members of the Co-operative Movement were, first and foremost, part of a large consumer organization. Consumerism and mutual aid came together through the wider movement. This became the *raison d'être* of the Co-operative Movement.

Underpinning this was a wider ideological element to the movement with an emphasis on social justice, equality and social inclusion. The Co-operative Movement of the early nineteenth century was influenced, though by no means dominated, by pioneers such as Robert Owen, who aimed to establish equitable labour exchanges so that men could mutually dispose of their property according to the real value of their labour. Eventually, this led to the development of community settlements such as Queenswood in Hampshire and New Lanark in Scotland, where the common ownership of property and the development of class co-operation were the guiding ideals.[7] By the 1840s these experiments had effectively failed.[8]

The main impetus for the movement thereafter came from the Rochdale Pioneers. Established in 1844, the Pioneers originally wanted to form a local store, provide homes for members, produce manufactured goods by unemployed members and establish a temperance hotel. The central rationale of the movement was to provide commercial services, guaranteeing standards and sharing the profits. They offered a pledge of food purity and true weights and measures. Also, each member was given a dividend, a share of the profits. Their business successes throughout the mid to late nineteenth century saw the movement expand across the country. They were especially strong in Lancashire and West Yorkshire. In 1891 the Royal Commission Report on Labour estimated that half the households in Oldham were members of the Co-op.[9] By 1914, the Co-operative retail trade alone was worth £87,964,229 and there were 1,385 societies with over three million members.[10] The Co-operative Movement of the early nineteenth century had tried to change the expansion of industrial capitalism by developing alternative communities, but these failed to make a lasting impact.[11] In the second half of the century they were more limited in scope and ambition, though they succeeded in providing millions of customers with quality-assured goods and a dividend.[12]

Although mutual aid in this sense was concerned with providing quality goods while sharing the profits, the Co-operative Movement expanded its activities into a number of areas. These included banking and insurance, as well as what became Britain's largest funeral service. But it was also a movement involved in a great deal more than buying and selling goods. The Co-op was part of a much wider

---

7   Hopkins, *Working-class Self-help*, p. 200.

8   G. Holyoake, *History of Co-operation* (Manchester, 1879).

9   Hopkins, *Working-class Self-help*, p. 214.

10   Ibid., p. 219.

11   Ibid., pp. 205–10, 228.

12   Ibid., p. 229.

'consumer' movement.[13] In this sense, consumerism was also about protecting citizens' rights in public services such as housing, health and education, about rights in the political arena.[14] The Co-op became actively involved in the politics of material culture, in protecting and promoting the rights of its members as consumers in the broad sense. Members were consumers of services, voters in the political system and part of a society who were entitled to enjoy the full rights of citizenship. In the first half of the twentieth century a number of leading members of the movement attempted to become politically active. Between 1860 and 1914, the movement was contained within a discourse dominated by the liberal bourgeoisie, who wanted to prevent it from becoming a vehicle for socialism and the trade unions.[15] Throughout the nineteenth century the Co-operative Movement became politically neutral, concentrating on consumer services rather than any wider social or political action. In the late nineteenth century Liberal members were concerned that politicization would mean a drift towards socialism. Therefore, the Co-operative Movement was little interested in politics, a fact underlined by the Congress of 1914 that carried a motion in favour of political neutrality.[16]

Yet the early twentieth century had already seen a change in attitude. Several members were taking an active interest in direct political action before 1914. The First World War increased the impetus, pushing the movement towards political action.[17] Interest in politics continued to develop after 1917 with support for the Labour Party and the creation of the Co-operative Party.[18] Moreover, organizations were formed before the War which were concerned with promoting rights. Most prominent was the Women's Guild, which was founded in 1883, and the Men's Guild, which was established in 1911. The Women's Guild was successful in taking the movement

---

13   There is a burgeoning interest in the history of consumerism, highlighted by the Cultures of Consumption research programme, based at Birkbeck, University of London and funded by the AHRC and the ESRC. In recent years research has focused on two main areas of study concerned with growth of trade and sale of consumer goods and the way in which goods were marketed and sold through, for example, the store. See J. Brewer, 'The Error of our Ways: Historians and the Birth of Consumer Society' (public lecture, Royal Society, London, 23 September 2003). However, as Trentmann points out, consumerism is at the centre of debates about freedom and social justice. There is a need to look at the broader concept and how it applies to other services, both commercial and public. See F. Trentmann, 'Beyond Consumerism: New Historical Perspectives on Consumption', *Journal of Contemporary History*, 39/3 (2004): 399–400; F. Trentmann (ed.), *The Making of the Consumer* (Oxford, 2006).

14   See, for example, M. Daunton and M. Hilton (eds), *The Politics of Consumption* (Oxford, 2001); Trentmann, 'Beyond Consumerism': 400; Brewer, 'The Error of our Ways', p. 12.

15   P. Gurney, 'The Middle-class Embrace: Language, Representation, and the Contest over Co-operative forms in Britain 1860–1914', *Victorian Studies*, 37/2 (1994): 253–86; P. Gurney, *Co-operative Culture and the Politics of Consumption in England, 1870–1930* (New York, 1996).

16   Hopkins, *Working-class Self-help*, p. 219.

17   S. Pollard, *The Co-operative Ideal, Then and Now* (Loughborough, 1978).

18   T. Adams, 'The Formation of the Co-operative Party Reconsidered', *International Review of Social History*, 32/1 (1987): 48–68.

to the poorer districts, reducing subscriptions, selling in smaller quantities and opening shops in poor areas. For them, consumer activity also meant promoting women's rights and encouraging women to become active in local government, the administration of the poor law and other social policy issues such as education and housing.[19] The Women's Guild enjoyed considerable success during the inter-war period. Membership reached 88,000 in 1938. The Guild embarked on a campaign to promote the interests of working-class women, a socialist-feminist agenda that was successful in exerting influence over the Labour and Co-operative parties.[20] Despite many obstacles, the Guild managed to give women a useful platform, enabling them to establish a place in the labour movement, giving them a vehicle for reformist feminist ideology and supporting their activism and pacifism.[21]

By the end of the First World War many within the Co-operative Movement viewed social and even political action as an extension of their consumer activities.[22] Members were consumers not simply of their own goods and services. Social justice and equality demanded widespread public and political action. This included education through the Workers Education Association, the promotion of members' rights through the Guilds and an attempt to influence politics directly through the Co-operative Party. Increased political action through the Guilds and Co-operative Party was to reach its height during the inter-war period as the Co-operative Movement became concerned with wider issues of social justice, equal opportunities and the promotion of effective democratic institutions. Mutual aid still meant mutual benefit: members were consumers buying into a service and expecting a return. They joined with the promise of individual benefits. What some leading members of the movement did, however, was to apply these principles to the wider social and political arena. This, in turn, was meant to lead to an inclusive society, equal rights and equal opportunities for every individual.

Citizenship was to be promoted through mutual aid. Members were to help each other to help themselves and the wider working-classes. Guild members were to become active citizens, spreading the ideals of the Co-operative Movement and supporting political action.[23] Some members of the Co-operative Movement became

---

19   P. Thane, *Foundations of the Welfare State* (Harrow, 1990), p. 31.

20   G. Scott, *Feminism and the Politics of Working Women* (London, 1998).

21   B. Blaszaks, 'The Women's Co-operative Guild 1883–1921', *International Social Science Review*, 61/2 (1986): 76–86; B. Blaszaks, *Matriarchs of England's Cooperative Movement: A Study in Gender Politics and Female Leadership, 1883–1921* (Westport, 2000); B. Blaszaks, 'The Gendered Geography of the English Co-operative Movement at the Turn of the Nineteenth Century', *Women's History Review* 9/3 (2000); N. Black, 'The Mother's International: The Women's Co-operative Guild and Feminist Pacifism', *Women's Studies International Forum*, 7/6 (1984): 467–76.

22   Adams, 'The Formation of the Co-operative Party Reconsidered'.

23   See, for example, T.H. Marshall, *Class, Citizenship and Social Development* (New York, 1965); C. Tilly, 'Citizenship, Identity and Social History', *International Review of Social History*, 40 (1990): 1–17; M. Steinberg, 'The great end of all government ... working people's construction of citizenship in early nineteenth century England and the matter of class', *International Review of Social History*, 40 (1990): 19–50. The latter two articles have extensive bibliographical references.

active in promoting the ideals of co-operation and, through it, the rights of its members and the poor and working classes across the spectrum of social policy. In 1920, the *Co-operative News* stated that all members should become engaged with the 'question of carrying the benefits of our movement to the very poorest of the population'.[24] This was to be achieved on several fronts, including the workplace, property ownership, education and political action. The Co-operative Movement was seen by many of its members as the vehicle for promoting these economic and social rights. It had a range of institutions that would enable it to carry out its aims. The idea of partnership in the workplace, for example, was seen to provide benefits for all members of the community. Co-partnership between workers and employers meant inclusion for everyone, a stakeholder society that would guarantee the rights of all members of society. One member, Edward Greening, writing in the *Co-operative News,* claimed that co-partnership between workers and employers created an environment where the worker 'works with a light heart', and feels he is no longer a 'mere wage hireling but a recognised factor in prosperity and success'. He claimed that the worker 'feels he has acquired a new status' and, because his opinion was sought, 'he soon has something at stake'.[25]

The Co-operative Movement actively promoted notions of citizenship, equal rights and social inclusion for working men and women. Besides the workplace, these affected all aspects of life, including home ownership, educational reform and direct political action. J.H. Thomas, Labour MP for Derby, for example, claimed that the Co-op Building Society offered the working classes the opportunity to create a sense of citizenship. He claimed that if it were possible for the working classes to become homeowners 'we should have done something to create a real sense of citizenship', and that the Co-operative Building Society was 'doing something towards solving the problem'.[26] Equal opportunity would also be achieved through both promoting and providing education. In June 1918, Mrs B. Williams, Secretary of the Southern Sectional Board of the Co-operative Union, demanded equal education for all. She claimed that education should provide equal opportunities for every boy and girl from now for the next 25 years. For her, education would 'put the final touch upon our scheme of liberty', as it would break down once and for all the 'caste and class systems which are so rightly condemned in our Co-operative programme'.[27] Education was the 'very foundation of democracy', the only way to extinguish social inequalities and the key to political action and social reform. She concluded that 'if we carried the education of democracy far enough we would have solved nearly all our problems'.[28]

The Co-operative Movement viewed social improvement, equal opportunity, education and citizenship as being interrelated. Ultimately, however, reform would

---

24   *Co-operative News* (3 January 1920), p. 12.

25   E. Greening, 'Co-partnership as a cure for the evil of strikes and misunderstandings', *Co-operative News* (7 February 1920).

26   J.H. Thomas, 'A real spirit of citizenship', Letter to Co-operative Permanent Building Society, *Co-operative News* (20 March 1920).

27   *Manchester and Salford Co-operative Herald* (June 1918).

28   Ibid.

be achieved through political action and the development of a democratic system. The movement was especially keen to exert influence over local government. This was seen as a means to ensure quality for the consumers of public services. Many in the movement believed that local governing bodies had enormous power at their command if they would only make proper use of it, and that a judicious expenditure of rates often meant better public-health services, better housing, better education, and a better overall mode of living.[29] Some felt that Co-operative members should make sure that their votes in local elections went to those who would bring the Co-operative spirit to the discharge of the functions of local government.[30] They also hoped to influence central government. The Co-operative Party was established for the purpose of securing direct representation on local councils as well as in Parliament. It aimed to safeguard effectually the interests of voluntary co-operation and to resist any legislative or administrative inequality which would hamper its progress.[31] Also, it wanted to make sure that the processes of production, distribution and exchange (including the land) should be organized on Co-operative lines in the interests of the whole community, and that the profiteering of private speculators and the trading community should be eliminated. Thus, the overriding objective was to promote the rights and interests of all 'consumers'. This included the abolition of taxes on all foodstuffs, good-quality housing for everyone (financed by government) and an education system 'recast on national lines which will afford equal opportunity of the highest education to all, the breaking down of the caste and class systems and the democratizing of State services'.[32]

These were all bold claims. Certainly, the size of the Co-op Movement cannot be denied. Also, the influence of the Women's Guild has been well documented. But the lasting impact of the Co-op Movement, and especially of the Men's Guild, needs to be explained. Despite its ambitions and undoubted growing strength during the inter-war period, the political influence of the movement, and the long-term success of the Men's Guild, proved to be decidedly restricted. This chapter will explore the growth of the Men's Guild in Britain's urban areas and suggest why, ultimately, the appeal of mutual aid was limited.

The Men's Guild: origins and growth

The Co-operative Guilds which emerged in the early twentieth century were a brave attempt to extend the principles of the movement to a wide consumer membership. As indicated, the most successful was the Women's Guild. Founded in 1883, the Women's Co-operative Guild achieved considerable success, reaching a membership peak of 88,000 in 1,800 branches by 1939.[33] During the inter-war period it gained a formidable reputation as a political campaigning organization for women, promoting the rights of working-class women, and attempting to empower its members through

---

29   *Co-operative News* (27 March 1920).
30   Ibid.
31   *Co-operative News* (22 May 1920).
32   *Bolton Co-operative Record* (1919).
33   Scott, *Feminism and the Politics of Working Women*, pp. 4–5.

its educational programme and political campaigns. The Men's Guild was formed much later, in 1911, with 12 branches and 515 members. The aims included promoting interest in and the study of Co-operative theory and practice and to assisting in the formation of Co-operative opinion with regard to the Co-operative solution of social problems.[34] The branches were also trying to promote a spirit of fellowship and comradeship among the members of the Guild, the members of each society and members of the movement generally. This was to be achieved by educating their members and encouraging social and political activity. Importantly, they emphasized the mutual dependence of the members of society and the interdependence of their welfare, and sought to arouse and develop an interest in the application of Co-operative principles in the solution of social problems.[35] By 1914 the Guild had more than trebled its membership, with 50 branches and 1,825 members. Most of the branches were engaged in propaganda work among trade unions with their mutual aim being the 'uplifting of labour'. The inter-war period saw sustained growth, with membership rising to 11,530 by 1939.

Table 12.1 The growth of the Men's Guild 1917–1939

Years	Branches	Members
1917	98	3,500
1919	126	3,909
1922	195	5,536
1929	233	5,075
1930	201	5,676
1934	272	8,820
1936	290	9,900
1939	321	11,530

The Guild made steady progress across the country.[36] Reports from the branches reflected the growing confidence of the Men's Guild as it expanded rapidly across the north-west of England and throughout Scotland.[37] Moreover, in the early 1920s the Guild was emboldened by what was believed to be a remarkable increase in membership that increased confidence of a bright future.[38] The post-war spirit gave them a new feeling of optimism and a belief that the time was right for the Men's Guild to promote Co-operative principles in all aspects of life. The need for the

---

34   National Co-operative Men's Guild (hereafter NCMG), *Annual Report*, 1914.

35   Ibid.

36   The full Council was W.R. Raf JP, W.H. Watkins (Plymouth), F.A. Gibbins (Brighton), A. Hollands (Willesden), E. Lawn (Leeds), F. Lonsdale (Kinning Park), A. Park (Failsworth), J. Penny (Sheffield), C.H. Russell (Birkenhead), H. Skeels (Walsall), A.J. Tapping (Derby), W.C. Potter (Ilford), and C.E. Wood (Manchester).

37   NCMG, *Annual Report*, 1920–21.

38   Ibid.

Guild was greater than ever before if a better world was to be secured for Guild members and society as a whole.[39] Such confident enthusiasm continued throughout the 1920s. The *Annual Report* of 1925–26 claimed that the previous twelve months constituted the best and most fruitful period in the history of the Guild, stating that 'every sign indicates that the Guild and its branches are now moulding the thought of many co-operators and so exercising a strong and growing influence upon the policy of the Co-operative Movement in this country'.[40] Like the Women's Guild, this interest and enthusiasm reached a peak in 1939.[41]

Promoting the rights of the citizen

The Men's Guild viewed their members as consumers in the wider sense of the term, and consumers demanded justice and equal rights. When applied to politics and social policy, this meant equal rights as active citizens. The Guild distributed its own newspaper and various other publications, established educational classes and supported political action. Their objective was to promote workers' rights. Such rights were felt to be inseparable from the principles of the Co-operative Movement. These principles were outlined at the Men's Guild Conference held in Manchester in February 1919. One of the delegates, A.J. Tapping from Derby, gave an address on the 'Men's Guilds and Their Work in Relation to Citizenship'. He claimed that the aims and objects of the organization included spreading the principles of co-operation and its application to all areas of life.[42] Tapping declared that it was necessary for the Guild to 'enter into the affairs of Government and apply to them the Co-operative principles and work'. He thought it was a duty to permeate and rouse public opinion, and that members had to 'act and raise our voices, so that we may attain our ends'.

For Tapping, an inseparable correlation existed between citizenship and the consumer-based principles of the Co-operative Movement. He argued that citizenship was the exercise of Co-operative principles as citizens of the town and country, and that employing these principles would 'lead to a well ordered life on Co-operative lines'. The key to promoting citizenship was education and involvement in local politics. Education would help members to 'do the right thing'. This had to be accompanied by an active interest in local politics. Co-operative principles would be employed to provide benefits for their members and the town as a whole. Guildmen were working 'for the good of all'. They were missionaries who were 'filled with the spirit of sacrifice'.[43]

This missionary spirit, it was hoped, would lead members to create a 'nobler civilisation', a better society (through Co-operative ideals) affecting all aspects of social life.[44] It was hoped that citizens would join the Men's Guild and embark on

39   Ibid.

40   NCMG, *Annual Report*, 1925–26.

41   NCMG, *Annual Report*, 1938–39.

42   *Bolton Co-operative Record* (May 1919).

43   Ibid.

44   W.B. Cattermole, 'Why Co-operative Employees should join the Men's Guild', *The Co-operative Guildman*, 4, 1 (January 1931).

a campaign for an improved world for all members of the Co-operative Movement
and the rest of the community. Members were buying into a better world which was
to be achieved through mutual aid. The Guild existed to promote citizenship in every
aspect of life – what leading members described as 'Co-operation without bounds or
limits'. Central to the Co-operative principles was the notion of an inclusive society,
or the 'Co-operation of all with all for the elevation of every individual and the
enrichment of our common human life'.[45] This was an audacious attempt to use a
mutual-aid organization to promote social and political justice and equality. The
Men's Guild was aiming at transforming society, at replacing the existing social
order by a nobler one. Through the creation of new forms of economic organization
and new systems of government, it would create 'nobler ethical standards and moral
codes'. This new society would be based on a system of fellowship and mutual aid.[46]
The Men's Guild was to be a key organization in exerting a growing influence over
society by promoting Co-operative policy and democracy.

Entering local government

The Men's Guild was trying to educate its members in the principles of citizenship
and to give them the confidence to take the message into the wider community,
leading to political action. Influencing local government was an obvious extension
of its work and a means of achieving its objectives. Members were instructed to
work and vote for the return of Co-operative activists to local government. A few
Guildmen played an active role in local politics. The 1921 Men's Guild *Annual
Report* described how the former secretary of the Midland District Council had
become a Birmingham City Councillor and was to seek a parliamentary seat
under the auspices of the Co-operative Party at the next election.[47] It claimed that
his success emphasized the fact that the Guild was bound to provide men to carry
on the work of the Co-operative Movement and that there was 'no better school
than the Men's Guild'. In the same *Annual Report*, the Mersey District described
how their Guildmen had taken an active part in the municipal elections and their
efforts had been regarded as a success.[48] The necessity of getting involved in politics
was emphasized in a letter to the branches in October 1921. The letter stressed the
importance of securing direct Co-operative representation on local administrative
bodies, and requested that members should take a keen interest in municipal affairs.
Guild members were also told that they could do a great deal by taking part in the
work of the party, by becoming grass-roots activists. Guildmen believed that in view
of the municipal elections in November, every effort had to be made to put forward
Co-operative candidates for election to the local authority.[49] Citizenship through
mutual aid could be achieved by getting actively involved in local government. The

---

45   W. Mercer, 'The Mission of the Guild Men and the Movement', *The Co-operative
Guildman*, 4, 8 (October 1931).

46   Ibid.

47   NCMG, *Annual Report*, 1920–21.

48   Ibid.

49   Ibid.

Report stated that just as men and women worked together in their societies for mutual good, so could they work together in the building up of municipal and other bodies that would bring Co-operative principles more into 'human life'. Buying in to the Men's Guild, helping others and helping yourself through mutual aid also meant achieving change through involvement with the local political system.

This was about the politics of consumption, of promoting the Co-operative ideal in all areas of life. It was to this end that members of the Men's Guild were meant to work. During the 1929 General Election, the *Guildman* called on members to become politically active. Guildmen were encouraged to prepare and pledge support for political action.[50] Members were informed that in those chosen few constituencies where Co-operative candidates were to be nominated, it was necessary for them to enlist as workers, to approach the local Party agent and to offer their services. Members were encouraged to write campaign material, distribute election pamphlets and carry out door-to-door canvassing. They had to awaken apathetic citizens and rouse them from their sleep.[51] Those who were good at public speaking were encouraged to gather information and prepare speeches.[52] If there were no Co-operative candidates, then Guildmen were told that they should support the Labour candidate, because they could do a great deal to ensure that the Labour candidate was one on whom Co-operators could wholeheartedly support and depend.

Political awareness and action was not restricted to elections. The Guilds discussed a range of social, economic and international topics. In 1931, for example, R. Southern published an article on 'The Men's Guild and the Means Test', in which he claimed that the application of the means test was striking at the very roots of working-class independence, and that members of the National Co-operative Men's Guild ought to know about what was going on.[53] Guildmen were urged to be politically active to solve this type of social problem. They were instructed to make sure that their voice and vote were used well in elections.

Education, education, education

The Men's Guild's educational programme also attempted to promote political awareness among its members. This was a central aim and objective. Mutual aid meant creating awareness of members' position in the political system. This would lead to action, to men improving their lives by helping themselves. As consumers of a mutual-aid service, they were purchasing self-awareness and self-improvement. From the early years the Guild members made it clear that they intended to extend formal and informal educational work by arranging classes and short courses of lectures. Education was the main plank in their platform. Education was to be provided for children as well as adult members.[54] In a letter to the branches of

---

50   *The Guildman*, 3, 13 (May 1929).

51   Ibid.

52   Ibid.

53   R. Southern, 'The Men's Guild and the Means Test', *The Co-operative Guildman*, 8 (October 1931).

54   *Bolton Co-operative Record* (January 1915).

February 1921, one member claimed that they needed 'thousands of classes for the children of our members; we need classes for adults; we need hundreds of week-end schools and summer schools'. He added that Co-operative education was not a luxury but an absolute necessity.[55]

The role of the Guilds in providing education to its members was never lost. This was always seen as the way of moulding politically active citizens who would take the mantle of equality and social justice into the social and political spheres. Education was preparation for the struggle in the politics of consumption. In 1960, Brian Groombridge published his *Report on the Co-operative Auxiliaries*, in which he claimed that the branches should be developing programmes which taught their members about international problems such as 'Peace and the Bomb, Food and Population, Colour and Commonwealth'. But the politics of consumption worked on the micro-as well as the macro-level. The Guild tried to support its members to become prudent consumers and active citizens, drawing on the principles of Co-operation for guidance in every aspect of life.[56] The central purpose of Guild education was to promote inclusion. In this sense, the politics of consumption was a struggle for equality and justice for all consumers in society. The Guilds existed to educate their members and to encourage social and political activity to emerge from that education.[57] Groombridge claimed that Britain's political and economic system resulted in the exclusion of the people from decisions which concerned them and that it was vital that Guilds continued to educate their members to take an informed and active interest in Co-operative democracy. The working classes, an obviously major consumer group, were still excluded from whole areas of social life, a fact which led to the impoverishment of both themselves and the rest of the community. Action through mutual aid was one way to secure change. In this view, the Guilds needed to be strong so that communities did not become split along class lines, with one group pre-empting to itself the rights, privileges and duties of citizenship. The work of the Guilds in educating and promoting citizenship among the working-classes was, therefore, important and relevant, a vital means of countering social exclusion. In the post-war years, it was claimed, the Guilds were more important because they helped to counteract the added exclusion of older people from active participation in social affairs and gave all members a sense of self-confidence, which, they believed, was the basis of social usefulness.[58]

Recreation, recreation, recreation

The Men's Guild attempted to empower its members by giving them the confidence to take action. This, they believed, could only come through education. Working men were trying to help others to join them in the wider crusade for social

---

55 A Letter to the Branches February 1921, 'Co-operative Representation on Local Administrative Bodies in London', *Co-operative Education*. (October 1921).

56 B. Groombridge, *Report on the Co-operative Auxiliaries*, Co-operative College Papers (Loughborough, 1960), p. 13.

57 Ibid., p. 36.

58 Ibid.

inclusion. However, the Guilds increasingly found themselves having to 'attract' men to join the branches. Recreation was seen to be a vital part of the Guilds' approach to winning and maintaining support. It was even thought to be a useful means of enticing children into the movement. In the first few years, local Guilds held children's classes, children's choirs, French classes and swimming galas, all designed to attract hundreds of children.[59] In Manchester, children were subjected to the delights of the Ardwick Industrial Band, a juggler, and a Punch and Judy show.[60] While it was believed by some that they had a moral duty to provide for the social and recreational needs of members' children, the hard fact was that even as early as the 1920s Guilds were asked to take the matter of social clubs and institutes seriously, because if the movement failed to provide for the wants of its members' children through recreational facilities, then there was a real danger that they would look elsewhere.[61] Entertainment for adult members was also seen as important. At the Leeds branch, which had a membership of nearly 1,000, there were five billiard tables in one room, a room for other games such as chess, draughts, dominoes and cards, and periodicals and refreshments. The branch also had a football club, a cricket club, an angling club and a cycling club, and playing fields where they intended to create tennis courts. It was even hoped that in the near future members would be able to compete at football, cricket, billiards and other games with members in other towns and counties. Competing in international matches for trophies provided by the movement was even considered a possibility.[62]

The leaders of the Men's Guild realized that if they failed to give potential members what they wanted, such as sport and recreational facilities, then they would be unable to attract members and so spread the gospel of citizenship and mutual aid. Members had choice and, as such, their demands had to be met. By their very nature, mutual-aid organizations lived or died by their ability to attract and keep members, just as any consumer organization depends on the continued interest of its customers or members. One letter to the branches from London pointed out that the movement was not doing all that was necessary for the people because there was 'another side of life which I think is just as necessary for the well being of the people as food and clothing are'. The writer claimed that recreation was equally important and that the Guilds had to give serious consideration to attracting members through sport and leisure because 'many football, cricket, bowls, tennis etc enthusiasts seek their games in other than Co-operator's spheres'. This was obviously a major concern. If the Guild could not meet the challenge by providing similar pursuits, then, as with any consumer organization, they would simply fade away. The movement needed to provide social and recreational clubs and societies to attract all age groups. Ideas

---

59   *Manchester and Salford Co-operative Herald* (April 1918).

60   Ibid. (June 1918).

61   Letter to the branch members from E. Lawn, Secretary of the Leeds Men's Guild, NCMG, *Annual Report*, 1920–21.

62   Ibid.

included organizing games between towns and countries and building holiday homes for members.[63]

Although the Men's Guild attempted to attract and keep members through entertainment and recreation, it also emphasized that, ultimately, it was attempting to educate men in the values of Co-operation. In this sense, it was copying many of the late Victorian missionary charities which realized that working men were turning to the pleasures of non-denominational social and recreational clubs.[64] Yet there was clearly a tension and irony in the Guild's tactics. Although it was a mutual-aid organization, it had to sell itself in order to attract members and educate them in principles meant to be of mutual benefit. The benefits on offer were concerned with promoting the rights of working men, but the real benefit that attracted many members was the promise of a recreational programme, of a leisure activity – rights, education and politics were of secondary importance.

Decline and fall: the limits of mutual-aid

The failure to attract enough members eventually led to the downfall of the Men's Guild. The steady growth of the Guild during the inter-war period ground to a sudden halt with the outbreak of the Second World War. Unfortunately for the Men's Guild, membership had peaked; it was never able to attract the kind of support enjoyed by the Women's Guild. Even at its high point in 1939, the Women's Guild's membership was eight times greater than that of the Men's Guild. Furthermore, inter-war growth was not only interrupted by the war, but was never to be repeated after 1945. Just as the First World War had halted progress, so the Second World War led to a suspension of all activities. Problems were highlighted from the start of the war. The *Annual Report* of 1938–39 stated that the war caused an immediate 'dislocation in educational bodies' and a reduction of more than one-sixth of the membership recorded in 1938. The Guild had to contend with the blackout, poor travelling facilities, the enrolment of members in ARP, the calling up of others to the armed Forces, excessive overtime and shift work.[65]

Whereas the Men's Guild was able to recover and expand after the First World War, the period after the Second World War witnessed rapid decline. While the membership in 1950 had staged a slight recovery to 189 branches with 4,800 members, by 1960 this had declined to only 85 branches with 1,461 members.[66] The Guild was criticized for being outdated and out of touch with the needs of the working classes in the modern world. It was part of wider criticism about the role and significance of the entire Co-operative Movement. The Movement was condemned

63   A Letter to the Branches February 1921, 'Co-operative Representation On Local Administrative Bodies in London' (October 1921), *Co-operative Education.*

64   See, for example, S. Yeo, *Religion and Voluntary Organizations in Crisis* (London, 1976); P. Shapely, *Charity and Power* (Manchester, 2000), pp. 21–40.

65   NCMG, *Annual Report*, 1938–39.

66   NCMG, *Annual Report*, 1961.

as being a child of the Victorian period and accused of becoming too small and dull to play any part in national affairs or to command the enthusiasm of the people.[67]

Concerns such as these haunted the entire Co-operative Movement throughout the 1950s. It was these concerns that led to Groombridge's report, published in October 1960. He pointed out that there now existed a mood of despair about recruitment. While there were still twelve million members of Co-operative Societies across the country, and although the number of Co-operators had increased by half in the previous 20 years, by contrast the auxiliaries (the different guilds and related associations) had lost half their members in the same period.[68] The drop was nothing short of catastrophic for the Men's Guild; it had 11,530 members in 1938 but only 1,488 in 1959.

The problems facing the Men's Guild were highlighted by its ageing membership. The failure to attract young people meant that becoming characterized as an aged movement was a real danger.[69] This was seen as the greatest single problem facing the development of the Guild. At the 1951 Annual General Meeting, James Leonard claimed that the Guilds tended to 'glorify age', and he wondered whether Guild members realized that young married people had a very different attitude to each other, to home and family life, than that which existed at the time the Women's and Men's Guilds were first formed.[70] The Men's Guilds was living in the past, and many of them were justifying their existence by a constant reference to past usefulness.[71] One young member, Jim Hinchcliff, stated that he wanted new members, more 'new YOUNG members', and that although the eternal cry was for younger blood it was clear that the conditions for obtaining it were relics of the past. He claimed that the Guild was suffering from a 'fossilized mentality which revolved in a milieu of out-dated slogans and the super abundance of fraternal greetings which told us all how good we were'.[72] Hinchcliff's message was blunt. The average Guildman was old, and, in that sense, part of a dying organization which was proving itself impotent to influence events.[73] There were even problems with the leadership. Some believed that the leaders were not only old but also generally men of a lesser calibre than in the past.[74] Groombridge's report claimed that the age level of the membership was universally regarded as lamentable and was partly responsible for the poor quality of the leadership and activities. The problem now was compounded by the image of the Guild. It was becoming an old man's organization and younger people were simply 'turned off'.[75]

---

67 'The Co-operative Movement in a Socialist Society', *The Guildman*, 22, 2 (November 1949).

68 Groombridge, *Report on the Co-operative Auxiliaries*.

69 R. Jones, *Guildman*, 2 (Summer 1951).

70 J. Leonard, 'The Future of the Auxiliaries', *Guildman*, 12 (Summer 1951).

71 Ibid.

72 J. Hinchcliff, 'OPINION: A Young Man looks at the Guild', *Guildman*, 6 (Summer 1952).

73 Ibid.

74 Ibid.

75 Ibid., p. 19.

Besides an ageing membership, the branches were criticized for being reduced to little more than glorified social clubs. This was a vicious circle. The fact was that the membership could only be sustained by organizing Guild meetings more and more as social clubs. Branches were forced to offer inducements by providing what was, in effect, basic entertainment and recreation.[76] Reacting to the decline in membership in 1947, the Tyneside District introduced free dances, coffee mornings for de-mobbed servicemen, and talks which were meant to be of wider interest, such as 'Travels out East'.[77] In some areas the provision of social activities was the only 'service' keeping members interested. In the Southern Section, even the Annual General Meeting was seen as popular only because it combined business with pleasure.[78] The entire meeting was turned into a family party just to make it more appealing. In an effort to increase membership, the Section even launched a fund to purchase a trophy so that the Guilds could be encouraged to make an even greater effort to enrol new members.[79] Some success was claimed in maintaining the same number of branches and suffering only a slight fall in membership.

But the fact remained that the idea of promoting the rights of working men was, for most, simply outdated. If the Guilds were attempting to promote the interests of the ordinary working man as the consumer of public services, then they had failed – there was simply no market for their particular brand. Even the recreation programmes were being criticized for becoming uninviting. Many branches were openly criticized for the poor quality of their programmes. At the Men's Guild AGM of 1952, delegates debated the future of the organization. M. Bennett called on Guildmen to 'cut out talks on beekeeping, horticulture, and the like'. The 1959 working party also underlined the failure by many branches to produce an effective programme which would pull in and motivate members. The Guilds were failing, both in terms of their educational programmes and, crucially, their ability to provide appealing social activities. These programmes were supposed to help members become enlightened citizens, promoting ideas of citizenship while drawing on the principles of Co-operation for guidance. They tried to do this by encouraging members to take an interest in such subjects as local affairs, government and international problems such as international peace, nuclear bombs, race and the Empire. Moreover, they were meant to motivate and instruct them so that they took an *active* interest in these issues.[80] However, Groombridge's research concluded that there were too many unsatisfactory programmes which were obsessed with business of a sectarian or parochial kind. The programmes offered by the branches were simply boring for younger people. As this was one of the main features of the Guilds – the means by which they hoped to attract and keep members (and traditionally the *raison d'être* for most members) – the future of the Guilds was critical. It was this, and not the idea of promoting working men's rights, that kept many members interested. Once this failed, then, obviously, membership began to decline. The

---

76   J. Leonard, 'The Future of the Auxiliaries', *Guildman*, 12 (Summer 1951).
77   *Memoirs from the Tyneside District, Diamond Jubilee Year*, 1926–86, p. 5.
78   E.S. Rudrum, 'Southern Section and its Work', *Guildman*, 12 (Summer 1953).
79   Ibid., p. 13.
80   Ibid.

attractiveness of branch programmes was one of the principal factors affecting the question of membership, especially with regard to new and younger members.[81] It was clear that a branch had to modernize its procedure and its programme. The titles of old favourites in branch programmes had echoes of the nineteenth century. They still included 'Faith Supper', 'Praise Night', 'Sing, Say or Pay'.[82] As Groombridge pointed out, these conjured up a 'faded, antique and moribund world to those who stand outside'. The problem was that while the world had moved on, the Guilds were still living in a pre-war age. However, they were now trying to compete with modern entertainment such as television. The working party concluded that 'there are many who blame television for luring away their potential members', but that they were trying to counter this threat by going into the entertainment industry themselves, that they were competing with the professionals. The sad fact was that their alternative programme of American teas, cake competitions, tombolas and beetle drives was failing to challenge television successfully.[83]

By 1960, the future of the Men's Guild was being openly questioned. One survey found that 47 out of 124 Society Presidents, and 12 out of 54 Education Secretaries, felt that the Guilds had served their purpose.[84] Senior members believed that it was only a matter of time before they ceased operating.[85] Times had changed, but the Guilds seemed hardly to have noticed. One Co-operative employee admitted that 'the Guilds ought to be wound up', while many of the Guild's secretaries themselves believed that they were actually damaging the image of Co-operation.[86]

Significantly, many still believed that the underlying purpose of the Guilds was potentially important and relevant. Gregory's survey concluded that the Guilds were still important 'internationally, nationally, Co-operatively, socially and personally'.[87] The aim of promoting citizenship for the working classes was still relevant in a society which had a political and economic system that resulted in the exclusion of the people from decisions which concerned them. In this respect, the need for the Guilds was as great as it ever was. Nevertheless, if they were to be of any future benefit, then the Guilds had to adapt to the modern world.[88]

Conclusion

The Men's Guild was established within the Co-operative Movement to promote the rights of working men. It attempted to educate through classes and propaganda, while also encouraging direct political action. Members were consumers of public services – mutual aid was viewed as one means of securing the rights of ordinary working men who were not getting the full benefits of these services or of the economic and

---

81   Ibid.
82   Ibid., p. 41.
83   Ibid., p. 53.
84   N.H. Gregory, 'Are the Auxiliaries needed?', *Discipline or Disaster* (1960), pp. 36–8.
85   Ibid.
86   Ibid.
87   Ibid.
88   Ibid.

political system as a whole. The Guild was concerned with encouraging its working-class members to become active citizens and to campaign for social equality, justice and an extension of democracy. They wanted an inclusive society. This was an organization run by working men for the benefit of working men. Although it never achieved the same success as the Women's Guild in terms of membership, it still attracted increasing numbers throughout the inter-war period.

However, after the Second World War, the Men's Guild struggled to generate the same levels of interest and support. Its demise mirrored that of the Women's Guild, which also went into steady decline after the war. The Women's Guild was already running into problems by 1939, and the decision by the leadership to become closely associated with the Labour and Co-operative Parties meant that it had to abandon its feminist agenda and so lost its drive and vitality.[89] The Men's Guild never even came to exert such influence or even generate such interest. Its problems were suggested in the inter-war period. Even then it was clear to many members that they needed to attract members by providing social activities. They had to entice members with the promise of recreational facilities. The idealism, the notion of promoting citizenship for working men, was not enough. The benefits were unappealing. Membership never rose above 11,500. After the war, the Guild was seen to be outdated and irrelevant. Its programme of events failed to attract members. The advent of television made it even more difficult to recruit men by providing social activities. Moreover, a strong Labour Party and robust trade unions, together with the creation of a fully comprehensive welfare state, meant that campaigns for citizenship were no longer relevant to the lives of most working-class men.

Looking at the Men's Guild is important for what it reveals about members of mutual-aid organizations and, arguably, recipients of any benefits, whether through charity or state. It shows a distinct outlook among the poor and working classes. Mutual aid was only necessary if a perceived need existed. Most mutual-aid societies in Britain suffered a serious decline in support after the creation of the welfare state.[90] Like charities, mutual-aid societies had to offer tangible and useful advantages. The Men's Guild was offering to promote workers' rights, but this was already being promoted by Labour and the unions. Moreover, citizenship was not seen as an issue in the modern post-war world where poverty and exclusion were being slain by central government and the welfare state.

However, even the inter-war period saw only limited support. The Co-operative Movement existed to provide commercial services because of the experiences of the nineteenth century, while trade unions were the vehicle for economic struggles and the Labour Party for political rights. Women did not have access to the same organizations. The Women's Guild, therefore, did fulfil a perceived need in promoting women's rights and notions of feminism. For most working-class men, there was only a limited perceived need for any further organizations. In the early 1960s, the Men's Guild changed to a mixed guild called the League of Co-operators, before finally in 1967 becoming part of the original mixed guild, the National Guild of Co-operators.

---

89   Scott, *Feminism and the Politics of Working Women*, p. 5.
90   See, for example, van der Linden (ed.), *Social Security*.

Although the Guild ultimately failed to have the desired impact, research into its work suggests the need to look at the limits of mutual aid as well as trumpeting its successes. Moreover, research into the vast Co-operative Movement highlights the limited number of studies that have been carried out in recent years. Yet it was of huge importance to the lives of millions in providing commercial services and in offering a range of social activities. These were all carried out at the local level and formed an integral part of working-class life.

CHAPTER THIRTEEN

Retelling the stories of clients of voluntary social work agencies in Britain after 1945

Pat Starkey

We rarely hear the voices of social-work clients in the post-war period. Narratives of their lives were constructed for them within social workers' files. Once constructed, these were not accessible to their central characters, who were consequently unable to correct misunderstandings, protest at misrepresentations or comment on the quality of the care they received. Social workers assessed both the nature of their problems and the effectiveness of services in their amelioration: any grievances the clients may have had were necessarily 'privatized and unexpressed'.[1] In the 1970s, attempts began to be made to address this one-sided record and to listen to the voices of selected clients of voluntary social-work agencies specializing in work with poor and disadvantaged families in urban areas. Although those works to be considered in this chapter were greeted with acclaim by the profession when they were published in the 1970s and 1980s, it will be argued that, in spite of their intention to listen to the clients, the authors were unable to break free from an approach which privileged their own views and professional concerns, and that this resulted in texts which reflected established power relations, informed by class, gender and professional and institutional status. As a result, in spite of methodologies designed to avoid such distortions, the voices of the clients were muffled by the concerns of the interviewers and the ambitions of the agencies, as well as by a failure to address the complexities of the interview situation.

Neglect of the clients' viewpoint had already been identified as a weakness in professional social work. A decade earlier, in characteristically caustic tone, Barbara Wootton had used a review article to castigate the 'godlike attributes of the social worker characteristic of the most up-to-date psychiatric image' epitomized, so she believed, in works such as Borgatta, Fenshel and Meyer's *Social Workers' Perceptions of Clients* and L. Pincus (ed.) *Marriage: Studies in Emotional Conflict and Growth*.[2] Wootton grudgingly conceded that another work she was reviewing, *Portrait of Social Work* by Rodgers and Dixon,[3] at least gave a 'concrete picture of what social workers actually do' rather than indulging in the 'unnecessary and

---

1   J. Mayer and N. Timms, *The Client Speaks. Working-class Impressions of Social Work* (London, 1970), pp. 3, 16.

2   E. Borgatta, D. Fenshel and H. Meyer, *Social Workers' Perceptions of Clients* (New York, 1960); L. Pincus (ed.), *Marriage: Studies in Emotional Conflict and Growth* (London, 1960).

3   B. Rodgers and J. Dixon, *Portrait of Social Work* (Oxford, 1960).

distasteful' interpretations she had identified in the other two works. But to her mind, even Rodgers and Dixon failed to view the relationship between client and social worker from the perspective of the person seeking help. As Wootton commented, their chapter 'Attitudes to social work', while purporting to consider clients' attitudes, had done little more than discuss social workers' views of themselves and of their senior colleagues.[4] Wootton's critique may have been harsh, but the nub of her complaint appears to have been borne out when other contemporary studies of social-work provision are considered. They, too, did little to redress the balance, merely reflecting the perceptions and concerns of the professional worker. The influential 1959 *Report of the Working Party on Social Workers in the Local Authority Health and Welfare Services*, or the *Younghusband Report*, which examined the recruitment and training of social workers, for example, had considered evidence from 76 organizations and individuals but did not find it necessary to discuss the quality of the services they provided with those who used them, in spite of the fact that members of its working party had accompanied social workers on some of their visits and, presumably, had met users of their services.[5] Similar omissions are evident in the 1968 *Report of the Committee on Local Authority and Allied Personal Social Services*, or the *Seebohm Report* , which suggested the reorganization of social-work services, but had also signally failed to ask the clients about their experiences.[6]

New research

The three pieces of research revisited in this chapter were believed at the time of their publication to be important and significant because they set out to counter the current trend and to foreground the experience of the client. They are Mayer and Timms's 1970 study, *The Client Speaks: Working Class Impressions of Social Work*,[7] Eric Sainsbury's 1975 work, *Social Work with Families. Perceptions of Social Casework among Clients of a Family Service Unit*[8] and Peter Phillimore's *Families Speaking*,[9] which was published in 1981. All three were conducted with the active co-operation of specific voluntary social-work agencies – the Family Welfare Association (FWA) worked with Mayer and Timms and Family Service Units (FSU) sponsored both

---

4   B. Wootton, 'The Image of the Social Worker', review article, *British Journal of Sociology*, 11 (1960): 382.

5   Ministry of Health and Department of Health for Scotland, *Report of the Working Party on Social Workers in the Local Authority Health and Welfare Services*, also known as *Younghusband Report* (HMSO, 1959), pp. 1ff.

6   *Report of the Committee on Local Authority and Allied Personal Social Services* (or *Seebohm Report*), Cmnd 3703 (HMSO, 1968); A. Sinfield, *Which way for social work?* (London, 1969), quoted in Mayer and Timms, *The Client Speaks*, p.2. See also Mayer and Timms, *The Client Speaks*, pp. 4, 8, 136.

7   Ibid.

8   E. Sainsbury, *Social Work with Families. Perceptions of social casework among clients of a Family Service Unit* (London, 1975).

9   P. Phillimore, *Families Speaking. A Study of Fifty-one Families' Views of Social Work* (London, 1981).

Sainsbury and Phillimore. Both agencies specialized in work with families in urban areas and all those interviewed lived in the poorer parts of British cities, although in different parts of the country: Mayer and Timms concentrated on London, Sainsbury's work was done in Sheffield, while Phillimore's respondents were selected from users of FSU services in several different cities. All those interviewed suffered from financial difficulties and had found themselves on the caseworkers' files because of the problems they faced or, frequently, that their lifestyles and family organization posed for health, housing and welfare authorities. Together all three works can be seen as part of a movement which aimed, in Sainsbury's words, to 'compare how the helping process looks from both ends',[10] and which signalled changes in attitude towards those who used social-work services. In addition to moves to discover the views of those on the receiving end of social-work intervention, this shift may also be seen clearly in the change of nomenclature: the 'cases' of the 1940s and 1950s had become the 'clients' of the 1970s and 1980s. In more recent times the accepted term has become 'service users'.

All three research projects employed semi-structured interview techniques. On the face of it, the encounters with clients were exercises in privileging the views of the powerless – people who were marginalized because of their inability to cope with what their neighbours might consider to be day-to-day problems, or whose economic situation was such that their ability to solve their difficulties was severely restricted. Most were women. They represented those who, as Wootton noted, were in need of the sort of social work that largely consisted 'in performing for the poorer classes services that the well-to-do provide for themselves'.[11]

The significance of timing

The timing of these studies is significant. Mayer and Timms conceded that social workers, embodying the aspirations of a profession that had developed rapidly in the years after the Second World War, had a vested interest in claiming the ability to discern what was best for the client.[12] Since the late 1940s, social work had been carving out a space for itself within welfare provision and, in the process, competing with other professions, notably public health, for influence, particularly in work with poor and deprived families in the least desirable residential areas of British cities.[13] Many of these were categorized as 'problem families' and had attracted the attention of Medical Officers of Health because the domestic disorder in which

10 Sainsbury, *Social Work with Families*, p. 1. See also Z. Butrym, *Medical Social Work in Action* (London, 1968); E. Goldberg, *Helping the Aged* (London, 1970); S. Rees, *Social Work Face to Face* (London, 1978); A. McKay, E. Goldberg and D. Fruin, 'Consumers and a Social Services Department', *Social Work Today*, 4 (1973): 16.

11 Wootton, 'The Image of the Social Worker', p. 380.

12 Mayer and Timms, *The Client Speaks*, p. 15.

13 See, for example, J. Welshman, 'In Search of the "Problem Family": public health and social work in England and Wales, 1940–1970', *Social History of Medicine*, 9 (1996); P. Starkey, 'The Medical Officer of Health, the social worker and the problem family, 1943 to 1968: the case of Family Service Units', *Social History of Medicine*, 11 (1998).

they were assumed to live was seen as a public-health issue. However, as local-authority departments and voluntary agencies increasingly employed social workers to support and socialize such families, a terrain was created where professional responsibility for the families was contested. In addition to claiming space for their professional expertise, therefore, the sponsors of the research were concerned to position particular voluntary agencies within the wider field of social-work provision. This may be seen as an attempt to redress the shift which increasingly favoured the statutory services, themselves expanding in the wake of post-war legislation and, in the process, easing the former charitable organizations from the central position they had hitherto enjoyed.

The competition between public-health and social-work departments was compounded by that between the voluntary and statutory social-work agencies. Both FWA and FSU had distinguished histories in the delivery of services to poor families. FWA had begun life as the Charity Organisation Society in 1869 and, although its sometimes inquisitorial and judgemental methods came more and more to attract criticism during the twentieth century, it could claim to have introduced to the relief of distress case-working methods which were to be used, even if in altered form, for decades. In 1942 the organization changed its name to Family Welfare Association,[14] a move which reflected changes in method and approach in the light of altered attitudes towards the welfare of children and families. Family Service Units had a shorter, but nevertheless distinguished, history that developed from the work of pacifists in Liverpool, Manchester and London during the Second World War. The 'intensive family casework' they pioneered with poor families suffering as a result of the bombing of already disadvantaged neighbourhoods so impressed the local authorities within whose areas they worked that the end of the war saw a large number of invitations to establish units in British cities, or even to provide staff to work within the new Children's Departments,[15] as the work of reconstruction got under way. Both FWA and FSU, therefore, conscious of the considerable impact they had had on the development of professional social-work practice in the immediate post-war period, had reason to believe themselves to be at the forefront of the development of innovative methods.[16]

The importance of both organizations began to diminish, however, in the face of increasing statutory involvement in social-work services. The 1948 Children Act, which had established Children's Departments and provided for the appointment of Children's Officers, had recognized the role of the voluntary agencies in the provision of care to children and families, but had given local authorities power to monitor their work. Furthermore, by the end of the 1950s, local authorities were increasingly providing services that had, hitherto, been offered by voluntary organizations. Together, these developments resulted in an alteration of the balance between statutory and voluntary provision, both in the size of their contribution and

---

14   See J. Lewis, *The Voluntary Sector, the State and Social Work in Britain. The Charity Organisation Society/Family Welfare Association since 1869* (Aldershot, 1995), *passim*.

15   See P. Starkey, *Families and Social Workers. The Work of Family Service Units 1940–1985* (Liverpool, 2000), pp. 8–44, 77–97.

16   Ibid., pp. 141ff.

their status in relation to each other. This was noted in the *Younghusband Report* of 1959, which claimed that those voluntary organizations providing casework services for families had become relatively unimportant when considered alongside local-authority provision, a process of which the committee appeared wholeheartedly to approve.

Furthermore, statutory departments were increasing their complement of trained staff, although from a very low base – in 1959, 89 per cent of social workers had no professional qualification.[17] This compared unfavourably with some voluntary agencies, for example FSU, which claimed to recruit trained social workers and, in addition, to provide rigorous training for its employees, although this carried no officially recognized qualification.[18] Unsurprisingly, the *Report* noted that this reduction in their importance was not entirely to the liking of the voluntary organizations. Younghusband claimed to have been given evidence of poor communication between the voluntary and statutory sectors, a reluctance on the part of the former to surrender its role to the state, and resistance to the suggestion that, in the interests of meeting various and complex needs, local authorities would increasingly take responsibility for 'established services which have previously been provided by a voluntary organization'.[19] Legislation such as the 1963 and 1969 Children and Young Persons Acts, and the 1971 Local Authority (Social Services) Reorganization Act had further thrown into question the role of the voluntary agencies, so that it is hardly surprising that they, perceiving a threat to their position as providers of specialist and often innovative services, were anxious to publicize the quality of their practice.

Voluntary agencies fight back

In the face of developments that appeared to want to dispense with, or at least reduce, their contribution, it was not surprising that some agencies reacted by attempting to fight back. Nor was it surprising that some assumed that favourable assessments by clients would demonstrate the extent to which the care offered by the voluntary sector was, in some cases, superior to that of local authority social-work departments. This was explicit in Mayer and Timms's work, which set out to discover why some people chose a voluntary agency when they looked for help, and specifically, why they chose the Family Welfare Association. They drew attention to the friendly atmosphere that clients enjoyed when visiting FWA offices and the more humane treatment they believed that they received there. That offered by the statutory agencies fell far short. For example, 'Mrs Wood' noted that the FWA worker invited her to sit down as she tried to explain her problems, whereas one of the Ministry of Social Security staff had left her to stand. And 'Mr Peel' had told the researchers that the FWA workers were ready to listen to clients but 'at the Social Security you don't want to know them and they don't want to know you'.[20]

---

17 *Report of the Working Party on Social Workers*, p. 21.
18 See Starkey, *Families and Social Workers*, pp. 141ff.
19 *Report of the Working Party on Social Workers*, pp. 298, 299.
20 Mayer and Timms, *The Client Speaks*, vii; cf. also, for example, ibid., p.108.

Although there was no discussion about the different functions of the agencies there compared – Social Security being largely concerned with the payment of benefits and FWA with welfare in its wider sense – it would appear that the respondents saw them as similar or, more probably, had chosen to ask them for similar sorts of help. This difference in approach was something that cut little ice with the Younghusband Committee, which made clear its view that statutory services were better able to assess and meet need, whereas the role of voluntary agencies was to experiment and, if the experiment proved successful, to pass the work to local authorities. It noted that in general the wisdom of handing over responsibility to a statutory service was appreciated by the voluntary sector,[21] though judging by the alarm shown by some voluntary agencies at the provisions of the Children and Young Persons Act of 1963, the committee might not have judged accurately their response.[22]

Informed client preference less overtly coloured the assumptions behind Sainsbury's work, although he aimed to discover clients' perceptions of 'good practice' and, in the process, was unable to resist making comparisons between Family Service Units and local authority social services as well as other voluntary agencies.[23] He did that, in spite of warning of the dangers of allowing clients to project their ambivalent feelings about their present plight on to social work agencies they had used in the past.[24] By asking clients currently or recently on the books of a particular agency to describe the characteristics of their preferred social worker, at the same time as acknowledging that the most recent worker was likely to receive greatest approval, he skewed the evidence in favour of the current agency. For example, one respondent was asked: 'Of all the visitors you've had, can you choose one who's your favourite?' That enquiry elicited a response that challenged the line of questioning: 'Well, no. I don't think that's quite fair, is it? ...'[25] Others, though, were prepared to grade their workers, although the criteria for assessing them was only partly to do with the service they provided:

> ... '[W]hich did you like most?' 'Little Linda, because she had a sweet face ... she was warm and open and friendly in everything and every way. She had some lovely attitudes. If I wanted to go to the Assistance Board, and they gave me short on my money, she'd be gentle and calm, get my money through, and that was it.'[26]

Commenting on Sainsbury's remarks, Phillimore argued that, by endorsing behaviour which he had earlier impugned as irrational, Sainsbury gave clients' statements about preferences for one agency or one worker rather than another both publicity and legitimacy.[27] Anxious to avoid this danger himself, Phillimore devoted his comparative chapter to institutional ethos rather than the attitudes of personnel, but had to admit the likelihood that the most recently consulted agency would be viewed

21 *Report of the Working Party on Social Workers*, p. 299.

22 See Starkey, *Families and Social Workers*, pp. 187ff.

23 See, for example, Sainsbury, *Social Work with Families*, pp. 17–36, 59, 87.

24 Ibid., pp. 33, 35–6, 91; cf. Phillimore, *Families Speaking*, p. 4.

25 Sainsbury, *Social Work with Families*, p. 152.

26 Ibid., p. 153.

27 Phillimore, *Families Speaking*, p. 4.

with more affection and approval. His comments that clients readily appreciated the advantages to them of FSU workers' smaller caseloads and informal organization may well have been objective assessments of client experience, but were still coloured by the fact that that experience was a recent one.[28] His respondents, too, commented on the difference in approach between the statutory services they had used and FSU. 'Social Services haven't got time, but the Family Service makes time', and 'You can go down any time you want, and it's there', were remarks that Phillimore recorded.[29] The questionnaire he used was designed in consultation with the Director and Assistant Director of FSU, whose close involvement in the project also extended to helping to devise the format adopted in the final report.[30] Although no attempt was made to conceal this intimate association of the agency's management with the project, the validity of the research as an independent exercise must be thrown into question.

Neither of the other two projects appears to have experienced such close control over the work, but none of the researchers seemed to have given much consideration to the anxiety of interviewees to please the person in front of them, whom they knew to be associated with the agency in question, and the potential of this connection to influence the way in which respondents chose to narrate their accounts. And the links were close. Sainsbury, for example, used the occasion of one interview to give the respondent the telephone number of the local FSU.[31] Nor did they consider the possibility that the close relationship might shape the way that they, as researchers, interpreted the responses. Phillimore's intention to compare Family Service Units with local-authority provision was more explicit than that in the other two studies,[32] reflecting the more focused nature of his enquiry, which was to produce evidence of FSU's work for presentation to the National Institute for Social Work Committee on the Role and Tasks of Social Workers in order to guarantee that the users' own views reached the Committee.

Changes in social-work theory

As well as promoting the cause of the voluntary sector, the texts reflect a further concern. This was associated with changes specific to social-work theory and practice which were the topic of anxious discussion within the profession, whatever the status of the agency. FSU had built its reputation on its ability to offer practical help to families in difficult situations. In its early days, workers rolled up their sleeves and assisted with basic household cleaning and decorating, as well as enabling families to claim any monetary and other allowances to which they were entitled.[33] FWA, in its attempts to encourage personal responsibility and independence, also emphasized the practical side of its work. But both had also employed psychodynamic methods in

---

28 Ibid., pp. 76ff.

29 Ibid., p. 77.

30 Ibid., p. 8.

31 Sainsbury, *Social Work with Families*, p. 163.

32 Phillimore, *Families Speaking*, pp. 2, 4.

33 Starkey, *Families and Social Workers*, pp. 17ff.

order to help clients to understand the 'real' causes of their distress. Psychodynamic social work, which worked from the premise that a client's problems were, at least in part, internal to herself and her relationships, had been widely used since the late 1940s. This had been influenced by developments in the United States, where teaching about unconscious motivation and the impact of infantile experience had begun to take hold in the inter-war period. From the late 1940s, FSU increasingly exposed its trainees to these methods and both the records of training courses and individual client case notes reflect this emphasis.[34] Almost inevitably, this method assumed the ability of social workers to discern the supposed underlying causes of clients' problems, and the inability of the client to exercise such discernment without assistance, creating a divide between the professional and the client which emphasized their respective roles and competencies.

As Mayer and Timms pointed out, practitioners believed clients to be unable to 'perceive clearly and without distortion the reality of the treatment situation',[35] and both FWA and FSU used methods which emphasized the responsibility of the worker to use his or her personality in the process of helping clients to come to terms with the difficulties facing them: as an influential textbook of the period stressed, every problem – even an explicit request for some form of material assistance, like a loan for the purchase of a new cooker – had an emotional component.[36] This led to what Sainsbury, Nixon and Phillips noted as the tendency of social workers to have more extensive goals than their clients appreciated: these were almost always in the area of family relationships and were not on the whole disclosed to clients.[37] Unaware of the worker's intentions and assumptions, clients were at a disadvantage. Moreover, as Mayer and Timms showed, psychoanalytically inspired casework inevitably encouraged practitioners to discount or explain away opinions that the client might have had, and many social workers were trained to assume that clients were unable to perceive clearly the treatment situation.[38] Should they entertain negative feelings about the treatment they received, there was a tendency to attribute these to the underlying problem. Such methods were subjected to serious attack throughout the 1970s from what was called 'radical social work': informed by an interest in sociology and sociological explanations, it dismissed what it saw as the sometimes tortuous reasoning behind psychotherapeutic work, looked to environmental factors such as poor housing and low income to explain the difficulties faced by many families, and rejected interventions which focused almost entirely on psychological factors. [39]

---

34   Ibid., pp. 70ff. Records of individual trainees can be found in the University of Liverpool, Department of Sociology, Social Policy and Social Work Studies, student records 1960. See also University of Liverpool Special Collections and Archives D495 (HQ) M5/3 for records of trainees at other colleges.

35   Mayer and Timms, *The Client Speaks*, p. 14.

36   F.P. Biestek, *The Casework Relationship* (London, 1959), p. 36; Starkey, *Families and Social Workers*, p. 92.

37   E. Sainsbury, S Nixon and D Phillips, *Social Work in Focus. Clients' and Social Workers' Perceptions in Long-term Social Work* (London, 1982), pp. 171ff.

38   Mayer and Timms, *The Client Speaks*, p. 14.

39   Ibid., p. 143.

Mayer and Timms found themselves at the point of meeting between these two theoretical positions; they were ready to reconsider, perhaps even to adapt, earlier conventions, but not to reject totally the 'insight-oriented' approach.[40] They argued that clients of voluntary agencies tended to define their own problems in the first instance and to choose where to go for help, but it is doubtful whether clients were always permitted to define their problems. As will be shown, those subjected to some forms of social work found their definitions altered so that they could be fitted into a particular theoretical framework. There can be little doubt that at base, and in spite of their criticism that some psychoanalytically oriented workers betrayed a sense of their own superiority of judgement, Mayer and Timms believed environmental and economic factors to be of less importance than, or at least reflective of, emotional difficulties.[41] They claimed that a combination of material aid and 'insight-oriented help' produced more satisfied clients,[42] something that appears to have been borne out by the other studies. However, they failed to consider the possibility that clients might have been prepared to tolerate the dissection of their inner lives and intimate relationships in order to qualify for the material help they believed that they needed and for which they had gone to the agency in the first place. The woman they characterized as the 'one exception' to their assumption that most satisfied clients appreciated the interest that workers showed in more intimate details of their lives was presented as atypical, and not given credit for challenging her social worker's 'obsession with feelings'.[43]

Her insistence through the course of a long interview was that her problem was purely financial. She was confused by the worker's initial assumption that '...we were having trouble with our marriage. You'd think I was going to leave my husband or he was going to leave me'. Yet this response was met with persistent questioning about whether the intervention had been successful and whether 'Mrs Mountford' would recommend FWA to others. Although she eventually conceded that talking about her problem had shown her that she could take steps to solve it herself, there was no discussion of the erroneous assumption that her 'real' problem was marital. Dissatisfied clients were sometimes blamed for failing to make clear the exact nature of their plight. 'Mrs Hunter', who had gone to FWA to ask for financial assistance, complained that 'all they seemed interested to me was that they just wanted to know my personal life, what we were like, what we argued over and that was all ...'. Although she had not felt able to tell the social worker that she had problems meeting her debts, she assumed that he would realize that she had gone to see him because she needed financial help and resented his interest in other aspects of her life. The social worker failed to perceive the cause of her distress, and 'Mrs Hunter' did not bother to return to the agency. Mayer and Timms commented that she had assumed wrongly that the worker would see the problem as she did, but did not suggest that the worker's original questioning should have elicited from her the true

---

40   Ibid., p. 143.

41   Ibid., pp. 12, 14, 141, 144.

42   Ibid., p. 106; Sainsbury, *Social Work with Families*, p. 28; Phillimore, *Families Speaking*, p. 21.

43   Mayer and Timms, *The Client Speaks*, p. 113.

nature of her difficulties.[44] To be fair, in their concluding chapter Mayer and Timms discussed ways in which caseworkers could more appropriately have responded to the problems that clients presented. Nevertheless, they came down firmly on the use of 'insight-oriented' methods, on the grounds that, regardless of short-term client satisfaction with 'supportive-directive' techniques that aimed to enable clients to solve their own difficulties, 'insight-oriented' methods provided the best hope of long term 're-socialization'.[45]

'Mrs Mountford' and 'Mrs Hunter' may have been unusual in their insistence that their social workers had failed to understand the nature of their problems. Although 'Mrs Hunter' decided not to continue in her quest for help, others, 'Mrs Mountford' among them, appear to have been prepared to pursue the satisfaction of their needs by choosing to play the game and to behave in ways calculated to achieve those ends. Sainsbury, Nixon and Phillips, in their 1982 study, highlighted one way in which they believed clients adapted their behaviour to the workers' preoccupations. They argued that 'a narrower range of subjects was discussed as cases progressed, and it seemed probable that many clients ceased to raise issues which, irrespective of their importance, seemed not to attract the worker's attention'.[46] Was the need to keep the social worker's attention a factor influencing the results of some surveys of client needs? Many interviewees had a lot of experience of talking to social workers. They knew how to respond – how to give the 'right answer'.

A table produced by Mayer and Timms suggesting that 34 per cent of clients were treated for 'marital discord' and 23 per cent for 'economic difficulties'[47] must be read carefully in the light of these observations. As the authors made clear, these were the problems on which the worker focused, but it was by no means certain that they were the problems for which the client originally sought – and perhaps continued to need – help.[48] Any changes in the fundamental assumptions of social-work practice must have had an impact on clients' experiences as clients, and on the stories that they wove about themselves in order to achieve the support they needed. But paucity of evidence makes the quest for descriptions of that impact difficult. Moreover, the widely recognized tendency for clients to assume the values of their workers – what Sainsbury called realignments in their recollections – would render many attempts useless because of the difficulty of separating the client's story from the one that she had been conditioned to accept.[49]

The tension between material assistance and psychological help, which was a feature of both the 1970s studies, was much less important to Phillimore's work. The interventions experienced by his respondents were more practical than insight-oriented, and focused on the care of children and the use of group work of various sorts, rather than on the solution of more intimate and personal problems. To a great extent that reflected the changing fashion in social-work intervention generally and

44   Ibid., pp. 116ff.
45   Ibid., p. 143.
46   Sainsbury, Nixon and Phillips, *Social Work in Focus*, p. 176.
47   Mayer and Timms, *The Client Speaks*, p. 25.
48   See, for example, the discussion in Sainsbury, *Social Work with Families*, pp. 46ff, 97.
49   Ibid., pp. 26, 34, 62, 73. See also Mayer and Timms, *The Client Speaks*, p. 9.

represented the type of work being done in most Family Service Units in the 1980s. Phillimore's approach also reflected his academic background as an anthropologist, whereas Mayer, Timms and Sainsbury had been trained in social work and social policy. Phillimore believed himself to be better able to accept the results of his interviews at face value, as the perceptions of people whose views society habitually discounts, rather than as a tool for evaluating a particular social-work service or providing suggestions for its modification.[50] There may well be some truth in that. But if that disciplinary distance allowed Phillimore more objectivity, his research, aiming to produce evidence for the National Institute for Social Work, did have an element of evaluation built into it. Moreover, he did not appear to consider the potential for distorting the evidence in the fact that his interviewees knew that he had been commissioned by Family Service Units and, unless they were profoundly dissatisfied, were unlikely too fiercely to criticize an agency of which they might have need in the future.[51]

Status, gender and class

Those reasons alone should give us cause to read critically the recorded comments of clients and encourage us to look for other clues to underlying presuppositions in the ways in which questions were framed and responses made. One of the first points to note is that interviewees were constructed as clients – their stories were those of people in a professional relationship with social workers. They had been selected by the agencies in order that they should describe their experiences. They had not approached the researchers to suggest that they had interesting stories to tell. By definition, they were people with problems and the nature of their interviews with the researchers, by constantly focusing on those problems and the strategies that had been adopted to relieve them, reinforced that status and encouraged them to compose their stories around the theme of the family difficulties that had resulted in encounters with social workers. The inherent power relations between the social workers and their clients and between interviewers and interviewees and their potential for influencing the outcome of either set of encounter are not discussed, but the world view of each cannot have failed to shape and colour the interview. For example, Mayer and Timms qualified the importance they attached to client opinion by making clear that the client cannot be 'sovereign' or an 'economic man' (*sic*) who has the freedom to shop around for services or the right to demand treatment that the social worker may believe to be 'therapeutically unsound'.[52] The use of quasi-medical language and the insistence that the caseworker has the right to overrule client preference resonates with Wootton's antipathy towards the 'god-like' caseworker who evinced a 'Daddy knows best' attitude.[53]

---

50   Phillimore, *Families Speaking*, p. 5.
51   See Sainsbury, *Social Work with Families*, p. 79.
52   Mayer and Timms, *The Client Speaks*, p. 3.
53   Wootton, 'The Image of the Social Worker', *passim*. See also B. Wootton, *Social Science and Social Pathology* (London, 1959), p. 273.

In addition to demonstrating their concern for the professional status of social work and the reputations of particular social-work agencies, all three pieces of research were coloured by the manner in which they were presented. By committing the interviews to print, the researchers changed an aural object – a conversation between two people – into a visual one, a text.[54] Moreover, the interviewees found themselves on unfamiliar territory. In the social-work situation, they would have assumed that what they revealed about their personal circumstances would have been delivered in private and treated as confidential. But as subjects for research, they were being invited to take part in a performance: their words were being recorded on tape and would be converted into text for strangers to read. An audience, of whom they knew little or nothing, was an invisible element in the interview. In addition, the researchers controlled and attempted to shape the way in which their readers understood those stories, in the first place by designing the questions and in the second by selecting extracts from the interviews and by offering their own interpretation of them.[55] And that is in addition to the 'tidying-up' of the account, the cutting out of pauses and repetitions, the imposition of grammatical forms on to speech which may not have been syntactically precise – what speech is? – and the insertion of punctuation in an attempt to make it more readable or to convey a particular meaning that the interviewer believed he had understood.

Apart from the dramatic difference in meaning that can sometimes be conveyed by the insertion of a comma, as Alessandro Portelli has shown, in normal speech narrators may switch from one rhythm to another and may employ pauses of irregular length and position to accentuate the emotional content as their attitude to the subject under discussion changes. Similarly, the speed of narration may alter for a variety of reasons, most of which will be evident in a face-to-face interview, but cannot accurately be conveyed in a transcript without considerable and dangerously interpretative commentary. These variations in speech pattern cannot be transcribed: they can be appreciated only by listening and watching.[56] Furthermore, a whole range of body language, including facial expressions suggesting anger, discomfort, pain or pleasure, so important a feature of normal conversations, is absent from these accounts.

Another feature of the transcriptions that gives pause is the absence of any reported swearing; however angry or upset the respondents may have been, none appears to have used strong language to convey the strength of her or his emotions. Perhaps that reflects the reality of the conversation between researcher and respondent, but it seems unlikely. All such impositions of order on what is essentially a disorderly medium contribute to what Raphael Samuel has called the 'decadence of transcription',[57] allowing the reader to impose a regularity that was not a feature

---

54 A. Portelli, 'What Makes Oral History Different?', in R. Perks and A. Thomson (eds), *The Oral History Reader* (London and New York, 1998), p. 64.

55 K.B. Orland, '"That's Not What I said": Interpretive Conflict in Oral Narrative research', in S. Gluck and D. Patai (eds), *Women's words. The feminist practice of oral history* (London and New York, 1991), p. 64.

56 Portelli, 'What Makes Oral History Different?', p. 65.

57 R. Samuel, 'Perils of the Transcript', in Perks and Thomson, *The Oral History Reader*, p. 389.

of the original encounter.[58] These distortions may be detected in our texts. Some of Sainsbury's respondents, for example, speak in carefully organized sentences that are unlikely accurately to reproduce the original patterns of speech.[59] Oral historians have alerted us to these dangers, common to all transcribed interviews, but they were compounded in the studies we are considering because the interviewer was frequently conducting interviews about interviews; the interviewer was himself dependent on clients' interpretations of interviews with their social workers.

The point of view of the other person or persons involved in the original interview – the social worker – is absent from the research. The short time in which he had to conduct his investigation – between late February and early April 1981 – meant that Phillimore was unable to interview any of the social workers whose clients had provided him with information, and there is no indication that he had been allowed access to social workers' notes. Although Sainsbury attempted to verify, or at least to compare, workers' accounts of events with those of their clients, it is significant that workers had a less clear memory of the detail of encounters.[60] This may reflect the sometimes sketchy note-keeping by social workers and the impossibility of detailed recall in the face of the size of their workloads, even in an agency like FSU which prided itself on expecting workers to be responsible for many fewer families than their local authority counterparts. It also suggests, however, that the meetings between clients and their workers were more significant events in the lives of the former in their efforts to make sense of their past, to create meanings from things that had happened to them and – crucially – to seek amelioration of their difficulties. At the very least, the experience of having an interested listener might have made the interview more memorable for the client. For their part, Mayer and Timms did speak to relevant workers and noted that this enabled them 'to obtain a fuller understanding of the ways in which misunderstandings develop and spiral in the casework situation', though they scarcely referred to these interviews in their text.[61]

As well as a failure to solicit, or at least to mention, social workers' impressions of their relationships with particular clients, assumptions about gender, revealed almost unconsciously in some of the commentaries, should lead us to consider the possibility of a serious distortion of the sound of the client's voice. All the researchers were male. Most of the respondents were female. Sainsbury had 17 couples and ten single women in his sample and used the inclusive term 'the families' to describe his respondents, but he admitted that more women than men were interviewed alone.[62] Phillimore noted that of the 51 households recommended to him by FSU, 16 were without a resident man, eight of the men were at work on the day he visited, the whereabouts of two were unknown, and two other of his women respondents were interviewed alone in the FSU offices. Four men deliberately avoided speaking to

58   Portelli, 'What Makes Oral History Different?', p. 65.
59   See, for example, Sainsbury, *Social Work with Families*, p. 69.
60   See, for example, the observations in Sainsbury, *Social Work with Families*, p. 58; Mayer and Timms, *The Client Speaks*, p. 66. See also the discussion about social workers' perceptions of clients' difficulties in Rees, *Social Work Face to Face*, Ch. 3.
61   Mayer and Timms, *The Client Speaks*, p. 32.
62   Sainsbury, *Social Work with Families*, pp. 48–9, 54.

him. Moreover, the constraints imposed on his research by a very tight timetable meant that there was little opportunity to rearrange the times of the interview if the man in the family was out at the time he called.[63] In total, he was able to interview 19 men. Mayer and Timms claimed that nine out of ten of their 61 interviewees were female. However, that did not deter them from using masculine pronouns, except in cases where there was a syntactical link to a named person.[64] This would have been normal convention in most official documents in the 1970s, and social workers who read the book when it was first published say that they did not notice this then, although they certainly would now.

Nevertheless, it illustrates the degree to which the researchers were themselves prisoners of conventions which denied the possibility that gender might be used as a tool for understanding and interpreting clients' responses. They do not appear to have considered the significance of according honorary membership of the male sex to the client to whose voice they professed to listen. Nor was consideration given to the nature of the narrative requested by the interviewer,[65] which required both that the woman submit herself to what has been called the androcentricity of oral history method,[66] and that she deal with the relation between her self and her social sphere and, consequently, with particular representations and expectations of women. Little scope for reflection was allowed, partly because of the projects' narrow foci and partly because they were conducted within traditional, that is masculine, paradigms with no opportunity to explore the attitudes and values that women might employ to give meaning to events. For example, it is clear from some of Phillimore's interviews that domestic activities – dealing with the children, paying household bills, performing domestic chores – were perceived as falling entirely within the woman's area of responsibility.[67] One respondent, possibly expressing an extreme point of view, complained that her husband, when asked by the social worker if he would consider staying at home occasionally to look after their children, answered:

> Oh no, I'm out with my friends tonight, I'm playing darts, I'm playing snooker and I'm up to the pub, and I'm seeing my friends, and she's staying tied to the sink and she'll stay and look after the kids.[68]

Phillimore also discussed the role of the woman as problem bearer for her family. Although, significantly, his treatment of the topic was contained within an exploration of men's reactions to social workers and the possible erosion of their sense of status when having to ask for help, he also demonstrated the ways in which women had internalized societal expectations. On the one hand, his respondents appeared to regret that their men folk missed out by failing to benefit from social-work intervention,

---

63   Ibid., p. 7. See also his Appendix 6, p. 90.

64   See, for example, Mayer and Timms, *The Client Speaks*, p. 114.

65   M-F. Chanfrault-Duchet, 'Narrative Structures, Social Models and Symbolic Representation in the Life Story', in Gluck and Patai, *Women's Words*, p. 78.

66   K. Minister, 'A Feminist Frame for Interviews', in Gluck and Patai, *Women's Words*, p. 31.

67   Phillimore, *Families Speaking*, p. 47.

68   Ibid., p. 52.

while on the other they tacitly acknowledged their right to distance themselves from their family difficulties.[69] Phillimore's respondents made clear that many men resented any 'interference' in their family and the possibility that any social-work intervention might undermine their rights and authority within the household. As one woman told him:

> She did her best to talk to him. She went into the kitchen to talk to him, she followed him outside and he just, you know, told her to get lost in a not very polite way for a man talking to a woman.[70]

The resentment is made more explicit in the response from another of Phillimore's interviewees:

> Personally, myself, social workers, I don't like them … There's only one party got anything to do with me, or what goes on in this house, and that's my wife. I says, 'If you ask any questions about the child, fair enough, you'll be told. But anything personal I won't tell you. That'll be kept to myself.' I says, 'that's my problem, not yours. If I do need help with anything, and I think you can help, then I'll ask.'[71]

The inclusion of these, largely negative, views of social workers help to demonstrate the authenticity of the research, though it has to be remembered that the women did not escape so easily and would not have been able so confidently to repulse social-work attention. Assumed to be the principal carers of the children, women almost always found themselves to be the targets of intervention.[72]

All three studies mentioned – only to skirt round – family problems arising from the poor health of some women.[73] While it is tempting to wonder whether discussion was avoided because this was of an obstetric or gynaecological nature, it appears more likely that some poor families were seriously affected by the depressive illness suffered by some women.[74] But factors contributing to mental distress, or discussion about courses of action taken by social workers to alleviate that, are not in evidence. It may, perhaps, be argued that the research was directed towards discovering more about client expectation and experience within a narrow professional encounter, but by failing to consider women as women, the researchers neglected an examination of the meaning that the majority of clients gave to that encounter and to the events which had led up to it. The experience of being a social-work client is one which produces complex and conflicting emotions. By adopting a mechanistic – masculine? – approach, the researchers denied themselves the opportunity to explore some of the complexities and conflicts associated with the use of the services of particular agencies.

In addition, class informed both the way in which respondents remembered and told their stories and the researchers' approach to their subject. As Joan Sangster has

---

69   Ibid., pp. 47ff, 55.
70   Phillimore, *Families Speaking*, p. 31.
71   Ibid., p. 48.
72   Ibid., pp. 46ff.
73   Sainsbury, *Social Work with Families*, pp. 46–7.
74   Ibid., pp. 28–9; Phillimore, *Families Speaking*, p. 47.

argued, both researchers and respondents are bound by the way in which cultural values shape the ordering and prioritizing of events – even notions of what is myth, history, fact or fiction.[75] This was only partly understood by the researchers in this case, whose class-based assumptions unconsciously demonstrated their own sense of middle-class superiority. Mayer and Timms reported that clients liked the 'superior' class background and accent of the worker,[76] but did not explore the reasons why. One of Sainsbury's respondents commented that her favourite social worker, 'Linda', had … 'a nice way of talking, nicely spoken…'.[77] Did so personal an attribute as accent give the client confidence by suggesting that the worker had received an appropriate level of education? Did it satisfy a sort of snobbery? Or did it reassure the workers in some way, perhaps allowing them to distance themselves from the sorts of difficulties that afflicted their clients? All three researchers used class to explain the difference in understanding between the client and the social worker about the nature of personal problems. The gap was explained as a function of different cognitive orientations to problem solving, informed by class differences.[78] Any dissatisfaction on the part of the client was attributed to her unsophisticated view of the causes of any situation and the low priority she gave to the therapeutic benefits of 'self-awareness'.[79]

The authors assumed that clients would be working-class and, therefore, less able to articulate and to conceptualize than middle-class people, although they immediately softened the judgement by arguing that this was not because working-class people could not solve problems, but that they solved them in different ways. Individual incapacity was held responsible for the client's inability to understand why a request for material aid – for money to pay the electricity bill, for example – was met with a probing into her internal world.[80] Such assumptions did not go entirely unchallenged. Eric Sainsbury, for example, expressed mild surprise that the respondents on his project were able to put across their views clearly and with a good deal of insight.[81] But on the whole, the voice of the client – as they heard it – confirmed researchers in their professional stance. As an anthropologist rather than a social worker by training, Phillimore was more straightforward and pointed out that a hierarchy of credibility assumed that people who used social work services had a version of reality that was 'intrinsically less acceptable than that of more credible people'.[82]

It is here, perhaps, that class and gender merge and reinforce the essential inequality between interviewers and interviewees. The interviews were conducted on the basis of unequal power and unequal control over the outcome, as all such interviews

---

75   J. Sangster, 'Telling our Stories. Feminist Debates and the Use of Oral History', in Perks and Thomson, *The Oral History Reader*, p. 89.

76   Mayer and Timms, *The Client Speaks*, p. 92.

77   Sainsbury, *Social Work with Families*, p. 153.

78   Mayer and Timms, *The Client Speaks*, p. 78.

79   Ibid., p. 155.

80   Ibid., pp. 120, 123, 140, 167.

81   Sainsbury, *Social Work with Families*, p. 5.

82   Phillimore, *Families Speaking*, p. 5. See also Portelli, 'What Makes Oral History Different?', p. 64.

are.[83] In this case the inequalities arose from gender – male interviewers, female respondents; class – educated middle-class interviewers, disadvantaged respondents; and professional and institutional status – professional interviewers with close links to the management and workers of the organization they were investigating, and clients who needed the services of that organization. But the consequences of that inequality extended beyond the interview. If notions of truth diverged significantly between interviewer and respondent, how was that incorporated into and interpreted in the research? It is at least conceivable that, in such a case, the interpretation of the interviewer assumed precedence in the written account.[84] There is no suggestion, for example, that the interviewees were consulted about those extracts of their interviews that were to be reproduced in print, or the accuracy of the interpretations placed on their conversations once the text was prepared for publication.

Conclusion

In spite of these flaws, there can be no doubt that the research of the 1970s and 1980s into the experiences of social-work clients represented a new departure in professional attitudes and that this was an important element in the evolution of social work services. The projects we have considered played no small part in alerting the profession to the necessity for information about the views of recipients of services and marked the beginning of a recognition that these were valid as indicators of the quality of those services. Nevertheless, in spite of their intentions, the researchers showed themselves unable to break free of either their own assumptions as middle-class, male professionals or the concerns of the agencies that sponsored their work, conscious that changes were afoot that had the potential to alter both the scale and the character of social work by voluntary organizations. The research signalled important changes in attitude, but because it was an element in a protracted struggle between the voluntary and statutory sectors, the voices it claimed to reproduce were as much those of the researchers as of the clients.

---

83   G. Kress and R. Fowler, quoted in Minister, 'A Feminist Frame for Interviews', p. 29.
84   Sangster, 'Telling our Stories', p. 93.

Index

Printed in Great Britain
by Amazon